America's BEST Zoos

A Travel Guide for Fans and Families

Allen W. Nyhuis and Jon Wassner

America's Best Zoos:
A Travel Guide for Fans and Families

Published by
The Intrepid Traveler
P.O. Box 531
Branford, CT 06405
http://www.intrepidtraveler.com

First Edition
Printed in the U.S.A.
Cover design by Foster & Foster
Interior design by Alfonso Robinson

ISBN: 978-1-887140-76-8
Library of Congress Control Number: 2007943954

10   9   8   7   6   5   4   3   2   1

Dedication

Allen dedicates this book to his dad, and to his Millie.

Jon dedicates this book to his grandmother, Yvonne Morehead.

THE AUTHORS IN THEIR OWN WORDS

ALLEN W. NYHUIS: I was born in California but grew up in Sheboygan, Wisconsin. I developed my love for travel and for zoos during my family's frequent zoo visits and  many cross-country vacations. After high school, I joined the U.S. Army and spent the better part of three years in Hawaii, training in field artillery. Living there stoked my interest in seeing more exotic locations and the fauna that inhabit them. Following my discharge, I earned my Bachelor's and Master's Degrees at the University of Wisconsin and then went to work for the U.S. Census Bureau for a year in the Washington area (my Master's is in Statistics). I moved to Indianapolis in 1984 when I began my career as a statistician in medical research.

My interest in zoos stayed with me as I grew up, married, and had children. In 1988, just about the time my children were getting old enough to enjoy zoos, the brand new Indianapolis Zoo opened, whetting my appetite still further. I started visiting zoos in other cities while on business trips and discovered how fascinating and different every zoo is. I wrote long, detailed descriptions of the zoos I visited to my brother and fellow zoo-lover, David. He finally told me I "ought to" write a book about zoos. So in 1994, I wrote *The Zoo Book: A Guide to America's Best*. I've been a member of the Association of Zoos & Aquariums for over fifteen years.

In addition to working full-time for Eli Lilly and visiting every zoo I possibly can – over two hundred worldwide so far – I teach statistics part-time as an Adjunct Professor for Indiana University's School of Public Health. My wife Kathy is kind enough to indulge me in my zoo habit. We are the proud parents of four children.

JON WASSNER: When I was three years old, I visited the Indianapolis Zoo with my mom and brother. At the giraffe pen, a giraffe leaned over the fence and licked me on the side of the face. Right then I knew my life's path would lead me back to a zoo.

As I grew up, my interest in zoos and animals grew with me. Family vacations were accompanied by at least one, and usually multiple, zoo visits. These continued until I reached college and began what I thought would be my long-awaited career in zoos. While earning my degree at Ball State University in Muncie, Indiana, I spent two summers working as a zookeeper intern, the first at the Potawatomi Zoo in South Bend, Indiana and the second at Chicago's Brookfield Zoo. I worked at the Indianapolis Zoo as a full-time zookeeper for Australian and African animals for a season following graduation. By then, I realized my interests lay more in zoo-exhibit design than in zookeeping.

My hobbies are visiting zoos – I've tallied sixty-nine zoos and aquariums in the United States so far – playing soccer, and traveling with my wife, Kelly. We live in Indianapolis with our cat, Maddie.

ACKNOWLEDGMENTS

THIS BOOK WOULD NOT HAVE HAPPENED WITHOUT THOUSANDS of miles of traveling, hundreds of hours walking through zoos, and thousands of hours researching and writing. Yet even with all of the hard work on our part, we could not have completed this book without the special help of many people across the nation.

First, we would like to thank the many zoo employees, from public relations specialists to zoo directors, at more than sixty zoos nationwide, who provided us with personalized tours, vital information, and photographs. We especially want to thank: Cindy Castelblanco in Miami; Jason Jacobs in Los Angeles; Terry Axline in Albuquerque; Julia McHugh in Santa Barbara; Dr. Lee Simmons and Jennifer Westfall in Omaha; Lee Ehmke and Tim Hill in Minnesota; Dr. Stuart Strahl and Sondra Katzen in Chicago; Charlie Abrego in Brownsville; Debbie Rios-Vanskike in San Antonio; Bruce Bohmke in Seattle; the okapi staff in Dallas; Virginia Edmonds in Tampa; and Brian Hill in Houston for their kind attention and help.

During our grand research tour of most of the zoos in this book in 2007, we both traveled all over the country, spending time with many friends and family members, who gave us a place to spend the night or helped us in other important ways. We would like to express our gratitude to: Amy Nyhuis in Virginia; Marty & Julia Nyhuis in West Virginia; Jen & John Reid in Arizona; Heide Nyhuis, her son, and Don & Lori Armerding and family in California; Amy & Heidi Anderson in Wisconsin; David & Jennifer Nyhuis and family in Washington; the Copps in Maryland; the DeGrootes in Utah; the Nelsons and Earl Miller in Indiana; Ian Munday in Michigan; the Ruehmers in Illinois; and the Niberts in Texas.

Of course, we very much appreciate our publishers, Kelly Monaghan and Sally Scanlon at The Intrepid Traveler, for their help, their confidence in us, and especially their willingness to take a chance on us with this book. We give a special nod of thanks to the very first reader of this book, our editor Alexis Elder. Her contributions have been invaluable. We also thank Speaker Newt Gingrich for taking time from his busy schedule to write an excellent and insightful Foreword.

Jon also would like to thank his co-author Allen for his guidance through the process of writing this book. He could not have written it alone, and is so glad Allen agreed to take on this venture. Likewise, Allen returns the thanks to Jon for giving him the energy and inspiration to go forward with this big project.

Allen wishes to express lifelong gratitude to his parents Wayne & Lois Nyhuis for their unfailing love and care for him over the years, and for instilling a love of zoos in him many, many years ago. Some of Allen's best zoo memories are with his dad. Allen also posthumously thanks his father-in-law Owen Wald for being the first one to believe in his ability to write a book like this.

Jon greatly appreciates his parents, Mollie & Bill Wassner, who have supported and fostered his love of zoos from a young age. Just as important are Jon's brothers, Jeremy and Joel Wassner, who among other things deserve considerable thanks for not complaining too much about all the family vacation zoo trips; his grandmother Yvonne Morehead for a life's worth of encouragement; and his in-laws, Don & Paula and Amy Fisher, for laughing at his jokes. Jon would also like to thank his extended family, the senior class members of the 2002 Clay High School boys soccer team, their families, Brian Rodick, and his first zookeeper mentor, Jeri Ellis.

Allen has four extremely important people to thank, his wonderful children, Jeremy, Mandy, Becky, and Millie: "Seeing the world through their eyes helped me see what a special place a zoo is, especially for families. Each of these children toured many of the zoos with me and provided the best company anyone could ask for. Millie even participated in touring zoos during the latter stages of the writing of this book. A big hug and thank you goes to each of these precious kids."

Jon gives his biggest thanks to his wife and best friend, Kelly: "There is no one else I'd rather take to the zoo, or come home to at night. Thanks for supporting the long travels, and I hope next time we can visit each zoo together."

Allen, most of all, thanks his sweet wife Kathy. She provided support while her husband was off traveling the nation, visiting zoos: "She gave me encouragement when I needed it most, and best of all, she has been my love and life partner for over 25 years now!"

Finally we thank our God and Creator for the ability and opportunity He has given us to write this book at this time. We humbly acknowledge His role in our lives and thank Him for any success we have.

Photo Credits

Speaker Newt Gingrich   p xiii   Callista Gingrich, Gingrich Productions

Animal Photos

Bonobo	p 13	San Diego Zoological Society
Fossa	p 13	Omaha's Henry Doorly Zoo
Giant otter	p 14	Philadelphia Zoo/Bob Simrak
Seahorses	p 19	Paul Riley
Moon jellyfish	p 20	Indianapolis Zoo
Otters	p 24	National Zoo
Polar bear	p 28	The Maryland Zoo
Child in nest	p 30	The Maryland Zoo
Child on lily pad	p 30	The Maryland Zoo
African wild dogs	p 31	Julie Larson Maher
White lions	p 39	Philadelphia Zoo/Jim Kochis
Zooballoon	p 41	Philadelphia Zoo
Snow leopards	p 46	Dan Crawley
Bird of paradise	p 51	anonymous
Sifaka	p 51	Chuck Dresner
Clouded leopard	p 51	Charlie Doggett
Echidna	p 51	Philadelphia Zoo/Andy Whiting
Panda photographers	p 52	National Zoo
Monorail	p 52	Ron Magill
Jaguar	p 57	Barry Rabinowitz
Rhino and girl	p 61	Allen W. Nyhuis
Crane	p 66	Ron Magill
Lorikeet feeding	p 69	©Busch Entertainment Corp., All rights reserved. Reproduced by permission.
Gorillas	p 77	Zoo Atlanta
Giant panda	p 78	Zoo Atlanta
Drills	p 79	Zoo Atlanta
Patas monkey	p 84	Tom Gillespie
Aquarium	p 87	Riverbanks Zoo
Red panda	p 90	Knoxville Zoo

Animal Photo Credits, cont'd.

CHINA exhibit	p 94	Memphis Zoo
Kayaking	p 102	John White
Train	p 104	Audubon Nature Institute
Skyfari	p 104	Zoological Society of San Diego
White alligator	p 106	Audubon Nature Institute
Snowy owls	p 113	Gavin Elliott, Tulsa Zoo Friends, Inc.
Wombat	p 142	Chicago Zoological Society/Jim Schulz
Aardvark	p 142	Chicago Zoological Society/Jim Schulz
Dolphin Dome	p 156	Paul Riley
Savanna	p 159	Zoo Staff, Binder Park Zoo
Gray wolf	p 170	Cleveland Metroparks Zoo
Hippoquarium	p 177	Andi Norman
Impala and vulture	p 182	Milwaukee County Zoo
Gorilla habitat	p 190	Sedgewick County Zoo
Maned wolves	p 192	Sedgewick County Zoo
Penguin exhibit	p 201	Gil Courson
Micronesian kingfisher	p 214	San Diego Zoological Society
Tree kangaroo	p 214	Sedgewick County Zoo
Flying fox bat	p 214	Oakland Zoo/Adam Fink Zookeeper
Elephant shrew	p 214	National Zoo
Coatimundi	p 214	Philadelphia Zoo/Jeff Chapman
Bighorn sheep	p 216	Phoenix Zoo
Desert Loop Trail	p 219	Randall Jason Landau
Hummingbirds	p 221	Randall Jason Landau
Giraffe feeding	p 223	Jenny Kerchner
Hyenas	p 226	Dave Parsons
Tiger	p 234	James Weston, Utah's Hogle Zoo
Siberian lynx	p 235	James Weston, Utah's Hogle Zoo
Rhino feeding	p 240	Zoological Society of San Diego
Mountain tapir	p 245	Jamie Pham
Child on statue	p 250	Oakland Zoo Staff
Blue iguanas	p 253	Zoological Society of San Diego
Koalas	p 256	Zoological Society of San Diego
Komodo dragon	p 257	Zoological Society of San Diego
Grizzly bear	p 259	San Francisco Zoo
Nene geese	p 262	anonymous zookeeper (i.e., no credit)

All other animal and zoo photos by Jon Wassner., including cover photos of komodo dragon, otter, grizzly bears, poison dart frog, and black mamba.

Table of Contents

Southern Zoos, cont'd.

South Central Zoos

Great Lakes Area Zoos

North Central Zoos

Southwestern and Western Zoos

West Coast Zoos

Appendices

Glossary

Animal Index

Maps

Foreword

By Newt Gingrich

LONG BEFORE I ASPIRED TO ENTER THE FIELD OF POLITICS, I wanted to be a zookeeper, then a zoo director. Adulthood did not dampen my love for animals or zoos – it created new opportunities for me to visit them. As I've traveled the nation and the world in my official and unofficial roles, I have often taken time out to go to the local zoo.

As I was growing up in Harrisburg, Pennsylvania, my relatives would take me to the big zoos in Philadelphia, Baltimore, and Washington, DC. They would also take me a few miles away to a small zoo in Hershey, Pennsylvania. I fell in love with seeing animals in all their glory and diversity. I found animals fascinating.

When I was ten, I went to an afternoon matinee of two animal films. When I came out of the movie, I saw a sign for City Hall. I promptly walked over and asked how Harrisburg could get a zoo. The kind, older park official (who had dated my grandmother forty years earlier) took the time to show me the records for the Harrisburg Zoo in the 1930s. He told me they had closed the zoo during World War II because of rationing and that my job was to come to the next city council and explain why Harrisburg needed a zoo. The next Tuesday, I was right there. The following day, the *Harrisburg Patriot-News* published a nice article about a young boy calling for a zoo. I was hooked on animals, zoos, and citizenship from that point on.

While representing my Georgia district in Congress, I had the pleasure of helping my hometown Zoo Atlanta with its fund-raising efforts. What I most enjoyed, however, was helping the zoo acquire important animals, such as Boma, the black rhino, relocated to Atlanta from a zoo in Czechoslovakia. I was especially honored to participate in the successful efforts to bring Yang Yang and Lun Lun, the giant pandas, from China to our zoo, and to assist in the zoo's acquisition of Komodo dragons.

Back in 1995, when I was Speaker of the House, my friend "Jungle Jack" Hanna, Director of the Columbus Zoo, brought some of his animals to the Capitol. Knowing I was a lover of zoos, Jack brought his traveling menagerie into my office for a visit. After a monkey, a rare Asian binturong, and hissing cockroaches had climbed all over me, a baby cougar eventually took a bite out of my chin. If only my political opponents at the time had been so gentle!

I am committed to zoos and to the environment, not only for the pleasures they bring, but also because I believe that we are called to be stewards of the natural world. We have an obligation to preserve and protect it, not only for future generations of human beings, but for all living things, including endangered animal species. That's why I played a key role in saving the Endangered Species Act during the late 1990s. More recently, Dr. Terry L. Maple, director of the Palm Beach Zoo, and I wrote a book, *A Contract with the Earth*, where we call for a bipartisan approach to environmentalism, for Americans to work together to solve our environmental problems.

But wildlife face diminishing habitats and dangerous poachers in the wild, so today zoos are vital to helping animals the world over. Ironically, my name has come up in connection with zoos and animal preservation recently, in an unexpected way. No, I'm not named after an amphibian found in zoo reptile houses. My name, Newt, is an Anglicized form of the Danish name, Knut. In Germany, there was a major crisis recently over a polar bear cub named Knut, one that received international attention. After he was abandoned by his mother, Knut would have been doomed to die, except for the Berlin Zoo's intervention, where staff hand-raised him. A German animal activist was outraged, claiming, "feeding by hand is not species-appropriate, but a gross violation of animal protection laws. The zoo must kill the bear!" The zoo disagreed, and there was a huge public outcry. The activist lost and thankfully, Knut won. I had the pleasure of meeting him while I was in Berlin in May of 2007. See below: I'm the one on the left.

That German activist's criticism that zoos are an unnatural and immoral interference with the course of nature is false. Zoos have been called a modern-day Noah's Ark, a place for animals to live and breed, safe from the "flood waters" of pollution, poaching, and habitat destruction. One of the great icons of the American West, the American bison, would no longer exist but for the efforts of zoos. Just over a hundred years ago, this species was on the brink of extinction. Then, the Bronx Zoo led efforts to gather the remaining animals for protection, breeding, and eventually to successfully return them to their native prairie lands. The Phoenix Zoo played an equally significant role in saving the Arabian oryx from extinction. In 1962, when there were only nine of these Arabian desert antelope remaining in the world, this Arizona zoo became the oryxes' refuge. Today, there are more than a thousand Arabian oryxes in zoos, and a few have even been returned to the wild. Americans can help these and other endangered species by

financially supporting zoos, becoming members of their local zoo, and by visiting zoos across the country.

But if you already have a good zoo nearby, why would you want to visit another zoo elsewhere in America? As this book's title suggests, this is a travel guide "for Fans and Families." I am a zoo fan. During my adult lifetime, I've lived near two excellent zoos – Zoo Atlanta and Washington's National Zoo. But no one zoo can possibly have everything. While my zoos in Atlanta and Washington are wonderful for watching giant pandas and orangutans, neither of them has koalas or polar bears. To see one of those enchanting creatures, I would need to go to San Diego, or some other zoo. Maybe I want the experience of watching massive hippos, looking graceful as they swim underwater. If I'm near Toledo, Ohio, I'm in luck! Each of the sixty zoos included here offers unique opportunities and experiences for animal-lovers, world travelers, and other zoo fans like me. In my travels, I have visited dozens of zoos across America and around the world. As I look forward to future zoo visits, I'll be able to consult the *Index* and reviews in this guidebook to help me find the animals and exhibits I'm most interested in seeing.

This is also a guide "for Families." To me, zoos are both a family value and a value for families. A family of four can spend an entire day at many zoos for under $50 – that's less than the cost of a single ticket at most of the big amusement parks around the nation. True, zoos don't offer the high-tech, white-knuckle thrill rides found in the big coaster parks. Instead, in a zoo you can hand-feed crackers to a giraffe, have a beautiful Australian parakeet land on your head, or pet the soft fur of a pygmy goat. Zoos may also have enchanting miniature steam trains, and sometimes a camel to ride. Allen and Jon make it clear that some zoos have extra special exhibits aimed directly at children. Readers with children should pay special attention to the reviews of the zoos in Chicago, Pittsburgh, Baltimore, Tampa, and even Fort Wayne, Indiana. If your family is ever close to one of these cities, I recommend that you take a trip to the zoo. Your children will thank you. I am looking forward to many exciting zoo trips with my two grandchildren, Maggie and Robert.

Zoos also give parents (and grandparents) special chances to teach their children about nature, about differences in animals, about which animals come from Africa and which come from Australia. Mom or Dad can teach these things in a fun, memorable way, and build family relationships at the same time. Even more important, a visit to a zoo can spark in a child a lifelong love for the magnificent animal heritage that is God's gift to His children. That is exactly what happened to me. That love, nurtured and cultivated, can blossom into a commitment to protect and save the environment that is home to us all.

— *Newt Gingrich*

Introduction

YEAR AFTER YEAR, ZOOS IN THE UNITED STATES ATTRACT MORE annual visitors than all major spectator sports combined. Of these millions of visitors, out-of-town tourists are usually only a small minority. According to a 2004 survey, roughly one fourth (28%) of zoo visitors are from outside the "normal" area. More specifically, just over a quarter of the visitors to America's zoos have driven more than two hours to get to the zoo. From this, we estimate that fewer than 10% of the visitors in an American zoo are truly tourists in the traditional sense.

There are, however, a few obvious exceptions – some zoos attract hordes of tourists. Disney's Animal Kingdom, for example, is part of the Walt Disney World® Resort, making it a clear tourist magnet. Busch Gardens Africa, in nearby Tampa, attracts many of the same vacationing visitors to Central Florida. In Southern California, San Diego's Zoo and Wild Animal Park compete with Disneyland and other major family attractions for vacation dollars. Elsewhere, a few smaller zoos such as the Caldwell Zoo in Texas and the Binder Park Zoo in Michigan are showing some success attracting new visitors from the busy highways that pass nearby. But these are still the exceptions. Most of America's zoos are completely overlooked as tourist attractions. For the most part, zoos are visited primarily by local school children and families.

It's a common misconception that all zoos are alike. This erroneous belief keeps many people from adding zoos to their travel itineraries. People ask, "We already have a good zoo in our hometown, so why should we want to see some other zoo?" The fact is, though, that each zoo is different, and some are unique. The tropical foliage at the Jacksonville Zoo is quite different from the evergreens of Portland's Oregon Zoo. An African savanna exhibit in the desert at the Phoenix Zoo is not at all similar to the savanna at the urban Lincoln Park Zoo in Chicago. Some zoo exhibits, such as the Bronx Zoo's Congo Gorilla Forest or the Lied Jungle in Omaha's Henry Doorly Zoo, are unparalleled. Koalas, okapis, giant otters, and even moose are displayed at very few zoos, and there are still fewer than half a dozen U.S. zoos where you can go to see a giant panda. Thus, visiting a new zoo is almost guaranteed to be a very different experience than a visit to your local zoo.

Together, we have visited all sixty of the "Best" zoos featured in this book, many of them more than once. We have visited these zoos as tourists, often with family members (including children) accompanying us, and we have been careful to notice what would interest the typical visitor. Our hope is that this book will inspire you to visit more zoos around our nation, and that it will make your experience of these zoos even more rewarding.

To summarize, we offer you the following three reasons to visit an out-of-town zoo:

1. The zoo is likely to display many animals you will not see at your local zoo, no matter how excellent your hometown zoo is.
2. Zoos are not only great places to learn about nature and zoology, but many also offer an excellent – and painless – geography lesson, displaying both the wildlife and culture of foreign lands.
3. While on vacation, a day at a zoo can be an excellent alternative to an expensive theme park. Many zoos offer rides and shows that are equal to or better than standard amusement park fare at a fraction of the price.

Current Trends at U.S. Zoos

Background

The first zoos in the United States opened in Philadelphia, New York, and Chicago just after the Civil War. By 1900, more than twenty public zoos were in operation, one as far west as Seattle. In the twentieth century, a large zoo became a major source of community pride for almost every major city, and for many mid-size and small cities as well. Putting together a zoo was like assembling a coin collection – the goal was to display one or two of as many different "items" as possible. The emphasis in these menageries was on quantity, not quality.

Exhibiting the maximum number of animals meant squeezing in as many cages as available space would allow, with little regard for the amount of room available for the animals inside. Outdoor cages featured thick iron bars and concrete floors. In the great animal houses of the day, cages were equipped with tile walls and concrete or tile floors; they were fronted with iron bars or glass. These cages enabled visitors to get very close looks at exotic animals. Tile walls and concrete floors also made the exhibits easy to clean, a benefit for zoo employees and, it was thought, the animals as well. Zoos believed that a clean exhibit made a healthy animal.

Breeding

Until the 1960s, breeding was not a high priority for zoos. If a popular animal died, the zoo would simply purchase a new one captured from the wild. Then suddenly, things were not so simple. Political instabilities and a desire to protect natural heritage prompted many nations to put stricter controls on collecting animals from the wild. Zoos were forced to acquire new animals from other zoos or to breed them themselves.

Another problem soon came to the attention of both zoos and the public. Popular animals such as tigers, cheetahs, rhinos, gorillas, and elephants were quickly becoming rare in the wild, with some dangerously close to extinction. By 1962, the world population of Arabian oryxes, a desert antelope from the Middle East, had fallen to single digits. The world's zoos banded together and saved this species from extinction. Similar efforts saved the Pere David's deer and Mongolian wild horse (also known as Przewalski's wild horse). With so many other animals in a similar predicament, the zoological world initiated Species Survival Plans (SSPs). These organized efforts use zoos' resources to save the most endangered animals. Today more than 160 mammals, birds, reptiles, amphibians, and invertebrates are part of the SSP program. Most of these animals, though very rare in the wild, are increasingly common in zoos. This is why so much zoological attention is paid to such seemingly innocuous species as Puerto Rican crested toads, Bali mynahs, and babirusa pigs.

Today, baby gorillas, elephants, rhinos, chimpanzees, and other exotic youngsters are common sights for zoo visitors, though they're still highlights of any trip. However, until 1956, gorillas had never reproduced in any zoo, and it had been nearly forty years since an elephant calf had been seen by zoo visitors. Today, as zoos emphasize saving species and breeding rare animals, visitors have more opportunities to see baby animals.

Wild animals didn't just spontaneously decide to mate and reproduce in zoos. Important changes had to be made. One important step was pairing up reproductive males and females of the various species. As part of the SSP, genetic research is used to match males and females that will, if successful, produce genetically optimal offspring for the continuation of the species.

Habitats

To encourage breeding, it was necessary to upgrade the animals' homes. The iron and concrete cages created a bare, sterile environment. This, plus the gawking of thousands of visitors, discouraged animals from performing natural behaviors, including mating. Research showed that if animals felt like they were in their native environments, they would also act like they were. With this in mind, zoos began to build wonderful naturalistic habitats for their inhabitants.

Across the country, zoos constructed habitats that replicated the African savanna, the North American prairie, the rocky Pacific coastline, the ice flows of the Arctic and Antarctic Circles, and the tropical rain forests of the world. One of the most important features of these re-created habitats was the use of living plants, preferably from the animals' native lands. When a zoo's climate ruled out the use of exotic plants, clever use was made of local look-alike species. Both animals and zoo visitors appreciated these natural habitats; today, the word "cage" is almost a dirty word in the zoo community.

The rain forest has become a very popular environment to recreate. In 1974, the Topeka Zoo opened a Tropical Rain Forest building under a large clear acrylic dome. Three years later, Wichita's Sedgwick County Zoo, also in Kansas, opened the larger and lusher Jungle building. Since then, massive rain forest buildings have popped up across the nation, culminating with the opening of Omaha's astonishing Lied

Jungle in 1992. These remarkable buildings are filled with palm, fig, banana, and other tropical trees, plus bamboo, ferns, flowering plants, waterfalls, flowing streams, free-flying colorful birds, and a variety of animals.

The rain forest buildings often utilize an exciting concept: multi-species exhibits, which display many types of animals in a single space, just as they live in the wild. African savanna exhibits now have giraffes, zebras, antelope, ostriches, and other mammals roaming the open veldt together with birds. Of course the meat-eating predators, such as lions and cheetahs, cannot be directly exposed to the zebras and antelope, their natural prey, but zoos have made it seem to happen. So-called "predator/prey" exhibits often utilize a hidden deep moat, below visitors' lines of sight, to separate natural enemies while making them appear to share the same exhibit.

Visiting today's zoos can be like stepping into a *National Geographic* wildlife special. Americans can now experience a realistic tour of the African savanna, the Amazon rain forest, or the Himalayan highlands. A revolutionary concept called "landscape immersion" puts people into the animals' environment, rather than vice versa. Modern technology allows for fog machines, realistic man-made rocks and trees, and recordings of animal calls and wild noises that allow visitors to not only see animals in a realistic rain forest setting, but also feel as if they are actually in the rain forest themselves. Exhibits can look, feel, sound, and even smell like the real thing. It wasn't always so.

Technology Provides a Better View

The major drawback to these naturalistic habitats was that the animals were sometimes difficult to see, as they hid in the dense vegetation or rocky crevices. Steps have been taken to remedy this problem. Heated rocks and watering holes tempt animals near visitor overlooks, and viewing caves that extend into enclosures are used to keep the animals in sight of visitors.

Modern advances in glass-making have provided larger, stronger, and even curved panels that give visitors unique views of zoo animals. Underwater viewing galleries are being built at zoos across the country. Visitors can now see seals and sea lions, walruses, dolphins, polar bears, penguins, otters, crocodiles, tapirs, jaguars, and even hippos swimming and diving underwater. In the Toledo Zoo's beautiful Hippoquarium, humans have even witnessed underwater hippo births.

Many zoos have gone "barless" and have removed all visible barriers between animals and visitors. Animals are exhibited on islands or separated from viewers by moats, streams, or ponds. Some of the animals that cannot be exhibited in this manner, such as birds and large cats, are shown behind ultra-thin harp (or piano) wire. This strong wire is thin enough that most cameras can focus right through it for a clear, barless picture.

The Conservation Message

The Association of Zoos and Aquariums (AZA) is the parent organization that officially accredits the nation's zoos and aquariums. To receive a highly coveted accreditation, a zoo must pass an on-site inspection by AZA representatives. Of the more than 2,400 animal exhibitors licensed by the U.S. Department of Agriculture, approximately ten percent have been accredited by the AZA.

One of the most important items evaluated during an AZA site visit is the zoo's educational program. Today's zoo is more than just a source of entertainment, or even a refuge for endangered animals. It is also a major educational center that hosts thousands of school children every year. Zoo exhibits are enhanced with attractive and interpretive graphics that list more than animal names; they provide important and interesting information about the animals and their native habitats. Many exhibits, especially in children's zoos, are equipped with hands-on activities that encourage learning by doing. Some of these exhibits compare human abilities with those of various animals. Others let kids imitate the animals on display, or learn about ecological concepts. Most animal shows presented in zoos are now called "demonstrations" and are primarily educational, though they're still lots of fun for visitors!

Zoos also have a very specific message to deliver. By introducing the public to the world's tremendous variety of animals and their native habitats, they hope to inspire people to better appreciate the animals and to help preserve them. Visitors are encouraged to recycle and conserve, and they are advised not to pollute and not to buy exotic animal products.

Visitors: The Bottom Line

In the last ten years, America's zoos have spent more than $1 billion on upgrades and improvements. While some zoos receive a measure of government financial support, all zoos depend upon a stable attendance rate and strong support from their community. Quite simply, zoos need visitors. Some zoos are attempting to attract them with theme-park-like rides such as monorails and sky rides. In the twenty-first-twenty-first-century zoo, new adventures to attract more visitors include: animal-feeding exhibits, usually with giraffes or birds; special exotic animal carousels; splash play parks; touch pools with stingrays, sharks, or starfish; and walk-through butterfly greenhouses. Because a nominal fee is often charged for these special attractions, they can also be a great source of additional revenue for the zoo. All in all, the variety of animals, exhibits, scenery, rides, and shows make zoos attractive destinations for vacationers, business travelers, and local residents alike.

Going to the Zoo

Planning Ahead

Many zoos in the United States are massive and can be overwhelming to the unprepared. One way to prepare for a visit is to call the zoo in advance or to visit its website. Request a map and brochure about the zoo (or print it out off the website), as well as its current hours and admission fees. (We do our best to list information that's current as we go to press, but prices and hours are always subject to change.) Then, using the map, plan a route through the zoo. Show your children the animals in the brochures or on the website to get them excited about their upcoming "safari."

Look over the zoo's review in this book. Take note of the exhibits listed as "Don't Miss" attractions. Then read through the narrative portion of the review, taking note of what interests each member of the family. Re-read the review on the way to the zoo as a reminder of what everyone wants to see.

What To Bring

At the zoo, just about anything you might need is available – for a price. Because prices can be steep, it's important to think about what to bring along.

A full day of walking zoo trails, especially at the larger zoos, can lead to very tired feet. Small children can become cranky and spoil everyone's fun. Bring along a stroller, or rent one from the zoo, to help alleviate this problem. Wagons can also be rented at many zoos and are becoming increasingly popular because more than one child, and older children, can ride. Whatever your mode of transportation, pack a few bandages for blisters.

While refreshments and meals from zoo snack bars and restaurants can be costly, they are also convenient and fun. If you want to save money by bringing your own picnic, check first to see if the zoo allows outside food to be brought in. Most, but not all, zoos have designated picnic areas on the grounds. Some of those that do not compensate by providing picnic tables just outside the entrance.

In summer, take precautions to protect yourself and your family from the sun. Bring sun hats, visors, and sunscreen to shield faces and limbs, and be sure you're drinking enough fluids to stay hydrated.

If you bring along a camera or camcorder, don't forget to bring extra film or a memory card, tapes, and batteries, as appropriate. Binoculars are also handy to have along. Some exhibits are so massive that you'll miss a lot if you're limited to what the naked eye can see.

Finally, give some consideration to what to wear on your zoo visit. Check the weather forecast and dress accordingly. If you're unsure, bring extra clothes in the car – just in case. Comfortable walking shoes are, of course, essential.

When To Go

In summer, it is important to arrive early. This is when the crowds are lightest, the temperatures are coolest, and the animals are most active.

Summer, however, is not the only time to go. Many people think that the zoo is not an enjoyable place unless the weather is warm and sunny, but the zoo can be just as much fun, maybe even more so, during bad weather. Inclement weather will reduce the crowds, so you won't have to strain to see over people. And with smaller crowds and cooler weather, the animals tend to be more active.

It is true that when the temperature is cold, fewer animals from Africa and tropical Asia will be outside (though some of these animals are surprisingly tough). Then again, when else but in winter can you see a polar bear or a snow leopard playing in a fresh blanket of snow? Many zoos, particularly the northern ones, have numerous warm indoor exhibits (which they keep air-conditioned in the summer). These buildings are, of course, not affected by the weather and are especially enjoyable when they're relatively empty.

Starting Your Tour

As you enter the zoo, pick up a map for everyone in your party. Children especially enjoy having their own map, and might even pick up a few map-reading skills as the day wears on!

Determine what exhibits each person wants to see most. Mark those exhibits on the map and then plan a route that leads to all of them. If the zoo has a circular layout, it's a good idea to go "against the flow," that is, to tour the zoo in a counter-clockwise direction (most people tend to move clockwise). You can avoid some crowd buildup this way.

As you check over the map, note the times of any animal shows, feedings, or keeper chats that sound interesting. Adjust your plans to arrive at these exhibits at the specified times.

Animal Viewing Tips

Use the following simple guidelines about animal activity to maximize your viewing experience:

1. Tigers and lions are among the most popular animals, but they are also among the zoo's least active. Just like your kitty at home, these cats sleep a lot – up to twenty hours a day. If these big cats are a must-see on your list, make them your first stop, as they tend to be most active at the beginning of the day.

2. Primates are usually the most active animals in the zoo. Almost any time of day is a good time to see playful monkeys and apes.

3. The middle of a summer day is a good time to visit indoor exhibits, such as aquariums, bird houses, or reptile houses. While the outdoor animals may be snoozing in the shade, these air-conditioned places are not only a good way to escape the heat, but the animals inside live in climate controlled environments which allow them the comfort to be active most of the day. Fish never stop swimming and birds follow a strict light cycle, which keeps them active throughout the day, but completely inactive at night. Reptiles, on the other hand, are low activity animals; they conserve energy by not moving much, which is why many only have to eat once a week (or less). There isn't typically a best or worst time to see snakes at the zoo, so consider yourself lucky when you do find these slithery creatures moving about.

4. Semi-aquatic animals, including polar bears and hippos, will often begin their day with a morning swim. If the zoo has underwater viewing of these animals, try to visit them early in the day.

5. Late afternoon is another excellent time to view active animals, as they are anxious to go in for the night (where they will be fed) and are thus likely to be up and moving about.

6. Summer is not the only time of year to visit a zoo. Animals such as snow leopards, Japanese macaques, and Amur tigers enjoy the winter season and are more likely to be active in colder weather.

Rules and Manners

Everyone should be aware of two simple rules. First, the animals should not be teased or intentionally disturbed. Some visitors like to tap on the glass or throw rocks at the animals to get their attention; both actions are strictly forbidden. Secondly, visitors should never feed the animals – not even grass – unless explicitly invited to do so. Zoo animals are on special diets designed for their optimal health. Violating either of these rules may harm the animals, embarrass your companions, and possibly result in being asked to leave.

At Chicago's Lincoln Park Zoo, you may get a look at a sad example of what can happen when a visitor fails to obey the rules. In 2006, disregarding the no-feeding rule, a visitor threw food to the gibbons near their outdoor enclosure. One ape reached through the fence to grab at the food, but his arm became stuck. Tragically, that arm had to be amputated from the elbow down. The gibbon has recovered remarkably well and is still (at press time) on exhibit, but he would still have two arms if not for one visitor's bad behavior. Remember this story when you are tempted to disregard the rules.

Shows

Most zoos offer animal shows, but their appeal can vary greatly. Some are of the caliber found at major theme parks like SeaWorld, while others are simple, informal demonstrations. One way to gauge the potential appeal of a show is to look at the size of its amphitheater. If it has a large seating capacity, it is probably popular. Almost any show featuring dolphins, sea lions, or elephants will be good. Of course, the smaller informal "keeper chat" presentations can be fascinating, too – and you may get a chance to chat with and have your questions answered by a real animal expert.

When taking very small children to a show, try to sit near the exit. Even the best entertainment can be boring to toddlers and babies, and you might need to make a fast getaway.

Dining

Seating at many zoo restaurants includes a captivating view of the animals. For example, Omaha's Henry Doorly Zoo has a 400-seat restaurant with glass panels that overlook the amazing Lied Jungle. A more simple, though equally pleasing, experience can be had in the outdoor seating area of the Montgomery Zoo's Overlook Café, where the lunchtime entertainment includes lions and zebras on one side, bison and elk on another, and Asian deer in a third direction.

The menu can be fun, too. Dolphin-shaped French fries or a "Happy Meal" with a zoo theme are exciting choices for children. Soft drinks may be served in colorful plastic souvenir cups that make great mementos for zoo-loving kids.

Zoo Membership

Since numerous visits to the zoo can get quite expensive, consider buying a zoo membership. It usually pays for itself in just two or three visits. Besides free admission, most zoos offer their members other advantages, such as inclusion in special events and discounts at the gift shop. Also, a **reciprocity program** among most zoos allows members to enter other zoos across the country at a discounted fare when they use their membership cards. Zoos that participate in this program are noted in the Fees section of each zoo review.

Animal Photography

Wildlife photography can be a wonderful hobby, and for most people, even professionals, zoos are often the best places to take animal pictures. Many of the animals in zoos are very hard to find in the wild, let alone to photograph. The most important thing to understand is that anyone can take great animal pictures, even without spending a fortune on expensive photography equipment. But getting a great picture means taking into account a number of factors that can change on a daily basis. Specifically, dream shots require timing, patience, and often a little research. Here are a few tips that should prove helpful in almost any situation:

Timing. By timing, we mean time of day, and specifically the lighting. Previously, we pointed out that the best time to see almost any outdoor animal is early in the morning, due to both the animals' activity levels and to the sunlight. Early morning light is usually the softest of the day; it almost lights the subject from within. On the other hand, midday light can be bright and harsh, and in the late afternoon, the setting sun creates problematic shadows. Cloud cover can be a bonus when it comes to lighting; the diffuse light illuminates evenly without creating harsh shadows. Be aware of these factors when composing a shot. But timing also can include attending planned zoo events that may increase your chances of getting a great picture. Most zoos feature educational shows, chats, and animal feedings. These informative interactive presentations also present excellent picture-taking opportunities.

Patience may be the most important factor in getting a good photo. Finding an animal in a zoo isn't always tough, but finding one in the right position can be quite difficult. If a gorilla is hiding behind a bush, or a leopard is perched high in a tree and nearly out sight, spend a few minutes waiting to see if it will move. Trying to find an animal in the right context, however, does not mean tapping on the glass to get its attention. (For one thing, glass-tapping is a big no-no in zoos, a clear violation of zoo manners and rules. Repeatedly tapping on their glass tanks can even harm some animals, such as reptiles.) Even though it will take longer, waiting for the right shot, instead of artificially creating it, is much more satisfying. The old adage that "persistence and patience pays off" certainly holds true in wildlife photography.

Angles and equipment. Modern zoo exhibits bring animals closer and closer to visitors, so even a disposable point-and-shoot camera can produce some nice shots. Quite often, these close encounters with animals are achieved through creative use of glass barriers. Unfortunately, the downside of glass is the potential for glare. The best way to eliminate glare is to take the picture from a forty-five-degree angle. For those willing to purchase more advanced equipment, a glare-reducing filter can significantly improve photos of animals taken through glass. If you are fortunate enough to have an SLR camera with detachable lenses, bring along a wide-angle lens to the zoo.

Popular Photography Magazine named the San Diego Wild Animal Park, Woodland Park Zoo, Minnesota Zoo, and Oregon Zoo, among others, as great photography sites. Each of these zoos has a specialty – an animal that can be photographed better there than anywhere else. At the San Diego Wild Animal Park, they recommend you photograph the lions; at Minnesota, the wolves and tigers. Before your next zoo visit, take a peek at the *Animals To Look For* chapter, as it recommends the best places to see some unusual animals, as well as some of your favorites. If you can't find what you're looking for, go to the specific zoo review and find out what that zoo is known for.

Zoos are in the business of recreating natural habitats. While close-up pictures of animals are certainly impressive, don't forget to include a few pictures that showcase their surroundings – you might even be able to convince someone you actually went on an African safari! You may also want to take some pictures of people watching animals, the botanical gardens that often grace zoo grounds, animal statues, or even the beautiful historic architecture at older zoos. There is a lot to photograph at the zoo besides the animals.

When Children Are Along

Educational Fun

It is no accident that many schools plan field trips to the zoo. Observing animals is educational, and kids can learn a lot by reading informative signs that not only identify the animals, but also describe where they come from, what they eat, and what is unusual about them. Read these signs to, or with, your children. An eight-year-old who knows that a koala is not a bear is one step ahead of the general population. Who knows – you may learn a thing or two yourself!

Many zoos take extra steps to make learning an enjoyable experience. At the St. Louis Zoo's River's Edge and the Fort Wayne Children's Zoo's Indonesian Rainforest, a card or flyer with pictures of all the creatures in the exhibit is given to each visitor, who is then challenged to find as many of these animals as possible. At most zoos, volunteers present a table full of animal artifacts for children to touch and examine. These might include a gorilla skull, an elephant tusk, or the fur of an exotic animal such as an okapi or snow leopard.

Rides

To a child, a zoo trip can be the best part of an entire vacation. A child visiting New York City might enjoy a day at the Bronx Zoo far more than a day at the Statue of Liberty. Keep this in mind when considering whether a ride on that little train is worth the money. It may not look so important through adult eyes, but it can look like a ride at Disneyland to a five-year-old.

Even if your budget is tight, do let the kids pick out at least one ride to enjoy. A ride on a camel, though short in duration, is long remembered by most children.

Sky rides and monorails are offered at only a few zoos, and they are every bit as fun as most theme park rides. Don't miss the opportunity to enjoy them. Especially when you consider the average cost of admission to a theme park, most of these zoo rides are real bargains.

Souvenirs

In the rush to get tired bodies home, don't overlook one of the highlights of a zoo visit for many children – selecting a souvenir at the gift shop. It doesn't require a lot of money to buy a child something special that will serve as a memento of a good time. A plastic animal figurine, an animal-shaped eraser, or even a few postcards depicting their favorite animals can be very special, even though they cost very little.

Other reasonably priced items for pint-sized collectors may include a smashed penny or a colorful sew-on patch. A zoo map is a souvenir that costs no money. They can be fun to collect, and make a nice display taped up on your child's bedroom wall.

Should you decide to spend a bit more and purchase a plush stuffed animal, consider making it one of the exotic animals that you saw at the zoo. Instead of a bear or a bunny, select a stuffed red panda or a black-and-white Malayan tapir. That's something you can't find at just any toy store!

Many zoos sell souvenir guidebooks for their facilities that make excellent, and inexpensive, keepsakes. It will be a reminder of your happy day at the zoo, and can also serve as a great animal reference book.

The money you spend on these souvenirs goes to a good cause. Zoos use gift shop profits to pay for facility upkeep and improvements.

Going Home

An important, but often ignored, rule is: don't overdo it! When planning an outing to your local zoo, remember that a few short visits are often more enjoyable than one long one. Potentially wonderful days at the zoo have been ruined by parents who insisted on seeing *everything*. When the children are worn out, call it a day and be thankful for the memories you've already made. If you missed exhibits that someone still wants to see, come back another day.

Animals To Look For

MOST ZOO VISITORS ARE QUITE FAMILIAR WITH ZEBRAS, GIRAFFES, elephants, seals, gorillas, lions, tigers, and bears. These animals are very popular, and are what most people expect to see at the zoo. Many other zoo animals, however, are not nearly as well-known to the average visitor.

SOME LESSER-KNOWN ANIMALS AND WHERE TO SEE THEM

This chapter aims to spotlight some unusual animals, along with a few you may know, but can't see at every zoo. These animals are easy to recognize once you know what to look for. We'll give you fun facts and information about each one. Most of them are found in only a few U.S. zoos, so consider it a privilege to come across one.

MAMMALS

Aardvarks *(See photo, page 142.)*
Aardvarks are unique enough to merit their own scientific Order (Tublidentata), thanks to their unusually shaped dental pattern. Their name translates, in Africaans, to "earth pig," a reference to their talent for digging. An aardvark's diet consists almost entirely of termites, and they are well-designed to catch them. Long claws help them break into hardened termite mounds, and their two-foot-long sticky tongues slurp up termites with ease. Most active at night, they're usually found in nocturnal exhibits.
Best Places to See Them: Omaha's Henry Doorly Zoo, Brookfield Zoo, Memphis Zoo.

Bearded Pigs
These aptly named Asian pigs sport bristly beards. Beards on males are thicker and reach the tip of the snout, while females have thinner, whisker-like beards that do not extend toward the tip of the snout. Bearded pigs are taller and more slender than most other swine. Thanks to this lighter build, they can jump over seven feet into the air. In the wild,  these pigs like to follow gibbons and orangutans, feeding on the figs dropped by the apes.

Best Places to See Them: San Diego Zoo, Lowry Park Zoo, Gladys Porter Zoo, Philadelphia Zoo.

Bonobos

Our closest living relatives (human and bonobo DNA are 99% identical), bonobos are among the most fascinating social creatures in the animal kingdom. Similar in appearance to the common chimpanzee and also known as the pygmy chimpanzee, the bonobo has a slighter build, a part in its hair, and very different social behavior. Most notably, bonobo troops are led by females, rather than males, and the species as a whole is significantly less aggressive than the common chimp.

Best Places to See Them: Columbus Zoo, San Diego Zoo, Milwaukee Zoo, Cincinnati Zoo.

Clouded Leopards   *(See photo, page 51.)*

These leopards, named for the cloud-like patterns in their fur, are native to the rain forests of Southeast Asia. These mid-sized cats are built for life in the trees. Their long tails help them maintain balance, and their rear feet are very flexible, allowing them to climb down trees head first with ease. Clouded leopards can be intimidating: no other cat has longer canine teeth relative to its body size. Researchers have discovered that zoos' breeding success with clouded leopards is greatly improved when they are housed far away from other large cats and provided with high places to perch throughout their habitat.

Best Places to See Them: Nashville Zoo, National Zoo.

Drills   *(See photo, page 79.)*

Drills are among the world's most endangered primates, found only in a few West African forests. Due to the popularity of Disney's 1994 film *The Lion King*, mandrills (like the character "Rafiki" in the film) have become a popular addition to zoos around the country. Drills look nearly identical to their mandrill cousins, except for their jet-black faces; the mandrill's visage is vivid blue and red. Unfortunately, drills are just as uncommon in zoos as in the wild. Male drills are more than twice the size of females and will intimidate intruders by pulling back their upper lips to reveal their three-inch canines.

Best Places to See Them: Zoo Atlanta, Columbus Zoo, Los Angeles Zoo.

Fossas

(Pronounced FOO-sas)

Another animal made famous by a movie (*Madagascar*), the fossa is the largest land predator on the island of

Madagascar. Although it strongly resembles a cat, it is most closely related to civets and genets, other agile Old World carnivores. In the wilds of Madagascar, fossas are lemurs' main predators, due to their ability to climb trees.

Best Places to See Them: Omaha's Henry Doorly Zoo, Cleveland Zoo.

Giant Otters

In many parts of South America, giant otters are called "lobos del rio," river wolves. Reaching lengths of up to six feet, they are the largest and longest of the world's thirteen otter species. In addition to its massive size, the giant otter is also distinctive for the yellow patch of fur on its neck. They live in groups, called "holts," of up to ten individuals, and are one of the few animals brave enough to hunt piranhas. Like all otters, giant otters are very playful and are lots of fun to watch. They are also the most vocal of the otters, emitting a high-pitched sound that's similar to a cat's meow.

Best Places to See Them: Philadelphia Zoo, Jacksonville Zoo.

Giant Pandas *(See photo, page 78.)*

Scientists argued for years about whether or not giant pandas are actually bears. The latest genetic studies show that pandas are, in fact, members of the bear family. They are closely related to South American spectacled bears. Giant pandas are only seen in a few American zoos because they are so expensive to keep. Pandas eat only certain types of bamboo leaves, and they eat a *lot*. Pandas have a sixth "finger," an extension of a wrist bone that helps hold on to bamboo, and strong jaws and teeth to bite through tough bamboo stems. In addition, American zoos that exhibit pandas have to pay one million dollars a year to China to help support conservation efforts for wild pandas.

Best Places to See Them: San Diego Zoo, National Zoo, Memphis Zoo, Zoo Atlanta.

Koalas *(See photo, page 256.)*

Koalas are not bears at all, but are, in fact, marsupials – like kangaroos. Tiny baby koalas live in their mother's pouch for six months before venturing out into the world. Despite their cute and cuddly appearance, koalas have deep, bellowing voices and can be quite aggressive. Koalas are very picky eaters, eating only leaves from certain eucalyptus trees. These leaves are so rich in moisture that koalas never have to drink.

Best Places to See Them: San Diego Zoo, Los Angeles Zoo, Rio Grande Zoo, Cleveland Zoo.

Manatees *(See photo, page 74.)*

Unfortunately, manatees are best known today as regular victims of speedboat traffic in Florida. These gentle giants, also known as sea cows, feed on floating plants in shallow waterways and are usually not fast enough to get out of the way of oncoming motorboats. While manatees can be quick underwater, they usually float so slowly that algae will grow on their backs. Nearly all manatees in zoos today are recovering from encounters with speedboats, and once an animal is rehabilitated, it is generally released back into the wild.

Best Places to See Them: Lowry Park Zoo, Columbus Zoo, Cincinnati Zoo.

Maned Wolves *(See photo, page 192.)*

Despite their name, maned wolves are more like foxes than wolves in both appearance and behavior. These long-legged canines are native to pampas (or tall grass) habitats of South America. Almost as striking as their stilt-like legs are their bright red fur coats. Like foxes, and unlike other wolves, maned wolves hunt rodents and live alone, rather than in packs. Over half of their diet in the wild consists of a tomato-like fruit called *lobeira*, which has been nicknamed "wolf fruit." Their non-predatory attitude towards larger species makes them great candidates for mixed-species exhibits in zoos. Thus, they are often found sharing space with typical prey species such as tapirs and giant anteaters.

Best Places to See Them: Oklahoma City Zoo, Louisville Zoo, Houston Zoo, Montgomery Zoo.

Okapis

(Pronounced o–KAH–pees)

Although they look like a cross between a horse and a zebra, these shy creatures from the central African rain forests are actually the only living relatives of giraffes. Despite lacking the giraffe's long neck, okapis share many significant characteristics with their savanna-dwelling cousins. Most notably, okapis have three-foot-long purple tongues, which they use to strip leaves from branches and to clean their ears. Male okapis have horns (called ossicones), which are also found on both male and female giraffes. Westerners did not discover the elusive and shy okapi until just over a hundred years ago, in 1901. For the first few weeks after birth, a mother okapi will leave her calves alone for most of the day, hiding them in the dense forest.

Best Places to See Them: Bronx Zoo, Dallas Zoo, Brookfield Zoo, Disney's Animal Kingdom.

Scimitar-Horned Oryxes *(See photo, page 121.)*

Zoos saved Arabian oryxes from extinction in the 1980s. Scimitar-horned oryxes may be the twenty-first-century equivalent. These beautiful desert antelope may have been hunted to extinction in the wild for their namesake horns, shaped much like the swords known as scimitars. Fortunately, there is a healthy captive population in zoos around the world, which should sustain the species until it can be reintroduced back into Africa's vast Sahara Desert. Conserving water is of the utmost importance to survival in such a harsh, dry environment. These oryxes do so by not sweating until their internal body temperature reaches an astounding 116 degrees Fahrenheit.

Best Places to See Them: San Diego Wild Animal Park, Dallas Zoo, San Francisco Zoo.

Sifakas *(See photo, page 51.)*

(Pronounced she–FAH–kas)

These acrobatic lemurs are most recognizable, at least to kids, as "Zoboomafoo," from the PBS television series of the same name. In real life, few primates can compare to sifakas in terms of agility. They can leap more than twenty feet from tree to tree, and hop like kangaroos when moving across the ground. Their eyes are bright yellow or orange, in striking contrast to their black and white fur. As with most lemurs, leaders of sifaka clans are typically females.

Best Places to See Them: St. Louis Zoo, Los Angeles Zoo, Philadelphia Zoo, Maryland Zoo.

Takins

(Pronounced TAH–kins)

The famed golden fleece sought by Jason and the Argonauts is believed to have come from a takin. The takin is native to the misty, mountainous bamboo forests of China, and is the national animal of Bhutan. Although similar to mountain goats in nature and appearance, they are most closely related to musk oxen. Two species are seen in American zoos: Sichuan takins, whose males have golden coats, and Mishmi takins, which have much darker brown coats.

Best Places to See Them: Minnesota Zoo, San Diego Zoo, St. Louis Zoo, Denver Zoo.

Wolverines *(See photo, page 164.)*

Wolverines are one of the largest members of the weasel family and, pound fo pound, may be the fiercest animal in the world. There are many documented instances of wolverines chasing bears away from their meals. Wolverines are active animals, covering more than twenty-five miles in a day, searching for animal carcasses on which to scavenge. Even frozen animals do not deter wolverines, as their jaws are strong enough to crunch through frozen meat and bones. These tough critters are found along the Arctic Circle in North America, Europe, and Asia. Wolverines are very shy, and are rarely sighted in the wild.

Best Places to See Them: Minnesota Zoo, Detroit Zoo, Columbus Zoo.

Wombats *(See photo, page 142.)*

Wombats are marsupials, like kangaroos and koalas, and are native to Australia. They are known for being slightly aggressive at times, and their thick build and burrowing tendencies have led to their nickname "bulldozers." While they do not eat anything particularly complicated, mostly just grasses, their digestive process can take up to fourteen days. A wombat pouch faces backward, which prevents these enthusiastic diggers from kicking dirt into their pouches.

Best Places to See Them: Brookfield Zoo, San Diego Zoo.

BIRDS

Birds of Paradise *(See photo, page 51.)*

There are forty-two species of birds of paradise, native to Pacific islands. Males have brilliant and colorful plumage, in contrast to the females, which are rather drab looking. Males court by showing off their beautiful feathers in choreographed shows that are among the most stunning displays in the animal kingdom. These birds were once hunted extensively for their feathers, which were used to decorate women's hats.

Best Places to See Them: San Diego Zoo, Toledo Zoo, Riverbanks Zoo, Honolulu Zoo.

Cassowaries *(See photo, page 80.)*

Cassowaries are one of four species of large flightless birds known as ratites. This native of New Guinea and Australia has a large casque (a hollow horn) on top of its head. Several different theories have been proposed to explain its purpose. One possibility is that it is attractive to mates; another is that it helps the birds push through the dense rain forest brush where they live. The rest of their heads and necks are beautifully colored with bright blue and red patterns. Cassowaries are dangerous birds; they can deliver strong kicks with their sharp-clawed feet.

Best Places to See Them: Gladys Porter Zoo, National Zoo, Los Angeles Zoo.

Harpy Eagles

These slate gray masters of flight are among the largest birds of prey. Native to the high canopies of Central and South American rain forests, these birds are famous for their ability to nab perching monkeys and sloths with ease. Like most birds of prey, females are larger than males; a female harpy eagle can weigh up to 20 pounds, nearly twice as much as a male. Both, however, are distinguished by crests of long feathers on the backs of their heads, which look like a crown when raised.

Best Places to See Them: Fort Worth Zoo, San Diego Zoo, Dallas Zoo.

Shoebill Storks *(See photo, page 51.)*

It's hard to find an odder-looking bird than the shoebill stork. Their bills resemble Dutch wooden shoes, and are used to catch lungfish, frogs, and snakes. Native to the wetlands of eastern Africa, shoebill storks are nearly four feet tall and will stand completely still, like statues, for hours at a time, as they stalk their prey. Little is known about their breeding habits since they nest in highly inaccessible papyrus swamps.

Best Places to See Them: Lowry Park Zoo, San Diego Wild Animal Park, San Diego Zoo.

REPTILES

Gharials

The gharial, also called a gavial, is a highly endangered crocodilian that was formerly native to the rivers of India, Nepal, Pakistan, and Myanmar. Today its range is restricted to isolated streams in Eastern India. Males are much larger than females; they can reach more than fifteen feet in length, making gharials one of the longest crocodiles in the world. They have long and very narrow snouts, filled with hundreds of sharp teeth.

Best Places to See Them: San Diego Zoo, Fort Worth Zoo, National Zoo, Honolulu Zoo.

Komodo Dragons *(See photo, page 257.)*

Komodo dragons are the largest lizards in the world. Measuring up to ten feet long and weighing up to 310 pounds, they are found only on a few remote islands in Indonesia. Komodos are excellent swimmers, and have been spotted swimming from island to island. They are famous for the deadly bacteria found in their saliva, which cause their bite victims to suffer slow and painful deaths. Adults are known to prey on juveniles, so young dragons live in trees until they are big enough to defend themselves.

Best Places to See Them: Disney's Animal Kingdom, Columbus Zoo, Los Angeles Zoo, Miami Metrozoo.

Tuataras

Tuataras are believed to be the closest living relatives of dinosaurs. These nocturnal lizard-like reptiles are native to New Zealand and some believe they have inhabited the earth for 200 million years. Often referred to as "living fossils," tuataras are also called "beakheads" for their uniquely shaped heads. The tuatara has a mysterious third eye on the top of its skull which is only visible in the young. The exact function of this eye baffles scientists even today. Tuataras mature very slowly, breed infrequently, and can live for more than a hundred years.

Best Places to See Them: Toledo Zoo, St. Louis Zoo, Dallas Zoo.

AMPHIBIANS

Japanese Giant Salamanders

These fifty-five-pound giants live in a very harsh environment. Dwelling at the bottom of cold mountain streams, these salamanders are covered in mucus that protects them from parasites. Their bodies are flat and streamlined, the better to swim in rapidly flowing waterways. Anything small that comes by, including crabs, mice, insects, and fish, will become food, though they can go several weeks without a meal.

Best Places to See Them: Omaha's Henry Doorly Zoo, National Zoo.

FISH

Archerfish   *(See photo, page 130.)*

Archerfish, native to Southeast Asian mangrove swamps, use a one-of-a-kind technique to hunt their prey. As insects fly over the water, an archerfish moves to the surface, waiting until the insect is directly above. It then spits a jet of water out of its mouth, knocking the insect out of the air and down to the water's surface for an easy meal. Archerfish can spit these water jets up to six feet, but they are most accurate at a range of three feet or less.

Best Places to See Them: Denver Zoo, Louisville Zoo, Houston Zoo.

Seahorses

With horse-like heads and kangaroo-like pouches, seahorses don't really look like fish. They do, however, have gills and tiny fins. There are thirty-two species of seahorse, ranging in size from the potbelly seahorse, which is more than a foot long, to the dwarf seahorse, which is smaller than a quarter. Seahorses are the only animals where the male delivers the babies. The female deposits her eggs into the male's pouch, where he proceeds to fertilize them. After several weeks, when the eggs hatch, he will "give birth."

Best Places to See Them: Indianapolis Zoo, Pittsburgh Zoo.

INVERTEBRATES

Cuttlefish

Despite the name, the cuttlefish is not actually a fish, but rather an eight-tentacled mollusk – like an octopus. Cuttlefish are often called "chameleons of the sea" because of their ability to rapidly change colors to match the surrounding terrain. These sea creatures are full of scientific marvels. For instance, cuttlefish have three hearts, one for each set of gills and one for the rest of the body. Because their maximum life expectancy is only two years, they are hard to keep in captivity.

Best Places to See Them: Pittsburgh Zoo, Point Defiance Zoo, National Zoo.

Moon Jellyfish

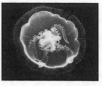

Jellyfish are one of the simplest, yet most fascinating, organisms on the planet. Watching a group of these translucent aquatic creatures as they glide through the water is a mesmerizing experience. Their "umbrellas" can reach nine inches across, with hundreds of thin stinging tentacles trailing down from their bases. There really isn't much to a jellyfish: 96% of its body is water.

Best Places to See Them: Toledo Zoo, Indianapolis Zoo, Omaha's Henry Doorly Zoo.

BEST PLACES TO SEE FAVORITE CREATURES

Alligators: Audubon Zoo, Omaha's Henry Doorly Zoo, Nashville Zoo, Busch Gardens Africa.

Beavers: Knoxville Zoo, Minnesota Zoo, Omaha's Henry Doorly Zoo, Arizona-Sonora Desert Museum.

Bison: Sedgwick County Zoo, Minnesota Zoo, North Carolina Zoo.

Camels: Minnesota Zoo, Miami Metrozoo, Bronx Zoo.

Chimpanzees: Kansas City Zoo, Dallas Zoo, Los Angeles Zoo, Busch Gardens Africa, Honolulu Zoo, North Carolina Zoo.

Elephants: San Diego Wild Animal Park, Indianapolis Zoo, Oakland Zoo, Oregon Zoo, Tulsa Zoo.

Giraffes: Cheyenne Mountain Zoo, San Diego Wild Animal Park, Brookfield Zoo.

Gorillas: Bronx Zoo, Zoo Atlanta, Lincoln Park Zoo, Louisville Zoo, Sedgwick County Zoo, Los Angeles Zoo, Gladys Porter Zoo.

Grizzly/Brown Bears: Woodland Park Zoo, San Francisco Zoo, Sedgwick County Zoo, Milwaukee Zoo, Minnesota Zoo.

Hippos: San Diego Zoo, Toledo Zoo, St. Louis Zoo, Busch Gardens Africa, Disney's Animal Kingdom.

Kangaroos: Kansas City Zoo, Fort Wayne Zoo, Cleveland Zoo.

Lions: Busch Gardens Africa, San Diego Wild Animal Park, Sedgwick County Zoo, Toledo Zoo.

Meerkats: Nashville Zoo, Houston Zoo, Sedgwick County Zoo, San Diego Zoo.

Orangutans: National Zoo, San Diego Zoo, Zoo Atlanta, Woodland Park Zoo.

Penguins: St. Louis Zoo, Milwaukee Zoo, Omaha's Henry Doorly Zoo, Indianapolis Zoo.

Polar Bears: Detroit Zoo, Pittsburgh Zoo, Toledo Zoo, Maryland Zoo.

Sea Lions: Memphis Zoo, Oregon Zoo, Rio Grande Zoo, Indianapolis Zoo, Audubon Zoo.

Tigers: Disney's Animal Kingdom, Bronx Zoo, Omaha's Henry Doorly Zoo, Utah's Hogle Zoo, Minnesota Zoo.

Wolves: Oklahoma City Zoo, Brookfield Zoo, Cleveland Zoo, Milwaukee Zoo.

Zebras: San Diego Wild Animal Park, Busch Gardens Africa, Phoenix Zoo.

How To Use This Book

We considered over two hundred American zoos to come up with the ninety-seven reviews in this book. Those we have selected as the top sixty are given detailed reviews. To help you find the best zoos in a particular area, or along a particular trip route, our zoo reviews are divided into seven geographic regions. We give our thirty-seven "Best of the Rest" zoos one-paragraph reviews at the end of the appropriate regional chapters.

The Zoo Reviews

At the beginning of each review, we list the zoo's official name, address, phone number, and website address along with a good deal of helpful information:

Hours and **Admission & Fees.** Use these as guidelines, not guarantees; hours can change on short notice and fees will almost certainly increase, some even before this book reaches the shelves of local bookstores, so be sure to check the zoo's website for the latest information. Zoos that admit members of other zoos free of charge or at reduced rates in a reciprocity program (see "Zoo Membership," page 9) are noted here.

Directions are meant to guide visitors to the zoo from major interstate highways. When available, interstate exit numbers are provided. If the zoo is conveniently accessible from a mass transit system, this is also noted.

We list some exhibits, shows, and rides in the **Don't Miss** section, to aid visitors who are short of time but want to see the best the zoo has to offer. Attractions are listed in descending order according to what we consider to be their entertainment value and uniqueness. If you have time for only a few items, start at the top of the list.

Special children's zoos and their youth-oriented displays, activities, playgrounds, petting areas, and animal feeding opportunities, along with most rides, are listed in the **For Kids** section. This should enable parents to plan ahead, knowing what is likely to appeal to their children.

Authors' Tips are hints, mostly from personal experience, to make touring the zoo easier, more efficient, and more fun. Step-saving tram and train rides are mentioned. Restaurants that provide interesting menu selections, or a unique or delightful dining atmosphere, are also included, as are special picnic sites, gift shops, and nearby attractions.

Most zoos offer entertaining animal shows and presentations. They are listed in the **Edutainment** ("*edu*cational enter*tainment*") section, along with a brief description.

Show times are usually listed on your zoo map, on an insert included with the map, or posted near the entrance gate. Ask an employee if you have questions.

In each zoo description, we devote the first paragraph or two to discussing interesting and important facts about the zoo, including its history.

Featured Exhibits contains a detailed description of the best exhibits listed in the "Don't Miss" section. The names of the exhibits are **boldfaced** when first introduced. The smaller sub-exhibits within the main exhibits are named in *italics*. These exhibits will often be described in the same order as the "Don't Miss" list – but not always. Sometimes it makes more logical sense to discuss the exhibits in the order in which you'll encounter them as you tour the zoo.

The remainder of the zoo's major exhibits are covered briefly in **Other Exhibits**. Names are boldfaced and italicized as above.

For the Kids expands on the capsule information offered in the "For Kids" section at the beginning of each zoo review.

The last section of each review is called **In Progress**, and includes information on exhibits that are in the works. This may, in some cases, include exhibits that will open within a few months of this book's publication.

How Each Regional Chapter Is Organized

Each chapter begins with a regional map that pinpoints the cities in which the featured zoos are located. The zoo reviews are arranged alphabetically, first by state and then by city (rather than alphabetically by zoo name). Thus in Eastern Zoos, we start with the District of Columbia, followed by Maryland, New York (Bronx and then Buffalo), Pennsylvania (Philadelphia, then Pittsburgh), and Rhode Island (Providence). The Best of the Rest zoos follow and are organized in the same way.

Other Information

Some technical terms, such as "kopje" and "pachyderm," are used frequently in the zoo reviews. Check the *Glossary* for definitions of these and other terms that may be unfamiliar.

The *Appendices* provide some perspective on how U.S. zoos compare to each other. There, we list list the "Top 10 U.S. Zoo Exhibits in 20 Categories." We also list what each of us considers the "25 Best U.S. Zoo Exhibits."

More Places to See Animals

Zoos aren't the only places you can see animals. The best of the wildlife parks, aquariums and aquatic parks, and other animal attractions in the United States, as well as three of Canada's best zoos, are highlighted in a free, downloadable supplement. You can access it online at our website.

www.AmericasBestZoos.com

Eastern Zoos

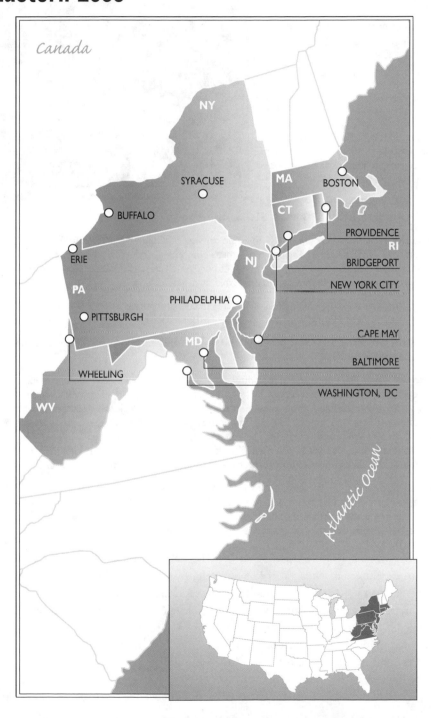

Canada

NY

SYRACUSE

BUFFALO

ERIE

PA

PITTSBURGH

WHEELING

WV

PHILADELPHIA

MD

NJ

MA

CT

BOSTON

PROVIDENCE

RI

BRIDGEPORT

NEW YORK CITY

CAPE MAY

BALTIMORE

WASHINGTON, DC

Atlantic Ocean

National Zoological Park

3001 Connecticut Avenue NW
Washington, DC 20008
(202) 673-4821
http://nationalzoo.si.edu

Hours: Grounds: 6:00 a.m.-8:00 p.m. daily, April-October (during Daylight Saving Time); 6:00 a.m.-6:00 p.m., rest of year. Buildings: 10:00 a.m.-6:00 p.m., April-October; 10:00 a.m.-4:30 p.m., rest of year. Buildings sometimes open earlier in summer.

Small-clawed otters watch visitors to the Asia Trail exhibit.

Admission & Fees: Free. Parking: $4 for the first hour, $12 for 2-3 hours, $16 for over 3 hours.

Directions: From downtown, go 2½ miles northwest on Connecticut Avenue. From the Capital Beltway (I-495), take Exit 33 and go 4½ miles south on Connecticut Avenue. Best idea: Take the Metro subway (Red line), getting off at either the Cleveland Park or Woodley Park-Zoo station, then walk a few blocks to the Zoo (this saves you the parking fee).

Don't Miss: Asia Trail (including Giant Panda Habitat), orangutans as they travel along the O-Line, Amazonia, Bird House, Small Mammal House, Beaver Valley.

For Kids: Kids' Farm, Tiger Tracks, educational displays and learning labs in Think Tank, the Bird House, Amazonia.

Authors' Tips: The entire zoo slopes downhill from its Connecticut Avenue entrance, where pedestrians and Metro riders enter, to its other entrance near Lion-Tiger Hill. Almost all of the animals are accessible from two connected paths: Olmsted Walk, which passes most of the indoor animal buildings, as well as Asia Trail; and the Valley Trail, which takes you past the bird exhibits, Beaver Valley, and Amazonia. The recommended route is to go up Olmsted Walk, and then down the steeper, shaded Valley Trail. This is a two-mile hike round-trip. Maps ($2 each) are available at the information station at the base of the hill or in the Visitor Center at the top.

Edutainment: There are over a dozen daily animal presentations, plus several others on certain days of the week. Highlights include elephant (11:00 a.m.) and sea lion (11:30 a.m.) training demonstrations, and feedings of eagles, fish, octopus, gorillas, otters, and sloth bears – all at their respective exhibits. Visit the zoo's website for specific times and shows.

FROM ALL ACROSS AMERICA, FAMILIES COME TO WASHINGTON, DC to experience its wide variety of patriotic, historic, and educational attractions. Many younger visitors find it difficult to fully appreciate the monuments, government buildings, and vast museums. What most children do enjoy is the National Zoo. Situated on 163 hilly acres along beautiful Rock Creek, the National Zoo is not just Washington's zoo, but one that belongs to all Americans. Its nearly 2½ million annual visitors confirm this status. It is part of the well-known Smithsonian Institution and funded by our federal taxes.

Many of the zoo's animal buildings were constructed over sixty years ago. Outside, they retain an historic charm, but inside most have been renovated, with modern, naturalistic exhibits. These buildings are surrounded by outdoor animal enclosures that are easy to miss (though you shouldn't). Look closely for them, especially those around the Reptile House, Great Ape House, and Bird House.

FEATURED EXHIBITS

It is fitting that the best exhibit, **Asia Trail**, features the zoo's most famous and popular animals, the giant pandas. These cuddly bears have been the face of the National Zoo since 1972, when President Nixon returned from China with two pandas. (Being our national zoo, this institution has traditionally been the recipient of animal gifts from foreign governments.) The original pandas are gone, but the current adult pair, Mei Xiang and Tian Tian, produced an adorable cub, Tai Shan, in 2005. Within the *Giant Panda Habitat*, their native Chinese terrain is mimicked using pools, streams, rocks, caves, fallen trees, and of course, bamboo. The pandas are usually visible from a bi-level path that runs past their two outdoor yards, or indoors in one of four exhibit rooms. The pandas are the stars here, but Asia Trail's six acres offer much more, including red pandas and an aquarium displaying a massive Japanese giant salamander, both further along the winding path. Other attractive animals on the Trail include beautiful clouded leopards, and small-clawed otters, which can be seen both above and below water in their long flowing stream. Small spotted fishing cats will sometimes demonstrate their hunting skills on the fish that live in their pool. Sloth bears anchor the other end of the Trail, in another large, glass-fronted rocky habitat. These shaggy bears draw big crowds when they suck their food through a long tube, in the same way that they would extract termites from mounds in the wild.

It is both thrilling and startling to see an orangutan overhead on the famous **O-Line** (Orangutan Transport System). The great apes use a 490-foot long, fifty-foot high, rubber-coated steel cable that runs along eight towers to swing or walk between Think Tank and the Great Ape House (described below), giving them a choice of location plus valuable natural exercise. They have access to the O-Line between 10:00 a.m. and 2:00 p.m., weather permitting, but the most likely time to see them is around 11:00 a.m. Visitors should note there are no ape restrooms along the O-Line, so be careful not to stand directly below passing orangutans!

Amazonia, a 15,000-square-foot glass-domed rain forest habitat, is the largest exhibit ever built at the National Zoo. Visitors enter the lower level, where a waterfall crashes into a pool full of freshwater stingrays at the beginning of the *Flooded Forest*. A long, cascading river aquarium displays Amazon River fish, including enormous arapaimas, one of the largest scaled freshwater fish in the world, and giant river turtles. Upstairs, the *Forest Walk* leads you back above the river and through a dense, mist-clouded jungle of fifty-foot trees, including a massive artificial kapok tree and many beautiful live bromeliad plants. While waterfowl are easily found in the stream, patience is required to spot the other colorful birds, a two-toed sloth, and titi and Goeldi's monkeys high above in the trees.

The **Bird House** is the centerpiece of an extensive bird collection and is one of America's best bird buildings. Inside, Raggiana birds of paradise, keel-billed toucans, and other tropical birds are displayed behind nearly invisible harp wire. Memorable exhibits include the walk-through *Indoor Flight Room* and a nocturnal exhibit of kiwis from New Zealand. (Few zoos display kiwis.) Outside, an impressive array of large birds includes stunning cassowaries from New Guinea, flamingos, and the residents of the *South American Run*, among them king vultures and lanky red-legged seriemas, one of the few birds that have eyelashes. Around the corner, four species of endangered cranes make up the *Crane Line*, while local fly-in herons stalk and wild ducks swim through the attractive *Wetlands* in front of the Bird House. Most impressive of all, a bridge leads to the famous ninety-foot-high *Great Flight Exhibit*, where more than a dozen beautiful avian species can stretch their wings.

The **Small Mammal House** is the best building of its kind in the nation. Inside, naturalistic exhibits showcase many small but fascinating animals most people have never heard of, such as prehensile-tailed porcupines, three-banded armadillos, black-footed ferrets, naked mole-rats, and a variety of small monkeys. The meerkats' arid desert habitat is a favorite here.

In the shady area known as **Beaver Valley,** river otters and, of course, beavers swim, play, and (in the beavers' case) build homes. Underwater viewing panels for both exhibits delight visitors with entertaining perspectives on these animated aquatic mammals. Other North American animals in this area include endangered Mexican wolves and the symbol of America, bald eagles. Further down the path, California sea lions and gray seals swim in rocky pools, habitats they share with brown pelicans.

OTHER EXHIBITS

Among the most celebrated projects here are the **free-ranging golden lion tamarin monkeys**, who, during the warmer months, roam freely on zoo property with no physical barriers to contain them. These furry little orange monkeys have the entire zoo for their range, but being territorial, they usually stay in the trees and ropes near their nest box. The rest of the zoo's primate collection is mostly distributed among two buildings and two outdoor exhibits. The **Great Ape House** displays gorillas and orangutans, both indoors and out. As noted above, orangutans can also be seen in **Think Tank**, along with distinctive Sulawesi macaques. In that educational building, many interactive displays demonstrate how researchers in behavioral sciences are studying the ways these animals think. Noisy gibbons and siamangs inhabit **Gibbon Ridge**, a mesh enclosure nestled in a grove of maple trees. Attractive **Lemur Island**, with its large waterfall, is the rocky home of two species of lemurs from Madagascar.

The **Cheetah Conservation Station** is representative of the zoo's efforts to save endangered animals. In a miniature African savanna, these sleek cats chase a mechanical lure at high speeds during regular exercise sessions. Also in this area, two varieties of desert antelope present a predator/prey backdrop for the cheetahs. Down the hill, the **Great Cats Exhibit** occupies a zoo landmark, *Lion-Tiger Hill*. Three large terraced habitats, encircled by the visitor path, provide naturalistic homes for the zoo's popular African lions and Sumatran tigers.

The **Elephant House** is the indoor/outdoor home of Asian elephants, Nile and pygmy hippos, and water-loving capybaras, the largest members of the rodent family. The pygmy hippos here are direct descendants of Billy, the first pygmy hippo in the U.S., who arrived here in 1927 as a gift to President Coolidge.

The **Reptile House** contains a large collection of snakes, lizards, tortoises, and other reptiles. Behind the building, a boardwalk through a swamp habitat passes a variety of alligators, crocodiles, and most notably, Komodo dragons, the world's largest lizards. The first dragons bred outside of Indonesia were hatched here. Also nearby is the indoor **Invertebrate Exhibit**, a diverse collection of invertebrates that includes jellyfish, coral, crabs, a giant octopus, various insects, and spiders. Most fascinating is the "super ant farm" filled with industrious leaf-cutter ants. Upon exiting the invertebrate display, visitors walk through the butterfly- and flower-filled *Pollinarium*.

Many other animals are scattered throughout the zoo, including caracal cats, coatimundis (raccoon relatives from Latin America), giant anteaters, peccaries (wild pigs), Mongolian wild horses (or Przewalski's wild horses), spectacled bears, long-legged maned wolves, emus, and tammar wallabies (kangaroo cousins).

FOR THE KIDS

At the bottom of the zoo, in the **Kids' Farm,** children can explore a real barn, learn where pizza ingredients come from in the *Pizza Garden*, play on the rubber-surfaced *Giant Pizza Playground*, and reach into corrals to pet dairy cattle, miniature donkeys, and small goats.

Animal artifacts, videos, touch-screen computers, and other displays are all utilized by the friendly staff to help educate children at the *Bird Resource Center* in the Bird House, the *Amazonia Science Gallery*, and in the Think Tank primate and research building.

Behind the Great Cats Exhibit, the *Tiger Tracks* trail uses innovative displays to help children compare themselves to the ferocious tigers nearby. You'll also find a small playground in this vicinity, behind the kid-pleasing prairie dog exhibit.

IN PROGRESS

In 2007, construction began on **Elephant Trails**, an innovative new home for the zoo's Asian elephants; a move made necessary because Kandula, a bull calf born here in 2001, is growing up! The old Elephant House from the 1930s will be modernized and extended to include a soft-floored *Elephant Community Center*, where the herd can socialize. Outside, among three large natural habitats, visitors will enjoy the *Elephant Camp* interpretive village, while the elephants will have access to the *Elephant Trek*, a long walking path into the forest, just for them! As we go to press, this exciting new exhibit is scheduled for completion in 2011.

The Maryland Zoo in Baltimore

1876 Mansion House Drive
Baltimore, Maryland 21217
(410) 366-5466
www.marylandzoo.org

Hours: 10:00 a.m.-4:00 p.m. daily. Closed January-February, on Thanksgiving, Christmas Day, and one day in June for their annual fund raiser.B

Don't miss Maryland Zoo's Polar Bear Watch exhibit.

Admission & Fees: Adults $15, seniors 65+ $12, children 2-11 $10. Carousel, climbing wall, and amusement rides $2 each, paid in tokens, available for $1 each at ticket booths on the zoo grounds. Camel ride $4, can be paid in cash or tokens.

Directions: From I-83, take Exit 7 West (Druid Park Lake Drive). Follow signs to the zoo along Druid Park Lake Drive. Turn right into the park at Gwynns Falls Parkway, then take a quick left onto Beachwood Road, which leads to the zoo.

Don't Miss: Polar Bear Watch, African Journey.

For Kids: Maryland Wilderness featuring the Children's Zoo.

Authors' Tips: It's a long walk from the entry area to the exhibits, so take the free Zoo tram. Convenient to the Children's Zoo, the Village Green complex has restaurants and an ATM.

Edutainment: Meet critters at an "Animal Outpost" presentation at Base Camp Discovery (across from the tram stop), or an "Education Outpost" encounter, held at three locations around the zoo. Puppet shows are popular with kids, and held four times per week in the Children's Zoo's Meeting Barn. "Wild Encounters" feature feeding and training of elephants, crocodiles, and penguins. "Keeper Chats" are 15-minute demonstrations, on weekends only, at the polar bear, giraffe, leopard, and chimpanzee exhibits. Check show schedule on the zoo map.

OPENED IN 1876, THE MARYLAND ZOO IS ONE OF THE OLDEST ZOOS in the nation. With its highly-rated children's zoo, innovative Polar Bear Watch, and excellent African Journey, the zoo is making a name for itself, out of the shadow of Washington's National Zoo just forty miles away.

When riding from the entry gate to the exhibits, take notice of the stately **Mansion House** on the left. This historic Victorian-era manor was built in 1801. It now holds the zoo's administrative offices, and on weekends it's a popular site for weddings.

FEATURED EXHIBITS

In the **Polar Bear Watch**, visitors are encouraged to pretend they are in Churchill, Manitoba, a town known as the "Polar Bear Capital of the World." These bears are a common sight in Churchill, on Canada's Hudson Bay, during the summer months. The winding path through this tundra setting passes mesh enclosures of snowy owls, common ravens, and arctic foxes. Just beyond these exhibits is a large underwater window for watching the polar bears swim. When one of these massive white bears is in this deep pool, it is a truly enchanting experience! Even better, however, is what waits above. The path winds uphill to the back door of a real Tundra Buggy®. This fifty-seven-foot-long, twenty-five-ton vehicle was actually used in Churchill to safely transport tourists to see wild polar bears. In Churchill, it costs over a thousand dollars for the opportunity to sit in one of the Buggy's padded seats and look out at the dangerous polar bears. Here, zoo visitors can sit in the same seats and look out the same windows at the zoo's polar bears for free. The Buggy takes visitors right into the middle of the bears' arctic habitat. As you descend from this realistic adventure, signs describe day-to-day life for children who live in the polar bears' native environment, up in Churchill. For example, one sign tells what to do if you're approached by a polar bear while trick-or-treating on Halloween.

African Journey has a remarkably diverse collection of species. At its entrance, vultures, crowned cranes, and marsh-dwelling sitatunga antelope peek through the tall grass near a fifteen-foot waterfall. Just past small exhibits of tortoises and crested porcupines, the *African Watering Hole* comes into view. Framed by tall rocky outcrops, this six-acre kopje exhibit is seen from a boardwalk that provides views of white rhinos, zebras, kudu antelope, gazelles, ostriches, and saddle-billed storks. The mesh-enclosed walk-through *African Aviary* encourages visitors to linger and admire a variety of African songbirds. There are large side-by-side enclosures for two very different spotted cats, African leopards and cheetahs. A side path leads through the tall grass to the warthog exhibit, almost hidden amongst the plant life. Giraffes and lions live in adjacent savanna yards. The lions can be seen through wide windows in the wall surrounding their enclosure. Visitors must cross a bridge to get to the three-acre African elephant complex, which includes two separate yards with large pools, and is best seen from a high observation deck. Members of North America's largest colony of African penguins are usually swimming in the waters of the deep moat surrounding *Rock Island*. Back near the giraffes, a breeding pair of their rare relatives, okapis, can be seen up close, near an enclosure of red-ruffed lemurs. The bamboo-lined path takes you deeper into the jungle, to the colossal *Chimpanzee Forest*. In a lush indoor environment, the zoo's prolific troop of chimps enjoys a large enclosure equipped with a variety of entertainment possibilities, while crowds gather at the wide windows to watch these lovable and funny apes. The walls are painted a deep green, making the tropical foliage seem even more abundant than it really is. Two other popular primates, black-and-white colobus monkeys and Coquerel's sifaka lemurs, also live here in large, tree-filled habitats. The highly endangered sifakas are powerful jumpers. It's great fun to watch them bounce around their enclosure. Near the door, slender-snouted crocodiles and colorful African cichlid fish swim in a glass-fronted tank. Outside, the chimpanzees are often seen in their well-planted enclosed yard.

FOR THE KIDS

The **Maryland Wilderness** *featuring The Children's Zoo* is one of the nation's best children's exhibits. This 8½-acre exhibit, occupying a previously untouched wilderness, has more than forty interactive exhibits that give kids the opportunity to jump, climb, and crawl just like the animals being displayed – all species native to Maryland. A boardwalk starts the adventure in the *Marsh Aviary*, a walk-through enclosure with herons, long-legged spoonbills, and other native waterbirds. Here, kids can climb into gourd-shaped oriole nests, sit in a heron's nest, and hop across the trickling stream on king-sized lily pads, providing classic photo opportunities for parents. At *Otter Falls*, a few steps lead down into a clear underwater acrylic tunnel where river otters can be seen, swimming directly overhead. Next door, a red fox lives in another naturalistic habitat, with snapping turtles in the water nearby. Behind the waterfall, the path continues into *The Cave*, where frogs, venomous snakes, and lots of bats live among realistic stalactites and stalagmites, and a jungle gym shaped like a woolly mammoth skeleton beckons. Just across a swinging rope bridge, the man-made *Giant Tree* houses a spiral staircase and close-up exhibits of more snakes. Adventurous children can exit the tree down a slide through a hollowed-out limb. The *Spinning Turtles* give kids a chance to see what wearing a turtle shell would feel like. Wildflowers fill the *Meadow*, where kids can climb through underground tunnels to pop up in clear plastic domes in the middle of the box turtle habitat. The highlight of the *Farmyard* area is the *KidZone* goat yard, where kids can pet these furry, friendly livestock. Inside the barn, there's a mechanical cow, a silo slide from the second floor, and more farm animals.

The *carousel* and *climbing wall* are popular attractions in the **Village Green** concession area, which also includes three carnival-style amusement park rides: the *Polar Bear Ride*, *Turbo Tubs*, and the *Hay Ride*. In the summer, there are also camel rides in African Journey, near the penguins. At the front of the zoo, the *Celebration Hill Playground* is fun for small kids.

IN PROGRESS

The zoo plans to add a giraffe feeding station to the African Journey area, scheduled to open in 2008 as we go to press. Eventually, the zoo hopes to include new exhibits for flamingos and prairie dogs. In the long term, they hope to double the size of the elephant exhibit and holding area, and otherwise enhance the space. This would allow them to add three more elephants to the herd. One part of this project would be the creation of an "elephant trek," a special walking path for the elephants to use.

Kids romp in the Children's Zoo's Marsh Aviary.

Bronx Zoo

Bronx River Parkway at Fordham
Road
Bronx, New York 10470
(718) 220-5090
www.bronxzoo.com

Hours: 10:00 a.m.-5:00 p.m. weekdays,
10:00 a.m.-5:30 p.m. weekends and holidays, April-late October; 10:00 a.m-4:30
p.m. daily, rest of year. Open until 9:00
p.m. during Holiday Lights. Last entry is a
half hour before closing time.

Admission & Fees: Adults $14, seniors 65+ $12, children 2-12 $10; base
admission is free on Wednesdays. Chil-

African wild dogs, newest residents of African Plains.

dren's Zoo $3; Congo Gorilla Forest $3
(when the weather is gorilla-friendly – otherwise, the indoor gorilla viewing is covered in the
basic admission); Wild Asia Monorail (April-October) $5; Skyfari aerial tram $3; Zoo Shuttle
$3 for rides all day, seniors free; camel ride (Memorial Day-October) $5; Butterfly Garden
(April-October) $3; Bug Carousel $2. Pay-One-Price Pass: Adults $25, seniors 65+ $21, children
2-12 $19. Parking $10.

Directions: From the Bronx River Parkway, take Exit 6 (Boston Road/Bronx Zoo), and then
follow signs to the zoo. By subway, take the #2 or #5 train to the West Farms Square/East
Tremont Avenue stop, or take the D Express train to the Fordham Road stop.

Don't Miss: Congo Gorilla Forest, JungleWorld, Wild Asia Monorail, Skyfari aerial tram, African
Plains (especially the Baboon Reserve), Himalayan Highlands, Tiger Mountain, World of Darkness, World of Birds, Seabird Colony Aviary.

For Kids: Children's Zoo, Skyfari aerial tram, Bug Carousel, camel ride.

Authors' Tips: Use the zoo's parking lot, as parking outside is limited and can be subject to
ticketing. Arrive early to enjoy as much of this huge zoo as possible. If there are children in your
group, don't plan to see everything in one day. The Zoo Shuttle offers step-saving transportation
around most of the zoo for a onetime fee. Unless you're arriving late, the Pay-One-Price Pass
(see above for prices) is cost efficient and easier than lining up to buy separate tickets all day.

Edutainment: "Animal enrichment programs" (training or feeding sessions) take place at
Tiger Mountain, World of Birds, Monkey House, the penguins in the Sea Bird Aviary, and the Sea
Lion Pool. The Wildlife Theater Players host performances in summer, while the Children's Zoo
Theater often has live animal demonstrations. Check the schedule on your zoo map.

SINCE NEW YORK CITY IS, BY FAR, THE LARGEST CITY IN THE U.S.A.,
it's no surprise it would have the nation's largest metropolitan zoo. The Bronx Zoo
is situated on 265 acres in the city's northernmost borough. Its enormous size gives
many of its animal residents more than enough room to roam, while human visitors
have a difficult task if they wish to see everything in one day. With over 4,000 animals,
this zoo has one of the largest animal populations in the nation, and with nearly 500
different species, it also has one of the most diverse collections.

Now over a hundred years old (it opened in 1899), this historic zoo offers the best of both old and new. Many of its buildings in the central Astor Court area display classical architecture, but most have been redesigned with ultra-modern interiors for the comfort of both animals and humans. This zoo has always been a trendsetter, and its innovative exhibits have been imitated by other zoos across the nation.

The Bronx Zoo is the hub of The Wildlife Conservation Society, a zoological society that also operates three smaller New York City zoos and the New York Aquarium. The society coordinates more than five hundred field projects in sixty nations. They hope their more than four million annual visitors will leave their parks with an interest in and compassion for wildlife.

FEATURED EXHIBITS

The **Congo Gorilla Forest**, a 6½-acre replica of a central African rain forest, is truly breathtaking! Using real and artificial jungle trees, rocky outcrops, crashing and trickling waterfalls, and over 15,000 tropical plants, the exhibit offers a unique jungle experience. As visitors walk the *Rain Forest Trail*, it even feels like the jungle, with a refreshing cool mist in the air. Huge, clear walls of glass give amazing views of the exhibit's magnificent animals. After a close-up view of black-and-white colobus monkeys, the trail enters a massive fallen tree. Through the tree roots, and then again from the *Ituri Field Camp*, elusive okapis are visible only a few feet away. Deeper in the jungle is the *Mandrill Forest*, with red river hogs, multi-colored Wolf's guenon monkeys, DeBrazza's monkeys, and mandrills – all colorful and rare species. Indoors, the *Treasures of the Rain Forest Gallery* has many terrarium and aquarium displays of reptiles, invertebrates, and fish of the African rain forest. Above the African rock python exhibit, a video screen demonstrates how these snakes detect body heat to find their prey by displaying a thermal image of the visitor viewing the screen. In the *Conservation Theater*, a seven-minute film shows the beauty and devastation of the Congo's rain forests. When the movie concludes, the screen is lifted, revealing a panoramic view of the zoo's resident gorillas. In the next room, a twenty-six-foot-wide window lets huge crowds gather to watch more than twenty of these great apes playing in their large hillside habitat, the *Great Gorilla Forest*. This is the largest breeding group of lowland gorillas in North America. Their reproductive success is obvious from the presence of many gorilla babies – the real crowd favorites here. After walking through a glass tunnel, with gorillas on both sides, visitors are asked to vote to choose how their $3 entrance fee will be directed for conservation of the Congo's rain forests.

One of this zoo's most world-renowned exhibits is the massive **JungleWorld** building. As one walks through its temple-like entrance, below hanging banners from Bali and India, there is a sense that this is a mystical place. The 783-foot wooden pathway passes through three distinct jungles (the *Scrub Forest, Mangrove Forest*, and *Rain Forest*), each dense with both live and artificial trees, vines, and other exotic plants. Behind the lush foliage, lifelike murals make the view seem more extensive than it really is. Five waterfalls drop into jungle streams and pools, while mist fills the air with steamy humidity. Within the three jungles, visitors can spot jungle birds, binturongs (often called "bear cats," though they are technically neither), tree kangaroos, small-clawed otters, Malayan tapirs, and silvered and ebony langur monkeys. Sleek black leopards seem dangerously close, but thick glass walls keep them in their enclosure. At the end of a cascading river is a deep pool, bordered by a seating area where visitors can relax and watch large freshwater fish swimming about. Above, the trees are filled with fruit bats, gibbons, and great hornbill birds. The three jungle habitats are separated by galleries displaying reptiles, amphibians, fish, insects, and small mammals of the Asian jungles.

The famous JungleWorld is only one part of the zoo's **Wild Asia** complex. *Asia Plaza*, with its pagoda-roofed pavilions, is modeled after an Asian bazaar, and includes a snack bar, souvenirs, camel rides, an outdoor amphitheater, and the *Wild Asia Monorail* station. In the specially designed one-sided monorail, riders sit facing out towards the exhibits, giving them superb views of the big, exotic, and mostly endangered species they glide past. The two-mile, twenty-minute tour crosses the Bronx River to the thirty-eight-acre Wild Asia preserve. The monorail silently passes Asian elephants, Indian rhinos, Indo-Chinese tigers, gaurs (wild cattle), Mongolian wild horses (or Przewalski's wild horses), and a wide variety of deer and antelope from Asia's forests and plains.

The **Himalayan Highlands** represents the wildlife and culture of Asia's mountainous regions in a convincing one-acre mountain habitat. An uphill trail winds through large boulders, crosses bridges over ravines, and follows Tibetan signposts to views of the red pandas and pretty Temminck's tragopan pheasants. Endangered snow leopards, often with cubs, are visible from many vantage points, in an exhibit often fronted only by nearly invisible harp wire.

At the entrance to **Tiger Mountain**, a forest path takes visitors to the Russian Far East, home of the world's largest cats, Siberian (aka Amur) tigers. From within two glass-walled pavilions, visitors can watch half a dozen awe-inspiring tigers as they roam their three-acre grassy forest or wade in their own *Tiger Swimming Hole*. Huge crowds will gather to watch a tiger gnaw on a horse bone during the daily enrichment programs. Graphics and cultural artifacts along the winding path to and from the pavilions educate visitors about all things tiger, including the need to save them from extinction.

When it opened, back in 1941, the **African Plains** was revolutionary – one of the first cageless zoo exhibits in America. The long, circular trail around this four-acre area is enhanced with inverted log fencing, simulated lava flows, and termite mounds. Animals in this wooded savanna include giraffes, zebras, ostriches, cheetahs, and several antelope species, including nyalas and slender-horned gazelles. A pride of lions overlooks the antelope in an excellent predator/prey exhibit. The newest residents here are the pack of well over a dozen African

Cheetah

wild dogs, perhaps the largest pack outside of Africa. The *Carter Giraffe Building* houses small duiker antelope and is the winter home of the zebras and giraffes. The highlight of the African Plains trail is the **Baboon Reserve**. This five-acre mountain exhibit depicts the Ethiopian highlands, home of gelada baboons. The male geladas are especially stunning with their bright red chests. Sharing the exhibit are Nubian ibexes (curly horned wild goats) and small rock hyraxes (nimble rodent-like creatures). A viewing cave allows visitors to get up close, and mounted coin-operated telescopes are available to see more distant animals. The adjacent *Somba Village* recreates an African market with thatched-roof mud houses, a souvenir stand, and a restaurant with an outdoor terrace that provides a great view of the baboons and ibexes. This is the zoo's most scenic place to eat.

When it opened in 1969, the **World of Darkness** was the first exhibit of its kind. Inside this tall black C-shaped building, deep red lighting is used to convince the many nocturnal animals that it is nighttime – their favorite (and most active) time of day. The sound of chirping crickets helps human visitors to imagine the same. One of the highlights of this place is the colony of naked mole-rats, crawling through a network of plastic tunnels. Other memorable animals include sand cats, douroucoulis (night monkeys), and of course, many, many fluttering bats!

The **World of Birds** is a strange-looking building, with outdoor catwalks connecting its two levels of avian exhibits. Among the hundreds of species here are dazzling birds of paradise, helmeted curassows, and rare St. Vincent Amazon parrots. All the birds are exhibited in naturalistic settings, many with nothing separating them from the viewers. The white-throated bee-eaters are remarkable for their ability to catch live crickets mid-flight, as they demonstrate during daily feeding sessions. Across the zoo, the sixty-foot-high walk-through **Seabird Colony Aviary** displays Magellanic penguins, rare sea gulls, and cormorants in a most appealing seashore setting that replicates the Patagonian coastline of South America.

OTHER EXHIBITS

The heart of this zoo is a landmark area called **Astor Court**, where California sea lions swim and play in their round, rocky pool, newly renovated in 2007. Nearby, the **Zoo Center** is a stately old structure, home to Bactrian camels and babirusas, wild pigs from Indonesia. All around this tall, domed building, jungle paths lead to observation points for the camels and babirusas. The old **Monkey House** nearby is still very popular. In exhibits lush with greenery and backed by painted dioramas, the collection of small South American monkeys includes pygmy marmosets, endangered golden lion tamarins, and Goeldi's monkeys, which are quite rare in zoos.

The 1899 **World of Reptiles** building, renovated in 2001, is not a typical reptile house. A broad collection of snakes, lizards, and turtles are housed in room-size habitats instead of the more usual small terrariums. One entire wall is dedicated to amphibians, including the axolotl, a Mexican salamander that breathes using gills. Other unique species here include endangered Chinese alligators and basilisk lizards, which can run on water on their hind legs.

Small mammals live in the **MouseHouse**. This building, especially favored by children, shelters one of the largest collections of rodents anywhere. Residents include giant cloud rats, flying squirrels, dwarf mongooses, and nine varieties of mice, including zebra mice. Nearby, in the **Butterfly Garden** greenhouse, more than a thousand butterflies of over fifty-five species seem to be everywhere! This rainbow of butterfly wings and flower blooms also features a koi pond, resting benches, and windows through which future butterflies can be seen, still in their cocoons.

The zoo's vast, highly rated collection of birds is spread throughout the grounds. In the **Aquatic Bird House** you'll find such favorites as spoonbills, kingfishers, and puffins. Just outside this building is a large flight cage for rare, primitive-looking adjutant storks. Nearby, the **Birds of Prey** aviary has a row of large flight cages housing Andean condors, golden and bald eagles, king vultures, and owls. Flamingos and native ducks live in the scenic **Wildfowl Marsh**.

King vulture

At **Bear Overlook**, polar bears and Kodiak bears attract crowds in front of their spacious grottoes. A large herd of American bison is nearly hidden behind the bushes in a pasture near Astor Court. (The Bronx Zoo played a major role in saving the bison from extinction in the early twentieth century.) The **Northern Ponds** have coin-operated telescopes for close-up views of trumpeter swans, ruddy ducks, and other North American waterfowl. Guanacos (related to llamas), Formosan sika deer, and rare Pere David's deer thrive in large herds in the **Rare Animal Range** across the zoo from these ponds.

FOR THE KIDS

The award-winning **Children's Zoo** is one of the nation's best. This three-acre space uses woodland, marsh, forest, and desert habitats to teach children about the homes, motion, defenses, and senses of animals. Kids can experience animal perspectives as they sit in a child-size heron's nest, pop up out of a prairie dog burrow, scoot through an otter log, play on a spider web, hop like a wallaby, climb up a porcupine tree, crawl into a turtle shell, and listen like a fennec fox through giant "ears." Nearby, these same animals watch the young humans imitating them. At the end of the path through this special place, children can pet and feed a variety of domestic animals.

On the thrilling **Skyfari** aerial tram, riders get a panoramic view of the entire zoo, and even the distant Manhattan skyline, from high above the Baboon Reserve. A camel ride is available in season at Wild Asia Plaza, while the **Bug Carousel** offers kids the chance to ride on giant insects.

IN PROGRESS

Scheduled to open in 2008, as we go to press, the new **Madagascar!** exhibit will also reopen one of the zoo's most historic buildings: Astor Court's 1903 Lion House. In naturalistic habitats, at least four species of endangered lemurs (ring-tailed, brown, red-ruffed, and blue-eyed black) will keep the exhibit's trees lively. Two lemur predators, Nile crocodiles and cat-like fossas, related to mongooses, will round out this display.

Buffalo Zoo

300 Parkside Avenue
Buffalo, New York 14214
(716) 837-3900
www.buffalozoo.org

Hours: Gates: 10:00 a.m.-5:00 p.m. daily, July August; 10:00 a.m.-4:00 p.m. daily, rest of year. Grounds remain open one hour after the gates close. Closed on Thanksgiving and Christmas Day, and on Mondays and Tuesdays in January and February.

Admission & Fees: Adults $8.50, seniors 63+ and children 2-14 $5. Train ride $1, carousel $1, giraffe and lorikeet feeding $1, parking $3.25. Note: you must purchase tokens (at the front gate or at a token booth in the zoo) for rides and parking: cash is not accepted. Participates in reciprocity program.

Japanese macaque is one of the zoo's Vanishing Animals.

Directions: From I-90 (NY Thruway), take Exit 51W (NY-33) and follow Kensington Expressway (NY-33) for 4.3 miles. Exit to Scajaquada Expressway (NY-198) and go west for 0.8 miles. Turn right onto Parkside Avenue, follow for 0.6 miles to the zoo. From I-190, take Exit 11 (Scajaquada Expressway/NY-198) west for 2.9 miles. Turn left onto Parkside Avenue, follow 0.6 miles to the zoo.

Don't Miss: Gorilla Habitat, Sea Lion Cove, Otter Creek, Vanishing Animals, Reptile House.

For Kids: Children's Zoo, Lorikeet Landing, carousel, kiddie train, Bone Zone, NOCO Playground, Living Tree House.

Authors' Tips: This mid-sized, 23½-acre zoo is easy to get around in. A visitor map is essential, however, as the maze of pathways can be confusing, especially during the construction of major exhibits. The zoo provides picnic tables in a park-like setting.

Edutainment: The zoo has a number of summer offerings. The "Wild About Wings" bird show is presented at the Gazebo Lawn area. Special elephant programs, held in the W.I.L.D. Place outdoor amphitheater, include "Bathtime With Buki," in which selected visitors help bathe an elephant, and "Elephant Art With Surapa," when visitors watch an elephant paint. Sea lion feeding demonstrations are held at Sea Lion Cove. Animal keeper talks, with various animals, are scheduled several times throughout the week. The Giraffe Feeding Station opens repeatedly throughout the day. Check your map for the day's schedule of these presentations.

WHILE WORLD-FAMOUS NIAGARA FALLS IS WHAT BRINGS MOST tourists to western New York, the Buffalo Zoo, just fifteen miles south, is another leading attraction. The zoo officially opened in 1875, exhibiting just a small herd of deer. This makes it one of the oldest zoos in the country. Despite its modest size, the zoo has the feel of a large wooded park and offers an extensive array of activities for children.

FEATURED EXHIBITS

The zoo's largest structure is known as the **Main Building** – a long, horseshoe-shaped structure. At one end is the **Gorilla Habitat**, the zoo's longtime premier exhibit. At the building's entrance foyer, visitors encounter *Diversity of Life*, a set of attractive exhibits of insects and crustaceans. The gorillas live in a rocky riverbank habitat that extends into the visitor area, so that viewers are immersed in the same environment as the apes. High above the gorilla family, under a glass roof, a waterfall crashes down through dense African broadleaf plants. All around the habitat, tall glass panels provide many views of the gorillas. Near the exhibit's exit, the *African River Aquarium* exhibits beautiful cichlid fish, swimming in an equally pretty pool with clear glass walls. Near the door is an exhibit of meerkats, which are very popular with visitors.

Just outside the Gorilla Habitat, **Vanishing Animals** is a set of six modern natural habitats for some very attractive threatened or endangered animal species. The animals here are easily visible through glass or thin mesh wire, and include serval cats, snow leopards, colorful baboon-like mandrills, Japanese macaque monkeys, and two other types of primates.

The impressive **Reptile House** is on the other end of the Main Building's horseshoe. When it first opened in 1942, zoo icon Marlin Perkins, then this zoo's curator, called it the "finest Reptile House in America." Today, it is still very good, with glass-fronted natural habitats enhanced by realistic background murals. Some of the memorable reptiles in the main hall include four types of rattlesnakes, king cobras, and American alligators.

Sea Lion Cove is a coastal habitat for the zoo's California sea lions. Two separate stairwells lead down to a tunnel-like viewing area, where the sea lions' underwater antics can be enjoyed through large windows. The rocky cove is surrounded by a 220-seat amphitheater, which hosts regularly scheduled feeding demonstrations. In the adjacent **Otter Creek** exhibit, you'll have another chance to watch aquatic mammals playing underwater – river otters, this time. Their naturalistic habitat, with a free-flowing stream and waterfall, displays many colorful educational graphics that explain the zoo's commendable goal of returning river otters into the wild throughout western New York.

OTHER EXHIBITS

Near the zoo's entrance, some very vocal Asian elephants live in a dusty habitat with a large pool. They will soon enjoy a major renovation of their **Elephant House**, which was built in 1912.

Scattered around the zoo are many unspectacular but spacious pens for an impressive collection of large mammals. Near the otters live herds of Scandinavian reindeer, mouflon sheep, and llama-like guanacos from South America. Across the path is a moated, mountain habitat for bighorn sheep. In another corner of the zoo, Indian rhinos and axis deer, which never lose their fawn-like spots, are situated across from the **Giraffe House** and its popular *Giraffe Feeding Station*, which is open seasonally. Finally, in the zoo's far corner are three African hoofstock yards, featuring three species of rare antelope: gemsboks, addax, and roan, as well as common zebras. And of course, the Buffalo Zoo has to have a small herd of buffalo (actually American bison).

The zoo's predators are also exhibited throughout the zoo. In the Main Building's outdoor Central Court, a deep moat separates lions and tigers from curious visitors. The big cats' grassy yards are enhanced with pools, tree branches and boulders for climbing, and a splashing waterfall. Among the Amur tigers on display is an orange-and-white "golden" tiger, a variety found only in zoos. As with white tigers, this golden shade is a rare coloration. It is believed that fewer than thirty of these beautiful golden cats exist in the world.

Across from Otter Creek, large rocky grottoes are the homes of polar bears, grizzly bears, and spectacled bears. Across from the bears, a set of enclosures holds maned wolves, and nearby small mammal grottoes contain red pandas and peccaries. In a modern, attractive habitat with multiple viewing points, spotted hyenas live within view of antelope, their natural prey.

Ecostation, in the midst of the Vanishing Animals habitats, is an interactive exhibit depicting a nature researcher's "base camp." Across the hall are three attractive animal habitats, with wallabies in the *Australian Scrub Forest*, little cotton-top tamarin monkeys in the *New World Rainforest*, and desert lizards and tortoises in the *American Southwest Desert*.

The **Boehm Porcelain Gallery**, displaying over eighty-five Boehm porcelain wildlife statues, all behind glass, offers a very different zoo experience – nature art!

FOR THE KIDS

The **Children's Zoo** displays exotic domestic animals, including zebu cattle, Sardinian donkeys, pygmy goats, and Ossabaw Island pigs, all ready for petting in basic steel pens. Kids can feed brilliantly colored Australian parrots in *Lorikeet Landing* (open seasonally), a tall mesh enclosure.

A musical carousel and kiddie train are inviting to small children. For free fun, there is the colorful **NOCO Playground**, and the **Bone Zone**, a super sandbox where children can dig to uncover realistic dinosaur bones. During inclement weather, the **Living Tree House** is a fun, high-tech education center for children.

IN PROGRESS

As this book goes to press, the amazing **South American Rain Forest** is already under construction, slated to open in July of 2008. Several tropical bird and monkey species will roam freely inside this 18,000-square-foot complex. A two-story waterfall will be the centerpiece of the habitat, and inhabitants will include giant anteaters, vampire bats, piranhas, spotted ocelot cats, anacondas, capybaras (giant water-dwelling rodents), and dwarf caimans.

Philadelphia Zoological Garden

3400 West Girard Avenue
Philadelphia, Pennsylvania 19104
(215) 243-1100
www.philadelphiazoo.org

Hours: 10:00 a.m.-5:00 p.m. daily, January-November; 9:30 a.m.-4:00 p.m. daily, December-February. Closed June 7, Thanksgiving, Christmas Eve and Day, and New Year's Eve and Day.

White lions are the most famous residents of Big Cat Falls, the zoo's premier exhibit.

Admission & Fees: Adults $17.95, children 2-11 $14.95, January-November; adults and children $12.95, December-February. Parking $10. Zooballoon $10; swan boat, camel safari, horse and pony rides $5 each; PZ Express $3; Wild Earth $2 weekdays, $5 weekends; PZ Panning Co. $5 small bag, $7 large bag. Participates in reciprocity program.

Directions: From I-76 take Exit 342 (Girard Avenue). The zoo is just off the exit from either direction; follow the signs. The SEPTA public transportation system services the zoo.

Don't Miss: Big Cat Falls, Carnivore Kingdom, Primate Reserve, African Plains, Reptile House, Bear Country, Zooballoon.

For Kids: Children's Zoo, Birds of Australia, camel safari, swan boat rides, PZ Express, Wild Earth, pony and draft horse rides, PZ Panning Co..

Authors' Tips: Zoo parking can be tough to find. Arrive as early as possible to get a parking space near the zoo. Several spacious lawns and a circular picnic grove make picnicking at the zoo an attractive option.

Edutainment: At the "Free Flight" bird show, visitors meet many different dynamic feathered creatures, from imposing eagles to colorful macaws to American backyard birds. Shows are presented Wednesday through Sunday.

"AMERICA'S FIRST ZOO," THE PHILADELPHIA ZOO WAS CHARTERED in 1859, although the Civil War delayed its opening until 1874. Reminders of the zoo's illustrious history are seen throughout the park, in the form of nineteenth-century Victorian buildings, animal sculptures, statues, and fountains. Today, it successfully maintains a delicate balance between preserving this historic heritage and exhibiting its impressive animal collection in some of the most modern and naturalistic habitats we've seen.

FEATURED EXHIBITS

Big Cat Falls, which was named "Exhibit of the Year" for 2007 by the AZA, uses the old Carnivora Building as the backdrop for each of its naturalistic outdoor cat exhibits. The biggest change for visitors familiar with the previous exhibit is that viewing is now through floor-to-ceiling glass windows rather than across deep moats.

In five separate yards – each utilizing plants native to a particular cat's homeland – the zoo displays lions, tigers, pumas, a black jaguar, and both Amur and snow leopards, which alternate time out in one exhibit. (The white lions are especially popular with guests and can often be seen resting near a row of termite mounds.) Each of these big cats travels from indoor housing to an outdoor exhibit area through a system of steel mesh tunnels known as "catwalks." These walks periodically pass over the visitor path that runs between the different exhibit yards. There are heated pools in the jaguar and tiger exhibits, to encourage these water-loving cats to swim year round. Visitors are presented with several different educational opportunities connecting their lives to the exhibit's big cats. At a research station, you can pretend to be a jaguar, hunting for prey and avoiding poachers. Kids can take a computerized personality test to learn what big cat they are most similar to, and then watch as a photograph of their face morphs into the face of their feline match. At *Big Cat Theater*, visitors can see wide screen movies chronicling the fascinating behavior of big cats.

A winding path leads around the huge boulders that encompass the **Carnivore Kingdom** exhibits. Long-tailed coatimundis, related to raccoons, are seen first, across from some lazy red pandas. Fishing cats are displayed in a bamboo grove, Canadian lynx among pine trees. The exhibit's highlight is a deep stream for a family of South American giant otters. As we write, this is the only breeding pair of these otters in the country. They and their offspring have a long glass-fronted pool to explore, as well as two smaller pools and a crashing waterfall. Unexpectedly, pelicans, which are also technically carnivorous, live in a marsh at the exhibit's end.

Tragedy stuck this zoo on the morning of Christmas Eve 1995, when the World of Primates building caught fire. None of the primates inside survived. Five years later, the **Primate Reserve** opened in its place. Now the apes, monkeys, and lemurs in this much larger facility enjoy tall, glass-fronted enclosures. Brightly colored steel walkways guide visitors along both upper and lower levels. Squirrel monkeys, spectacled langur monkeys, ruffed lemurs, and tamarin monkeys all have intricate networks of ropes and branches to play on. Orangutans and gorillas have indoor habitats, but are best seen in their outdoor yards. The orangutans share their tree-dominated exhibit with gibbons, while the gorillas wander among fallen trees. Also on the outdoor walking path are energetic sifaka lemurs, a lemur island, and exhibits of tiny tamarin monkeys.

The exhibits of the **African Plains** are spacious and lie along both sides of the visitor path. Zebras and curve-horned sable antelope share a long, narrow yard. A herd of reticulated giraffes is next, and square-lipped white rhinos live in a nearby paddock. Across the path, an expansive grassland habitat is home to ostriches, gazelles, and slender secretary birds. On the other side of the Carnivore Kingdom exhibit, the *African Outpost* offers a great view of hillside habitats for cheetahs and African wild dogs. Guinea baboons and colobus monkeys are also displayed here, in net enclosures.

The **Reptile and Amphibian House** is another stately old building with a magnificent interior where more than 120 species of reptiles and amphibians are displayed. Top exhibits include *King Cobra's Temple* and *Everglades*, an exhibit where daily thunderstorms occur in the alligator and crocodile habitats; check the schedule inside the building for times. Outside on *Tortoise Trail*, a Galapagos tortoise lives near equally large Aldabra tortoises from the Seychelles islands, off the coast of Africa. Also outside is the *Reptile Exercise Yard*, where turtles, snakes, and lizards from the zoo's education department can bask in the summer sun.

Bear Country, with its spacious meadow habitats for bears from three continents, is a popular destination. It is no surprise that the polar bears receive the most attention, especially at the underwater window into their 200,000-gallon pool. South American spectacled bears and Asian sloth bears each have exhibits here as well.

Since the first American passenger balloon flight occurred in Philadelphia, it seems fitting that this zoo has a permanent hot air balloon ride. Reaching heights of over 400 feet, **Zooballoon** is an excellent opportunity to get a spectacular look at the zoo grounds and historic Philadelphia. Voyages on this 72-foot-wide, 124-foot-high balloon last about ten minutes.

OTHER EXHIBITS

The **Small Mammal House** is best known in the zoo world for the occupants of its nocturnal wing. Five different species of bats are exhibited, including intriguing vampire bats. In another wing, pig-like aardvarks can be observed both above ground and underground in their burrow. Nearby are egg-laying Australian echidnas (also known as spiny anteaters), a colony of meerkats, and grass-climbing harvest mice. The **Rare Animal Conservation Center** is a rather ordinary-looking building that holds some of the zoo's most interesting animals: naked mole-rats (in what looks like a giant ant farm), elephant shrews, tree kangaroos, lemurs, and fruit bats.

Jagged rock walls separate outdoor yards at the **Pachyderm House**. Indian rhinos, Nile hippos, and an okapi, a rare relative of the giraffe, can be seen in their respective yards or inside the aging building.

The **Australian Outback** includes red kangaroos, Bennett's wallabies, emus, and Cape Barren geese in an open pen. Animals from **South America**, including giant anteaters, llamas, and capybaras, which are enormous aquatic rodents, are displayed in two adjacent yards. Next door, you'll see rare Bornean bearded pigs. **Monkey Junction**, with its agile spider monkeys, is right inside the zoo entrance. Prairie dogs perch on dirt mounds near the far end of the zoo.

In **Bird Valley,** pools display exotic waterfowl; endangered Humboldt penguins and flamingos are the standout residents. Beautiful **Bird Lake**, overgrown with water plants and willow trees, is home to hundreds of ducks, geese, and swans. Other bird exhibits include large flight cages for Andean condors, hornbills, and bald eagles.

FOR THE KIDS

The **Children's Zoo** offers a wonderful variety of animal experiences, with shows and demonstrations all day long. At *Backyard Bugs*, a summer insect zoo, tarantulas and giant stick insects are fun to observe. Crowds gather at the duck feeding pond, the Scottish Highland cattle pen, the farmyard, and the sheep and goat contact yard. When it gets hot, the *Ice Cream Parlor* just might be the most popular place of all.

In an open-air aviary, **Birds of Australia** lets visitors feed nectar to colorful lorikeet parrots. Miniature train rides are available on the **PZ Express**. Under the willow trees on Swan Lake, the **swan paddle boats** are popular with kids and adults. Children can also ride camels, ponies, and draft horses at this zoo. A 3-D virtual reality ride, **Wild Earth**, offers a simulated adventure through the African plains. In **My Wild Backyard**, kids can help plant flowers, make crafts, and search for ladybugs. The **PZ Panning Co.** provides an opportunity to pan a stream for gems to take home.

IN PROGRESS

Future projects at the zoo include remodeling the current 1916 Bird House into an expanded **Avian Center** and updating the Children's Zoo. Plans call for both exhibits to reopen when the zoo celebrates its 150th anniversary in 2014.

Pittsburgh Zoo and PPG Aquarium

I Wild Place
Pittsburgh, Pennsylvania 15206
(412) 665-3639
www.pittsburghzoo.org

Hours: 9:00 a.m.-6:00 p.m. daily, Memorial Day weekend-Labor Day; 9:00 a.m.-5:00 p.m. daily, April-Memorial Day and Labor Day-December; 9:00 a.m.-4:00 p.m. daily, January-March. Last admission one hour before closing. Closed Thanksgiving, Christmas Day, and New Year's Day.

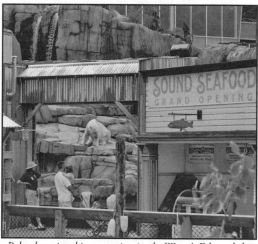

Polar bear is a big attraction in the Water's Edge exhibit.

Admission & Fees: Adults $10, seniors 60+ $9, children 2-13 $8, April-November. Adults $8, seniors and children $7, December-March. Tram: $2 adults and children, $1 seniors; carousel, train, and Kid's Kingdom rides $1.

Directions: Take I-279 to Route 28 (Exit 8B southbound, Exit 7C northbound). Follow Route 28 for over five miles to the Highland Bridge exit. Cross bridge to Butler Street, turning left. At the first light, Baker Street, turn right. Bear left to enter the zoo parking lot.

Don't Miss: Water's Edge, PPG Aquarium, African Savanna, Tropical Forest.

For Kids: Kid's Kingdom (including Worlds of Discovery), Sumatran Express Train, carousel.

Authors' Tips: The zoo is built on a steep hill and can be a "bear" to walk. Buy a wristband to ride the tram all day; it makes getting from place to place much easier than traveling on foot. Trams arrive at each of eight marked stops approximately every twenty minutes.

Edutainment: "Meet the Staff" discussions are held daily in summer at all of the zoo's major exhibits. Amphitheater shows are held four times daily in both the Kid's Kingdom and African Savanna amphitheaters, where small animals come out for up-close encounters. "Zoo Keys" can be purchased for $2; they unlock animal stories and songs at twenty-five locations within the zoo.

THE HISTORIC PITTSBURGH ZOO, WHICH OPENED IN 1898, HAS become one of America's most modern zoos. While some of its historic architecture remains, most of its exhibits have either been built or renovated since the 1980s as part of an extensive master plan.

Located on Pittsburgh's northeast side, the zoo lies on the steep slopes of the Allegheny River Valley. The resulting hilly terrain makes the gigantic escalator, which transports visitors from the entrance gate to **The Village** plaza, an amenity that's much appreciated. To some children, this oversized escalator is an attraction in itself.

FEATURED EXHIBITS

Water's Edge blends fascinating aquatic animals with a cultural theme. Habitats for polar bears, sea otters, and walruses border a fictional fishing village named "Pier Town." Your journey begins with a look into the polar bear cave. Two windows overlook the bears' rocky, rolling terrain, before your path curves into town. Each of the town's colorful buildings, including a market and town hall, displays tips on how to help protect the environment. After giving you an overview of the polar bears' pool, the path leads to *Sea Otter Cove*. These larger-than-expected aquatic mammals are famous for using rocks to crack open clam shells as they float on their backs. Enjoy your time here: very few zoos exhibit sea otters. The same is true for the residents of the next habitat, *Walrus Island*. Just past a fishing boat, after above-water views, an underwater tunnel passes directly through the polar bear pool. This thirty-foot passage, where bears swim above and around their guests, is only the second of its kind. Next, a ten-foot-high glass panel showcases the kelp forest habitat of the sea otters. Finally, visitors enter a forty-foot glass tunnel through the 280,000-gallon walrus pool. Like the polar bear tunnel, this is a unique exhibit among zoos.

Pittsburgh has long been one of only a few zoos with an aquarium, as the **PPG Aquarium**, which opened in 2000, replaced the old AquaZoo. A crashing waterfall and outdoor tank of native Allegheny River fish invite visitors into the current wave-shaped structure. Leafy sea dragons in a circular kelp-filled tank are the first aquatic wonder you'll see in this home to aquatic creatures from all corners of the earth, including Antarctic penguins. A key attraction here is the row of tanks displaying venomous fish, including rockfish and lionfish. The building's highlight, however, is the two-story shark tank. Large sharks swim with eels and hundreds of fish as visitors watch from an elevated platform or from ground level. When an attendant is present, you can touch stingrays in their shallow pool. Attendant or not, be sure to check out this pool's crawl-through tunnel, from which kids can see the stingrays at their own level, on the ocean bottom. Finally, a huge Amazonian pool displays pacu (piranha relatives) and gigantic arapaima fish, as well as freshwater stingrays. The tropical plants towering over the water create a realistic rain forest atmosphere.

Outdoors, a long, winding stream separates visitors from the animals of the **African Savanna**. Dwarf crocodiles float in a shallow pool in front of endangered black rhinos. As the path climbs, the rhinos come into view again, as do African lions. A grassland at the base of a steep cliff provides a great space for the king of the jungle to survey his surroundings. Zebras, ostriches, and two gazelle species share a shady, rolling yard. African elephants, which have historically had difficulty breeding in captivity, thrive here. A realistic termite mound catches the eye in an outdoor habitat the elephants seem to share with the antelope and a herd of giraffes, though hidden barriers keep them apart. Jackson, a bull elephant here, fathered more African elephant calves than any other bull in America.

The **Tropical Forest**, a five-acre indoor/outdoor primate complex, is the place to find the zoo's most energetic animals. Inside, tropical plants line a walkway that leads to a number of thirty-foot-high habitats under a central translucent roof. Additional plants behind each exhibit enhance the rain forest experience. Primates from Asia (gibbons), Africa (colobus monkeys and mandrills), and South America (howler monkeys) are represented, as well as two lemur species from Madagascar. Two great apes, orangutans and gorillas, are displayed in dimly lit enclosures, with thick trees for to climb. The gorilla troop, one of the country's largest, is often found outside in its 1½-acre grassy meadow.

OTHER EXHIBITS

Asian Forest is the first exhibit most visitors see. Furry snow leopards rest in crevices in their rocky domain. Neighboring Amur tigers prowl a conifer forest as a waterfall crashes into the stream below. A viewing window brings visitors close to the big cats at the top of the valley. Across from the tigers, the landscape shifts quickly from northern forest to steamy jungle for the Komodo dragon exhibit. A long window lets visitors peer into the dragons' indoor holding space and outdoor yard filled with fountain grasses. Amur leopards are also featured here, in a tall hillside exhibit near the African Savanna path.

Built into the valley are four massive, rocky grottoes with deep pools. These **Bear Dens** are home to Kodiak, spectacled, and black bears. Just across from the dens, a shaded boardwalk overlooks the **African Ravine**, home to a pack of African wild dogs.

FOR THE KIDS

When the Pittsburgh Zoo built the seven-acre **Kid's Kingdom** in the mid 1990s, their goal was to create the best children's zoo in the country. With its many close animal encounters, exciting activities that let you mimic animals, and even a few fun rides, they may very well have met that goal. The adventure begins at the beautiful *Sea Lion Pool*, where playful sea lions swim under two waterfalls and a spouting fountain. A wide underwater window allows face-to-face encounters. In the *Animal Motions Playground,* a gigantic spiderweb net is always crawling with energetic children. When kids reach the high platform above, they have a choice about how to come back down – via the milder *Penguin Slide* or the longer and faster enclosed *Otter Slides*. In a walk-through deer yard, kids can gently stroke Bambi's relatives, white-tailed deer. The walk-through kangaroo yard is another great petting opportunity. On the high *Canopy Walk*, a boardwalk takes children to see animals at a treetop-level view, including a porcupine who's usually up at the top of his tree. Birds fly overhead in the enclosed walk-through *Flight Deck*. Most kids enjoy the swaying rope bridge, especially when their parents find it "scary." Along this path, take a peek into habitats for a skunk and a great horned owl. You can also look down into the pond exhibits and spot perennial kid favorites, river otters and beavers. Parents can relax and grab a bite to eat at the *Animal Connections* restaurant, while their children enjoy a surrounding playground of the same name. Uniquely themed playground structures include the "gibbon rope climb" and the "naked mole-rat tunnel." Nearby, carnival-style kids' rides have adventure themes, including the *Safari Cars* and the small *Log Ride*. Upon entering the **Worlds of Discovery** pavilion, visitors walk through an underwater tunnel, as huge fish and alligators swim above and all around you. Among the small animals exhibited here are leaf-cutter ants and naked mole-rats, the latter visible as they scurry through clear plastic tubes. In the dark, forty-foot-long *Bat Flyway*, it's a thrill to having bats flying very close to you separated only by thin, almost-invisible piano wire. Near this building's exit, kids have the chance to "burrow" underneath the *Meerkat Exhibit*, and pop up inside the habitat in a clear acrylic dome, just inches from real meerkats. Back outside, the *Domestication* section features side-by-side paddocks with domestic animals from three different continents: a camel, llamas, and reindeer. Just across the path is a small contact yard with one last chance to pet friendly animals: goats, this time.

A small **Carousel** looks inviting in the entrance Village area, while just beyond the giant escalator is the **Sumatran Express Train** ride.

IN PROGRESS

Although it will not be on zoo grounds, nor be open to the public on a daily basis, construction of the **International Conservation Center** will make this zoo a leader in the preservation of endangered species. Currently being built on 724 acres of land in nearby Somerset County, the center will focus on the management and propagation of African elephants. Eventually, twenty elephants will roam in large open paddocks. The space and care available at this center will be crucial to saving the elephant from extinction. This center will also allow the zoo to expand its efforts in breeding cheetahs, black rhinos, African wild dogs, and Grevy's zebras.

On zoo grounds, seven unused acres will eventually be the home of a new reptile house and other yet-to-be determined animal exhibits.

Roger Williams Park Zoo

Snow leopards in Marco Polo Silk Road.

1000 Elmwood Avenue
Providence, Rhode Island 02907
(401) 785-3510
www.rogerwilliamsparkzoo.org

Hours: 9:00 a.m.-5:00 p.m. daily, mid-April to October; 9:00 a.m.-4:00 p.m. daily, rest of year. Last admission half an hour before closing. Closed Thanksgiving, Christmas Eve and Day.

Admission & Fees: Adults $12, seniors 62+ $8, children 3-12 $6.

Directions: From I-95 South, take Exit 17 (US-1 South). Turn left onto Elmwood Avenue, and follow 1.9 miles to zoo. From I-95 North, take Exit 16 (Elmwood Ave). Turn left onto Elmwood Avenue, and follow for 0.5 miles to zoo.

Don't Miss: Marco Polo Silk Road, Plains of Africa, Tropical America, Australasia.

For Kids: Farmyard, Carousel Village (outside the zoo).

Authors' Tips: Carousel Village, which features a Victorian carousel, bumper boats, a play-ground, and pony rides, is on the grounds of Roger Williams Park, though not in the zoo. Also in the park is the Museum of Natural History.

Edutainment: Special farm-themed presentations and activities are held regularly in the Farm-yard. Zoo docents host "Yakety Yak" animal interviews at various exhibits. Interactive presentations by the Wild Bunch traveling performers are held throughout the zoo. Listen for announcements of times and places for these programs.

THE ROGER WILLIAMS PARK ZOO IS NOT ONLY ONE OF THE TOP tourist attractions in Rhode Island, but also, in our humble opinion, the best zoo in the region. No less than the *Boston Globe* has called it "New England's great zoo." It is certainly the most complete zoo in New England, not only in terms of the expected cast of characters, but also in terms of geographic diversity, with sections here representing five different continents. This zoo is also making a name for itself with its significant contributions to critically endangered species. Animals it is helping to save include African elephants, snow leopards, babirusa pigs, and red wolves. These efforts aren't just restricted to zoo grounds, either: the zoo's Conservation Department contributes to the Tree Kangaroo Conservation Project down in Papua, New Guinea.

FEATURED EXHIBITS

The **Marco Polo Silk Road** is the zoo's most unique exhibit. Its opening in 1996 marked the beginning of the zoo's goal to build a "biopark" – a facility that combines features from a region's history, culture, and animals to tell a story. In this exhibit, the "story" is explorer Marco Polo's thirteenth-century journey to Asia. In this well-themed area, you'll meet some of the animals Polo himself might have seen (and perhaps collected) during his three-year odyssey. The adventure begins in a courtyard, painted to resemble Marco Polo's hometown: Venice, including a canal, as it appeared in 1271. An adjacent side room off the courtyard portrays what Polo's boat might have looked like. A winding downhill trail takes visitors through the woods to see such Asian animals as dromedary camels, moon bears, snow leopards, and rare red-crowned cranes. The moon bears are highly entertaining, playing in a large rocky hillside habitat that's outfitted with a trickling waterfall and a deep pool. They are usually called Asian black bears, but "moon bear" sounds much more exotic!

The **Plains of Africa** exhibit is almost unavoidable, right at the front of the zoo. An archway sign reads "Welcome to Africa," and leads visitors to the Grant's zebras. From the main path, separate side trails run to the animal enclosures, making each a new adventure. Animals here, visible from within attractive viewing blinds, include African wild dogs, aoudads (Barbary sheep), and wildebeest. To see the beautiful crowned cranes, visitors must walk through artificial boulders set in a savanna kopje landscape. The stars here, though, are the Masai giraffes and African elephants. The elephants draw big crowds when they cool off in their large pool. The *African Pavilion* exhibits an elephant skull, educational graphic displays, a video of a giraffe birth, and indoor quarters for the giraffes and elephants.

At **Tropical America**, an unlikely old structure has been creatively converted into a convincingly realistic rain forest habitat, with free-roaming tropical birds, monkeys, prehensile-tailed porcupines, and a two-toed sloth. Climb up to the canopy skywalk: it's usually the best way to find the smaller monkeys – golden lion and cotton-top tamarins. Side exhibits display white-faced saki monkeys, a giant green anaconda snake, a cave of fluttering Jamaican fruit bats, and a variety of smaller creatures of the jungle. Outside this building, Chilean flamingos wade in a pool near the new habitat for giant anteaters, just built in 2007.

The official name of the **Australasia** exhibit is "Australasia: Where Worlds Collide, Where Worlds Divide." This indoor/outdoor complex displays animals from the islands of New Guinea, Indonesia, the Philippines, and the island continent of Australia. Indoor habitats for the region's reptiles, birds, fish, and Matschie's tree kangaroos are in the exhibit's central building. Outside, a ring of habitats includes wild Indonesian babirusa pigs, wallabies, laughing kookaburras, and a walk-through aviary of Asian birds. Children can climb through tunnels to pop up in clear acrylic domes inside the raccoon-like binturongs' habitat. Nearby, an enclosure equipped with ropes and tree branches to swing from is well utilized by a troop of excitable white-cheeked gibbons. Not far away, you'll find a yard filled with gray kangaroos and emus.

OTHER EXHIBITS

In the **North America** section, the current feature exhibit is the bald eagle habitat (new in 2007), with its own flowing streambed. Down the path, the red wolves are often hard to find in their densely wooded enclosure, but the hunt is worth it. This zoo is involved in a coordinated effort to save these wolves from extinction. At the bottom of a hill, pronghorn antelope and American bison live across from each other in large prairie yards. Further on, the collared peccaries (or javelinas), a species of wild pig, are always entertaining, and the harbor seals are even more fun to watch through their underwater window. Above the seals is a tropically planted pool for two species that are not actually from this continent, Humboldt penguins (native to South America) and white-breasted cormorants (Africa). The very popular penguins can be seen from an overhanging platform near an arctic fox habitat.

Madagascar, an adjoining set of enclosures, features radiated tortoises and three varieties of endangered lemurs, including mongoose lemurs, which are rarely seen in zoos. Next door, a small building displays rare Asian turtles. Walking the quarter-mile **Wetlands Trail** is a relaxing way to end a zoo visit. Along the way, you can spot native wildlife such as herons and turtles.

FOR THE KIDS

In the **Farmyard**, children can learn about farming and farm animals through hands-on activities. In front of bright red barns, petting corrals hold rare and exotic breeds of livestock, including Dexter cattle, Guinea hogs, Nigerian dwarf goats, Santa Cruz sheep, Sicilian donkeys, European rabbits, and Rhode Island white chickens. Signs featuring the Farmyard's mascot, "Fred the Field Mouse," teach kids about eco-friendly farming techniques.

IN PROGRESS

The new bald eagle enclosure is the first stage of a new exhibit, the **North American Trail.** When complete, this area will provide improved habitats for all of the zoo's animals from this continent, plus two new species of owls. In addition, polar bears, featured on the zoo's logo, will return to a new world-class exhibit that will be nine times larger than their old home. Farther along, the master plan calls for more new exhibits, including a **New England Trail** and **Children's Play Zoo**. The latter should include a fun two-story tree house, climbing structures, and approachable animals.

BEST OF THE REST

Connecticut's Beardsley Zoo

1875 Noble Avenue
Bridgeport, Connecticut 06610
(203) 394-6565
www.beardsleyzoo.org

This zoo, the only one in Connecticut, focuses primarily on animals from North and South America. In the *Rainforest Building*, free-flying tropical birds, a caiman crocodile pond, ocelots, and monkeys are just some of the South American species that inhabit the lush jungle. Other animals from South America – llamas, maned wolves, Andean condors, and spectacled bears – are spread throughout the zoo. The *Hoofstock Trail* features animals from closer to home, including pronghorn antelope and bison. Other North American animals, such as wolves, foxes, lynx, and prairie dogs, live in exhibits throughout the zoo. The only major species here that's not from the Americas are the Amur tigers, from Asia. The *New England Farmyard* has a contact yard with goats, as well as a nice collection of domestic farm animals.

Franklin Park Zoo

1 Franklin Park Road
Boston, Massachusetts 02121
(617) 541-5466
www.franklinparkzoo.org

The *Tropical Forest* building at this zoo, set in Boston's historic Franklin Park, is often called one of the nation's best zoo exhibits. Inside, a troop of gorillas share lush jungle space with tapirs, warthogs, bats, and a variety of tropical birds and reptiles. *Kalahari Kingdom* and *Tiger Tales* are beautiful modern exhibits for lions and tigers, including, at press time, a white tiger. In *Bird's World*, built in 1913, four naturalistic indoor habitats display a wide variety of feathered creatures. Another highlight is a pair of central African savanna exhibits, featuring giraffes, zebras, ostriches, wildebeest, and Nubian ibexes, a type of mountain goat.

Cape May County Park & Zoo

707 North Route 9
Cape May Court House, New Jersey 08210
(609) 465-5271
www.capemaycountyzoo.org

Located at the southern tip of New Jersey, this small-town zoo attracts well over half a million visitors each year. Reasons for its popularity include free admission, the *World of Birds* aviary, a reptile house with over seventy-five species, and a thirty-acre *African Savanna* with giraffes, zebras, and antelope. The *Cat Exhibit* features lions, tigers, cougars, cheetahs, and two types of leopards. There are also over a dozen types of primates, red pandas, and bison displayed at this popular zoo.

Central Park Zoo

830 5th Avenue
New York, New York 10021
(212) 439-6500
www.nyzoosandaquarium.com/cpz

Located in America's most famous urban park, this zoo opened in 1864, making it one of the oldest in the country. Run by the same zoological society that runs the massive Bronx Zoo, this tiny facility fills its six acres with impressive and high-tech exhibits. The best known is the popular *Polar Zone*, where polar bears enjoy a rocky naturalistic habitat with underwater viewing. Penguins and puffins are displayed in similar icy habitats, while the steamy two-story *Rain Forest* building features a lush jungle with displays of colobus monkeys, small tamarin monkeys, free-flying tropical birds, and a fascinating exhibit of leaf-cutter ants. Outdoors, highlights include red pandas, snow monkeys (aka Japanese macaques), river otters, and an iconic central court sea lion pool. In 1997, the *Tisch Children's Zoo* was added, giving kids a variety of opportunities to play and to pet animals.

Rosamond Gifford Zoo at Burnet Park

I Conservation Place
Syracuse, New York 13204
(315) 435-8511
www.rosamondgiffordzoo.org

Most of this zoo is arranged in two distinct sections, an unusual layout. The indoor section has four exhibit areas, in separate buildings connected under one roof. *USS Antiquities* explores the beginnings of life on the planet, and exhibits mostly reptiles. *Diversity of Birds* is a tall walk-through aviary with dozens of tropical birds. The *Adaptation of Animals* hall uses displays of bats, naked mole-rats, and more to show how animals adapt to survive. The *Social Animals* building displays animals who live in families, including lions, meerkats, and various monkeys. Outside, the *Domestic Animals* area includes Asian elephants, animals that are often domesticated in Asia. In our opinion, the best feature here is a winding *Wildlife Trail*, which includes spacious open habitats for more than twenty mostly cold-weather animals. On this half-mile trail, you'll see, among other creatures, penguins, yaks, tigers, wolves, bison, snow leopards, red pandas, and spectacled bears.

Erie Zoological Gardens

423 West 38th Street
Erie, Pennsylvania 16508
(814) 864-4091
www.eriezoo.org

A surprisingly extensive collection of animals is packed into this tiny fifteen-acre zoo. In and around the zoo's *Main Building*, you'll find a naked mole-rat exhibit, meerkats, jaguars, leopards, a variety of small animals, and a gorilla. Under a forty-foot jungle temple, *Wild Asia* is the beautiful home of orangutans, siamangs, red pandas, and more. *Kiboka Outpost* is a well-themed exhibit area that displays African animals, including white rhinos, zebras, warthogs, cheetahs, and some smaller creatures. Near a giraffe exhibit, a set of grottoes displays polar bears, lions, and a white Bengal tiger. Across Mill Creek, *Children's Adventure* is, in our opinion, one of the best children's zoos in America. Activities for kids abound in this fascinating area, which includes kid-friendly exhibits of penguins, alligators, and kangaroos. Children's Adventure also includes a train ride, a carousel, multiple contact yards, and a play area for kids with toys and stuffed animals.

Oglebay Good Zoo

Route 88 North
Wheeling, West Virginia 26003
(304) 243-4000
www.oglebay-resort.com/goodzoo

Part of the well known Oglebay Resort on West Virginia's Panhandle, this small zoo, designed especially for children, is named "Good" in memory of Philip Mayer Good, a seven-year-old nature-lover. Almost all of the animals exhibited here are small or cute (or both). Some of these kid favorites include spectacled bears, red pandas, tamarin monkeys, meerkats, naked mole-rats, and an ocelot cat. The best exhibits here are those for river otters, endangered red wolves, and bald eagles, all shown in naturalistic habitats. The Benedum Planetarium, which presents astronomical star shows on a big screen, is also on site.

Zoos Feature Many Interesting Animals

Above (l-r): Shoebill stork, Bird of paradise, Sifaka.
Left: Clouded leopard.
Below: Echidna.

Giant Panda habitat in National Zoo's Asia Trail exhibit attracts lots of photographers.

Tired of walking? Many zoos offer alternatives. Miami Metrozoo's monorail, for example, offers air-conditioning along with good views of most of its animals. You can hop on and off all day long.

Southern Zoos

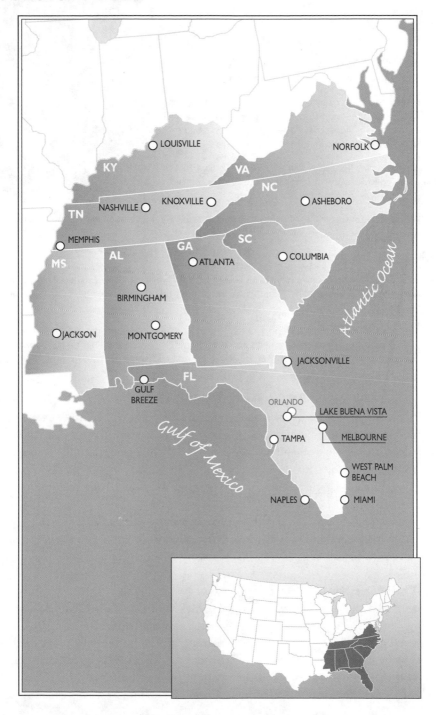

Montgomery Zoo

2301 Coliseum Parkway
Montgomery, Alabama 36110
(334) 240-4588
montgomeryal.gov/depts/zoo.aspx

Hours: 9:00 a.m.-5:00 p.m. daily, last admission 4:30 p.m. Closed on Thanksgiving, Christmas, and New Year's Day.

Admission & Fees: Adults $8, seniors 65+ and children 3-12 $5. Combo admission to zoo and Mann Museum: adults $12, seniors and children $8. AAA and military discounts. Train ride $2. Participates in reciprocity program.

Directions: From I-65, take Exit 173 (AL-152 East/North Boulevard). Follow Route 152E for 4.2 miles. Turn right onto Coliseum Parkway. Zoo is immediately on the right.

Greater kudu in African Realm.

Don't Miss: African Realm, North American Realm, Asian Realm, South American Realm, Overlook Café.

For Kids: Train ride, playground.

Authors' Tips: Plan on eating a meal here. Dining at the Overlook Café is a special part of the zoo experience (see below). The Mann Museum is air-conditioned; a visit here can be a nice break in the middle of a hot day.

Edutainment: On Saturdays in June and July, the zoo offers a "Behind the Scenes" tour. For $15 ($12 for members), guests are taken into several holding barns, including the elephant barn, and even get to hand-feed the elephants. Tours are limited to twelve guests at a time.

A VISIT TO THE MONTGOMERY ZOO CAN BE AN EXCELLENT wildlife geography lesson, as its residents are divided into five continental realms. Surprisingly, one of the highlights of this zoo is its restaurant, the centrally located **Overlook Café**. While its menu has standard (and slightly overpriced) fast food, the view from its seating area makes this place special. On a circular open-air deck, guests can sit and watch the animals of the African savanna, the North American prairie, and the Asian plains.

Located on the north side of Alabama's capital, the zoo expanded by a factor of six (from six to forty acres) in 1991. This means over eighty percent of this zoo is virtually new, by zoo-world standards.

FEATURED EXHIBITS

From the Overlook Café, the **African Realm**'s most obvious residents are a pride of lions, who calmly watch over savanna animals they would normally tear apart. Only a water moat, filled by a pair of waterfalls, separates the lions from the prolific herd of giraffes. As you follow the path counterclockwise, you'll encounter cheetahs in a grassy yard, also housed right across from their natural prey, the antelope of the savanna. The best views of the large central savanna, however, are from a pair of shaded visitor stations. Zebras, imposing marabou storks, crowned cranes, dama gazelles, and kudu and other antelope species roam this realistic African veldt. In the distance (they're easy to miss), a pair of pygmy hippos floats in one of the water moats. A short side trail leads to a large enclosure of the realm's only non-African animals, jet-black siamang gibbons from Asia. A small troop of playful chimpanzees lives on a nearby island, enhanced with ropes and poles and another tall cascade. For the best view of the zoo's African elephants, take a long ramp up to the top level of a double-decker viewing station. The elephants have an attractive habitat, with a wide, splashing waterfall. Later, you can view them again from behind the falls. The elephant herd includes the first calf to be born in the state of Alabama. From the lower level of the elephant and savanna viewing station, tiny dik-dik antelope are visible in a raised yard. Just over the fence is a small colony of African black-footed penguins. They're close enough to touch, but a sign warns you not to try this – they bite!

The pathway through the **North American Realm** is heavily forested, and the tall mature trees provide refreshing shade. From the first viewing station, Canadian lynx and cougars are displayed side-by-side behind thin harp wire. The cougars make up half of another predator/prey display; their prey, the deer and other animals of the upcoming prairie exhibit, can be seen on the other side of the big cats' habitat. Across the path is a tall wire aviary housing majestic bald eagles. Next door is this realm's main event, the new *North American River Otter* exhibit, which opened in 2007. The playful otters can be seen from two levels: a boardwalk completely surrounding the exhibit, or underwater through wide glass windows. The cinnamon-colored "black" bears (same species, different coloration) have a very attractive habitat, enhanced with a beautiful cascading stream that splashes down through the middle of the area. Scattered about the sprawling prairie exhibit are American bison (commonly called "buffalo"), elk, bighorn sheep, white-tailed deer, and wild turkeys.

As you enter from Africa, the **Asian Realm** begins with a long yard for Indian rhinos. These one-horned rhinos are often spotted cooling themselves in their deep pool or in a mud wallow. Around the corner is the waterfall-enhanced habitat for a pair of white Bengal tigers. These beautiful blue-eyed white tigers can be seen behind thin harp wire or through windows. Like most of the zoo's big cats, the tigers have the opportunity to watch some of their natural prey in the nearby Asian plain. In a wide open yard, creatures of the steppe grasslands of central Asia are represented by a wide variety of hoofstock, including blackbuck antelope, spotted axis deer, and a breeding group of bantengs, a type of wild cattle. Tall sarus cranes also roam here.

While the **South American Realm** does not have the best exhibits of the five realms, it does have the most complete array of species. It begins just inside the zoo's entrance with the *Flight Cage*, a tall walk-through aviary modeled after the famous 1904 World's Fair aviary in St. Louis. The colorful array of birds inside includes long-legged scarlet ibises and roseate spoonbills, Coscoroba swans, blue-gray tanagers, and a variety of South American ducks. Smaller cages exhibit toco toucans, various macaws and other parrots, king vultures, Andean condors, squirrel monkeys, and small marmoset monkeys. A new habitat that opened in 2007 features mustached emperor tamarins, another small monkey. A small concrete pool displays American alligators, while flamingos and black-necked swans live in a slightly larger pool across the path. The South American realm's most impressive exhibit is a lushly planted, fully enclosed grassy habitat for spectacled bears. Across from the bears, a round island offers spider monkeys a variety of poles and ropes to climb and play on. In the realm's corner is a shady mixed-species yard with a pair of unusual animals: long-legged maned wolves and giant anteaters. Next door is a small but interesting reptile house displaying geckos, monitor lizards, pancake tortoises, rat snakes, and more. A muscular black jaguar is clearly visible through thin wire in yet another lush habitat, while a nearby enclosure displays smaller ocelot cats. The jaguars would have to strain to see their prey in the *South American Hoof Stock* yard, where llamas, rheas (tall flightless birds), and agoutis (small rodents) roam.

OTHER EXHIBITS

Animals from a fifth continent are exhibited in the small **Australian Realm**. Inside this gated exhibit, visitors move along an arcing boardwalk that overlooks the spacious Australian yard. Red kangaroos, black swans, and flightless emus live in this tree-filled grassy habitat. Inside the boardwalk arc is a mud hole habitat for a pair of warthogs, an African species.

The **Mann Wildlife Learning Museum** is part of this zoo, but it can be toured separately (or skipped). This small natural history museum offers an extensive display of taxidermy specimens, the collection of George P. Mann, a nationally famous conservationist and bow hunter. The many three-dimensional displays include a complete collection of all of North America's deer and bear species, plus just about any other American animal you can think of.

FOR THE KIDS

With the exception of a small, shady playground, the zoo does not yet (as this book goes to press) have a children's zoo area, though one is planned. The main feature for kids is an attractive miniature **train** ride. The twelve-minute ride loops through the entire zoo, going around the scenic lake and through tunnels. It allows for glimpses of four continents' animals.

IN PROGRESS

While a site has been selected, no date has been set for completion of a new children's area, the **Discovery Center** . The new state-of-the-art play area will replace the existing playground and include zoo-related learning tools, games, and rides for all ages. The zoo plans to feature pretty toco toucans in a larger and improved exhibit that's scheduled to open in 2008 as we go to press.

Jacksonville Zoo and Gardens

370 Zoo Parkway
Jacksonville, Florida 32218
(904) 757-4463
www.jacksonvillezoo.org

Jacksonville is famous for its jaguars.

Hours: 9:00 a.m.-5:00 p.m. daily. Open until 6:00 p.m. on weekends and holidays, March-Labor Day. Closed Thanksgiving and Christmas Day.

Admission & Fees: Adults $12, children 3-12 $7.50, seniors 65+ $10, military and AAA members receive a 10% discount. Zoo Train: adults $4, children $2; wildlife carousel $2; giraffe feeding $2; lorikeet feeding $1, "Behind the Scenes" tour $25.

Directions: From I-95, take Exit 358A (Heckscher Drive/Zoo Parkway). Follow Zoo Parkway for 1 mile to zoo, on the right.

Don't Miss: Range of the Jaguar, Plains of East Africa, Great Apes, Wild Florida.

For Kids: Play Park, Zoo Train, wildlife carousel.

Authors' Tips: A meal in the South American-themed Palm Plaza Café is an enchanting experience: South American food is on the menu (it's somewhat similar to Mexican cuisine). Try to get a table close to the tall windows into the jaguar exhibit. The Trout River Grill is another nice, air-conditioned place to eat.

Edutainment: The zoo has long been known locally and in the zoo world for its "Elephant Encounters" presentations, held daily (twice a day on weekends) at the Elephant Plaza. The "Bald Eagle Chat" is also held daily. A variety of less frequent zookeeper talks include presentations involving reptiles, bats, bonobos, rhinos, and jaguars. Most of these are held only on weekends. The Saturday afternoon alligator feedings are popular with visitors. A tour of the animal hospital is available twice a day on weekends. Three-hour "Behind the Scenes" tours give visitors a look at how the African and South American animals are cared for, both on and off exhibit.

ASK ANY FOOTBALL FAN WHAT ANIMAL THEY MOST ASSOCIATE with Jacksonville and the response will be, "jaguars." Ask any zoo fan the same question and the response will be the same. This zoo has a long and successful history breeding these South American cats. The NFL Jaguars' owner, Wayne Weaver, an honorary zoo board member, has personally helped build this zoo's world-class jaguar exhibit.

Still, when entering this beautiful zoo – lush with palms, banana plants, and other tropical foliage – an African theme is most obvious. The entry gate is part of the large **Main Camp Safari Lodge**, which also includes a gift shop, food kiosk, and meeting rooms. The Lodge boasts a 26,000-square-foot thatched roof that was created by Zulu craftsmen from South Africa. It is one of the largest thatched structures in North America and is truly impressive! Arriving visitors get the message that an exotic adventure is about to begin.

FEATURED EXHIBITS

The **Range of the Jaguar** is more than an exhibit of Jacksonville's iconic animal; it is also one of the finest South American-themed exhibits in the nation. In *Palm Plaza*, a beautiful tiered fountain, ancient statues, and Spanish-style red tiles on the buildings (including the restroom) make visitors feel as though they've been transported to South America. Of course, the key exhibit here is the lush jaguar habitat, which can be seen from both sides. This hemisphere's largest cats roam a tropically planted space in front of the ruins of a Mayan stone temple. In front of these water-loving felines, a glass-fronted pond is filled with giant pacu fish and peacock bass. The big cats sometimes watch the fish from an overhanging log, and will occasionally take a dip in the pool. At press time, the Jacksonville Zoo had the largest collection of jaguars in the nation. A *Lost Temple* exhibit takes visitors inside the Mayan temple, behind the jaguars, where the winding halls are lined with ancient bricks and lit by lanterns. The many exhibits of reptiles, fish, and other South American creatures include a venomous bushmaster snake, a giant green anaconda, tiny cotton-top tamarin and pygmy marmoset monkeys, and a stalactite-filled vampire bat exhibit. Back outside the temple, the *River's Edge* is a mixed-species streamside habitat for capybaras (a species of large aquatic rodent), giant anteaters, and a Baird's tapir. Black howler monkeys hang out on a low rocky ledge above them. In the *Emerald Forest Aviary*, South American birds are the focus, including guira cuckoos, scarlet ibises, and a large flock of endangered Inca terns. There are also tiny Chilean pudu deer in this tropical forest habitat, but the main feature is a glass-fronted exhibit of giant otters. This is one of only a handful of zoos to exhibit this largest of the otter species.

Just beyond the zoo's African-themed entry area, the **Plains of East Africa** uses a 1,400-foot boardwalk to present a wide variety of animals from this continent. The elevated walkway overlooks warthogs on one side and a Nile crocodile marsh on the other. A spacious shaded yard exhibits impala and bongo antelope, as well as ground hornbill birds. Opposite this, tall saddle-billed storks from Africa can be compared to their native Floridian cousins: local endangered wood storks like to drop in for a visit; as many as 100 nesting pairs have chosen this place for their breeding home. Cheetahs are displayed in a 300-foot-long open yard at a turn in the boardwalk. The largest yard, at 2½ acres, is home to two antelope species, ostriches, and white rhinos. Imposing Cape buffalo occupy a nearby paddock of their own. Few zoos exhibit these nasty-tempered and dangerous animals. In *Elephant Plaza*, a set of mesh enclosures contains vultures and other African birds, large fruit bats, and a kopje habitat for small klipspringer antelope. Located in a bright orange African hut, *Reptiles of the Seronera* has an impressive collection of venomous snakes, including cobras and an assortment of vipers, all displayed with beautiful background murals. At the building's end is a naked mole-rat exhibit. The raised *Seronera Overlook* brings you eye-to-eye with elephants, living in a three-quarter-acre grassy yard with an eight-foot deep pool. *Mahali Pa Simba* is a shady sprawling one-acre habitat for lions, who can be seen from three different points, including up close from within a shelter. Opposite the lions, a tall enclosure displays attractive colobus monkeys, while a leopard lives at the boardwalk's end.

In **Great Apes**, visitors first encounter gorillas, who can be seen in their large grassy yard through a wide window. Across the path is an overlook into a lush island habitat for lemurs, both ring-tailed and ruffed varieties. Another viewing station gives views in three directions of the gorillas, who live in a sprawling grassy yard. The back rock walls of the gorilla enclosure are painted to add to the realism to the exhibit. Across the path, a high overlook gives a sweeping view of the habitat for the baboon-like mandrills. The highlight of this area is a habitat for gorillas and bonobos, again separated by a hidden barrier. The bonobos, also called pygmy chimpanzees, are highly entertaining as they cavort on their playground, wade in the water, and try to interact with their human visitors. The gorillas have a more densely planted yard than the bonobos, but both of the habitats have crashing waterfalls. A trek through a bamboo forest leads to a treetop-level view of siamangs, one of the loudest primates.

The **Wild Florida** exhibit, situated on 2½ acres of natural wetlands, displays a nice variety of Sunshine State wildlife, including two of Florida's most endangered animals. You enter the complex through a bright blue pavilion with a large porch, which overhangs the alligators' natural bog habitat. Inside this attractive pavilion is the *Reptile House at Wild Florida*, which displays twenty-five species of reptiles and amphibians native to Florida. Residents include an eastern indigo snake, water moccasins, and side-by side exhibits that let Floridians compare the harmless scarlet king snake with a venomous coral snake. You can keep them straight with this helpful mnemonic: "Red on yellow, kill a fellow, red on black, good for Jack." The outdoor tour begins with Florida panthers, a slender, highly endangered subspecies of puma. Along the path, a barn owl, black bears, bald eagles, white-tailed deer, and rare red wolves are displayed in densely planted habitats that nonetheless offer great viewing opportunities. The river otter exhibit is popular with visitors; it is equipped with underwater windows and a concrete slide that drops into the water. Connected to the exhibit is a rocky habitat for bobcats, natural predators of otters. Near the end of the wetlands walk is a small pool for impressive whooping cranes, which are among the most endangered birds in the world.

OTHER EXHIBITS

The **River Valley** aviary, near the zoo's entrance, marks the beginning of the African adventure. This tall walk-through aviary, with a nearly transparent roof, is lushly planted with tropical foliage and includes a tall trickling waterfall. The nearly twenty species of African birds on display include colorful turacos, African spoonbills, and lesser flamingos. There are smaller rocky enclosures for saddle-billed storks and milky eagle owls right outside. Just beyond the other impressive African habitats, **Giraffe Overlook** has an elevated thatched-roof viewing platform, providing an excellent view of a savanna yard for giraffes and greater kudu antelope. At 2½ acres, there is room here for up to twelve of these towering mammals. At select times, for a small fee, you can feed the giraffes a handful of browse (leafy branches).

At the far end of the zoo, follow a one-way trail through the **Australian Adventure**, past fenced exhibits of wallabies and a cassowary, a flightless bird from New Guinea that can disembowel a person with a single powerful kick. In the large walk-through free-flight aviary at the beginning of this area, visitors can feed nectar to dozens of beautiful lorikeets. Near the jaguars, the main path passes a large pond exhibit with American **flamingos** and two types of **swans**, who swim among giant lily pads.

The zoo is attracting new visitors with its botanical gardens, a focus that's now reflected in its name. **Savanna Blooms**, near the giraffes, is a low formal garden showcasing beautiful African plants and flowers. Opened in 2007, the **Gardens of Trout River Plaza** is a classical garden with an elegant central celebratory fountain surrounded by lush garden beds, Grecian-style living columns with flowering urns, and a vine-planted trellis.

FOR THE KIDS

The new **Play Park**, which opened in 2006, is a major attraction for families. Kids enter by negotiating one of two hedge mazes, the first of many fun adventures. The central *Splash Ground* may be the most popular spot in the park; children can climb on nearly full-size replicas of whales, dolphins, sea turtles, and a manatee, all of which spurt water from their spouts, tails, and mouths. In the *Discovery Building*, kids can put on puppet shows, dress up in animal costumes, check out a kid-sized veterinary clinic with real x-rays, or do arts and crafts. In the animal care contact yard, children can pet and groom pygmy goats. There are three tree houses to explore, one with a bird nest to climb into, all built above a rubberized floor. More adventures lie in store at the animal exhibits: Kids can climb into a tunnel window to watch otters swimming above them, or swing on vines in front of the squirrel monkeys.

The **Zoo Train** encircles the entire zoo. Tickets are good all day, so you can use it for transportation between the front entrance Main Camp and the Play Park. The **wildlife carousel** looks like a classic merry-go-round, but its mounts are all endangered animals.

IN PROGRESS

As we go to press, we hear that the former koala house will soon be transformed into an **Amphibian Research Conservation Center**, where the zoo will pursue a breeding program for endangered frogs, toads, and salamanders. There are also plans in discussion to add hippos to the Plains of East Africa.

The next addition to the zoo's gardens will be the **Asian Bamboo Garden**, where an Asian pavilion will be surrounded by winding paths lined with exotic plants and flowers, a reflecting pond filled with lotus blossoms, and a misty garden of bamboo. A new Komodo dragon exhibit is in the works after that. At press time, the bamboo garden is scheduled to open in 2008, and the Komodo dragon exhibit in 2009. In the years following, an exciting new **Monsoon Asia** exhibit should expand the Asian-themed exhibits described above. From an elevated boardwalk, visitors will see tigers, gibbons, sun bears, and more. There will also be an Asian village plaza with a restaurant, gift shop, and restrooms.

Disney's Animal Kingdom

2901 Osceola Parkway
Lake Buena Vista, Florida 32830
(407) 824-4321
http://disneyworld.disney.go.com
(listed under "Parks")

Hours: 9:00 a.m.-8:00 p.m. daily in summer, 9:00 a.m.-5:00 or 6:00 p.m. the rest of the year, with longer hours during holiday weeks. Call or check website for hours during your visit.

Admission & Fees: Adults $71, children 3-9 $60. Parking $11. Multi-day tickets for all Walt Disney World parks, with the ParkHopper option, are better deals per day.

Visitors can see rhinos on the Kilimanjaro Safaris ride.

Directions: From I-4, take Exit 65 (Animal Kingdom) and follow signs within Disney property for 5 miles. From Florida's Turnpike, take Exit 249 (Osceola Parkway). Follow Dart Road, which becomes Osceola Parkway, for 14 miles.

Don't Miss: Kilimanjaro Safaris, Maharajah Jungle Trek, Pangani Forest Exploration Trail. Also, theme park rides and shows: Expedition Everest, It's Tough to be a Bug!, Finding Nemo –The Musical, Festival of the Lion King, DINOSAUR, Kali River Rapids.

For Kids: Affection Section, Habitat Habit!, Kids Discovery Club stations, The Boneyard, TriceraTop Spin, Disney Character Greeting Trails.

Authors' Tips: This is Disney World, so lines can be long, especially during the summer and holiday weeks. To cut down on time in line, use the FASTPASS system for popular attractions, like Kilimanjaro Safaris. To save time, pick up a FASTPASS for Kilimanjaro or Everest, then spend the time until your designated ride time seeing the animal trails in Africa or Asia. There are many excellent dining choices, with wonderful atmosphere. Among the best are the Rainforest Café, Flame Tree Barbecue, and McDonalds food in DinoLand U.S.A. Most people visit this park as part of a Disney World vacation. If this is you, note that there is an excellent aquarium (The Seas with Nemo & Friends – also a ride) at Epcot. It even exhibits manatees!

Edutainment: Of course, the entertainment is "Disney quality" – first class! The "Flights of Wonder" bird show gives a humorous look at a wide variety of birds, including an amazing talking parrot, a pied crow that takes a dollar from a guest's hand, a crowned crane, and a bald eagle. In "Pocahontas and Her Forest Friends," the Disney Indian princess sings her classic "Colors of the Wind" as native North American wildlife including a raccoon, porcupine, skunk, snake, free-flying birds, and other animals join Pocahontas in her plea to help save the world's forests. These shows are held many times daily. Animal training sessions are presented daily in Pocahontas' amphitheater. Check the insert inside your park map for times and locations.

DISNEY'S ANIMAL KINGDOM OPENED IN 1998, AS THE FOURTH theme park at the Walt Disney World® Resort (WDW), the number one tourist destination in the world. Before Animal Kingdom, there was the classic Jungle Cruise ride; before that, there were Disney's "True Life Adventure" films. Animals have always been important to the Disney Company, and in fact to Walt Disney himself. It was only natural that, eventually, Disney would build a first-class zoo.

But Disney's Animal Kingdom is much more than a zoo. It is also a popular theme park, with amazing rides and shows – many of which do not include live animals. Because this is a zoo guidebook, this chapter will only briefly describe those attractions that are more theme park than zoo. (Consult our publisher's *The Hassle-Free Walt Disney World® Vacation*, updated annually, for details on those.)

Like many Disney theme parks, Disney's Animal Kingdom is laid out in a "hub and spokes" design, with a central "land" (**Discovery Island** and its spectacular *Tree of Life*) as the hub and five other lands connected by bridges (spokes). Walking through the plazas of these themed lands is like being transported to distant lands: authentic African or Asian buildings, artifacts, and music create an exotic atmosphere. The attention to detail is incredible. The décor in the *Africa* and *Asia* lands may be the most realistic anywhere outside of those continents. In fact, some of the buildings were constructed by native craftsmen.

FEATURED EXHIBITS

A ride on **Kilimanjaro Safaris** is the one true "must do" in this park. While walking through the long queue area (where there's often a long wait), overhead video monitors explain that this is *Harambe Reserve*, a place where poaching is a serious problem. You'll take the tour aboard a thirty-six-passenger safari jeep, as an energetic driver-guide points out the animals all around. Once the vehicle enters the 110-acre savanna, you will see no fences or walls. All of the barriers which keep the animals safely separated are hidden remarkably well, making this the most authentic safari adventure you can take without making a trans-Atlantic flight! There are more than thirty different species of African animals to look for, but odds are you will never see all of them in one trip. This makes every ride different, depending on where the animals are and on who your driver is; some of the guides are from Africa. The first animals you usually see are beautiful bongo antelope, elusive okapis, and black rhinos. Both hippos and Nile crocodiles are visible in separate river habitats. Winding through the dense vegetation, the tour vehicle emerges into an open savanna, with views of giraffes, ostriches, wildebeest, and many different antelope. Up on a high rock formation, a family of colorful mandrills seems to be watching the herd of elephants across the road. The jeep passes close to watering holes that bring white rhinos, zebras, warthogs, flamingos, and more antelope into view. Tall, rocky kopje formations give the cheetahs and lions tempting views of the antelope below them. But of course, this is Disney. This isn't just a well-rounded zoo safari – there's a story line that develops as the tour progresses. Along the way, the jeep splashes through flooded roads, crosses a collapsing bridge, and eventually ends up in a high-speed chase, helping to trap some evil elephant poachers. This is all very exciting for the kids, but for adults, the realistic safari is memorable enough.

Visitors usually enjoy the **Pangani Forest Exploration Trail** immediately before or after the safari ride. At the first observation site in this five-acre lush tropical exhibit, colobus monkeys are visible in a treetop canopy mesh enclosure. Nearby, exotic okapis are displayed in a forest clearing. In a small research field hut, people often miss the displays of animal artifacts, because many find themselves fascinated by a colony of naked mole-rats, the world's only hairless rodents. Outside the hut, the path passes a set of pools filled with hundreds of beautiful cichlid fish. A large walk-through aviary features bearded barbets, carmine bee-eaters, and other rare African birds, all flying overhead. Another open-air shelter shields a large window into the underwater world of hippos, who swim with cichlid fish that keep the pool clean. In this educational shelter, a hippopotamus skull reveals the gigantic teeth that make hippos the number one man-killer in Africa. Further up the trail, a large shaded overlook offers a view of some interesting savanna animals, including gerenuk gazelles, often called "giraffe-gazelles" because of their long necks, and the always-popular meerkats, made famous by the Disney film *The Lion King*. Most guests end up congregating in the *Gorilla Research Camp*, especially at the slanted glass window where a silverback-led family of gorillas often hangs out quite close by. Outside, from a swaying suspension bridge, the gorilla family can be seen across a gorge to the right, while to the left, a separate bachelor group of gorillas lives on a grassy hillside with a crashing waterfall.

In *Asia*, the fictional Kingdom of Anandapur hosts the **Maharajah Jungle Trek**, a self-guided walk through the Royal Forest, with very well done replicas of an ancient palace, hunting lodge, and religious temples – all lying in ruins and mostly reclaimed by the wildlife of India and Southeast Asia. Just outside the entrance to this half-mile walk, guests can see (and hear) a pair of ape islands, home to siamangs and white-checked gibbons. The loud siamangs are often visible directly above, swinging on a rope across the moat to a high tower above the visitors. Inside the Royal Forest, the first animal you'll encounter is a Komodo dragon. This huge lizard from Indonesia, displayed in a rocky pit with a waterfall, is visible from three separate viewing points. Around the bend, in a similar habitat with a small pool, there is a large black-and-white Malayan tapir. Adventurous guests will next enter a brightly painted hut that replicates an Indonesian community hall, where more than thirty large bats are only separated from visitors by thin wire. These Rodrigues and Malayan flying foxes usually hang upside down from crisscrossing vines, but sometimes they take flight, showing off their six-foot wingspan. There are several spots for viewing the Asian tigers: from high overhead, from a bridge, or up close through glass. While you're on this bamboo trail, be sure to take note of the Asian architecture and artwork. The painted murals in the tiger area are gorgeous. Across the bridge from the tigers is an open field that's home to Elds deer, blackbuck antelope, and bulky bantengs, a type of wild cattle. Along the trail, hundreds of colorful prayer flags hang above, as a large domed great hall comes into sight. Inside the hall are fountains, pools, and more than fifty species of beautiful Asian birds. Using the illustrated identification card, you can find such species as golden pheasants, fruit doves, and fairy bluebirds.

The wildest rides in the park are also in *Asia*. **Expedition Everest: Legend of the Forbidden Mountain** is one of the best roller coasters in all of Disney World. Its surrounding environs are thoroughly decorated as a Himalayan mountain village, because this wild coaster features a face-to-face encounter with the Yeti, the Asian version of the Abominable Snowman. Around the corner, **Kali River Rapids** is a whitewater raft ride on the fictional Chakranadi River. Aboard a twelve-person round raft, riders are virtually guaranteed to get soaked, and will float by a burning rain forest. Over in DinoLand U.S.A., riders for **DINOSAUR** pass through a queue area that resembles a dinosaur museum. Then you board a time travel vehicle and are taken for a wild, bumpy, dark journey through a steamy prehistoric jungle filled with hungry dinosaurs.

One of the park's most popular attractions is **It's Tough to be a Bug!**, a 3-D movie adventure. To get to this insect-themed show, follow a trail downhill into the roots of the gigantic *Tree of Life*. Animal-lovers should slow down to admire the hundreds of different animals carved into this massive man-made tree. The hilarious show features Flik, an ant from the Disney·Pixar film *A Bug's Life*, and an extensive cast of other animated bugs.

In two colossal amphitheaters, the park holds Broadway-quality musicals based on two of Disney's biggest-ever movies. In a tent-like setting, **Festival of the Lion King** features characters and songs from *The Lion King*, as well as acrobats, fire dancers, and more. In a larger indoor theater, **Finding Nemo – The Musical** features the characters of the film *Finding Nemo*, along with some new songs to accompany the story and some incredible special effects. These shows fill up fast, so arrive early for a good seat.

OTHER EXHIBITS

Just beyond the park's entrance is a series of animal habitats, called the **Oasis Exhibits**, which many guests bypass and never see. Emerging from either the left or right main path, a maze of side trails leads to more than a dozen open-view animal exhibits. The Oasis area is the most densely planted section in the park, with more than 850 species of trees alone. Among this lush jungle vegetation, there are habitats for giant anteaters, wild babirusa pigs from Indonesia, tiny muntjac deer, iguanas, and an assortment of exotic ducks and parrots, as well as numerous streams and waterfalls.

A bridge leads from the Oasis to the central Discovery Island, where the towering Tree of Life (see above) dominates the landscape. All around the tree are short trails that lead to unusual small animals. These **Discovery Island Trails** feature nice, clear views of red kangaroos, Axis deer, lemurs, African crested porcupines, Galapagos tortoises, flamingos and other exotic birds. The highlight of this area is an underwater viewing cave for small-clawed otters.

A ride on the **Wildlife Express Train** makes a refreshing break from hours of walking. This old-fashioned steam train has piles of luggage up on its roof. Since you board in the *Africa* section, the "story" behind this locomotive is that it transports adventurers across the African continent. On board, all seats face outward. The short tour passes the night holding barns for many of the park's large animals. The railroad's ultimate destination is the **Conservation Station**, the highlight of *Rafiki's Planet Watch*. You enter this fascinating building beneath a huge colorful mural of endangered animals. Inside, visitors are given an extensive behind-the-scenes look at how animals are cared for in Animal Kingdom. Interactive exhibits and videos here are both entertaining and educational. Sound booths let you hear the sounds of the rain forest, as well as the sound of a chain saw destroying the jungle. Visitors can watch from behind glass as sick and injured animals are cared for, while the *Nutrition Center* shows the different foods animals are fed. A variety of reptiles, amphibians, insects, and small mammals are displayed all about in small exhibits, and sometimes animal handlers will bring out an animal to meet visitors.

In **DinoLand U.S.A.**, there are exhibits of an American crocodile, Asian brown tortoises, and Abdim's storks. The *Dino-Rama* section has a fun, kitschy, 1950s roadside fair atmosphere. The *Fossil Fun Games* are ordinary carnival games, where guests test their skill to win prizes. *Primeval Whirl*, a mild spinning roller coaster, is popular with both kids and adults.

FOR THE KIDS

Just outside the Conservation Station is **Affection Section**, a brightly colored contact yard with goats and sheep. You'll also meet Guinea hogs, a llama, a Dexter cow, and other domestic animals in fenced corrals. Children don't just pet the animals; a basket full of brushes encourages them to brush the fur of the friendly goats. Located between the train and Conservation Station, **Habitat Habit!** is a forest trail that features informative graphics about conservation and a nice exhibit of endangered cotton-top tamarin monkeys.

At six locations around the park, the **Kids Discovery Club** sites are interactive learning stations for children ages three to eight. At these stations, they can examine clues left behind by African animals, piece together dinosaur fossils, look for insects, and engage in other fun activities. As they complete each simple task, they get a special stamp in their free Kids Discovery Club field guide.

The park's best playground is *The Boneyard*, a gigantic high-tech play area in DinoLand U.S.A. The area includes an extensive climbing structure, soft rubberized flooring, and life-size dinosaur skeletons embedded into the walls of the playground. Children line up to try *TriceraTop Spin*, a ride which emulates the famous Disney "Dumbo" ride, except instead of cartoon elephants, kids ride on friendly looking dinosaurs.

Because this is Disney World, after all, costumed characters, including Mickey Mouse, roam the park and are available for pictures, autographs, and hugs. The best place to find these characters is at the four *Greeting Trails* in the **Camp Minnie-Mickey** section. All of the characters can also be seen in the daily late afternoon parade.

IN PROGRESS

While Disney has not announced any future plans for its Animal Kingdom at press time, an attractive restaurant is under construction as this book goes to print. Scheduled to open in 2008, the Yak & Yeti Restaurant will continue the Himalayan foothills atmosphere of its *Asia* location. Featuring both table and counter service dining options, it should make it easy to believe you are feasting in Himalayan Asia.

Miami Metrozoo

1 Zoo Boulevard
12400 SW 152nd Street
Miami, Florida 33177
(305) 251-0400
www.miamimetrozoo.com

Hours: 9:30 a.m.-5:30 p.m. daily. Ticket booths close at 4:00 p.m. See website for special holiday hours.

Admission & Fees: Adults $13.95, seniors 65+ $12.95, children 3-12 $9.95, military and AAA members $1 discount. Monorail $3 for an all-day pass. Multi-seat two-hour "Safari Cycle" rentals: $44 for a small cycle (seats three adults and two children), $64 for a large (six adults, two children); each additional hour is $22 for a small, $32 for a large. Behind-the-scenes tram tour $4.95. Participates in reciprocity program.

Sarus crane in Wings of Asia.

Directions: Located on Miami's far southwest side. From the Florida Turnpike (Highway 821), take the Homestead Extension Exit 16. Turn right (west) on SW 152nd Street, follow ¼ mile, then turn left at SW 124 Avenue, following the signs into the zoo. From U.S. Highway 1, take the 152nd Street Exit and follow 3 miles west to zoo. Miami's zoo bus, the "Coral Reef Express," offers express service from the Dadeland South Metrorail station in Miami.

Don't Miss: Zoofari Monorail, Wings of Asia, koalas, African exhibits, Asian River Life, Asian exhibits, Tiger Temple.

For Kids: Children's Zoo, Splash Pads, Dr. Wilde's World.

Authors' Tips: A complete walk around this huge zoo is more than three miles, making the air-conditioned Zoofari Monorail almost essential. For a onetime fee, riders can hop on and off all day. It provides a narrated tour with good views of most animals. Four elevated monorail stations are well-spaced for convenient touring. To account for Miami's hot weather, water fountains, soda machines, splash pads, and "cool zone" misters are located throughout the grounds. A guided behind-the-scenes tram tour is also available a few times daily.

Edutainment: In the large central amphitheater, reptiles, free-flying birds of prey, and a rare king cheetah star in the popular "Wildlife Show," held three times daily. In the Children's Zoo, "Diego's Discovery Den Show" features a variety of animals, and the life-size character Diego, star of the popular TV show *Go, Diego, Go!*, in twenty-minute shows once daily during the week and twice daily on weekends. Informal keeper talks are scheduled regularly at various exhibits around the zoo. The giraffes and pelicans can be fed for a small fee at their exhibits.

CONSIDERED BY MANY TO BE ONE OF THE WORLD'S GREAT ZOOS, the new (relocated) Miami Metrozoo opened in 1981 on 740 inland acres. Ironically, a primary reason for relocating was that its coastal Key Biscayne former location was considered too vulnerable to the area's frequent hurricanes. Sadly, on August 24, 1992, when Hurricane Andrew hit southern Florida with its 187-miles-per-hour winds, this zoo was directly in its path. Due to the staff's extraordinary preparations, animal losses were remarkably light, but the structures and landscaping sustained over $15 million in damages. Thanks to the dedication of the zoo staff, generous donations from across the country, and the passage of time, the zoo is finally out of its rebuilding mode and once again growing. Still, reminders of that sad day can be found around the zoo.

One lasting memory of a visit here is the zoo's amazing number of large animals. With nearly 300 developed acres, this is one of the nation's largest zoos. All of this space provides large exhibit areas for its residents and the capability to display more pachyderms and other large animals than almost any other U.S. zoo. With most of its animals living in spacious natural habitats, and only hidden moats separating visitors from the animals, the Miami Metrozoo is called a "cageless" zoo. This was made possible because, as one of the nation's newest zoos, it was built from the ground up using modern exhibit technology. Of course, Florida's mild, semitropical climate is ideal for the zoo's lush tropical foliage, including orchids and palms.

FEATURED EXHIBITS

The worst damage from Hurricane Andrew was the complete destruction of the zoo's premier exhibit, the magnificent **Wings of Asia**. Eleven years later, in 2003, this superb walk-through aviary was finally back, rebuilt bigger and better than before. Today a sixty-five-foot-high, hurricane-proofed mesh roof covers the simulated Southeast Asian rain forest. More than 300 colorful birds of seventy different species fly, walk, and swim around their human visitors, who can climb to high observation points, go behind one of the five waterfalls, or simply relax while watching the stream's exotic Asian fish inside its air-conditioned indoor gallery. Memorable birds include Great Indian hornbills, Raggiana birds of paradise, blue-masked leafbirds, and five-foot-tall sarus cranes. Near the aviary's entrance, the small *Field Research Center* building offers a video, fossils, and other displays that explore the relationship between birds and dinosaurs.

Most of the spacious exhibits at this zoo are distributed along one of two geographical loops that originate from the central Amphitheater. More than sixteen **African exhibits** are scattered along the southern loop (currently unfinished). Chimpanzees, gorillas, and a large troop of black-and-white colobus monkeys inhabit large, sloping, grassy yards with artificial trees to climb. African elephants and black rhinos live next to each other in spacious grassy areas with large watering holes. At the start of this trail, the pygmy hippo exhibit has a deep pool. A multi-species savanna exhibit includes giraffes, zebras, gazelles, ostriches, and vultures in an expansive open grassland. Across the path is a breeding group of okapis, rare multi-colored giraffe cousins. The unparalleled variety of African antelope seen along this path includes kudus, waterbucks, nyalas, and giant elands. Most interesting, however, are the skinny gerenuks, who will stand up on their hind legs to nibble leaves from tree branches above them. Exhibits of smaller animals feature African porcupines and bat-eared foxes. Mixed in on this loop are a couple of South American exhibits, with guanacos (rare llama relatives), rheas (ostrich-like birds), and Andean condors.

Asian exhibits dominate the other winding loop, which also includes African and South American exhibits. The Asian elephant exhibit makes this one of only a few zoos to have two elephant displays. Indian rhinos and Malayan tapirs are nearby in spacious yards, and three bear species (sun bears, sloth bears, and Himalayan black bears) can cool off in deep pools. Orangutans are seen in a wide yard equipped with climbing poles and ropes, but the closest view of these apes is through a glass panel in a viewing cave. Three types of wild cattle (anoa, bantengs, and gaurs), onagers (wild donkeys), Bactrian (two-humped) and dromedary (one-humped) camels, spotted hyenas, and a wide variety of Asian deer and antelope (including Arabian oryxes) live in natural habitats along this loop. African lions and Cape hunting dogs (also known as African wild dogs) are found in grassy yards strewn with rocks. The lions can be seen up close through another viewing cave. Additional African antelope species, including rare gemsbok, also live in this mostly Asian area. Latin American animals here include Baird's tapirs, howler monkeys, saki monkeys, squirrel monkeys, and highly endangered Cuban crocodiles.

One of the highlights of the Asian loop is the bi-level **Asian River Life** exhibit, including the *Komodo Dragon Encounter* – an exhibit of the world's largest lizards, native to Indonesia. Passing an ornamental sign and a wide waterfall, visitors enter a rocky cave, where they encounter clouded leopards and a blood python. A higher observation level overlooks a muddy riverbank with muntjacs (small deer), Malayan water monitor lizards, and a family of playful small-clawed otters. The otters are enjoyable to watch as they frolic underwater.

Koalas are the highlight of the short **Australian Exhibits** trail. (This was the first U.S. zoo outside of California to exhibit these popular marsupials.) The cuddly koalas are displayed in a glass-fronted indoor habitat. Also in this area are red kangaroos, tree kangaroos, and New Guinea singing dogs, whose unusual upper lip formation allows them to "sing" with wolf-like howls.

Miami Metrozoo's most photographed exhibit is the **Tiger Temple**, near the front of the zoo. A very convincing replica of an ancient Cambodian temple provides a great background, while the tigers roam the grassy field in the foreground. The rare white Bengal tiger is especially popular here. A sign in front of the exhibit tells the story of Naomi Browning, a twelve-year-old zoo volunteer killed by Hurricane Andrew. This exhibit is dedicated to her memory.

OTHER EXHIBITS

A beautiful tropical lagoon filled with Caribbean flamingos gives a great first impression to visitors entering the zoo. Nearby, a long yard is filled with both live and artificial banyan trees, providing a suitable home for vocal siamangs and gibbons. Ring-tailed lemurs inhabit another banyan tree exhibit across the path. Also in this vicinity is a short path with three more exhibits of African antelope, including impressive bongos.

A mini-loop extending from the Amphitheatre offers five exhibits, highlighted by two types of wild pigs – red river hogs and popular warthogs. The *Giant Land Tortoise Exhibit* is dotted with both Galapagos and Aldabra tortoises.

FOR THE KIDS

The sparkling **Children's Zoo** offers kids a chance to see and touch many of their favorite animals. Inside *Toadstool*, small reptiles and amphibians are on display in a small air-conditioned room. Outside, the meerkats are especially popular. There's also a snack bar, *Diego's Discovery Den*, a small playground, remote control boats, an endangered animal carousel, a *Splash Pad* play area, and a small petting corral with white roosters, a turkey, and a pot-bellied pig. Elsewhere in the zoo, another playground and *Splash Pad* play area are by the *Lakeside Grille*.

Centrally located **Dr. Wilde's World** is an education center where different regions and cultures of the world are introduced in rotating exhibits. This huge air-conditioned indoor gallery educates using live animals, games, puzzles, and other fun interactive elements, such as microscopes.

IN PROGRESS

There is much excitement in south Florida over the projected opening of **Amazon and Beyond**, a twenty-seven-acre exhibit of plants and wildlife from tropical America. This may prove the nation's best exhibit of South American animals – and it will certainly be the largest! The keystone species here will be giant river otters, which are displayed in only a very few U.S. zoos. Other exciting species within this exhibit area will include jaguars, harpy eagles, Orinoco crocodiles, and anaconda snakes. South American animals already distributed around the zoo will be relocated to this fascinating new exhibit area. At press time, it is scheduled to open in November of 2008. Check the zoo's website for the latest information on this exciting new attraction.

Busch Gardens Africa

3000 East Busch Boulevard
Tampa, Florida 33612
(888) 800-5447
www.buschgardens.com

Hours: Normal hours are 10:00 a.m.-6:00 p.m., with extended hours in summer, during holiday periods, and on select weekends. Call or check the website for hours before your visit.

Admission & Fees: Adults $64.95, children 3-9 $54.95. Discounts for guests with disabilities, seniors, military, and AAA members. Inquire in advance or at the gate. Parking $9. Lory feeding $3. For those who want closer encounters with the Serengeti animals, more extensive tours are available for higher fees. If you're on a Florida vacation, there are multi-day tickets and package deals that include SeaWorld, Busch Gardens' sister park in Orlando.

Feeding Australian lorikeets in Lory Landing.

Directions: From I-75, take Exit 265 (Fowler Avenue). Go west on Fowler Avenue for 4.6 miles, then turn left onto McKinley Drive and follow for 1.5 miles to parking lot entrance on the left. From I-275, take Exit 51 (Fowler Avenue). Go east on Fowler Avenue for 2.5 miles, then turn right onto McKinley Drive and follow for 1.5 miles to parking lot entrance on the right.

Don't Miss: Serengeti Plain, Edge of Africa, Rhino Rally, Myombe Reserve. Also, theme park rides and shows: SheiKra, Montu, Kumba, Gwazi, Tanganyika Tidal Wave, Pirates 4-D, KaTonga.

For Kids: Land of the Dragons, kiddie rides, Carousel Caravan.

Authors' Tips: Of the park's many atmospheric restaurants, Crown Colony is by far the best. Looking like an elegant British resort, this first-rate restaurant has table-service dining in the air-conditioned dining room and out on the breezy patio, an excellent menu (including fresh seafood), and an unparalleled view of the Serengeti Plain's animals. It's advisable to bring along a change of clothes, as getting totally soaked is the norm on the park's many water rides.

Edutainment: "Critter Castaways" is a fun musical show featuring dogs, cats, flying birds, a tamandua (lesser anteater), a kangaroo, and other exotic animals. There are a wide variety of "Meet the Keeper" presentations at nearly all of the park's animal habitats, each held multiple times daily. Check the insert inside the park map for times and locations.

AN AMUSEMENT PARK IN THE BUSCH ENTERTAINMENT CORP. family, which includes the SeaWorld parks, Busch Gardens Africa is a full-scale theme park combining animal exhibits, shows, shopping bazaars, restaurants, and more than a dozen thrill rides, all in a most believable African atmosphere. Around the park, seven African-themed "lands" each have their own unique flavor. Arriving guests enter through *Morocco*, where lofty Arab-style buildings give things an authentic North African flavor. *Bird Gardens*, with its many bird habitats, was the extent of the original park when it opened in 1959 as a free hospitality garden for the on site brewery. The central *Nairobi* section hosts a wide variety of animal exhibits, from elephants to reptiles. *Congo, Stanleyville, Timbuktu*, and *Egypt* focus mainly on wild and wet thrill rides.

FEATURED EXHIBITS

When it opened in 1965, the **Serengeti Plain** was the first of its kind, a revolutionary new way of displaying African savanna animals – all together in one massive habitat. The current version of the sixty-five-acre Serengeti is remarkable for its realism. Its many acres are landscaped to maximize viewing opportunities of its hundreds of animals, while native African trees and grass are used to create scenery that is truly African. This savanna can be seen in many different ways, but the best two methods are from above via the high-flying **Skyride** or from ground level aboard the **Serengeti Express Railway** steam train. The train makes a two-mile loop around the park perimeter, beyond the Serengeti. You can board at three different stations. As it enters the Serengeti Plain from the south, the first animals you'll see are flamingos, followed by a herd of giraffes, usually being fed by a truckload of paying visitors. Along the way, you may spot a wide variety of antelope, including swift-footed impala, spiral-horned addax, bulky elands, and elegant bongos. The assortment of land birds includes African crowned cranes and ostriches. As the train crosses over a watering pool, larger animals come into sight, including white rhinos, Cape buffalo,

Ankole cattle, and herds of zebras. While the Skyride can be boarded in two locations, the Crown Colony station is best for seeing the savanna animals. From one of these high-flying gondolas, the view – of the Serengeti, elephants, Rhino Rally (see below), and even the roller coasters – is spectacular. Unless you have a fear of heights, we recommend that you see the Serengeti from both the train and the Skyride. *Note*: The Montu roller coaster provides another good, but brief, view.

The **Edge of Africa** is a spectacular walk-through journey featuring close encounters with some of Africa's most popular animals. Tents and safari-painted Land Rovers are parked all over the exhibit, to confirm that you are "going on safari." At the trail head, a thatched-roof hut provides trail guides for identifying the animals. The first species you'll meet include flamingos and pelicans, imposing vultures, and meerkats, which are usually hiding among dirt mounds. From here, there are good views of the giraffes, antelope, and large birds in the Serengeti. Next, at the superb lion exhibit, it looks as if a Land Rover has crashed into the wide glass window. While parents look through the glass at the nearby lions, their children can crawl into the Land Rover to see the lions up close, directly through the vehicle's windows. At times, a lion climbs up onto the vehicle, a real thrill for the kids inside! Spotted hyenas are seen next door from a long, deep viewing cave. The trail's highlight is a giant pool, housing hippos on one side and Nile crocodiles on the other. From a sheltered viewing station, the pool is a beautiful rainbow of color, created by hundreds of pretty African cichlid fish. These daring fish swim alongside the crocodiles and hippos, who are especially fun to watch underwater. At the trail's end, ring-tailed lemurs occupy an attractive habitat overlooking the hippo pool.

For animal lovers, **Rhino Rally** is the best thrill ride in the park. It combines a wild adventure safari with close animal encounters. Passengers ride on a specially equipped Land Rover with a hilarious driver-guide. Along the bumpy, winding trail, the vehicle passes Asian elephants, flamingos, Cape buffalo, zebras, crocodiles, various antelope, and of course, rhinos. Spoiler alert! The adventure comes to an unexpected climax when a rickety pontoon bridge gives way to a flash flood and the vehicle and its seventeen passengers find themselves spiraling down the river. The driver blames this mishap on the "navigator," the unfortunate passenger riding shotgun. For those who might forget that this is a theme park, this ride can be terrifying!

It's hard to believe such a lush jungle setting could exist in the middle of a coaster park, but it does at **Myombe Reserve**. The winding walkway leads to a beautiful habitat for a large troop of chimpanzees. Their rocky, terraced home includes crashing waterfalls, pools, towering palms, and grassy meadows. Most popular with visitors, however, is the large viewing cave with a wide slanting window, where the chimps can be seen up close. From there, the path leads through the *Research Outpost*, then on to an equally beautiful – and very similar – habitat for gorillas. Again, the best views of these great apes are from a pair of huge viewing caves, both with wide windows that slant outward. An overhead video presents information about the apes.

To the surprise of zoo fans, the park's wild roller coasters actually draw more visitors than the animals. None of the seven coasters looks more terrifying than

SheiKra, a floorless vertical dive coaster that takes riders 200 feet in the air, then drops them straight down at a ninety-degree angle, eventually splashing into a pool of water. In **Egypt**, *Montu*, one of the world's tallest inverted coasters, is famous for its inverse diving loop. **Congo's** *Kumba* is a longtime favorite, with one of the world's largest vertical loops. Finally, *Gwazi* is the park's enormous wooden coaster, actually a dueling roller coaster. There are three water rides, none wetter than *Tanganyika Tidal Wave*, which creates a wall of water at the end of a fifty-five-foot drop.

Most popular of the excellent entertainment available is the *Pirates 4-D* movie, the hilarious swashbuckling film starring Leslie Nielsen as "Captain Lucky." *Ka Tonga: Musical Tales From the Jungle* is a Broadway-style extravaganza with music, dancing, acrobats, handheld puppets, and story-telling, all presenting traditional African stories and legends.

OTHER EXHIBITS

Bird Gardens, the park's original site, now plays host to an array of pretty bird-related exhibits. *Eagle Canyon* is a short wooded loop where bald and golden eagles look especially regal in their rocky grottoes. Not far away, *Flamingo Island* features dozens of Caribbean flamingos in a peaceful lagoon. Black-necked swans swim in a nearby koi pond. At the *Aviary Walk-Thru*, a short path leads through a habitat for a variety of beautiful birds, including scarlet ibises and blue-billed ruddy ducks. *Lory Landing* is another walk-through aviary, this time with the opportunity to hand-feed multi-colored Australian lorikeets. It also has other unusual birds, such as demoiselle cranes and some larger parrot species. Across from the dragon-themed children's area, **Living Dragons** is the home of a massive Komodo dragon. Also here, in glass-fronted habitats, are large monitor lizards and iguanas. Behind the lory aviary is a South American animal yard, where the residents include giant anteaters.

In **Nairobi**, *Curiosity Caverns*, a long cave-like exhibition of small animals and reptiles, houses cotton-top tamarin monkeys, pythons, an indigo snake, and venomous Mexican beaded lizards. The nocturnal section features a spacious cavern that's home to fluttering fruit bats. Glass-fronted alligator and caiman exhibits are just outside, in front of the Caverns. *Jambo Junction* serves as an exhibit of the park's many animal ambassadors, friendly creatures that act as the "face" of Busch Gardens for media presentations. In open corrals and behind glass, some of the creatures here include snakes, opossums, owls and a llama. Out front, an open yard with a low fence displays a large group of giant Aldabra tortoises. The *Elephant Habitat* is easily visible, as it is slightly elevated above the path. Asian elephants live in a 1½-acre open yard, enhanced by waterfalls and large watering holes. Across from the elephants, a group of dromedary camels (with just one hump) dwell in a beautiful sprawling habitat, visible from many viewing spots. More alligators can be found in a sizeable swamp exhibit near the front of the park.

Football fans will recognize the residents of the *Clydesdale Hamlet*: they're the famous Anheuser-Busch Clydesdales, stars of the football game commercials. These magnificent horses can be found either in their stables or out in their exercise yard.

Another horse-related exhibit, the official *Show Jumping Hall of Fame*, is nearby, honoring the 40 people and 15 horses who have made the greatest contributions to this sport. Across from the Clydesdales, there is a small waterfowl pond where residents include rare Hawaiian Nene geese.

Other theme park rides include: the *Scorpion*, a small roller coaster with some high-speed 360-degree loops; *Cheetah Chase*, a milder (22 mph) "wild mouse" single-car coaster; and the *Phoenix*, a looping, swinging, dizzying giant ship. *Congo River Rapids* is an excellent way to cool off on hot days; its round multi-passenger rafts negotiate a wild whitewater river. *Stanley Falls Flume*, an old-fashioned log flume ride with a forty-three-foot drop, doesn't get riders too wet. In Congo, *Ubanga-Banga Bumper Cars* is self-explanatory – a classic bumper car ride. Appropriately located in Egypt, *King Tut's Tomb* is a replica of King Tutankhamen's burial site as it looked during excavation in the 1920s.

Aside from the featured entertainment described above, the park offers additional shows several times daily. At press time, they offer musical reviews featuring 1940s swing music and a variety of popular music, from disco to country.

FOR THE KIDS

The number one children's area is the **Land of the Dragons**, where costumed dragon characters welcome kids to play in a three-story-high tree house, a bouncing house, a sand play area, special slides, and assorted carnival-style kiddie rides. In the *Dragon's Tale Theater*, a fun stage show starring Dumphrey the dragon, is presented several times daily.

More traditional *kiddie rides* are available in **Timbuktu**, which is also home to a very pretty merry-go-round, *Carousel Caravan*.

IN PROGRESS

Scheduled for completion in 2008 as we go to press, **Jungala** will become the park's only animal habitat complex to focus mostly on Asian animals. Bengal tigers will be the feature species of this four-acre lush jungle exhibit in the *Congo*. Guests will see these big cats from viewing caves, some of them with underwater views of the tigers' plunge pool. From a tree-top viewing platform, orangutans will entertain visitors as they play in their specially designed tree house. *Kulu Canopy* will be a multi-species habitat with gibbons, flying fox bats, and gharials, rare Asian crocodiles. Within a jungle village, two new rides should be popular: *The Wild Surge*, which will launch passengers high above a waterfall; and *Jungle Flyers*, a zip line ride. Themed restaurants and *Tree Top Trails*, a family play zone, will round out the new area.

Tampa's Lowry Park Zoo

1101 West Sligh Avenue
Tampa, Florida 33604
(813) 935-8552
www.lowryparkzoo.com

Hours: 9:30 a.m.-5:00 p.m. daily. Closed on Thanksgiving and Christmas Day.

Admission & Fees: Adults $18.95, seniors 60+ $17.95, children 3-11 $14.50. River Odyssey Ecotour: adults $14, seniors 60+ $13, children 3-11 $10. (Buy zoo and ecotour tickets together for

An overlook offers a good view of two manatees, or "sea cows." See close-up, below.

$2 off the total price). Treetop Skyfari $4, Safari ride $3, Flyin' Bananas ride $3, Muster ride $2, Tasmanian Tower $3, Pony Trek $2, Camel Caravan $3, Jungle Carousel $2. Note: All rides must be paid in tokens. Tokens are $1 each, and may be purchased from machines found near each ride and at the main entrance. Lorikeet feeding $1, stingray feeding $2, giraffe feeding $2, rhino feeding $2 (weekends only). Participates in reciprocity program.

Directions: From I-4, take Exit 26 (I-275 North), and follow I-275 north to Exit 48 (Sligh Avenue). Turn left onto Sligh Avenue and head west for 1 mile. Zoo parking lot is on the right.

Don't Miss: Safari Africa, Asian Gardens, Manatee & Aquatic Center, Native Florida Wildlife Center, Primate World.

For Kids: Stingray Bay, Wallaroo Station, Treetop Skyfari, Camel Caravan ride, Lorikeet Landing, Jungle Carousel, Manatee Fountain.

Authors' Tips: If you plan to do several of the zoo's nine rides and special attractions, save money with an unlimited ride wristband ($18, $14 for members), available at the main entrance. Take the opportunity to feed four different animals here: giraffes, lorikeets, stingrays, and white rhinos.

Edutainment: A "Manatee Encounter Show" at the Manatee Amphitheater is held twice daily. The "Spirits of the Sky," featuring eleven birds of prey, includes bald eagles and Andean condors, and runs twice daily (except on Wednesdays). Keeper chats and other demonstrations are held by the Asian rhino and meerkat exhibits, and in Primate World; locations and primates rotate daily. Public penguin feedings are held twice daily, and alligator feedings are held on weekend afternoons.

ORIGINALLY ESTABLISHED IN THE LATE 1930S, LOWRY PARK ZOO existed for many years in the shadow of Busch Gardens, Tampa's other wildlife park. After closing for renovations in 1984, the zoo reopened in 1988. Every current exhibit has been built in the past two decades, so the zoo is still very new. The biggest boost to the zoo's reputation came in 2004, when *Child Magazine* rated it the most family friendly zoo in America. With many close-up creature encounters, a variety of entertaining rides, and a spectacular animal collection, this distinction is well deserved.

FEATURED EXHIBITS

Safari Africa is the zoo's largest new exhibit in twenty years. After you pass below the exhibit's huge, distinctive entry sign, a tunnel leads you to *Africa Plaza*, where the path runs past some of Africa's most popular animals. A meerkat mob climbs termite mounds behind the safari-themed restrooms. Warthogs enjoy a bi-level habitat next to a mixed-species grassland exhibit of lesser kudus and gerenuks (both slim antelope species), crowned cranes, ground hornbills (carnivorous land birds), and petite duiker antelope. Giraffes and zebras can be seen from ground level, before you head up to the giraffe feeding area. Whether you're feeding them or not, all guests can see the giraffes face-to-face from this platform. On the other side of the giraffes' rock wall is the elephant watering hole, where the elephant herd comes to drink. In the distance, visitors may see a large bull elephant in a separate enclosure. Nearby, thatch-roofed huts provide shade for white rhinos. Visitors next enter *Ituri Forest*, a replica of a central African jungle. A large lake separates *Lemur Island* from a flock of African flamingos. The sheltered path curves to a netted aviary with rarely seen shoebill storks. Nearby, cheetahs are visible from a deck. Further along, a branch of the elevated boardwalk trail extends into the okapi exhibit, while wading pygmy hippos and tuft-eared red river hogs are visible in the opposite direction. The **Safari Ride**, which boards in the Africa Plaza, is a fifteen-minute behind-the-scenes look at this area, with an especially close view of the elephants.

Newly renovated in 2007, **Asian Gardens** is themed with the exotic architecture of Southeast Asia. A wooden hut gives Malayan tapirs and tall sarus cranes a shady place to rest. Aptly named bearded pigs rustle among pine needles next to their natural predators, clouded leopards. Two other rare wild hogs, babirusa and Visayan warty pigs, can be seen nearby. The path then climbs to an overlook of Asian one-horned rhinos. Just around the corner, a Balinese-style balcony overlooks the *Sulawesi Aviary*, home to tufted deer and a dozen colorful bird species from the Indonesian island of Sulawesi. Past a small exhibit of anoa cattle, the path leads to a viewing cave for the sloth bear and tiger habitats. The zoo rotates different felines through the tiger exhibit – you may see a family of white Bengal tigers, or a solitary Sumatran tiger. The tour ends with a close encounter with Komodo dragons.

Undoubtedly, Lowry Park is most famous for its manatee conservation efforts. The **Manatee & Aquatic Center** is the best place in the country to see these endangered and beloved sea cows. First, there's a glimpse at the *Manatee Rehabilitation Center*, the world's only licensed nonprofit manatee hospital. The zoo has treated over 190 manatees since 1991. After a multi-step process, rehabilitated manatees are released back into Florida's warm waters. Three outdoor pools hold rescued manatees that are too sick or injured to survive in the wild. A ramp leads to the *Manatee Encounter Amphitheater*, where manatees munch on floating lettuce. River otters frolic in a pool along the way inside to underwater views of the manatees. Soothing music creates a relaxing environment to watch the slow-moving sea cows swim with turtles and hundreds of fish. Snapping turtles, moray eels, and several venomous snakes are just a few residents of a long row of aquariums and terrariums in the manatee exhibit building. Outside, the *Key West Deck* gives one last look at the manatee pools, as well as a view of a flock of brown pelicans.

A long elevated boardwalk takes visitors through the **Native Florida Wildlife Center,** where it seems that every animal ever to inhabit the Sunshine State is exhibited. First up is a pair of bald eagles in an uncovered enclosure: both raptors are unable to fly due to irreparable injuries. White-tailed deer and sandhill cranes follow, in an open exhibit across from American bison and wild turkeys. Continuing downhill, visitors get a look at red wolves, black bears, gray foxes, and a large group of skunks. Caribbean flamingos have a lagoon next to aviaries of more pink, long-legged waterbirds (roseate spoonbills, this time), as well as burrowing owls and American kestrels (falcons the size of robins). American alligators and a Florida panther, two iconic Florida species, are both exhibited here – the alligators in a shady pond, the panther among dense undergrowth. Finally, American crocodiles, North America's only crocodile, and slight Key deer, found only in the Florida Keys, are exhibited, the latter displayed with critically endangered whooping cranes.

Nearly every habitat in **Primate World** features a refreshing waterfall. Bornean orangutans and spot-nosed guenon monkeys are just a few of the endangered species here. African species include Wolf's guenons, chimpanzees and baboon-like mandrills. On island habitats, the colobus monkeys and siamangs enjoy tall climbing structures. Smaller exhibits display tiny tamarin and marmoset monkeys from South America.

OTHER EXHIBITS

Just outside the tunnel to Safari Africa lies **Penguin Beach** and its resident flock of black-footed penguins. Designed to replicate Boulders Beach in Cape Town, South Africa, which 3,000 penguins share with human beachgoers, the exhibit comes complete with a lifeguard chair and a colorful cabana on the white sand.

The huge walk-through **Free Flight Aviary** houses several hundred birds. The most memorable residents are a toco toucan and several noisy red-legged seriemas. Non-avian inhabitants here include sloths and a small colony of fruit bats. Side enclosures display hornbills (attractive birds with long curved bills) and colorful macaw parrots.

FOR THE KIDS

Stingray Bay is a fantastic opportunity to touch and feed stingrays. Over forty Atlantic, cownose, and southern stingrays swim in a 16,000-gallon oval pool. Use two fingers to touch the backs of these fascinating benthic, or bottom-dwelling, creatures as they swim by. The more adventurous can buy a raw shrimp platter. To feed the rays, place your hand on the bottom of the pool, lodging the shrimp tail between your second and third fingers. A stingray will swim over your hand and suck the shrimp up into its mouth. A truly incredible experience – don't miss it!

Wallaroo Station is an Australia-themed children's area. Spread across its 4½ acres are activities galore for little guys and gals. In addition to the 'roos in *Kangaroo Walkabout*, there are also emus, flying fox bats, New Guinea singing dogs, and laughing kookaburras. Kids can splash around in the *Billabong* pond, but the real entertainment here is the rides. Most entertaining are *Muster,* a jeep ride around a flock of sheep, and *Tasmanian Tower,* a twenty-five-foot rock-climbing wall. On *Flyin' Bananas*, an airborne vehicle can be steered up and down during flight. You'll also find an *Outback Pony Trek* here, as well as a traditional contact yard with goats to pet.

Next to the Komodo dragons, at **Lorikeet Landing**, kids can feed parrots. Get another perspective on the zoo by riding the **Treetop Skyfari**, an eighteen-minute round-trip journey that begins in the Africa Plaza. The ride goes directly over the Free Flight Aviary, Wallaroo Station, and most of Asian Gardens' animals. Check out the **Jungle Carousel** in a central plaza, near the entrance to Safari Africa. Near the white rhinos, you can ride dromedary (single-humped) camels. At the entrance plaza, the **Manatee Fountain** is surrounded by jets of water shooting up from the ground. This open area is a great place for kids to cool off in the summer, while parents relax on the benches surrounding the manatee statue.

IN PROGRESS

As we go to press, Spring 2008 is scheduled to bring a new water flume ride, where visitors will board a rustic boat afloat in a stream, to be carried up a wood-mill trough, over the treetops and thirty feet above the ground. After a series of switchbacks along the top of the track, the boat will rapidly plunge to a splashy finale into an albino alligator exhibit. There are also plans for more animal exhibits in Safari Africa.

Zoo Atlanta

800 Cherokee Avenue SE
Atlanta, Georgia 30315
(404) 624-5678
www.zooatlanta.org

Hours: 9:30 a.m.-4:30 p.m. daily, to 5:30 p.m. weekends during Daylight Saving Time. Grounds stay open one hour after closing time, year round. Closed Thanksgiving and Christmas Day.

Silverback gorillas dwell in the African Rain Forest

Admission & Fees: Adults $17.99, seniors 55+ $13.99, children 3-11 $12.99. Rides and Rock Climber $2 each; combined carousel/train ticket $3; unlimited ride wristband $6.50 (members $5.50).

Directions: Located in Grant Park. From downtown, take I-20 east to Exit 59A (Zoo Atlanta/Cyclorama). Turn right onto Boulevard and follow for half a mile. Parking lot is on the left. By MARTA public transportation, take bus route 97, also known as the A-Z route because it serves both the aquarium and the zoo.

Don't Miss: Pandas, African Rain Forest, African Plains, Orangutans of Ketambe, Asian Forest.

For Kids: KIDZone (Children's Zoo, Outback Station), Wild Like Me.

Authors' Tips: College students with valid ID get a break on admission. We highly recommend picking up a zoo/aquarium combo ticket, as the Georgia Aquarium is excellent.

Edutainment: "It's a Jungle Out There" familiarizes guests with local animals. "Rainforest Researcher Show" challenges the animal IQ of guests, and "Monkey or Ape" is a guided walking tour of the zoo's excellent primate habitats. Other activities include elephant training demonstrations and gorilla and orangutan feedings. A schedule is included with your zoo map.

DATING BACK TO THE CIVIL WAR, ATLANTA HAS A HISTORY OF rising from the ashes, and its zoo has a similar story. First opened in 1889, the former Municipal Zoo is the South's oldest zoo. Unfortunately, in 1984 the Humane Society of the United States named it "one of the nation's ten worst zoos." In response, the city hired new management (including Terry L. Maple, PhD, later president of the Association of Zoos & Aquariums), and began a multi-million dollar face lift of the grounds. The ultimate goal was to move the animals out of bar-and-concrete cages and into natural habitats. Willie B., the famous gorilla, became a symbol of this zoo's rebirth. He is now gone (though commemorated with a life-size bronze sculpture), but he left behind one of America's best gorilla habitats. Zoo Atlanta solidified its world-class status when it joined a very short list of zoos in the nation to display giant pandas.

Although the animal collection here isn't incredibly large, the quality of the exhibits is outstanding. Each outdoor habitat is beautifully landscaped and designed to closely mimic wild habitats.

FEATURED EXHIBITS

It took ten years to break through diplomatic red tape, but in 1999, Zoo Atlanta opened the **Giant Pandas** exhibit, welcoming Lun Lun and Yang Yang from China.

This pair's arrival improved the zoo's attendance, but not as much as the attendance boost following the birth of cub Mei Lan in 2006. Pandas are notoriously difficult to breed, so her birth was incredibly rare among American zoos, and a great accomplishment. The pandas roam in either of two outdoor canyons, with resting platforms right in front of the public. If they're not outside when you visit, they may be in their climate-controlled  building, visible through glass windows. A covered visitor waiting space, the *Panda Veranda*, is beautifully decorated with authentic Chinese motifs, making this a truly exotic experience. Panda videos are shown to the patient panda fans in this veranda building.

The **African Rain Forest** was among the first projects of the zoo's resurrection, and was built specifically for the late Willie B. After spending 27 lonely years in a small concrete cage, this majestic silverback gorilla finally felt grass beneath his feet and met another gorilla. Spread across the exhibit's 1½ acres are four unique habitats separated by hidden moats. Each habitat is designed to resemble a clearing in the Cameroon rain forest, and different angles along the visitor path reveal several different perspectives. Bamboo plants enhance the tropical atmosphere. The more than twenty gorillas can be observed from many excellent vantage points as they forage for food and care for their babies. The *Takemenda Research Camp* has an overlook platform for gorilla-watching, and the *Willie B. Gorilla Conservation Center* has both a seating area behind a wide window for close-up views and a continuous video presentation on gorillas.

The **Monkeys of Makokou** is another lush habitat, this time for black-faced drills (once considered baboons), mona monkeys, Wolf's guenons, and two types of lemurs. Atlanta's drills are currently the only breeding group of this species in the nation. You can watch the monkeys from both an outdoor platform and a window in the interpretive building for *The Living Treehouse*, a walk-through aviary with fifteen species of colorful African birds, including pheasant-like turacos and red-billed hornbills, that also houses some of the smaller primate species.

Drills

Another African locale is re-created in *Masai Mara*, part of the **African Plains** exhibit complex. Named for a savanna game reserve in Kenya, this five-acre mixed-species grassland is, among other things, home to a pair of black rhinos. Only a small moat separates the rhinos from giraffes, zebras, waterbucks, bongo antelope, and a variety of large African birds. *Mzima Springs*, also part of the African Plains, features "red" elephants. The African elephants dwell in a large yard with a pool of mud where they like to wallow, and so they're usually covered with Georgia's bright red clay! Learn more in *Nyumba Ya Tembo* (House of Elephants), an interpretive building with informative graphics where scheduled elephant training shows take place. Elsewhere in Mzima Springs, lions often bask on kopje rock outcrops, and are best seen behind glass from a covered viewing station. The *Kalahari Connections* exhibit, new in 2007, displays the stars of the Disney movie *The Lion King*: warthogs and meerkats.

Not far from the gorillas are **The Orangutans of Ketambe**, the largest group of these great red apes in the country. Both Bornean and Sumatran orangutans live here, in a replica of an Indonesian rain forest. Visitors can attempt to distinguish between them as the apes swing amongst ropes and trees. (Bornean orangs have dark red fur, compared to the lighter orange hair of the Sumatran orangs.) In one of the three outdoor yards, a central tree presents an opportunity for visitors to watch a most intriguing enrichment exercise. During demonstrations, orangs climb up the *Orangutan Learning Tree* to reach a video game for some brain-stretching fun that promotes psychological well-being. A companion video screen in the visitor area shows how the ape is doing in the game!

The *Harimau Hutan Tiger Forest* is another habitat featuring Indonesian animals. The Tiger Forest is a part of the large **Asian Forest** complex, which also includes the aforementioned giant panda and orangutan exhibits. At Tiger Forest, the visitor area offers seating and a wide window to observe rare Sumatran tigers as they range through their lush, grassy, hillside yard. Amongst bamboo groves, rocky crevices, and waterfalls, the dark orange tigers can be difficult to spot. Elsewhere in the Asian Forest, in neighboring forest and marsh habitats, a clouded leopard, Komodo dragon, small-clawed otters, and a red panda can all be seen.

OTHER EXHIBITS

The exhibits in the **World of Reptiles** building are rather ordinary, but the extensive collection of reptiles and amphibians is anything but. An assortment of rattlesnakes, cobras, vipers, and mambas are part of one of the most extensive collections of venomous snakes we've ever seen. Lesser known deadly serpents include bushmasters, death adders, urutus, and Australian taipans. Thin-snouted gharials have a large pool at one end of the building. Guatemalan beaded lizards, the world's most endangered reptile, are also showcased here.

In **Flamingo Plaza**, at the front of the zoo, a flock of Chilean flamingos wades in a pretty pool in front of a lush, green background of marsh plants. The nearby visitor services building is modeled after an African hut and features a thirty-foot-high thatched roof.

FOR THE KIDS

Cassowary

KIDZone (Kids' Interactive Discovery Zone) is split into two sections. In the *Children's Zoo*, kids can board the *Zoo Express Train*, ride the *Endangered Species Carousel*, or attempt to scale the twenty-four-foot *Rock Climber* wall. Smaller tykes will enjoy the new *Zoo! Playground*, with play apparatus just for their size and age level. Animals in this area include exotic birds and giant tortoises. *Outback Station* is the home of many Australian animals, including imposing cassowaries (one of four species of large flightless birds called ratites), kangaroos, and wallabies. The few non-Aussie animals here include small tamarin monkeys and a wetlands habitat with American alligators.

Wild Like Me is a fun indoor play space where kids are challenged to compare their physical attributes to those of animals, such as an elephant's strength or a giraffe's height.

IN PROGRESS

Having contemplated and rejected plans to move the zoo three miles south to a slightly larger site, the zoo board is now working on revising the current master plan for future development of its grounds.

Louisville Zoo

1100 Trevillian Way
Louisville, Kentucky 40213
(502) 459-2181
www.louisvillezoo.org

Hours: 10:00 a.m.-5:00 p.m., March-Labor Day; 10:00 a.m.-4:00 p.m., rest of year. Must exit by one hour after closing time. Closed Thanksgiving, Christmas Day, and New Year's Day.

A pygmy hippo in the Gorilla Forest's "Hippo Falls."

Admission & Fees: March-October: adults $11.95, seniors 60+ $9.95, children 3-11 $8.50; November-February: adults $10.95, seniors 60+ $8.95, children 3-11 $7.95. Train $2.50 ($1.50 half-way), ZooTram $2, carousel $1.50, flight simulator ride $4.

Directions: From I-264 (Watterson Expressway), take Exit 14 (Poplar Level Road/KY-684). Turn left onto Poplar Level Road, then right onto Trevillian Way. Zoo is on the right.

Don't Miss: Gorilla Forest, Islands, African exhibits, Wallaroo Walkabout, HerpAquarium.

For Kids: Glacier Run Splash Park, MetaZoo, Boma Village, Express ZooTrain, Conservation Carousel, Outpost Playground, Billabong Playabout, Morphis flight simulator ride.

Authors' Tips: For step-saving transportation, ride the ZooTram all day long for a one-time fee. Try to stop by the Islands exhibit at least twice, as the zoo rotates different species through this habitat as the day progresses.

Edutainment: Among the many regularly scheduled animal programs are "Elephant Aerobics," a gorilla program, meerkat enrichment, a pygmy hippo program, and keeper talks held in the HerpAquarium and Islands Pavilion. Check the schedule in your map for show times.

ONE OF THE MOST POPULAR ATTRACTIONS OF KENTUCKY'S largest city, the 133-acre Louisville Zoo is one of America's newest zoos. Its youth is an advantage because, when it opened in 1969, a new exhibit philosophy was afoot in the zoo world. Because of this, most of the zoo's animals enjoy open, barless enclosures. Designated as the official state zoo in 1980, it has built on its solid foundation and grown by leaps and bounds. Within this modern zoo, the higher elevations offer sweeping views of the exhibits at the foot of its long grassy slopes.

FEATURED EXHIBITS

Many zoos in surrounding states have great gorilla exhibits, so when **Gorilla Forest** opened in 2002, it had a lot to live up to. With two large outdoor yards and a building that immerses visitors in the apes' environment, it succeeds admirably. Along a winding path, microscope-shaped clues reveal secrets about the gorillas' African rain forest. *Mbeli Bai* is a hillside retreat filled with plants for gorillas to hide behind or snack on, according to their preference. ("Bai" is the pygmy word for "forest clearing.") The circular *Gorilla Sanctuary* has three separate living spaces, with floor-to-ceiling glass windows giving the impression that you're surrounded by gorillas.

Overhead paths connect the living spaces, allowing apes to cross over their visitors as they move from one space to another. Back outside, the *Arundo Bai* habitat is visible from an interactive *Researcher's Station*, where visitors can participate in behavioral observations. Also part of this exhibit, *Hippo Falls* is a terraced habitat for pygmy hippos. Its stream splits into four mini-waterfalls and eventually creates a deep pool for the hippos, with a glass window providing underwater viewing for visitors.

The Islands complex is a groundbreaking exhibit that rotates five Asian species – tapirs, babirusa pigs, tigers, siamang gibbons, and orangutans – through three outdoor yards and an indoor day room. Alternating habitats gives the animals behavioral enrichment because they encounter a different environment with different scents each day. The adjoining *Islands Pavilion* building showcases more animals confined to the world's islands. Bleeding heart doves and Bali mynahs dwell along the *Forest Bird Trail,* across from Rodrigues fruit bats. Cuban crocodiles, among the world's most endangered reptiles, swim next to the habitat for equally rare Komodo dragons. During the summer, these dragons have an outdoor exhibit by the HerpAquarium, described below. Rockhopper penguins and Inca terns reside in a chilled Pavilion habitat. Back outside, in the main courtyard, Japanese red-crowned cranes and Aldabra tortoises each have their own habitat.

Many exhibits for **African animals** are spread across a high plateau. White rhinos and warthogs each enjoy mud wallows. From a nearby cliff, lions can watch Masai giraffes, dromedary camels, and mountain zebras in neighboring paddocks. Rock hyraxes, which look like large guinea pigs but are most closely related to elephants, Stellar's sea eagles, and a large collection of arachnids, including tarantulas, are exhibited in the *Giraffe Building*, of all places. The elephant exhibit is the home of the zoo's biggest star, Scotty. His 2007 birth was the zoo's first success with breeding elephants. Chestnut-colored bongo antelope are displayed together with crowned cranes and storks, while ostriches, highly endangered Mhorr gazelles, and addax (spiral-horned desert antelope) reside in nearby enclosures. Near the African Outpost restaurant, adjacent meerkat and naked mole-rat exhibits are popular with visitors.

In **Wallaroo Walkabout**, visitors are immersed in the habitat of wallabies and their larger relatives, wallaroos, where only a short rope fence separates the Australian marsupials from their human visitors. Aboriginal paintings grace several central rocks in their enclosure. A set of bird displays holds kookaburras, blue-faced honeyeaters, emus, and Cape Barren geese. In *Lorikeet Landing*, tropical parrots have learned to land on people who drop by to feed them. Nectar is available to feed the birds, which are separated into flocks by gender.

Perfect lorikeet

King Louie, a white alligator, is the most popular resident in the **HerpAquarium**, a combination aquarium and reptile house with a glass roof. Asian archerfish on display here are aptly named, as they hunt by spitting streams of water at insect targets hovering above. The reptiles here are displayed according to their native habitats in the *Forest Biome*, *Savanna Biome*, and *Desert Biome*, where the *Nocturnal Desert* displays vampire bats (actually mammals) in a dark old mineshaft. The building's last five exhibits all feature extremely endangered species – including Madagascar boas and Missouri hellbenders (large salamanders).

OTHER EXHIBITS

Cats of the Americas features jaguars and Brazilian ocelots, two endangered spotted felines. Across the boardwalk from the cats, you'll find bald eagles and a pool of flamingos. America's largest exhibit of long-legged maned wolves lies close to snow leopards, pumas, hyacinth macaws, and ibises (curve-billed water birds). Rheas and guanacos (llama-like camel relatives) share a grassy hillside in **South America**.

Between the African and Australian animals, visitors enjoy an elevated vantage point overlooking both polar bears and Amur tigers. In an exhibit spread over two small islands, rarely seen wooly monkeys have plenty of ropes to climb on. Three types of lemurs occupy a mountain habitat near the zoo's entrance.

FOR THE KIDS

Glacier Run Splash Park is a great place to cool off on hot summer days. All around a climb-on fishing boat, dozens of waterspouts are mounted on the ground and in statues of various arctic animals. Some spouts can be activated by switches, something the kids take to enthusiastically. Every few minutes, the boat's mast explodes with water, drenching everyone below. Kids can also enjoy more traditional playgrounds, **Outpost Playground** and **Billabong Playabout**.

Both an education center and a classroom, **MetaZoo** displays many small critters, including local pond residents, such as bluegills, turtles, and leopard frogs. A mammoth skull also draws a lot of attention. **Boma Village** is an African-themed petting zoo where visitors can interact with goats and donkeys.

The **Express ZooTrain** circles the entire zoo, passing through five different underground tunnels along the way. Riders can get on or off at the halfway point, near Wallaroo Walkabout. The **Conservation Carousel** is fun for small children, while the **Morphis** flight simulator ride entertains older kids.

IN PROGRESS

An Australian addition was just the first part of a number of changes planned for the lower valley of the zoo. The **Amur tigers** will get an expanded habitat, before the zoo opens its next major project, **Glacier Run**. Set in a northern mining community where a glacier has run aground, this state-of-the art immersion exhibit will feature polar bears, sea otters, seals, sea lions, and Stellar's sea eagles. Part of this complex, *Glacier Run Sanctuary*, will eventually be home to arctic foxes, reindeer, and other northern animals. As we go to press, Glacier Run is scheduled for completion by 2010.

North Carolina Zoo

4403 Zoo Parkway
Asheboro, North Carolina 27205
(336) 879-7250
www.nczoo.org

Hours: 9:00 a.m.-5:00 p.m. daily, April-October; 9:00 a.m.-4:00 p.m. daily, rest of year. Closed Christmas Day and during severe weather conditions.

Admission & Fees: Adults $10, seniors 62+ and college students with valid ID $8, children 2-12 $6. SimEx Reactor 4-D simulator ride $3, carousel $2. Participates in reciprocity program.

Patas monkey surveys visitors from Patas Monkey Island.

Directions: From I-85 southbound, take Exit 122 (I-73/U.S. Hwy 220) South. Follow Highway 220 for 23 miles to Asheboro. From I-85 northbound, take Exit 96 (U.S. Hwy 64) East. Follow Highway 64 for 23 miles to Asheboro. In Asheboro, follow signs to N.C. Highway 159 (Zoo Parkway), turn right, and go south 4.4 miles to the zoo entrance.

Don't Miss: Rocky Coast, African Plains, Forest Aviary, Sonora Desert, Kitera Forest Chimpanzee Reserve, Cypress Swamp, Forest Glade, Forest Edge.

For Kids: KidZone, Garden Friends Playground, Carousel, SimEx Reactor 4-D simulator ride.

Authors' Tips: A complete circuit of the African region is a two-mile walk, while the North American region is three miles. A free tram provides transportation around the entire zoo, picking up and dropping off at four convenient stops. The animals are not visible from the tram – it's strictly for transport. The zoo has two separate entrances (in Africa and North America), each with its own parking lot. A free shuttle connects the two parking lots, so visitors can walk through the entire zoo, then quickly bus back to their car. If you have a choice, use the African region lot: it's better shaded. Picnic areas are available at each entrance, as are lockers to store your lunch while touring the zoo. Binoculars are useful for viewing distant animals.

Edutainment: Live animal encounters are common in KidZone. Special programs or concerts are sometimes scheduled in the large outdoor amphitheater, by the Africa entrance.

WITH 500 OF ITS NEARLY 1,500 TOTAL ACRES DEVELOPED, THE North Carolina Zoo is the nation's largest walk-through zoo. As the first state-supported zoo in the United States, it was placed in a central location in rural Randolph County, accessible to the state's three largest metropolitan areas. Thanks to its immense size, most of the zoo's animals enjoy large natural habitats.

This zoo is famous for its attention to detail in creating exhibits that closely mimic the wild habitats where the animals are found in the wild. A paved footpath leads visitors through a mature Piedmont forest. Off the main path, side trails lead to the exhibits, most of which are not visible from the main path or within view of each other, making each animal habitat an exciting adventure.

FEATURED EXHIBITS

The **Forest Edge**, near the Africa entrance, is the first exhibit many visitors see. This hillside habitat features giraffes, zebras, and ostriches that wander in and out of view of four different overlooks. The tall grass, boulders, and termite mounds in this exhibit give a realistic feel to the display.

Resembling an open forest clearing, the **Forest Glade** habitat provides its family of gorillas with volcanic boulders to play around, a stream to drink from, and many edible plants to dine on. The gorillas often come quite close to the sheltered viewing windows.

An authentic-looking road gate guards the **Kitera Forest Chimpanzee Reserve**, where one of the nation's largest troops of chimpanzees dwells. These apes are visible, through wide viewing windows, from the *Ranger Station* and the *Education Center*, both filled with artifacts and educational displays. Within the sprawling enclosure, termite mounds, fallen trees, and vines are scattered throughout the tall grass. When the chimps desire privacy, they can disappear over a hill, away from view.

An overlook gives an introductory view of the expansive thirty-seven-acre **African Plains,** the zoo's most impressive exhibit. On its own, it is as large as many entire zoos. The panoramic view extends to the horizon, and its grassy slopes and watering holes could easily be mistaken for the real African veldt. Seven kinds of antelope can be identified (use the coin-operated binoculars for a closer view), including gemsbok and rare fringe-eared oryx. Two species of land birds, ostriches and gorgeous saddle-billed storks, can also be seen in the distance. The lumbering white rhinos, this habitat's newest residents, are the easiest animals to spot in this vast savanna.

Both bird-watchers and casual observers often react with similar amazement at the beauty inside the **Forest Aviary,** a giant domed greenhouse. Colorful mounted placards are available to help visitors identify the more than thirty bird species that fly and hide among the palm, banana, fig, and screw pine trees. Visitors can walk along the winding pathway through this dense indoor rain forest, or just relax on a bench and spot the colorful birds. Some gems to look for include scarlet ibises, violet-backed starlings, turquoise tanagers, and fairy bluebirds. A stand of Chilean flamingoes wades in a pond outside the Aviary's entrance.

The North American region's top feature is the **Rocky Coast**, an arctic world re-created using jagged rocks, waterfalls, streams, and deep pools with wide underground observation windows for harbor seals and sea lions, in one direction, and playful polar bears in the other. Between these two popular habitats is the *Alaskan Seabirds* exhibit, where parakeet auklets, thick-billed murres, and horned puffins dive from a twenty-eight-foot cliff into their icy glass-fronted pool. Mesh enclosures display peregrine falcons and arctic foxes at opposite ends of this exhibit area.

The path to the glass-domed **Sonora Desert** exhibit is lined with cacti, yucca, and other attractive desert plants. Inside, the arid landscapes of the American Southwest are accurately replicated under an eighty-five-foot-diameter dome. Many desert reptiles and birds, including hummingbirds, move freely among the sand and cacti. An enclosed exhibit features roadrunners and other birds, while spotted ocelot cats draw a lot of attention behind a wide glass wall. Tucked into the artificial rock surface are many glass-fronted exhibits of small desert dwellers, such as rattlesnakes, scorpions, and Gila monsters. Features of the dimly lit nocturnal gallery include cacomistles (ringtail cats) and vampire bats.

Near the North American entrance, the **Cypress Swamp** features a long, meandering boardwalk through a convincingly Florida-like swampland. At least six types of ducks swim among bald cypress trees and cattails on either side of the walkway. Eventually, visitors will spot alligators, either floating in the water or sunning on shore. A shaded kiosk houses various pond turtles, salamanders, snakes, and gigantic alligator snapping turtles, all behind glass. Cougars can be seen from another kiosk, one that looks out on a naturalistic habitat studded with fallen trees, streams, and large boulders. On the way out of the swamp, visitors can stop to study the insect-eating Venus fly traps and pitcher plants of the *Carnivorous Plant Garden.*

OTHER EXHIBITS

Back in Africa, at the **Lion Habitat,** a pride of lions can be seen through a lion-level viewing window, or from a high vantage point overlooking their rocky grotto. Up the main footpath, the porcine residents of the **Red River Hog Habitat** seem to enjoy scurrying back and forth through their forested exhibit. On **Patas Monkey Island**, a dominant male monkey guards his harem of females, just as he would in the African savanna.

The excellence of the zoo is exemplified in the often overlooked **Streamside** complex. Within its two buildings and accompanying outdoor enclosures live many animals native to North Carolina. Fishermen especially seem to enjoy checking out the brook trout, longnose gars, bluegills, and other native fish, displayed in a curved-glass aquarium that allows these game fish to swim overhead. Other animals behind glass here include a variety of frogs, turtles, and snakes, particularly native venomous snakes. Playful river otters are visible both underwater and above, while nearby sleepy bobcats are often spotted napping up on their rocky ledge.

Near the zoo's highest elevation, the **Prairie** simulates the Western plains, with both elk and American bison roaming its eleven acres of real prairie grass. Concrete bleachers give visitors a chance to relax with a panoramic view. In separate wooded habitats, the **Black Bears**, **Grizzly Bears**, and **Red Wolves** exhibits display their namesakes in attractive enclosures, each with its own waterfall and deep pool for these large and wilderness-loving species. The **Marsh** offers a short stroll through a real native marshland, with evidence of local wildlife, including beavers.

As we go to press, the once-excellent **African Pavilion** is being phased out and should be empty by the end of 2008. While a number of its many small animal residents will be moved to other zoos, its colobus and DeBrazza's monkeys will probably join the Patas monkeys on their attractive island exhibit. Outside the Pavilion, the **Hamadryas baboon exhibit** is likely to remain. A large troop of baboons is thriving in this island habitat. In fact, it has become one of the largest baboon exhibits anywhere, as they have produced many adorable baby baboons.

FOR THE KIDS

KidZone in North America is an innovative area designed to put children in touch with nature. With opportunities to build, dig, climb, draw, and dress up, a child could spend hours here, learning about animals. A pair of Galapagos tortoises lives here, and keepers often bring out a live animal to pet. The *What in the World Is It?* maze is both educational and fun. Not far away, the colorful **Garden Friends Playground** is an enjoyable place to romp.

In the central Junction Plaza, the **Endangered Species Carousel** attracts small children, while the **SimEx Reactor 4-D Ride**, near the North American entrance, appeals to older children.

IN PROGRESS

Construction is already underway on the **Watani Grasslands Reserve**, an expanded and modernized habitat for the zoo's African elephants. Upon completion (slated at press time for April 2008), this expansion will give the elephants a new, state-of-the-art barn and a full seven acres to roam. To gain this space, the zoo's white rhinoceroses were moved to the forty-acre African Plains, and they too have had their barn expanded. The zoo hopes to eventually keep herds of up to ten elephants and ten rhinos, which should increase the breeding success of these endangered animals. Until the exhibit's completion, the elephants remain on display in the old **Elephant Habitat**.

Riverbanks Zoo and Garden

500 Wildlife Parkway
Columbia, South Carolina 29210
(803) 779-8717
www.riverbanks.org

A small part of the zoo's spectacular Ocean Gallery.

Hours: 9:00 a.m.-5:00 p.m. daily; to 6:00 p.m. on weekends March-September. Closed on Thanksgiving and Christmas Day.

Admission & Fees: Adults $9.75, seniors 62+ $8.25, children 3-12 $7.25. Use "safari bucks" to pay for activities: they sell for $1 each, or 10 Safari bucks for $8. Safari bucks are available at any ticket booth. Endangered species carousel $1 (or one Safari buck), 3-D Adventure $2, pony ride $4, giraffe feeding $1.

Directions: From I-126, take Exit 7 (Graystone Boulevard), then proceed south on Graystone Boulevard. Take an immediate left onto Rivermont Drive. Follow signs to the zoo.

Don't Miss: Ndoki Forest, Koala Knockabout, Birdhouse at Riverbanks, Aquarium/Reptile Complex (ARC), African Plains, Riverbanks Conservation Outpost.

For Kids: Riverbanks Farm, pony rides, Endangered Species Carousel, 3-D Adventure Theater.

Authors' Tips: The botanical garden here is just as impressive as the zoo. Both zoo professionals and the botanical garden community generally consider this to be one of the best in the country. A tram runs regularly between zoo and garden, and the two facilities are also linked by a bridge across the Saluda River. The 70-acre garden includes a rose garden, a bog garden, a day lily garden, and more. There is also more than a mile of palmetto-covered trails to walk.

Edutainment: Riverbanks has featured public penguin feedings since its inception, and this daily tradition continues. Keeper chats are held at the gorilla and sea lion exhibits. The "Amazing Animals" show, which highlights birds, is held on a stage just outside the Birdhouse. One of the most popular shows here is the aquarium dive demonstration in the Aquarium/Reptile Complex's Indo-Pacific coral reef tank.

RIVERBANKS ZOO AND GARDEN IS NOT ONLY SOUTH CAROLINA'S only major zoo, but also the state's biggest tourist attraction. Even though metro Columbia has barely a half million residents, this 170-acre zoo hosts over 850,000 visitors each year, making it – per capita – one of the most-visited zoos in America.

FEATURED EXHIBITS

Named after a Central African river, the **Ndoki Forest** exhibit has become home to the zoo's first great apes. A bachelor troop of muscular gorillas inhabits a thick jungle hillside. From a sheltered viewing station, visitors can look both into the apes' indoor day room, and out at their forest clearing. The clearing is surrounded by dense brush, so getting clear views of the gorillas can be a bit difficult. Despite the challenge, the view from a second open overlook of their habitat is beautiful. The visitor path leads to an African village, where elephants are visible in the distance. In the foreground, however, is an elaborate habitat for meerkats that's designed with their behavioral enrichment in mind. These energetic mongoose relatives (aka suricates) can explore among tall grasses, termite mounds, and lots of deep dirt that's perfect for digging. Beyond the village, you'll get a much better look at the elephants. Red clay rock walls form the backdrop for their half-acre habitat, which is outfitted with a large pool. The elephants often toss dirt onto their backs to protect their skin from the relentless South Carolina sun. Nearby, an eclectic mix of African birds in a tall grass habitat completes the adventure. The ground hornbill birds and vultures often perch atop a safari jeep parked inside their enclosure.

Koala Knockabout makes Riverbanks one of only a handful of zoos with a permanent display of koalas. The zoo's koalas were acquired through South Carolina's sister-state relationship with Queensland, an Australian state working hard to protect koalas. In this exhibit, the popular marsupials are displayed behind glass in a small building, along with Australian reptiles and fish. Outside, red-necked wallabies have a lush habitat. Visitors can also enter a nearby lorikeet aviary, where they can feed several species of these colorful parrots, including dusky lories and emerald lorikeets.

Visitors cross a lagoon full of flamingos to enter the **Birdhouse at Riverbanks**. Inside, three geographically themed habitats showcase a number of fascinating birds. Enormous great hornbills are the stars of the *Asian Trek*. Bali mynahs and birds of paradise are nearly as stunning. In another exhibit, featuring crowned pigeons, fairy bluebirds, peacock pheasants, and bleeding heart doves, periodic simulated rainstorms make this jungle trail experience more realistic. *Savanna Camp* focuses on birds of the arid grasslands. Sunbitterns, toucanets, and mot-mots inhabit the South American section, while pretty bee-eaters represent Africa. *Penguin Coast* is home to three Antarctic penguin species: king, rockhopper, and gentoo. A sixty-five-foot-long window makes above- and below-water viewing of their rocky habitat effortless for visitors. For those small enough to crawl through it, a tunnel leads to a view into the penguins' burrow.

The **Aquarium/Reptile Complex**, usually referred to as the ARC, displays more than 1,200 animals in four galleries. The *South Carolina Gallery* features twenty-four individual terrariums for native fish, reptiles, and amphibians. The *Desert Gallery*, the largest of the four, features a room-sized diorama of sand and cacti, inhabited by various Sonoran Desert lizards, including rare and venomous Gila monsters. Across the hall, sandfish (lizards from Africa) "swim" through the sand. Some of the world's most beautiful – and most deadly – reptiles and amphibians are on display in the *Tropical Gallery*: green mambas, king cobras, and poison dart frogs. This gallery also includes the *Tropical Habitat*, with a walk through a lush glass-domed rain forest that's home to mostly Amazonian species, including giant anaconda snakes, electric eels, and piranhas. Critically endangered false gharial crocodiles from Asia, also called tomistomas, dwell here in a dark stream. The real gem of the ARC, however, is the *Ocean Gallery*. Crystal clear, non-reflective windows allow floor-to-ceiling views of sharks, moray eels, and more than 400 colorful reef fish in the spectacular 55,000-gallon *Pacific Coral Reef* tank. A smaller 6,000-gallon tank re-creates a Caribbean coral reef. Injured loggerhead sea turtles have their own exhibit, where they recuperate and grow until they're healthy enough to be returned to the wild. The exhibit of moon jellies (a species of jellyfish) is also worth checking out.

A long pathway spans the length of the **African Plains**, a two-acre replica of the African savanna. Herds of reticulated giraffes and Grant's zebras, and a couple of ostriches, live in an arid mixed-species exhibit. A raised circular pagoda allows visitors to hand feed the giraffes.

Inside an enclosed tunnel is a row of exhibits called the **Riverbanks Conservation Outpost**. South American primates here include pygmy marmoset monkeys, black howler monkeys, gray titi and white-faced saki monkeys, and golden lion tamarin monkeys. Black-footed cats also live here, as do sloths, Rodrigues fruit bats, agoutis (wild relatives of domestic guinea pigs), and fishing cats. The fishing cats are especially fun to watch when goldfish are released into their flooded forest pool.

OTHER EXHIBITS

Large mammal exhibits are found throughout the zoo. On one side of the zoo's entrance plaza is a grotto for grizzly bears. The other side has four grottoes holding Amur tigers, lions, spotted hyenas, and Hamadryas baboons. The baboon exhibit, renovated in 2007, replicates a real habitat in Kenya's Samburu Park, where baboons have taken over a collapsed bridge. A Nile hippo and warthogs have neighboring yards near the Ndoki Forest exhibit. Opposite the grizzly bears, an attractive sea lion pool allows these graceful mammals to swim under and past rocky ledges. A deep moat encircles two rocky, tree-studded **Siamang Islands**. You'll find another island habitat, this one for ring-tailed lemurs, across from the flamingos. Naked mole-rats can be seen in the **Discovery Center**, while an American alligator drifts in a swamp and Galapagos tortoises live near the hippo.

FOR THE KIDS

The **Riverbanks Farm** gives children the chance to learn about life on a farm. Corrals hold sheep, dairy and beef cattle, and Belgian horses for through-the-fence petting, while the contact ring lets kids (both human and goat) interact up close. A special exhibit, the *Backyard Garden*, shows some of the food products grown in local South Carolina gardens. Pony rides are available just outside the barn. Not far from the farm is an **Endangered Species Carousel**. The **3-D Adventure Theater** offers virtual reality journeys, with shows that change periodically.

IN PROGRESS

Riverbanks Zoo and Garden is currently in the planning stages for several new exhibits that they hope to open within the next five years. No details are available at press time. Check their website for the most current information on these projects.

Knoxville Zoological Gardens

3500 Knoxville Zoo Drive
Knoxville, Tennessee 37914
(865) 637-5331
www.knoxville-zoo.org

Hours: 9:30 a.m.-6:00 p.m. daily in summer; 9:30 a.m.-4:30 p.m. weekdays, 9:30 a.m.-6:00 p.m. weekends in spring and fall; 9:30 a.m.-4:30 p.m. daily in winter. Call or check website for specific dates. Closed on Christmas Day.

Red panda takes it easy in cage-free Red Panda Village.

Admission & Fees: Adults $16.95, seniors 65+ and children 2-12 $12.95. If you enter the zoo after 3:00 p.m., the next day's admission will be free. Carousel $2. Camel ride: adults $4, children under 12 $3. Parking $4. Participates in reciprocity program.

Directions: From I-40 eastbound, take Exit 392 (US-11W South). From I-40 westbound, take Exit 392A (US-11W South). Merge onto US-11W/Rutledge Pike, then quickly turn right onto Timothy Avenue. Follow Timothy Avenue, which becomes Knoxville Zoo Drive, to the zoo.

Don't Miss: Black Bear Falls, African Forest, Reptile Center, Red Panda Village, African Elephant Preserve, river otters, white rhinos, the Bird Show.

For Kids: Kids Cove, camel ride.

Authors' Tips: The Night Club nocturnal exhibit in Kids Cove is REALLY dark – but worth seeing. Let your eyes adjust before moving, or you may walk into something. This is a very hilly zoo: they say it takes 10,000 steps to walk the whole thing. So wear good walking shoes! If you're not too tuckered out, the shady 0.3-mile Nature Trail is a relaxing way to end your tour.

Edutainment: In the 300-seat outdoor amphitheater, the "Bird Show" is a longtime classic. This free-flight show features more than a dozen birds that demonstrate their unique natural behaviors. The star of the show is "Einstein," a female African gray parrot with a vocabulary of over 200 words – she was a guest on *The Tonight Show* with Jay Leno. These popular shows are held three times daily (except on Mondays) in summer and on weekends in spring and fall. Short "Zoo Encounters" and keeper chats are held around the zoo daily during the summer. Check the schedule posted at the Crossroads for show times and locations.

LOCATED NOT FAR FROM THE APPALACHIAN MOUNTAINS IN Eastern Tennessee, the Knoxville Zoo takes full advantage of its natural terrain. Many exhibits are built along steep hillsides or surrounded by thick forests. From the grounds, visitors enjoy panoramic views of the mountains in the distance. Located less than a mile off of I-40, this pretty zoo makes a great stop on a Smoky Mountains vacation. It's well known for its breeding success with some high profile animals, including white rhinos and red pandas, as well as a number of lesser-known but endangered reptiles.

FEATURED EXHIBITS

The first environment every visitor encounters is **Black Bear Falls**, the zoo's tribute to the famous black bears of nearby Great Smoky Mountains National Park. With its many trees and four misty, crashing twenty-foot waterfalls, the exhibit captures the feel of a spectacular national park. In our humble opinion, this may well be the best single-species exhibit in America! The playful black bears can be seen from three distinct viewing areas, including a high overlook across the entire habitat. In a glassed-in viewing cave next to the bears' pool, bluegrass music sets the mood of the Smokies, while visitors read about the history of the Smoky Mountain bears, and about current conservation efforts. A unique forty-foot log tunnel gives visitors a view from deep inside the bears' habitat.

The wooded **African Forest** is an indoor/outdoor complex of naturalistic habitats for gorillas and chimpanzees. Both of these popular great apes can be seen up close in their indoor homes through large windows, or outdoors in their large yards. At *Chimp Ridge,* a gigantic glass window looks over a large grassy hillside habitat for these intelligent apes. Children can learn about the different vocalizations chimps make at the nearby interactive sound wall. *Gorilla Valley* provides resident gorillas with a one-acre outdoor habitat that resembles their native African home. The ape exhibits are connected by a thatched-roofed bridge, from which red river hogs are visible.

With more than four hundred reptiles of nearly ninety species, the zoo is justly proud of its **Reptile Center**. A unique open-air exhibit displays an albino rattlesnake, cobras, vipers, and other reptiles in glass cylinders mounted in rows along the exterior of a stone-covered building. Visitors can look over the plexiglass walls of open enclosures of alligator snapping turtles, alligators, and venomous Gila monsters. Gigantic Aldabra tortoises are one of several species in the open yards of *Tortoise Territory*. Also of interest is the *Southern Appalachian Bog Exhibit*, where protected Tennessee bog turtles live in a large, man-made bog and have produced over 165 offspring since 1988. The nearby *Turtle Marsh* displays other native turtles.

The Boyd Family Red Panda Village, finished in 2007, is a new indoor/outdoor exhibit of one of this zoo's trademark animals. The Knoxville Zoo is famous for its breeding success with these cuddly critters, and is, in fact, number one in the nation for red panda births. This new habitat, with space for up to eight pandas, features a walk-in aviary-style area where pandas can be seen without any barriers, as they lounge on logs above the heads of visitors. Attractive graphics highlight the zoo's success with this species.

At the **Stokely African Elephant Preserve**, the herd's spacious yard, equipped with a mud hole and three pools, is accompanied by a modern indoor barn, which provides a padded, heated floor for the comfort of its inhabitants. America's first African elephant birth took place here in 1978.

Often spotted performing underwater aerobics at the front of their deep pool, **river otters** dwell in a well-shaded naturalistic habitat at the top of a steep hill. Around a bend in the path, visitors encounter **white rhinoceroses,** another of the zoo's premier animals. These rhinos, exhibited in a large open field with many elevated overlooks, often have new rhino calves. Close to thirty have been born here, making Knoxville one of the nation's leaders in conservation efforts for this endangered species.

OTHER EXHIBITS

The spacious, arid **Grasslands Africa!** exhibit offers views from many angles. Here, giraffes and three varieties of African antelope roam in the shade of a thirty-foot-tall artificial baobab tree, while zebras occupy a separate enclosure across the path. Near a permanently parked safari Land Rover (which would make for a great photo op), coin-operated binoculars are available for closer looks of these savanna animals. Next to the zebras, **Meerkat Lookout** is a popular spot with children. The mob of meerkats is visible through two low glass walls. Black-and-orange colored ground hornbill birds enjoy a view of the other African animals from their adjacent habitat.

The broad collection of big cats, found in the thick woods, include beautiful tigers (among them a rare Indo-Chinese tiger and a blue-eyed white Bengal tiger) and a large pride of lions, all distributed among several cat exhibits. Rare snow leopards occupy another forest environment. Bobcats are displayed in a smaller enclosure. But by far the best cat habitat is *Cheetah Savanna,* a naturalistic one-acre setting for athletic cheetahs. Visitors can watch these speedy felines from a high overlook, or close up through ground-level windows into the enclosure. Also predators, although not cats, African wild dogs are exhibited in this same forested area.

At the **Penguin Rock** indoor habitat, African penguins are displayed behind a long row of windows, which are sometimes difficult to see through due to glare from the sun. **La Plaza** is the home of a variety of South American animals, including alpacas, armadillos, sloths, and little marmoset monkeys. The most popular residents of this area, however, are the prairie dogs. Pop-up windows let kids emerge in the middle of their exhibit. In the **Birds of Central America** walk-through aviary, you'll find many colorful birds, including roseate spoonbills. Bald eagles and red wolves live in large mesh enclosures set into the woods. Both of these animals have required major intervention to escape extinction, and both species are being reintroduced into the wild in the nearby Great Smoky Mountains. Scattered around the zoo are gibbons, blue monkeys, and a variety of birds, including sandhill cranes and Andean condors.

FOR THE KIDS

Kids' Cove is one of the nation's best children's zoos. Modeled on an early 1900s-era Appalachian farm, this rustic setting is literally filled with exciting adventures for kids. Activities and attractions include a 500-square-foot sandbox, a climbing wall, a swinging bridge, a rope spider web to climb, a fiberglass milking cow, log and waterfall slides, giant eggs and nests to crawl into, and a water play area with frog statues that squirt water. *Clayton's Play Cabin* houses a giant climbing structure with a high spiral slide. On the *Fuzzy-Go-Round* carousel, children can choose an exotic animal to ride. In a walk-through aviary, songbirds from Tennessee fly overhead, and a beaver pond lies below. You can watch the enchanting beavers both underwater and inside their dark den. The *Night Club* is a fun, but very dark, nocturnal exhibit of skunks, bats, and raccoons. In the upper loft of the *Barn*, there are small exhibits of rats, mice, snakes, spiders and barn owls. Other animals at Kids' Cove include rabbits, chickens, Guinea hogs, and, in the *Barnyard* contact yard, goats, sheep, and a llama, all available for petting.

During warmer months, camel rides are offered near the Grasslands Africa! area.

IN PROGRESS

The most immediate improvements are reconstructions of the lion, tiger, and African wild dog exhibits. Already underway, these updated exhibits will include a new holding area and improved visitor viewing, all scheduled (at press time) for completion in 2009-2010. These animals will remain on display during construction.

The two-story **Amphibian and Reptile Conservation Center**, scheduled to open in 2011 as we go to press, promises to be one of the best and most innovative displays of reptiles anywhere. The second floor will feature a gallery of natural habitat exhibits, while the first floor will give visitors a chance to see off-exhibit reptiles receiving special care: pregnant mothers, newborns, and those receiving medical treatment. The Center should allow the zoo to expand its already-excellent reptile collection by an additional fifty species.

Memphis Zoo

2000 Prentiss Place
Memphis, Tennessee 38112
(901) 276-9453
www.memphiszoo.org

Colorful koi swim in CHINA's central pond.

Hours: 9:00 a.m.-6:00 p.m. daily, March-October; 9:00 a.m.-5:00 p.m. daily, November-February. Last admission one hour before closing. Closed Thanksgiving, Christmas Eve, and Christmas Day.

Admission & Fees: Adults $13, seniors 60+ $12, children 2-11 $8. Butterfly garden $1, zoo tram $1 for all-day pass, Farm Train and children's rides $1, carousel $2. Note: Rides are closed November-February. Parking $3. Participates in reciprocity program.

Directions: Centrally located in Overton Park. From I-40 eastbound, take Exit 1F (TN-14). Turn right onto North Bellevue Boulevard, then left onto North Parkway. Follow for 1.3 miles, then turn right onto North McLean Boulevard. Turn left onto Galloway Avenue, and follow into the zoo parking lot. From I-40 westbound, as you enter Memphis, I-40 becomes Sam Cooper Boulevard. Turn right on East Parkway North, then a quick left onto North Parkway. Follow for 0.9 miles, then turn left onto North McLean Boulevard. Turn left onto Galloway Avenue, and follow into the zoo parking lot.

Don't Miss: CHINA, Northwest Passage, Cat Country, Primate Canyon, Animals of the Night, Tropical Bird House, Dragon's Lair.

For Kids: Once Upon A Farm, children's rides, Endangered Species Carousel, Cat House Café playground.

Authors' Tips: The zoo tram takes a circular route around the zoo, allowing visitors to get on and off at six stops. The Cat House Café is an attractive place for lunch, and has a good view of the gibbons outside.

Edutainment: Sea lion shows in the Northwest Passage's impressive Sea Lion Amphitheater are held three times daily throughout the summer, and are very nearly theme park quality entertainment. Other enjoyable shows include "Wild Wonders," "Living with Venomous Snakes," and feedings of polar bears, penguins, Komodo dragons, and other animals. Keeper chats are held throughout the zoo. Check the schedule on your zoo map.

MEMPHIS IS NAMED AFTER THE ANCIENT CITY IN EGYPT. THE ZOO commemorates this connection with its dazzling Egyptian entrance complex, where visitors pass through the Avenue of Animals, featuring white animal sculptures on both sides of the path. They then enter the zoo through a massive Egyptian gate decorated with ancient hieroglyphics. Inside this gate, an orientation courtyard features a forty-foot obelisk with a reflecting pool, a mock Nile River with seven small cataract waterfalls, palm and banana trees, and a pyramid-shaped fountain.

But Egypt isn't the only destination here: the Memphis Zoo offers a round-the-world tour. Other exotic stops include China, North America's Pacific Northwest, and Indonesia.

FEATURED EXHIBITS

The highlight of **CHINA**, one of the best total immersion exhibits we've ever seen, is its pair of giant pandas, Ya Ya and Le Le, who arrived in early 2003. At the entrance, a fifty-foot Chinese pagoda immediately confirms that this is a very special place. In the beautiful courtyard, a pair of white marble Beijing lions, imported from China, regally stands guard over the entire area. Everything is trimmed with bright red, the traditional color of China. After the loud chiming of a bronze gong, a set of doors opens and guests are welcomed into a heavily ornamented theater, where they watch a movie about giant pandas – a film made especially for this exhibit. After this, visitors emerge into a formal garden, planted with native Chinese foliage. Mandarin ducks and other Oriental waterfowl swim in a central pond, populated with koi goldfish. Across the pond is a habitat for small-clawed otters and white-cheeked gibbons, both native to China (as are all the animals in this exhibit). In another direction across the pond lies the first of two outdoor natural habitats for the giant pandas. When it is too hot for them outside, they can be seen through glass walls from a massive open air pavilion. The visitor area is lit by Chinese lanterns, while the pandas are comfortable inside in a habitat enhanced by trees, rock work, and bamboo. Beyond the pavilion, François' langur monkeys live behind another glass window, while a large open yard displays white-naped cranes, and rare Pere David's deer – an animal surviving only in zoos. Three pheasantries are scattered about, displaying beautiful birds from the Orient. Near the exhibit's exit, visitors can look through a window into the *Research Station*, where the zoo compiles data on and video of the pandas. A special gift shop sells Chinese- and panda-themed souvenirs.

The zoo marked its hundredth anniversary with the 2006 opening of **Northwest Passage**, one of its best exhibits yet. The journey begins among six towering, brightly painted totem poles. Native American artwork and sounds are prevalent throughout this three-acre slice of North America's Pacific Northwest region. A busy covered gallery has spectacular underwater viewing of polar bears and sea lions through a long wall of floor-to-ceiling glass. Children can climb into an inverted bubble window for closer looks at the sea lions. The polar bears are also visible from an overlook of their large tundra habitat. Of course, the best view of the playful sea lions may be in the 500-seat *Sea Lion Amphitheater*, where they educate and perform in daily shows throughout the summer. Black bears and a large mesh flight cage housing bald eagles and ravens round out this impressive exhibit.

Cat Country exhibits ten different felines from three continents, often opposite their natural prey, in settings that closely replicate their natural homes. Visitors enter this area by walking through an ancient Egyptian temple. In the Asian area, spotted leopards and clouded leopards are visible through thin high-tension wire. Across a water moat, a pair of Bengal tigers, including a rare white tiger, prowl by the ruins of an ancient city and a crashing waterfall. Down the trail, snow leopards live within view of their natural prey: muntjac deer and red pandas. Latin American jaguars and pumas are also exhibited near their prey: water-dwelling capybaras, the world's largest rodents. Smaller spotted ocelot cats live nearby. African displays include small exhibits of caracal lynx and fennec foxes, followed by wide-open savanna habitats for cheetahs and lions. Their potential prey – klipspringer antelope and meerkats – inhabit rock outcroppings known as kopjes.

The five-acre **Primate Canyon** is a set of natural habitats for gorillas, orangutans, siamang gibbons, colobus monkeys, Sulawesi macaque monkeys, and two other primate species. Exhibited among natural features, including trickling streams, waterfalls, and rock caves, the cultures of the primates' homelands are represented by an Oriental pagoda and a replica of an African fishing village. Most of these monkeys and apes have towering poles, ropes, and trees to climb and swing on.

One of the nation's best nocturnal exhibits, **Animals of the Night** features over twenty-five fascinating animal species. The zoo ensures that these night-loving creatures will be active during visitor hours by reversing the animals' biological clocks, lighting the building overnight and keeping it dim during the day. The building's center is the glassed-in *Bat Flight* exhibit, with more than 400 bats. Other interesting displays include large aardvarks, armadillos, a cave exhibit of vampire bats, and a cross-sectional look at naked mole-rats' underground tunnel network.

In the **Tropical Bird House**, two long hallways of exotic bird exhibits include fruit doves, tanagers, kingfishers, lorikeets, toucans, and other jewel-colored birds. These colorful exhibits boast hand-painted murals as background walls. Two walk-through aviaries, filled with free-flying birds, resemble lush rain forests.

The **Dragon's Lair** is an Indonesia-themed exhibit for Komodo dragons, the world's largest lizards. Under small palms, the three huge dragons are visible through tall glass windows.

OTHER EXHIBITS

The hub of the **African Veldt** area is a display of bongo antelope, Grant's gazelles, crowned cranes, and ostriches in a sprawling, shaded, grassy yard spotted with watering holes and termite mounds. Across the path, savanna enclosures hold zebras and several elegant varieties of antelope, including bonteboks, Nile lechwes, and scimitar-horned oryxes. A large herd of giraffes occupies another open yard. Also nearby are white rhino and African elephant exhibits. The elephants enjoy a pool deep enough to fully submerge themselves.

Denizens of the Deep South is an above ground and underwater swamp exhibit of an American alligator. Nearby, in the **World of Waterfowl**, you can see flamingos, black-necked swans, and various ducks from two wooden bridges. Open during warm weather, **Butterflies: In Living Color** is a beautiful mesh-covered garden and pond, with nearly a thousand butterflies fluttering in every direction. Of its thirty-four Southern U.S. species, the most prominent may be the stunning zebra longwings.

A large troop of **bonobos** (or pygmy chimpanzees), among the rarest primates), lives in an indoor/outdoor exhibit across from CHINA. Mother and daughter **hippos** are usually submerged in their pools. This zoo is sometimes referred to as the hippo capital of the world, because more hippos have been born here than at any other zoo.

Reptile fans should not miss the **Herpetarium**, where rows of terrariums are embedded in the rock walls. Smaller exhibits, grouped into four geographical regions, include king cobras, Chinese alligators, nine types of pythons, and a wide variety of frogs. Over thirty African black-footed penguins live on **Penguin Rock**, a rocky island habitat they share with cormorants. The octagonal **Round Barn** displays a variety of African animals in wedge-shaped yards. The path encircling the barn passes giraffe-necked gerenuk gazelles, three miniature antelope species, red river hogs, warthogs, and ground hornbill birds. The **Aquarium** has over thirty small tanks with 156 species of both freshwater and saltwater animals, including many fish native to the Amazon river. Other exhibits include a swan pool and a yard for giant Aldabra tortoises.

FOR THE KIDS

The goal of **Once Upon A Farm**, the main children's area, is to take visitors back in time to a nineteenth-century farm. Miniature versions of domestic pigs, cattle, donkeys, rabbits, and goats can be seen and (usually) petted. Many interesting farm structures surround a long duck pond, including a gristmill, water wheel, windmill, silo, and some old-fashioned barns. The chicken coop includes an incubation area with adorable chicks on display. After climbing through a tunnel, kids pop up in a clear acrylic bubble dome inside the prairie dog exhibit. The air-conditioned *Expo Building* has fascinating displays on weaving, canning, gardening, and even blacksmithing. On the *Farm Train* ride, visitors enjoy two laps around the entire farmstead on an old-fashioned miniature railroad.

The **Children's Rides** area offers a carousel and five other carnival-style kiddie rides. Elsewhere, the newer **Endangered Species Carousel** has many rare animals to choose from, including giant pandas and other Chinese species, a tribute to the nearby CHINA exhibit. The **Cat House Café playground** lets children play while parents finish lunch.

IN PROGRESS

The next adventure here will be **Teton Trek**, a three-acre exhibit that will show visitors the wildlife and scenery of the Yellowstone National Park area. The Yellowstone experience will begin in the *Old Faithful Entry Plaza*, complete with a twenty-five-foot geyser that children can play in. To get to the animals, visitors will walk through the two-story *Great Lodge*, modeled after Yellowstone's historic Old Faithful Inn. Outside, grizzly bears will be visible from a bridge near towering Firehole Falls, and by the Firehole River, where the bears can catch live fish. Timber wolves and a herd of elk will dwell nearby. A natural marsh will be home to trumpeter swans and sandhill cranes. This exciting exhibit is scheduled to open in 2009 as we go to press.

If construction proceeds according to schedule, the **Zambezi River Hippo Camp** will open a year later, in 2010. This will be yet another "take you there" adventure. This time, visitors will travel to a fishing village along the banks of Africa's Zambezi River. Nile crocodiles and the zoo's famous hippos will be visible from both underwater and above. In an upland forest habitat, rare okapis will be an exciting addition to the zoo. The path will end with an enclosure of African flamingos wading in a tidal flat.

Nashville Zoo at Grassmere

3777 Nolensville Road
Nashville, Tennessee 37211
(615) 833-1534
www.nashvillezoo.org

Don't miss Nashville's meerkats.

Hours: 9:00 a.m.-6:00 p.m. daily, April-October 15; 9:00 a.m.-4:00 p.m. daily, rest of year.

Admission & Fees: Adults $13, seniors 65+ $11, children 3-12 $8. Lorikeet nectar $1; carousel $2.

Directions: From I-24, take Exit 54 (Briley Parkway/TN-155). Go west on Briley Parkway for 1.1 miles, then turn left onto Nolensville Road. Follow Nolensville Road for 1.5 miles to zoo. From I-440, take Exit 6 (US-31A S/US-41A S). Turn onto Nolensville Road, head south, and follow for 2.3 miles to zoo.

Don't Miss: Bamboo Trail, African Savanna, Unseen New World, Alligator Cove, Meerkat Exhibit, Entry Village.

For Kids: Critter Encounters, Wild Animal Carousel, Lorikeet Landing, Jungle Gym.

Authors' Tips: The Zoofari Café offers an appealing menu, plus a nice seating area. Regularly scheduled tours are available in the historic 1810 Croft Home during summer, less frequently the rest of the year. No tours are given on Tuesdays or Wednesdays.

Edutainment: In a large amphitheater next to the Unseen World, three entertaining twenty-minute animal shows are offered seasonally, including "Practice Makes Perfect," a personal look at animal training; "Wings of the World," a popular bird show with parrots and hawks that fly over the audience; and "It's a Wild Life," an entertaining show with a varying cast of animal characters that often includes wild cats and reptiles. "Meet the Keeper" chats, featuring a wide variety of animals, are held around the zoo, including an elephant presentation and alligator and tiger feedings. Check your zoo map and enclosed flyer for specific times and locations.

ONE OF THE NATION'S NEWEST ZOOS, NASHVILLE OPENED at its present site in 1997. Previously, the grounds had hosted the Grassmere Wildlife Park, a small facility with mostly North American animals. When financial problems forced Grassmere to close in 1995, the grounds were offered to the then-small Nashville Zoo. Due to its youth, almost all of its exhibits are nearly brand new, built using the most modern exhibit technology to make almost every exhibit look like a gorgeous natural habitat. Because of this, the Nashville Zoo is considered by many in the zoo world to be one of the most beautiful zoos in the nation.

FEATURED EXHIBITS

As you enter the zoo along lushly planted pathways, you know this will be a special experience. In the **Entry Village**, the buildings, including the restrooms, are African in style, most with thatched roofs. The gift shop has a tall conical roof. The centerpiece of this area is a pair of *Gibbon Islands*, where the zoo's only apes, white-cheeked gibbons and siamangs, can usually be seen high in the towering trees and ropes of their island habitats. This is often the first exhibit arriving guests see, and most are noticeably impressed by this beautifully landscaped habitat. As visitors enter and exit the zoo, they also pass a pair of bird exhibits that are easy to overlook, but shouldn't be missed! In one, gorgeous bright blue hyacinth macaws rest on an overhanging branch in front of some pretty waterfalls. Many families stop here for a memorable photograph. Not far away, imposing red-crowned cranes live in a similarly lush habitat.

The beautiful **Bamboo Trail** is named for the thick, tall bamboo forest that lines both sides of the path. A picturesque trickling stream flows alongside the trail, occasionally coming into view. The first exhibit is an aviary for rhinoceros hornbill birds, visible in the trees through thin, almost transparent, mesh. Two bamboo forest inhabitants, red pandas and clouded leopards, are the focus of a small pavilion. Inside this attractive small building, Asian music plays softly and Chinese artifacts are displayed on the walls. The striking clouded leopards prowl behind a glass wall. These brown spotted cats are often quite active, chasing each other up and down the tall trees of their habitat. On the other side of the path, adorable red pandas can sometimes be a challenge to find among the thick foliage in their habitat. The music and attractive animals mean that the pavilion's seating area is usually popular, as visitors find this a most relaxing place to sit and admire the gorgeous creatures on display. Up the trail, Schmidt's guenon monkeys, with distinctive white noses, are fun to watch from a wide viewing station behind a see-through mesh barrier. Another attractive primate species, ring-tailed lemurs, are displayed in a similar enclosure nearby. A dangerous cassowary, a tall flightless bird from New Guinea whose kick can disembowel a human, lives in a sunken habitat below the trail. Near the beginning of this bamboo-themed path, cougars live in a large, lush hillside habitat, where only thin harp wire separates them from human visitors.

At the entrance to the **African Savanna** exhibits, a sign welcomes visitors to Tanzania, the east African nation where you'd find this set of habitats. The pathway is lined with tall grass and bamboo, while African music sets the mood. Along the trail, three research camps offer safari-style tents where visitors can sit and relax in the shade as they learn about elephants. The three-acre elephant habitat is, quite frankly, spectacular. Their expansive grassy field is enhanced with giant boulders and a large wading pool. To allow for better views, given its immense size, this habitat has many viewing points, including from *Shamba Market*, an African village with thatch-covered buildings. Masai giraffes are also visible from the village in their adjacent 1½-acre habitat. To accommodate these tall animals, a dozen even taller shade trees are scattered throughout their yard. Red river hogs inhabit a smaller yard near the exit.

On the ground floor of the large central Croft Center building, the **Unseen New World** is primarily a reptile and amphibian exhibit (and one of the nation's best), but it also displays fish, birds, arthropods, and a few small mammals. This exhibit showcases the often-unseen small creatures of the Western Hemisphere. In the initial *West Indies* section, three pretty saltwater aquariums display beautiful reef fish from the Caribbean. A beach scene with a realistic mural background is the home of large rhinoceros iguanas. More lizards from the Caribbean islands are displayed nearby, in smaller terrarium habitats. The *North America* section's most attractive exhibit is a large desert habitat with spiny-tailed iguanas and desert tortoises. A gallery of venomous creatures includes rattlesnakes, a copperhead, Gila monsters, and a pair of venomous arachnids: black widow and brown recluse spiders. Large and unusual salamanders are spotlighted, including foot-long hellbenders and strange-looking axolotls. The initial exhibit of *Central and South America* is a nocturnal cave populated by leaf-nosed bats. Back in the light, among the many reptiles here, the dwarf caiman crocodiles and giant anaconda are the largest on exhibit. A long aquarium focuses on animals from the Amazon River region, including long arowana fish, piranhas, mata mata turtles, and green basilisk lizards. A second gallery of venomous animals displays eyelash viper and bushmaster snakes, poison arrow frogs, and tarantulas. You'll go through a small walk-through jungle aviary before leaving the building.

Alligator Cove begins with a bayou-style shack, where visitors get an overview of a swampy pool, home to more than fifteen juvenile American alligators. On the path encircling the pool, you'll come to a rock wall with a terrific underwater window offering a view of these three-foot 'gators. The sight of so many active alligators swimming and hovering in the water is a real treat!

The **Corrieri Meerkat Exhibit** may be the nation's best display of these crowd-pleasing creatures. The well-populated meerkat colony has a long sloping yard, full of dirt for them to burrow in. They also tend to enjoy the many artificial termite mounds, where they stand upright to scout their territory. The entire habitat is surrounded by clear glass walls, but you'll get the best view by climbing underneath to a pop up in a glass "bubble" in the midst of the meerkats. Just down the trail, attractive saddle-billed storks are visible from a bridge as they wade in their thickly planted pond.

OTHER EXHIBITS

Currently, the zoo's largest exhibit is the **African Field**, an open forest clearing that's home to zebras, ostriches, and eland antelope. A wide fenced viewing area provides a good view of this veldt environment. Just up the trail, you'll encounter a pack of African wild dogs in their hilly yard. As you cross a nearby bridge, a deep valley habitat for Bengal tigers lies to one side. A rippling stream and waterfall make the tigers' hillside exhibit feel both natural and refreshing. Not far away, Eurasian lynx are displayed behind mesh netting in another hillside enclosure. Near the entrance to the Bamboo Trail, in a forested mixed-species habitat, pretty African crowned cranes live together with striking bongo antelope.

The **Grassmere Farm**, in the corner of the zoo, is the site of the *Croft Home*, a farmhouse that has stood here for nearly 200 years. Behind the house, the *Gardens* are kept the way they looked in the 1880s, and a nearby shed holds antique farming tools. The house, of course, was part of a working farm, and a large weathered barn and long fenced animal corrals stand behind it. The corrals hold sheep, cattle, and two breeds of horses.

FOR THE KIDS

Critter Encounters is a spacious open area where goats, sheep, alpacas, and a donkey can all be petted. Side exhibits display pretty toucans, hornbill birds, guinea fowl, and a duck pond.

The **Patton Family Wild Animal Carousel** offers thirty-nine exotic and endangered hand-carved animals for children to ride. Next door, **Lorikeet Landing** is a large walk-through aviary with more than fifty Australian lorikeets. Visitors can purchase small cups of nectar to feed these brightly colored birds. There are also a few equally beautiful pheasant-like African turacos flying freely about.

The **Jungle Gym** is the largest community-built playground of its kind in the nation. More than 6,000 volunteers worked together to build this amazing structure. The massive playground has enough room for more than a thousand children at a time. Its many features include the *Tree of Life,* a thirty-five-foot-tall tree house, tubular slides, a giant snake tunnel, a hippo kids can climb into, swinging suspension bridges, and a *Jungle Village.* Also nearby are an enclosed toddler's play area with foam flooring, a large covered picnic pavilion, and the *Rain Room,* where kids can cool off under a refreshing mist.

IN PROGRESS

As is apparent on the zoo's visitor map, there is a lot of undeveloped land here, and the zoo has great plans for populating this space with exciting new exhibits. The first of these plans calls for a very large area focusing on the animals of Central and South America. The focal point of this exhibit will be a sizeable Brazilian rain forest building. This new area would double the zoo's animal collection and include giant anteaters, jaguars, capybaras, tapirs, various monkeys, tropical birds, frogs, fish, and much more. It is scheduled for completion in 2010 as we go to press.

BEST OF THE REST

Birmingham Zoo

2630 Cahaba Road
Birmingham, Alabama 35223
(205) 879-0409
www.birminghamzoo.com

Birds are a specialty of this mid-sized zoo. Along with two enormous waterfowl pools just inside the front gate, there are also a pelican exhibit, a flamingo pool, and small aviaries all across the zoo. The *Primates* building displays gorillas, orangutans, mandrills, and more. The *Predators* building features white Bengal and Indo-Chinese tigers, as well as a variety of unusual small cats, including adorable Arabian sand cats. The "Sea Lion Splash" show is very popular with visitors. There's also a *Reptiles* house, an alligator swamp, and a *Savanna* exhibit. The zoo's main attraction is a spectacular new *Children's Zoo*. Completed in 2005, its highlight is *Alabama Wilds,* a walk through the woods to see native Alabama animals such as river otters, beavers, and skunks. The zoo recently announced plans for a major expansion with *Trails of Africa*, a new multi-species habitat that will display rhinos, giraffes, zebras, antelope, and most notably, a bachelor herd of bull elephants – rarely seen in zoos.

The ZOO Northwest Florida

5701 Gulf Breeze Parkway
Gulf Breeze, Florida 32563
(850) 932-2229
www.thezoonorthwestflorida.org

Located on Florida's Gulf Coast Panhandle, this zoo suffered back-to-back hits from Hurricanes Ivan and Dennis. Despite this, it still manages to display an excellent collection of animals for such a small zoo. A boardwalk leads past exhibits featuring orangutans, Komodo dragons, alligators, and African wild dogs, to an overlook onto *Gorilla Island*, where the giant apes live near companion islands for chimpanzees and colobus monkeys. A ride on the nearby *Safari Line Ltd.* train is a must; it's the only way to get a good look at the thirty wild acres that are home to free-roaming wildebeest, pygmy hippos, and more. Elsewhere, notable animals include lions, tigers, bears, giraffes, and gibbons.

Brevard Zoo

8225 North Wickham Road
Melbourne, Florida 32940
(321) 254-9453
www.brevardzoo.org

This beautiful small-town zoo displays its animal collection along five different trails, each extending from a central loop around a flamingo pool. *Expedition Africa* takes visitors to see giraffes, white rhinos, antelope, and a

Visitors here can kayak among African animals.

variety of African bird species. *Austral-Asia* passes kangaroos, emus, dingoes, fruit bats, an aviary filled with exotic birds, and cassowaries (large colorful flightless birds). In *Wild Florida*, gigantic American crocodiles and alligators lurk, as well as red wolves, otters, foxes, birds of prey, and deer that visitors can hand feed. *La Selva Rainforest* displays animals of the Amazon jungle, including a jaguar, tapirs, giant anteaters, monkeys, birds, and capybaras (giant aquatic rodents), and – from the Andes – llamas and rheas, large flightless birds. A fifth trail leads to the *Paws On* contact yard. What makes this zoo unique, however, is the opportunity to go kayaking inside the zoo. Adventurers can kayak among African animals, or take a guided tour upriver through the Florida wilderness.

Naples Zoo at Caribbean Gardens

1590 Goodlette Road North
Naples, Florida 34102
(239) 262-5409
www.napleszoo.com

This small zoo is only half an hour from the Everglades, which is obvious when you tour the beautiful grounds, a lush tropical marshland. Along a looping trail around *Alligator Bay*, visitors will see rare and endangered carnivores, including Malayan tigers, Florida panthers, African wild dogs, hyenas, serval cats, and African leopards. Antelope and red river hogs can be seen at the *African Oasis*, while zebras are displayed nearby. The real thrill at this zoo is a *Primate Expedition* cruise on a pontoon boat. On this relaxing guided boat tour on Lake Victoria, gibbons, siamangs, lemurs, spider monkeys, and other primates are all visible, each species on its own tropical island.

Palm Beach Zoo at Dreher Park

1301 Summit Boulevard
West Palm Beach, Florida 33405
(561) 547-9453
www.palmbeachzoo.org

Led by Dr. Terry Maple, the man credited with rebuilding Zoo Atlanta, this small zoo is making similar improvements. At its core is a three-acre *Tropics of the Americas* exhibit. Arranged around a breathtakingly realistic Mayan pyramid, jaguars, tapirs, bush dogs, giant anteaters, and capybaras (giant aquatic rodents) are just some of the Latin American species on exhibit. Nearby, trails through the *Florida Wetlands* pass alligators, black bears, otters, and endangered Florida panthers. Across the zoo, the *Australia/Asia* section features Malayan tigers, kangaroos, and a variety of Australian birds. Various primates are displayed around the zoo, some on tropical island habitats. The zoo also presents an intriguing "Wings Over Water" bird show.

Jackson Zoological Park

2918 West Capitol Street
Jackson, Mississippi 39209
(601) 352-2580
www.jacksonzoo.org

Housed on fifty-two acres, Mississippi's largest zoo has an excellent collection of endangered animals. Its signature exhibit is *Wilderness Mississippi*, completed in 2006. The more than three hundred animals include pelicans, river otters, alligators, cougars, black bears, beavers, several venomous snakes, and a variety of native birds. Chimpanzees and pygmy hippos live in the *African Rain Forest*, while *Jewels of South America* displays small primates, birds, and reptiles. Orangutans, elephants, two rare tiger species, rhinoceroses, giraffes, and lesser known species like golden-bellied mangabey monkeys and tapirs are also exhibited. Highlights of the *Discovery Zoo* children's area are an interactive lorikeet feeding aviary and *Discovery Reef* aquarium.

Virginia Zoological Park

3500 Granby Street
Norfolk, Virginia 23504
(757) 441-2374
www.virginiazoo.org

Norfolk is home to the state's only major zoo. Its eight-acre *African Okavango Delta Exhibit* includes a very authentic *African Village*, with thatch-roof buildings modeled after those in Botswana. The exhibit's many African animals include elephants, white rhinos, giraffes, zebras, baboon-like mandrills, red river hogs, ostriches, and antelope, as well as smaller reptiles and birds from Africa. The *Tsodilo Hills* exhibits include meerkats and a beautiful lion habitat. A more recent focus on North American animals has led to the addition of bison and prairie dogs. Other zoo exhibits include the large *Nocturnal Habitats/Reptiles* building and the new *Red Panda Paradise* exhibit, opened in 2007. *Trail of the Tiger*, planned for 2010, will be a major exhibit with a strong Asian theme. Inhabitants will include Sumatran tigers, sun bears, and Malayan tapirs. A unique feature will be an orangutan-activated shower that the red apes will be able to turn on over passing zoo visitors – soaking them!

Monorails, Trains – Even Sky Rides – Add Fun to Zoo Visits

Minnesota Zoo's monorail. Audubon Zoo's train. San Diego Zoo's Skyfari.

South Central Zoos

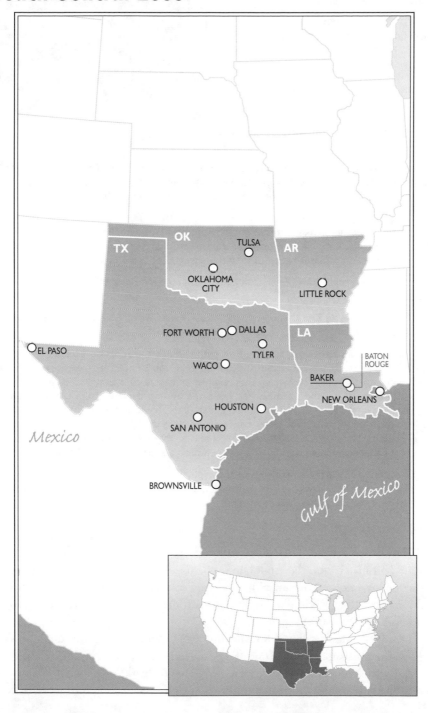

TX
OK
AR
LA

TULSA
OKLAHOMA CITY
LITTLE ROCK
FORT WORTH   DALLAS
TYLER
WACO
EL PASO
BATON ROUGE
BAKER
NEW ORLEANS
HOUSTON
SAN ANTONIO

Mexico

BROWNSVILLE

Gulf of Mexico

Audubon Park and Zoological Garden

6500 Magazine Street
New Orleans, Louisiana 70118
(800) 774-7394
www.auduboninstitute.org

Hours: 10:00 a.m.-4:00 p.m. Tuesday-Friday, 10:00 a.m.-5:00 p.m. Saturday and Sunday. Closed Mondays, Mardi Gras (which falls 46 days before Easter), Thanksgiving, Christmas Eve and Day.

White alligators seen at the Louisiana Swamp.

Admission & Fees: Adults $12.50, seniors 65+ $9.50, children 2-12 $7.50. Combo tickets for Zoo, Aquarium, and/or IMAX theater available. Swamp Train $4, carousel $2, rock climbing wall $5, simulator ride $5, all day ride pass (carousel, rock wall, train) $20, one time combo ticket for same $10.

Directions: From I-10, take Exit 232 (Carrollton Avenue) South. Follow Carrollton Avenue south for 2.2 miles. Turn left onto Leake Avenue, also called River Road. Follow Leake Avenue for 1 mile, then bear left as it becomes Magazine Street. Zoo is 0.4 miles ahead on right.

Don't Miss: Louisiana Swamp, Asian Domain, Jaguar Jungle, World of Primates, African Savanna, Reptile Encounter.

For Kids: Embraceable Zoo, Discovery Walk, Monkey Hill, Swamp Train, carousel, rock climbing wall, simulator ride.

Authors' Tips: Your zoo map lists the best path through the zoo. Visit exhibits in the numbered order to enjoy the best tour and ensure that you'll enter each exhibit as intended (instead of back to front). The Swamp Train, a white tram that runs along visitor paths, departs every 30 minutes from the Carousel and Louisiana Swamp depots. In the Louisiana Swamp exhibit, the Cypress Knee Café is a must-try restaurant. Try local favorites like gumbo in the wooden cabin, or eat outside at picnic tables overlooking the alligator swamp. The zoo is part of the Audubon Nature Institute, which also includes an IMAX Theater and the Aquarium of the Americas. Combination admission packages are available at each of these institutions.

Edutainment: On Wednesdays March-October, public alligator feedings take place in the Louisiana Swamp. Sea lion shows are held daily. Informal animal demonstrations are given throughout the day at the Discovery Walk (see below).

SINCE 2005, THE CITY OF NEW ORLEANS HAS BECOME ASSOCIATED with Hurricane Katrina. That devastating storm forever changed this city on the bayou. Fortunately for the Audubon Zoo, its excellent preparation kept animal collection losses to a minimum, although it did sustain significant damage to the trees and grounds. Much credit goes to the zoo staff, many of whom stayed at the zoo to weather the storm with the animals.

Despite the destruction of Katrina, this zoo, located in beautiful Audubon Park, right on the Mississippi River, is one of the South's best. Called a "zoological ghetto" in the 1970s, it rebounded after extensive renovations. The park's lush animal habitats now match the charm of its French architecture, statues, fountains, and moss-covered oaks.

FEATURED EXHIBITS

The zoo's best exhibit re-creates the region's most common ecosystem. This doesn't mean it's minimalist, however: the **Louisiana Swamp** is one of the premier themed exhibits in the country. An elevated boardwalk winds past exhibits featuring the diverse wildlife of the Louisiana bayous: black bears, cougars, raccoons, bobcats, rat-like nutrias, otters, red foxes, and, of course, alligators. Signs of human presence in the bayou include abandoned shrimp boats and houseboats floating in the swamp, and Cajun shacks built along the swamp's edge. An open building, *Le Cypriere*, displays some of the venomous snakes and other reptiles and amphibians of the bayou. Local insects and fish, including toothy alligator gars, are also housed here. The zoo's most famous residents, white alligators, live here as well. These beautiful blue-eyed 'gators were found in a local marsh. Their bright coloring is easily spotted by potential prey, which diminishes their ability to hunt, meaning these 'gators would not survive in the wild.

The **Asian Domain** is often the first exhibit guests visit. It showcases the exotic foreign animals the Louisiana Swamp lacks. Your journey begins at an Asian elephant exhibit, where these smaller-eared pachyderms can wade in a deep pool. The path then slowly rises, passing exhibits for milky storks, crested porcupines, sun bears, two species of cranes, and wild babirusa pigs, before reaching the white Bengal tigers, which can be seen in a moated valley across from barasingha swamp deer and double-humped Bactrian camels. Rhinoceros hornbill birds have a spacious flight cage near exhibits for two more fearsome felines: Amur leopards, shown behind harp wire, and lions, who live in a densely planted valley.

At **Jaguar Jungle**, rain forest habitats are built around replicas of ancient Mayan ruins. The tour begins at a food market that's overrun with cotton-top tamarin monkeys. Maguari storks and roseate spoonbill birds wade in a neighboring lagoon. As visitors continue along the forested pathway, the sight of stone heads and the sound of beating drums heightens the sense of anticipation. Bushy-tailed giant anteaters are first on the bill; they explore several termite mounds in their mulch-covered yard. Just beyond a stone gate, a covered sand dig site gives kids the opportunity look for Mayan artifacts. Black-handed spider monkeys swing past detailed temple ruins. From behind waist high glass panels, visitors can watch these prehensile-tailed monkeys romp on their island, which is well supplied with trees and ropes to swing from. Your walk eventually leads to the jaguar enclosure, where these spotted cats often rest on log perches and fallen trees.

The **World of Primates** begins with an animal that fits in by name, but not by species – monkey-tailed skinks. These lizards use their prehensile tails to hang onto branches, much like the howler monkeys and white-faced saki monkeys you'll see later on. In an interesting mix of glass, island, and moated enclosures, an impressive collection of primates is exhibited. The most unusual monkey here is an African talapoin, rarely seen in zoos. Also from Africa are colobus monkeys, Diana monkeys, and black-and-white ruffed lemurs, which come from Madagascar, off Africa's eastern coast. Golden lion tamarin monkeys, cotton-top tamarin monkeys and common marmoset monkeys live in smaller habitats. Siamang gibbons are the zoo's only lesser apes, while two great apes, orangutans and gorillas, enjoy the largest exhibits at trail's end.

The **African Savanna** is divided into several areas, each named after real African game reserves. At *Amboseli*, common eland, the world's largest antelope, and considerably smaller Thompson's gazelles both roam an expansive grassland. Across the path at *Masai Mara*, white pelicans wade in a lake that separates white rhinos from plains zebras. White-tailed wildebeests share a dusty exhibit with the zebras. A small pack of colorful African wild dogs are part of the *Serengeti* display. Kori bustards, the world's heaviest flying birds, and crowned cranes meander through a long yard with giraffes at *Twiga Terrace*. Although not really savanna animals, red river hogs are also displayed in this area.

In the *Dragon's Lair* in **Reptile Encounter**, Komodo dragons are shown in two outdoor enclosures: the larger for adults, and a smaller one for juveniles. Also shown outdoors, false gharial crocodiles wallow in a shaded pool. Inside the building, you'll find descriptions of the "magnificent seven," the only seven snake species that can reach twenty feet in length. Three are exhibited here: green anacondas and reticulated pythons (the two longest), and king cobras (the longest venomous snake). Stretched out along the ceiling above is a replica of the largest snake ever captured, a thirty-eight-foot-long green anaconda. From here, the path curves past Chinese alligators, day geckos, and a pentagonal aquarium for pig-nosed Fly River turtles from Australia. The latest snake and turtle hatchlings and baby American alligators are featured in the *Reptile Nursery*. Fifteen of the building's sixteen rattlesnakes live in *Rattlesnake Canyon*, a narrated exhibit near the exit. Venomous Gila monster lizards also inhabit a desert habitat along the canyon walls. Outside, you'll see rare Grand Cayman blue iguanas.

OTHER EXHIBITS

John J. Audubon, the zoo's namesake, is commemorated with a statue on the grounds. Famous for his paintings of birds, he certainly would enjoy the **Tropical Bird House**, a re-creation of a South American rain forest under a glass roof. Most of the more than forty bird species fly freely around a fallen kapok tree. Along the wall is a row of harp-wire enclosures for toucans, Bali mynahs, and other beautiful birds. Nearly as interesting as the birds is the entry foyer, where fascinating artistic examples of cultural artifacts made from bird feathers are showcased.

Classical columns tower over the **Odenheimer Sea Lion Complex.** It was this exhibit that sustained the most damage during Hurricane Katrina, and it was closed for two years following. Two separate pools can be seen from surrounding pathways, from a bridge overlooking both pools, and from underwater windows below. A large rocky outcropping rises above water level in one pool, providing the sea lions with a place to rest. The other pool is set up for sea lion shows, which are best seen from a covered amphitheater.

At the center of the **Australian Outback** is a lush walk-through aviary that displays laughing kookaburras. Other animals from down under include emus, wallabies, and kangaroos. Animals in the **South American Pampas** are shown on both sides of a walkway. Across a deep lake, visitors can spot tapirs, flamingos, and capybaras (huge aquatic rodents). Much closer is a herd of guanacos, related to llamas. Near the entrance to the zoo, more flamingos are displayed, as are endangered whooping cranes.

FOR THE KIDS

At the **Embraceable Zoo**, kids can interact with barnyard animals, including goats, sheep, and chickens. To reach this petting area, visitors pass through *Discovery Walk*, a hedge maze where keepers bring out small mammals, reptiles, and birds for close inspection.

Originally constructed in the 1930s, **Monkey Hill** has since received an overhaul. Because New Orleans is built on low flat country, legend has it that this hill was constructed to show kids what a hill looks like. Now the highest point in the city, its five-story tree house includes a complex maze of ropes and bridges for kids to play on.

On the **rock climbing wall**, kids get two chances to scale the wall and ring a bell at the top. The **Endangered Species Carousel** features more than sixty exotic animals to ride. Expeditions on the **Safari simulator ride** alternate between five different intense adventures.

IN PROGRESS

The zoo hopes to add an interactive bird feeding exhibit and a "wet zoo" water park in the near future. An expansion of the elephant exhibit is also in the planning stages.

Oklahoma City Zoological Park

2101 NE 50th Street
Oklahoma City, Oklahoma 73111
(405) 424-3344
www.okczoo.com

Entrance to the Oklahoma Trails exhibit.

Hours: 9:00 a.m.-6:00 p.m. daily, Memorial Day-Labor Day, buildings close at 8:00 p.m., grounds at dusk; 9:00 a.m.-5:00 p.m. daily, rest of year, buildings and grounds close at dusk. Closed Thanksgiving, Christmas, and New Year's Day.

Admission & Fees: Adults $7, seniors 65+ and children 3-11 $4. "Fins and Feathers" show: adults $2, children $1; Safari Tram: adults $3, children $2; rock climbing wall $2; paddleboats $5; Centennial Choo Choo: adults $2, children $1; children's train $1; Endangered Species Carousel $2; fish to feed sea lions $2; lorikeet nectar $2. Pay-One-Price, ride all day package: adults $10, children $8. This includes admission to the "Fins and Feathers" show and all rides. Surrey tandem bike rental: $7 for 30 minutes, $3.50 for each additional 15 minutes (must be 25 or older to rent).

Directions: From I-35, take Exit 132A (NE 50ᵗʰ Street) West, then follow 50ᵗʰ Street for 1 mile to the zoo. From I-44, take Exit 129 (Martin Luther King Avenue), follow Martin Luther King Avenue south for 1 mile, turn left onto North East 50ᵗʰ Street, and follow to zoo.

Don't Miss: Oklahoma Trails, Cat Forest, Noble Aquatic Center: Aquaticus, Great EscApe, Wild Dog Drive, Giraffe Loop.

For Kids: Adventure Zone, Endangered Species Carousel, Centennial Choo Choo Train, children's train, ExpLorikeet Adventure, swan paddleboats, Jungle Gym, rock climbing wall.

Authors' Tips: ExpLorikeet Adventure closes from noon to 1:30 p.m. every day for cleaning, and shuts down for the day at 4:00 p.m., so make this an early stop. The zoo covers more than 100 acres and, at points, can be difficult to walk. The paths to the Aquatic Center and Bison Hill are especially grueling. Consider riding the Safari Tram, which gives a narrated tour of the hoofed animal section. For easier touring, each zoo pathway is named after the animals exhibited in that area. For exercise, rent a Surrey Bike (weekends only) at a kiosk near Cat Forest.

Edutainment: The "Fins and Feathers" show at the Aquatic Center Performance Arena combines exotic birds with California sea lions in a creative presentation. Shows run Fridays through Sundays, and a free training session is held on Wednesdays and Thursdays. Afterwards, you can purchase fish to feed the sea lions. Elephant demonstrations are held every Saturday and Sunday, weather permitting. Near the Oklahoma Trails bison habitat, an indoor parlor exhibit features close to 100 historical photos from 1890-1920, many donated by zoo staff.

OVER A HUNDRED YEARS OLD, THE OKLAHOMA CITY ZOO IS THE most visited tourist attraction in the state. But the limited collection had become outdated by the early 1980s. In 1988, a master plan was drafted to improve the zoo. With an eighth-of-a-cent sales tax approved in 1990, the zoo promised it would focus on the "ABC's of the animal kingdom," apes, bears, and cats. It took seventeen years, but with the opening of Oklahoma Trails in 2007, the zoo has brought naturalistic habitats for the "ABC" animals to the zoo.

FEATURED EXHIBITS

Oklahoma Trails takes zoo exhibit theming to a new level. Over 800 animals live in this eight-acre re-creation of Oklahoma's eleven life zones, or ecosystems. Each new habitat is introduced with a beautifully carved Native American-inspired sign, describing the details and location of each of the state's life zones. Authentic vegetation from each region helps identify each habitat. Your journey begins at *Black Mesa,* the state's highest elevation in western Oklahoma's Rocky Mountain foothills. Swift foxes hide among boulders, bobcats rest behind shrubs, and cougars prowl a rolling plain. At the *Shortgrass Prairie*, white-tailed deer and wild turkeys roam a sloping grassland. Deer predators – coyotes and Mexican gray wolves (extinct in Oklahoma since the 1930s) – spy on the deer herd in the *Shinnery Oak Savanna*, a set of woodland habitats. In the *Mixed Grass Prairie*, the state's largest region, a large free-flight aviary showcases native birds, including quails and bobwhites, as well as seasonal residents, Caspian terns. Side exhibits inside the aviary hold turkey vultures, ring-necked pheasants, roadrunners, and raccoons. Animals of the *Arkansas Valley* night, displayed in a nocturnal barn, include great horned owls, fruit bats, flying squirrels, and raccoon-like ringtails (or cacomistles), all displayed in barn exhibits illuminated by black lights. Back outside in the *Tallgrass Prairie*, badgers and prairie dogs burrow in front of grazing bison and pronghorns. The grizzly bears at *Cross Timbers* are showstoppers. Towering trees dot the bears' rugged landscape in their panoramic habitat. Guests can watch the bears swim in the stream below from an elevated boardwalk, or through glass as they wade in a smaller pool. A twenty-five-foot replica of Turner Falls crashes from the side of the *Big Rivers* building. Inside, there is an 18,000-gallon aquarium with bass, paddlefish, and gars. At the other end of Big Rivers, river otters and beavers rest on a rocky shoreline and swim in their shallow stream. Between these aquatic mammals are reptiles and amphibians from around the state, including rattlesnakes, tree frogs, and salamanders. Also inside is a first look at the *Ozark Highlands*, where black bears roam a huge open field. Outside, the boardwalk follows the curve of the exhibit, so you rarely lose sight of the bears. Eventually, you reach a bald eagle in a circular grove. Southeastern Oklahoma's *Ouachita Mountains* features a small elk herd living in an open sloping yard. Across the path in a thicket, red wolves are visible from high above. Finally, an alligator-infested pond represents a *Cypress Swamp*. Also in this swamp is a Model T truck, one of many antique artifacts along the trail.

Cat Forest displays nine feline species in four acres of spacious naturalistic environments. Jaguars, ocelots, and servals each have tiered net-covered habitats outside the *Small Cat* building. Inside, graphics detail the unique characteristics of some lesser-known members of the cat family. Glass-fronted habitats showcase black-footed cats and desert-dwelling caracal lynx. Bordering *Zoo Lake*, the outdoor enclosure for the secretive snow leopards can be viewed through thick trees from two sides. This complex's second building is for tigers. Fishing cats are also displayed inside, next to a wide view of the dense Sumatran tiger habitat. Outside, visitors get another look at this exhibit, which is nearly divided by a thickly planted hill. Bordered by bamboo, the path continues to a second, narrower tiger habitat. The adventurous can take a path cut through the thick bamboo to learn more about tiger survival in Asia. Across from the exhibit's entrance is *Lion Overlook*, where a majestic lion is almost certain to be resting on a high rocky outcropping. These regal cats can also be seen through a sheltered window.

Great EscApe is one of only a few zoo exhibits in the country to display three types of great apes. Habitats for orangutans, chimpanzees, and two gorilla groups are situated in rocky forest clearings. Each of these four outdoor exhibits has unique features, but all are positioned on a hillside, raised above the visitor path. Beautiful walkways surround each of the exhibits and lead to a pair of interpretive buildings. Inside, long windows look out onto thatch-roof-shaded portions of the apes' outdoor habitats and into their indoor playrooms.

The **Noble Aquatic Center: Aquaticus** is one of the zoo's premier exhibits. First up is a large seal pool that resembles a rocky California cove. Two lower level galleries, reached by carpeted ramps, showcase more aquatic creatures. You'll find underwater viewing of the harbor seals and an indoor California sea lion pool near a trout stream. Cuttlefish, four-eyed fish, electric eels, and archerfish are some of the nearly six hundred aquatic creatures here. Coral reefs, with both soft and hard corals, are also featured, as well as zebra moray eels.

The long row of canines on **Wild Dog Drive** is the nation's largest and most diverse display of wild dogs. Each of the eight open, grassy yards is landscaped with bushes and trees. Overlooks are strategically placed at watering holes, and visitors view the dogs without visual barriers. Occupants of these innovative exhibits include rarely seen bush dogs, black-backed jackals, maned wolves, and small bat-eared foxes. African wild dogs, spotted hyenas, and Mexican gray wolves are also featured. One yard is occupied by felines – sleek, quick cheetahs.

The **Giraffe Loop** is home to a number of popular African animals, and also offers another look into the backs of some of the Oklahoma Trails habitats. Rothschild's giraffes, ostriches, nyala antelope, and ground hornbill birds live in a sprawling tall grass savanna. A neighboring yard exhibits Grant's gazelles, crowned cranes, guinea fowl, spurred tortoises, and Grevy's zebras. Two beautiful forest-dwellers, okapis (related to giraffes) and chestnut-colored bongo antelope, are also displayed here, along with yellow-backed duiker antelope. Warthogs live in a small yard across the train tracks.

OTHER EXHIBITS

Island Life highlights the fragility of isolated island ecosystems. Abaco Island boas, Javan hump-headed lizards, crocodile monitor lizards, New Caledonian giant geckos, and Puerto Rican crested toads are all featured inside. A Galapagos tortoise yard is outside, as are waterfowl ponds with black-necked swans, Philippine ducks, Hawaiian Nene geese, and American flamingos. Andean condors and harpy eagles live in tall flight cages nearby.

Historically, this zoo has been most famous in the zoo world for its hoofstock collection. **Bison Hill** is home to many of these hoofed residents, including sable antelope, gerenuk gazelles, greater kudu antelope, bontebok antelope, and Somali wild ass, which are very rare in U.S. zoos. The largest single habitat at the zoo is a thickly planted ravine, home to Indo-Chinese gorals (a type of small mountain goat), and hog deer, sika deer, and tufted deer.

Pygmy hippos, Indian and black rhinos, and Asian elephants are displayed in spacious outdoor yards and inside the **Pachyderm Building**. Along its interior walkway, there are large animals on one side and a row of small bird cages on the other. Also inside is **Butterflies: Wings of Wonder**, a walk-through garden with twelve species of American butterflies. Wild local fly-in butterflies are often seen in the **Butterfly Garden**, a winding maze of paths through butterfly friendly plantings on a sloping hillside.

A row of small grottoes borders Zoo Lake. They're home to meerkats, tiny pudu deer, red pandas, and crested porcupines. Yards near the children's zoo display red river hogs, kangaroos, and giant anteaters. The **Dan Moran Aviary**, a small indoor rain forest, displays colorful fairy bluebirds, pheasant-like Lady Ross turacos, and ruddy ducks.

The **Herpetarium** is well known in the zoo world for its chameleon collection. Other unusual animals here include striped Australian woma snakes, Kaznakov's vipers from the Caspian Sea region, snake-necked turtles, spitting cobras, and a wide variety of frogs. A wall display of salamanders includes rare crocodile newts, giant hellbenders, sirens, axolotls with frilly branches extending from their gills, and eel-like three-toed amphiumas.

FOR THE KIDS

The **Adventure Zone** rests along the shores of Zoo Lake. There's a *rock climbing wall*, a *children's train*, and *Endangered Species Carousel* in this open meadow. *Swan paddleboats* are available for rent at a nearby dock. The *Centennial Choo Choo Train* passes through the Asian deer ravine, and provides a good look at the giraffes. The *Jungle Gym* is a massive 30,000-square-foot playground.

ExpLorikeet Adventure is a walk-through aviary with colorful Australian parrots. The exhibit includes several species of these parrots, each uniquely and colorfully patterned. For an additional fee, kids can feed the birds a cup of nectar.

IN PROGRESS

The zoo plans to open a new **children's zoo** in 2009 as we go to press. By 2013, they also plan to open a new **Asian area** that uses the zoo's Asian elephants as a focal point. An expanded herd of elephants would be moved to a new site on the property, where they would enjoy three times the space of their current exhibit.

Tulsa Zoo and Living Museum

6241 East 36th Street North
Tulsa, Oklahoma 74115
(918) 669-6600
www.tulsazoo.org

Hours: 9:00 a.m.-5:00 p.m. daily, grounds open to 6:00 p.m. Closed Christmas and the third Friday in June.

Admission & Fees: Adults $6.04, seniors 55+ $4.03, children 3-11 $3.02. Mohawk Park entrance fee: $2 weekends and holidays April-October. Train: $1 each way, $2 round trip; carousel $1. Participates in reciprocity program.

Snowy owls in their Arctic/Tundra habitat.

Directions: From Cherokee Expressway (US-75), exit onto Highway 11 East (36th Street). Follow 36th Street for 1.8 miles to Mohawk Park and zoo. From I-44 eastbound, take Exit 223A (I-244). Follow I-244 north through Tulsa for 4.6 miles to Exit 4B (US-75/US-64/OK-51). On US-75, follow above directions to the zoo. From I-44 westbound, continue through Tulsa onto I-244. From I-244, take Exit 12B (Tulsa International Airport) and get on Highway OK-11. Follow

Highway OK-11 for 3.9 miles, then take the North Yale Avenue exit. Go north on Yale Avenue for 0.4 miles, then turn right onto East 36th Street. Follow for 0.6 miles to Mohawk Park and zoo. From Mingo Valley Expressway (U.S.169), exit at 46th Street West. Follow East 46th Street for 1.2 miles, when it becomes North Port Road. Continue for another 2.1 miles, when it becomes East 36th Street. Stay on 36th Street for another 0.2 miles to Mohawk Park and zoo.

Don't Miss: North American Living Museum, Tropical American Rainforest, Elephant Encounter (including museum), Chimpanzee Connection, East African Savanna, Conservation Center.

For Kids: Children's Zoo, Discovery Center, playground, miniature train, wildlife carousel, Nature Exchange.

Authors' Tips: Look for red-shirted volunteer guides in the Tropical Rainforest. These experienced and informative individuals will enhance your experience here. Don't miss the wooden deck by the tortoises that looks out across a beautiful wetland.

Edutainment: In 2007, the zoo opened the Elephant Demonstration Yard, which is fronted by a concrete-row amphitheater at the Elephant Encounter exhibit. In this small yard, the zoo's female elephants perform in a daily demonstration. Animal feedings take place at the Aldabra tortoise and penguin exhibits. Animal demonstrations in the Discovery Center are held at 1:30 p.m. daily from April-October, and on weekends the rest of the year.

AS ITS NAME IMPLIES, THIS ZOO IS ALSO ACCREDITED AS A MUSEUM by the American Association of Museums, and fittingly, many of its animal exhibits are accompanied by the natural history of the animal and/or its native region. In 2004, in an online voting contest promoting the new *Zoo Tycoon* computer game, the Tulsa Zoo was voted "America's Favorite Zoo." The zoo is located in Mohawk Park, one of the country's largest municipal parks.

FEATURED EXHIBITS

The award-winning **LaFortune North American Living Museum** is one of the country's most unusual and educational zoo exhibits. The museum is a four-building complex connected by elevated walkways. Each building represents one of the four major regions of North America, and each building's exterior is covered with tiny colored stones that match the environment portrayed inside. In addition to featuring live animals, attractive graphics, and popular interactive exhibits, this museum also displays minerals, fossils, and Native American artifacts.

In front of the white **Arctic/Tundra** building, a polar bear exhibit includes an underwater window. Inside, near the building's entrance, the *Time Gallery* has interpretive geology displays, among them an earthquake simulator that reproduces an earthquake that's a level six on the Richter scale, and a ten-foot-long dinosaur replica known as "Terrible Claw." Arctic foxes and snowy owls live here in rocky arctic habitats. The *Life in the Arctic Seas* aquarium displays white starfish and sea anemones.

Inside the brown **Southwest Desert** building, you'll pass the *Desert Rainfall Exhibit* on the way to a walk-through desert room landscaped with saguaros and other cacti and mesquite bushes, and populated with roadrunners, cactus wrens, and other free-flying desert birds. A gallery of desert reptiles, including Gila monsters and rattlesnakes, is laid out along the wall. The *Sea of Cortez* marine aquarium showcases colorful fish from the Gulf of California, and a kit fox and cacomistle (aka ringtail cat) are exhibited in rocky nocturnal habitats. Collared peccaries (aka javelinas), a kind of wild pig, can be seen outside, at the exit.

On the way to the green *Eastern Forest* building, white-tailed deer and wild turkeys come into view in a marshy exhibit planted with tall grass. Inside, electronic displays show the seasonal changes of forests, and an 8,000-gallon *Fishes of the Great Lakes* aquarium teems with gars and other freshwater fish. A trickling waterfall marks the beginning of the award-winning *Cave* exhibit. Among the realistic stalactites and stalagmites are exhibits of bats, blind crayfish, and blind salamanders. In the novel *Cave Formations* display, visitors use a panel of buttons to light up various geological formations. Animals of the forest – skunks, raccoons, bobcats, and a great horned owl – are featured in nocturnal exhibits. Tall harp wire aviaries house forest songbirds. Forest reptiles are exhibited near these birds. Outside, bald eagles and an enclosure of black bears are visible from the bridgewalk.

A tour of the gray *Southern Lowlands* building begins with displays of carnivorous plants and large swamp snakes. Just inside the door is *Bioluminescence: Nature's Light Show*, a darkened room showcasing fireflies, flashlight fish, fungi, railroad worms, and other creatures that glow in the dark. On the *Great Swamp Walk,* visitors follow a meandering boardwalk through a cypress swamp, with a large alligator snapping turtle pool to the left and a tall free-flight aviary of herons, ibises, and spoonbill birds to the right. A large coral reef aquarium displays colorful fish from the Gulf of Mexico – most notably the Atlantic spadefish, for which this facility is famous in the zoo world. The grant that the zoo won for being named "America's Favorite Zoo" was used to create *Cajun's Bayou*, an alligator swamp just outside, where the 'gators nap in front of an old bait shack

A replica of a 3,000-year-old Olmec stone head sits outside the **Tropical American Rainforest**. Inside, thousands of live plants and free-roaming marmoset monkeys, birds, and agoutis, forest-dwelling rodents related to domestic guinea pigs, thrive in eighty-degree humidity. Under a glass roof that lets in plenty of natural light, murals inspired by ancient Mayan culture are painted on the crumbling stone walls surrounding the Central and South American animals. The opening exhibits are set in a flooded forest environment. Anacondas, caiman crocodiles, tamarin monkeys, stingrays, and huge pacu fish are visible from inside a hollowed-out tree. Eyelash vipers, boas, and insects inhabit small exhibits carved into the rock wall. A peach palm, whose long sharp thorns are used as tips for blow darts in native cultures, sits in front of a noisy troop of howler monkeys. The most creative of the building's individual exhibits is the poison dart frog habitat. Opposite a closer view of the howler monkeys, a multitude of these brilliantly colored frogs can be seen barrier-free in the mist-shrouded jungle brush. These colorful creatures hop about just inches from guests. A pair of sloths has free range of the building, but their food supply generally keeps them in a tree close to the winding trail. Spectacled owls and Amazon parrots live in side-by-side harp wire aviaries. The indoor/outdoor jaguar exhibit uses ancient ruins as a backdrop to the cats' shallow pool. Scarlet ibises wade in a lagoon that surrounds a tree full of golden-headed lion tamarin monkeys in the last exhibit, before you reenter the real world.

At **Elephant Encounter**, the outdoor viewing station into the bulls' yard is enclosed for the visitors' safety, as these Asian bull elephants have been known to throw things. The view of the larger elephant cow yard is much better, with a long overlook that stretches the width of the exhibit. The *Elephant Center* lies between the two. It offers another view into each yard, and an informative elephant museum with a life-size prehistoric mammoth hunt diorama and interpretive displays that describe the cultural and biological history of elephants in Africa and Asia.

Chimpanzee Connection is an indoor/outdoor habitat for a growing troop of chimps (the Tulsa Zoo has a successful breeding program). *Chimp Island*, surrounded by a water-filled moat, is enhanced with natural vegetation, artificial termite mounds, and tunnel passageways. One tunnel leads inside to their indoor habitat. During inclement weather, visitors can watch them from a plush indoor viewing area with tall windows. Both inside and out, the chimps are provided with plenty of climbing equipment. Chimpanzees are known as the first animals (other than humans) that were discovered to make tools: they'll strip the leaves off twigs and use them to "fish" termites out of a termite mound. Here, this skill is well demonstrated on a termite mound that straddles the visitor and chimp sides of the glass. Kids can pretend to be chimpanzees by sticking magnetic rods into holes in the mound to fish for "ants," while keepers can put treats into the chimps' side. It makes for an interesting comparison of species.

With over three acres of grassland, the panoramic **East African Savanna** is the best of the outdoor exhibits. Zebras, Grant's gazelles, crowned cranes, marabou storks, ostriches, and Egyptian geese occupy a sloping central yard flanked on both sides by large, open paddocks with Cape buffalo, one of the most feared African animals, and greater kudu antelope. Another open savanna yard for giraffes lies across the path. A small wooden building overlooks a rolling cheetah yard and a mob of meerkats. Nearby, white rhinos roam a larger field. Another small building is home to giant Aldabra tortoises. Adding to the zoo's cultural museum of exhibits is the *Maasai Village*, where a thorny-bush barrier surrounds several thatch-covered huts, each introducing a different aspect of African life.

The multi-purpose **Conservation Center** is the nucleus of the primate, bird, reptile, and fish collections. The building's primates include ruffed lemurs, Diana monkeys, saki monkeys, and another troop of golden-headed lion tamarin monkeys. All have both indoor and outdoor enclosures. Three types of macaws, red-legged seriema birds, and Caribbean flamingos are exhibited along the building's outside walls. Inside, more glass-fronted aviaries display wrinkled hornbill birds, eclectus parrots, toucans, plush crested jays, and other brilliantly colored birds. Favorite exhibits in the reptile section include water dragons, rough-necked monitor lizards, Fiji banded iguanas, several rare Asian turtles, a huge African bullfrog, a blue iguana, and puff adder snakes. A centrally located tank displays huge Asian fish. Newly hatched reptile youngsters are placed close to the window in an extensive *Reptile Nursery*.

OTHER EXHIBITS

The Kodiak and Andean (also known as spectacled) **bear grottoes** have pools for their comfort. Past these grottoes is a troop of black-and-white ruffed lemurs. The **Great Cats** area has two large, grassy grottoes for African lions and Amur tigers and a rocky evergreen habitat for snow leopards.

A pathway surrounding the **black-footed penguin habitat** gives a variety of views into the aquatic birds' rocky streambed. Visitors can watch the penguins swimming or preening their feathers on a beach from several different vantage points. The path rises above the water level on both sides of the **sea lion pool**, giving great views of these active pinnipeds. Siamang gibbons and spectacled langur monkeys are best seen when they are on a bridge connecting their night building to a densely planted island. Adjacent to their building is a small playground that challenges kids to walk and swing like gibbons.

FOR THE KIDS

The **Children's Zoo** is built around a red barn that houses guinea pigs, rabbits, and chickens. Outdoor barnyard corrals are home to wild turkeys, Guinea hogs, llamas, and donkeys. Notable small exhibits include a prairie dog colony and a kangaroo/emu yard. At the *Otter Grotto,* kids can watch playful river otters frolic in their pool at the foot of a splashing waterfall.

Small Oklahoma creatures are exhibited in the **Helmerich Discovery Center**. Volunteers bring out fascinating animals like hissing cockroaches and reptiles so visitors can take a closer look. Also inside is *Nature's Attic,* an animal presentation theater that's open from 11:00 a.m. to 12:30 p.m. on weekdays, and from 1:00 p.m. to 3:00 p.m. on weekends. The **Helmerich Playground**, just behind the rhinos, is a fun place to explore. Natural artifacts (such as shells, rocks, and fossils) that kids find and bring in can be traded at the **Nature Exchange**.

A ride on a bright red **miniature train** provides a tour around the perimeter of most of the zoo's eighty-four acres. Young ones can ride their favorite animals on the **wildlife carousel**.

IN PROGRESS

As we go to press, a renovation of the **California sea lion** exhibit is planned for 2009. Both the sea lions and visitors will benefit from this larger exhibit. A key element of this project will be an underwater viewing area.

Gladys Porter Zoo

500 Ringgold Street
Brownsville, Texas 78520
(956) 546-7187
www.gpz.org

Hours: 9:00 a.m.-5:00 p.m. Monday-Friday, 9:00 a.m.-5:30 p.m. weekends; grounds open until dusk.

Admission & Fees: Adults $9, seniors 65+ $7.50, children 2-13 $6. Safari Express tour train: adults $2, children $1; bird feeding $1. Parking $2.50. Participates in reciprocity program.

Directions: From US-77/US-83 Expressway, take the 6th Street exit. Follow for 0.3 miles south to Ringgold Street, and turn right to arrive at the zoo.

Young orangutan lives in Indo-Australia area.

Don't Miss: Africa, Indo-Australia, Herpetarium, Tropical America, Realm of the Dragon, Free-Flight Aviary, Asia.

For Kids: Small World Petting Zoo.

Authors' Tips: The Safari Express tour train only runs on Sunday afternoons. Despite its small size (only 31 acres), there's a lot to see at this zoo and it's mostly outdoors. Take advantage of the many water fountains to keep yourself hydrated, as it gets very hot during the summer.

Edutainment: Special educational programs featuring sea lions are presented in a 200-seat amphitheater next to the sea lion exhibit.

OPENED IN 1971, THE GLADYS PORTER ZOO IS FOUND IN A MOST unlikely place – at the southern tip of Texas, just across the border from Mexico. It was planned, built, stocked, and equipped by the Earl C. Sams Foundation and then donated to the city of Brownsville. Mr. Sams was the chairman of the board for the J.C.Penney Company. Gladys Porter, his daughter, oversaw the establishment of her namesake zoo.

From the beginning, this zoo's primary goal has been to serve as a "survival center" for rare and endangered species. This is apparent in its impressive collection of rarely displayed animals. Many of the creatures here are found nowhere else in the United States. The zoo has had excellent success breeding these endangered species, so baby animals are a common sight.

The raw natural beauty of this zoo is the result of its location in the semi-tropical lower Rio Grande Valley. The mild climate is ideal for supporting abundant palm and mesquite trees, bougainvillea vines, hibiscus shrubs, and other tropical plants. The lush botanical collection here is nearly as impressive as the animal collection. The most notable geological features are the "resacas," the waterways left behind by the Rio Grande River after spring floods. The flowing resacas on the grounds form the moats that surround most of the exhibits. These natural waterways are spanned by a maze of wooden boardwalks that, along with the splendid use of naturalistic rock work, create a stunning zoological panorama.

FEATURED EXHIBITS

Most of the large animals are organized into four geographic zones, their exhibit areas carved out by the resaca waterways. The largest continental zone is **Africa**, which covers nearly half the zoo. At the front of the zoo is an island exhibit for the zoo's signature animal and star of its logo, the gorilla. A multi-generation family of these apes enjoys a multi-level wooden playground, but interestingly, they also like playing in the shallow stream that runs through their steep moat. The oldest gorillas can be seen in a separate exhibit, where a number of windows allow visitors to get very close to these majestic elders. The zoo's famous collection of African hoofstock includes large savannas for giraffes, zebras, Arabian oryxes, bongo antelope, greater kudu antelope, and bontebok antelope. Smaller enclosures exhibit some smaller, more unusual antelope, including yellow-backed duikers and the nation's only displays of harnessed bushbuck and Jentinck's duiker antelope. Brightly colored mandrills and slender serval cats live behind wide windows in side-by-side grottoes. Africa's fiercest predators – lions and hunting dogs (or African wild dogs) – can be seen up close through windows, or from a distance along the path. The predator enclosures overlook the giraffes and sable antelope. One of the better photo ops in the zoo is at the gorgeous pygmy hippo exhibit, which features several beautiful cascading waterfalls behind its deep pools. Further down the boardwalk you'll find chimpanzees, several lemur islands, white rhinos, and camels that rest underneath a unique and interesting concrete "tree."

Visitors pass through a stone arch to enter **Indo-Australia**, which begins with islands inhabited by white-handed gibbons and a large family of orangutans. The highlight of the Indo-Australia zone is the *Australian Exhibit* building, where mouse-like kowaris, possum-like ground cuscus, Matschie's tree kangaroos, rat-like bettongs, and sugar gliders, which resemble flying squirrels, are just some of the interesting small marsupials found in picturesque glass-fronted habitats. A small, owl-like tawny frogmouth bird and a colony of bats are exhibited in nocturnal displays. More Australian birds, kookaburas and salmon-crested cockatoos, are found just outside in small aviaries. A nearby side yard houses the much larger but equally beautiful cassowaries, flightless birds that can grow up to six feet tall. Past an overlook into a grassy kangaroo yard, visitors can enter the *Indo-Australia Bird Walkabout*, a spiraling walk-through aviary with cockatiels and parakeets. For an interactive experience, purchase a seed stick to feed the birds. Saltwater crocodiles, the world's largest reptile, float in a large pool next to Philippine (also known as Mindoro) crocodiles. More Mindoro crocodiles have been born here than anywhere else outside of the Philippines.

The Gladys Porter Zoo's **Herpetarium** is well known in the zoological world. The zoo has received much acclaim for its breeding of king cobras, monitor lizards, and radiated and star tortoises. Alligators float beneath a trickling waterfall in the building's largest habitat, while unusual animals on display include marine toads, several geckos, venomous black and green mamba snakes, spitting cobras, and Aruba Island rattlesnakes. There are arachnid displays featuring spiders and scorpions at the building's entrance.

Tropical America displays a variety of South and Central American animals in seven exhibits. The two waterfowl displays, on opposite sides of a lagoon, feature loud goose-like crested screamers and three types of flamingos. An outdoor gallery features birds of prey, caracara and king vultures, in tall flight cages across from a number of adult Galapagos tortoises (their hatchlings and eggs are visible in the Herpetarium) and *Macaw Canyon*, a huge aviary for three species of these large parrots. Black and Mexican spider monkeys live on adjacent islands. A few North American animals – white-tailed deer, and a giant aviary with great horned owls and bald eagles – are scattered throughout this area.

Across from the gorillas in the entry plaza is the **Realm of the Dragon**, a cave habitat for Komodo dragons. This exhibit is beautifully landscaped with logs and several small trees in front of a red rock wall. A tall window stretches the entire length of the cave, making viewing of these monstrous lizards very easy.

The lush **Free-Flight Aviary** is tucked in a corner of Tropical America. Within this screened-in structure is a dense jungle of trees, ferns, and freely flying tropical birds in a rainbow of colors, including fairy bluebirds, green jays, scarlet ibises, roseate spoonbills, golden pheasants, and several exotic ducks. Separate aviaries display beautiful pheasant-like turacos, conure parrots, and mot-mots, which are related to kingfishers.

In the **Asia** zone, there are great views from the boardwalk bridges of large, open habitats for endangered hoofstock: Przewalski's wild horses and wild Asian gaur cattle. The pathways also circle a pair of primate islands populated by pileated gibbons and siamangs. A final island exhibits rarely seen greater adjutant storks.

OTHER EXHIBITS

Not far from the zoo's entrance are three large **Bear Grottoes**. Two exotic bears – sun bears from Asia and South American spectacled bears – inhabit these spectacular grottoes, each equipped with a cooling pool. California sea lions have a pool of their own nearby, complete with an island and a beach for basking. In a glass-fronted building across the path, the Angolan colobus monkeys and white-faced saki monkeys are easy to miss but worth checking out.

The **Aquatic Wing**, attached to the Herpetarium, is behind an outdoor koi pond. Notable displays include sea turtles from the nearby Gulf of Mexico, alligator snapping turtles and mata mata turtles, Rio Grande siren salamanders, and freshwater tanks of native Texas fish, including spotted gars and largemouth bass.

More crocodilians live in a row of swampy habitats near the gorillas. Cuban crocodiles and American alligators are exhibited here, next to a flock of flamingos. Other reptiles around the zoo include radiated tortoises from Madagascar, smooth-fronted caiman crocodiles, and critically endangered Grand Cayman blue iguanas.

A large yard across from the Herpetarium exhibits several Bengal tigers. A pair of darker Sumatran tigers, rarer than their Bengal cousins, rotates time on exhibit with the more active Bengals. Another endangered Asian species, Bornean bearded pigs, roam a muddy grotto and murky stream near bushbuck antelope.

The **Texas Aviary** is a row of open-air aviaries that display scarlet ibises, macaws, roadrunners, curassows (which resemble pheasants), endangered thick-billed parrots, and more. Surrounding these aviaries are exhibits of red brocket deer, ground hornbill birds, cranes, and storks.

FOR THE KIDS

To enter the **Small World Petting Zoo**, visitors must walk through an adobe arch that resembles the front of an old Spanish mission. Here, behind the large *Nursery* windows, catch a glimpse of baby apes, monkeys, and other newborn animals – some still in incubators. In the contact yard, kids can pet pygmy goats, while other barnyard animals such as miniature mules and sheep live in nearby pens. Three types of tiny tamarin monkeys, including rarely seen red-handed tamarins, are found in a series of open-air mesh enclosures. Other monkeys here include white-faced saki, howler, and spider. The assortment of small mammals here includes several meerkat mobs, chinchillas, guinea pigs, ferrets, Egyptian spiny mice, and Mongolian gerbils.

IN PROGRESS

At press time, the zoo plans to build a larger **Aquarium** on the site of the existing Aquatic Wing. In addition to adding larger tanks, the new facility will focus mostly on native Texan marine species. One such animal, the Kemp's Ridley sea turtle, will be featured in particular, as the zoo has done extensive conservation work for this species on both Mexican and Texan beaches. Eventually, the zoo would like to bring leopards to the zoo.

Dallas Zoo

650 South R.L. Thornton Freeway (I-35E)
Dallas, Texas 75203
(214) 946-5154
www.dallaszoo.com

Hours: 9:00 a.m.-5:00 p.m. daily. Closed Christmas Day.

Admission & Fees: Adults $8.75, seniors 65+ $5, children 3-11 $5.75. "Zoo Ranger" hand-held automated tour $6.95, monorail $2.50, carousel $2. Parking $5. Participates in reciprocity program.

Directions: Located 3 miles south of downtown. From I-35E southbound, take Exit 425C (Marsalis Avenue). Take the north

Scimitar-horned oryx lives in Wilds of Africa's desert.

service road for 0.3 miles, then turn right at the giant giraffe statue and enter the zoo parking lot. From I-30, take Exit 44B (I-35E-S) and follow directions for I-35E southbound. You can also take the DART Red Line train to the Zoo. DART riders receive a discount on zoo admission, so hold on to your train ticket!

Don't Miss: Wilds of Africa (including monorail and nature trail), Endangered Tiger Habitat, Bird, Reptile, and Amphibian Building, Wings of Wonder, Otter Outpost, Primate Place.

For Kids: Children's Zoo, Endangered Species Carousel.

Authors' Tips: Although the zoo stays open until 5:00 p.m., the last monorail ride leaves at 4:30. It is, however, best to ride the monorail early in the day, despite the bright sun in your face for half of the ride, as this is the time when the animals are most active. The monorail closes during the summer, from mid-July to the Friday before Labor Day, due to the heat. It may also close at noon on hot days throughout the year.

Edutainment: Daily events include "Keeper Encounters" with warthogs, rhinos, tigers, elephants, otters, chimps, and birds, as well as Nile crocodile feedings. Check your zoo map for show times. Training windows at the gorilla and chimpanzee habitats let visitors watch interactions between keepers and apes. Visitors can rent "Zoo Rangers" at a kiosk near Lemur Lookout. These GPS-guided hand-held video screens provide a unique tour of the zoo, narrated by a local TV news anchor. The touch-operated screens automatically play video clips upon reaching various exhibits. After the clip, a short quiz is available. The system also gives directions to the nearest bathrooms and restaurants, as well as a schedule of the day's events.

BOTH THE OLDEST AND LARGEST ZOO IN TEXAS, THE DALLAS ZOO is divided into two very different sections. **ZooNorth** is the original zoo, and several of its seventy-year-old structures are still intact. There has, however, been a major effort to replace or renovate these facilities; in fact, in the past decade, the entire ZooNorth has been renovated or recreated. The **Wilds of Africa** section, an impressive twenty-five-acre expansion, opened in 1990.

FEATURED EXHIBITS

The **Wilds of Africa** is, without question, the zoo's premier exhibit. At its entrance, African black-footed penguins swim in a glass rotunda near mandrills, which occupy a large rocky habitat where side windows allow for close-up viewing. In the mesh *Acacia Springs Aviary*, guinea fowl, lilac-breasted rollers, mousebirds, and African pygmy falcons fly among thin branches. Beyond the aviary, visitors enter an African village, where flamingos wade in a nearby lagoon. The village, which includes a café and authentic African artwork, sets the mood for the upcoming main attractions.

The only way to see most of the Wilds of Africa is by **monorail**. Cruising along at a mere three miles per hour, all seats face the animals, so everyone gets a good view. At the start of the tour, the highlight of the *Forest Habitat* is a group of elusive okapis, antelope-like relatives of giraffes, in a dense forested enclosure. There's a dramatic change in the landscape as the monorail enters the *Mountain Habitat*, where klipspringer antelope and goat-like Nubian ibexes perch on a steep slope, quite close to the riders. The *Woodland Habitat* features common eland antelope and bontebok antelope, and a herd of pygmy goats. In the *Predator-Prey Exhibit*, enclosures for caracal lynx (the predators) and tiny dik-dik antelope (the prey) lie very close to the monorail and to each other. The *River Habitat*, which represents a habitat along the Nile, is the most spectacular of the monorail exhibits. The monorail track parallels a bend in the wide, cascading river that's inhabited by waterbuck antelope, and white pelicans, Goliath herons, and other wading birds. After passing behind a double waterfall, where you'll be cooled by the mist, the terrain becomes noticeably drier at the *Desert Habitat*. Behind a row of cacti, two separate habitats exhibit scimitar-horned oryxes (a species of antelope thought to be extinct in the wild), sand gazelles, addra gazelles, and ostriches. Popular animals within the *Bush Habitat* include Grevy's zebras, slender long-necked gerenuk gazelles, Thompson's gazelles, and greater kudu and impala antelope. A huge baobab tree is the centerpiece for an enclosure housing jet-black ground hornbill birds, vultures, and scavenging marabou storks. As the track curves toward the chimpanzee habitat, look out ahead of the front car for a great view of downtown Dallas. The upcoming view of the chimpanzees, however, is even better. The height and beauty of their exhibit is best appreciated from the monorail. Finally, before the monorail rolls into the station, it passes Nile crocodiles and wattled cranes.

Although it's not as exotic as a monorail ride, the **Nature Trail** is just as impressive and provides a closer look at some of the animals you'd see from the elevated track. Like the monorail, the trail begins in the *Forest Habitat*. Okapis have a densely planted stream-filled enclosure near some eye-catching saddlebill storks. The Dallas Zoo has had tremendous success breeding both of these rain forest creatures. Up the trail, massive boulders make up a *Kopje*, where meerkats, rock hyraxes (rodent-like rock dwellers), and nimble klipspringer antelope dwell. A side path through the kopje boulders is a favorite with children and leads to a great view of the kopje birds display. Also on the trail, the *Martin Forest Aviary* is a lushly planted walk-through aviary that's home to buffalo weavers, hammerkops, rose-ringed parakeets, and other colorful African birds. The *Chimpanzee Habitat*, among the newest exhibits in the Wilds of Africa, provides its residents with a remarkably realistic rain forest home. Set on a half-acre of sloping hillside, the chimps can climb several tall trees or perch atop the rocks that surround a waterfall. Nearby, several Nile crocodiles live in a murky pool at *Crocodile Isle*. The *Hamon Gorilla Conservation Research Center* is visible from a deck overlooking the Aldabra tortoises. Two gorilla groups live in the north and south habitats, separated by the renovated interpretive and research building that re-opened in 2007. From the Research Center, visitors can look out at the densely planted hillside habitats through twenty-foot-wide windows. A chalkboard inside lists the location of individual gorillas by name on the day of your visit. A video monitor keeps the staff and visitors informed about each gorilla's activities. Each habitat can be seen from several overlooks, and through glass from inside bunker-like structures designed to keep contact minimal between humans and the sensitive gorillas, who are easily stressed by constant interaction with visitors.

Rhinoceros iguanas inhabit a rocky enclosure outside the **Bird, Reptile, and Amphibian Building**. Inside, the main hallway forks into several corridors, where most of the building's creatures reside. In the central hallway, Chinese alligators and several chameleon species can be seen. The extensive collection of reptiles includes green and black mamba snakes (both highly venomous), a number of rare vipers, Argentine racer turtles, and tuataras, a unique lizard-like reptile. Tiny mantella frogs, Vietnamese mossy frogs, and Texas blind salamanders are some of the more interesting amphibians. Two hallways show off birds, including green jays, wood partridges, and Bali mynahs. More birds live in the humid *Rainforest Aviary*, which features bright orange cock-of-the-rocks, sun bitterns, and a macaw, all under a glass-topped dome.

Sumatran tigers, which have strikingly dark coats, enjoy a long exhibit with varying elevations in the **Endangered Tiger Habitat**. At each end, viewing shelters look into a dense forest. The shelter is on one end at ground level, near a small pool that lures the tigers close. As they follow the boardwalk, visitors can peer into the exhibit through bars made of thick bamboo stalks. The spaces between the bamboo bars sometimes reveal a lurking tiger, and demonstrates just how difficult spotting a tiger in the wild can be. The final stop here is the other viewing hut, which is elevated above the tigers' valley.

Birds of prey are featured in **Wings of Wonder**. A 2007 renovation provided the large birds with new perches, taller and deeper enclosures, and larger nesting areas. Bald eagles, ornate hawk eagles, harpy eagles, spectacled owls, Andean condors, and three types of vultures (black, king and turkey) can be compared and contrasted.

The **Norsworthy Otter Outpost** is the delightful home of Asian small-clawed otters, the smallest of the world's thirteen otter species. These curious weasel relatives can be seen through glass in a deep pool, or at the bottom of the stream that runs through their bamboo-filled exhibit. When they're not exploring outside, they're usually sleeping in their den.

Primate Place is a row of tall enclosures for several species of monkeys and lesser apes. Colobus monkeys, gibbons, DeBrazza's guenon monkeys, spectacled langur monkeys, and mona monkeys can swing and climb on branches and ropes. The newest habitat here is *Tamarin Treetops*, with two small but densely planted exhibits for cotton-top and golden lion tamarin monkeys.

OTHER EXHIBITS

Bug U! is a small building for North American insects. The leaf-cutter ant exhibit is especially fascinating. A diagram describes the social structure and design of the ants' chambers. A video camera follows the colony's queen ant. Surrounding exhibits include brown recluse spiders, velvet ants, centipedes and many other native Texas invertebrates.

Three species of lemurs inhabit an island at **Lemur Lookout**, where visitors can watch the lemurs from beneath two misty trellises in the entrance plaza. Kangaroos and wallabies are exhibited in front of beautiful Aboriginal art. Perentie monitors, Australia's largest monitor lizards, live a glass-fronted sand pit near the kangaroo overlook. The Dallas Zoo is the only zoo in the Western Hemisphere to exhibit Perentie monitors and the only zoo outside Australia to breed them in captivity.

The **Large Mammal Building** is the indoor/outdoor home of African elephants and giraffes. Australian emus have a grassy yard at the back of the building. **Cat Row** features lions, snow leopards, and ocelots near the *Cat Green* picnic area. **The Hill** has gravel yards for black rhinos, llamas, double-humped Bactrian camels, red river hogs, Arabian oryxes and bongo antelope, desert bighorn sheep, cheetahs, warthogs, and cassowaries, big colorful ground-dwelling birds. Along the **Snout Route** you'll meet animals with unique noses. Odd-looking, pig-like collared peccaries (or javelinas), giant anteaters, tapirs, petite Gunther's dik-dik antelope, and crested porcupines are all visible across small moats. A wide pool at the front of ZooNorth is populated by flamingos, pelicans, and wading birds, while more exotic avians can be seen in **Bird Valley**. Red-crowned cranes, cat-like fossas, which are predators of lemurs, and Galapagos tortoises also have exhibits in ZooNorth.

FOR THE KIDS

The extensive **Lacerte Family Children's Zoo** is lots of fun for kids. At the *Farm*, miniature donkeys, ponies, and pigs all have outdoor pens arranged around a big red barn, while rabbits and guinea pigs live inside. Unusual African animals are featured in the *Underzone*. Kids can crawl into bubble windows to pop up inside exhibits for mongooses and Jackson's hornbill birds, while agama lizards and naked mole-rats dig in nearby exhibits. Kids can play animal games inside the *Discovery House*, and trade nature artifacts (shells, rocks, etc.) at the *Nature Exchange*. While interactive bird-feeding exhibits have become common in American zoos, the unique residents of *Travis and Zach's Bird Landing* set this aviary apart from similar attractions elsewhere. guira cuckoos, crowned pigeons, pheasants, and metallic-colored woodhoopoes, related to kingfishers, are just some of the many hungry species inside. Kids have the option of feeding insects or seed sticks to the birds, another unique touch. Signs in the aviary help kids match their food of choice to a specific bird species.

Children also enjoy the **Endangered Species Carousel**, by the zoo entrance.

IN PROGRESS

As we go to press, the zoo plans to open a sloth bear exhibit near one of the tiger viewing huts sometime in 2008. Plans also call for a long-awaited expansion to **Wilds of Africa** in 2009. This newly acquired area will nearly double the size of the current African exhibit, and would allow the zoo to move its largest animals into new habitats. Elephants, giraffes, and lions will be the main attractions of this twenty-acre addition, which we expect to be as stunning as the rest of the Wilds of Africa. Warthogs, rhinos, and cheetahs may also be a part of this expanded exhibit.

Fort Worth Zoo

1989 Colonial Parkway
Fort Worth, Texas 76110
(817) 759-7555
www.fortworthzoo.com

Roseate spoonbills inhabit Texas Wild!'s Gulf Coast.

Hours: 10:00 a.m.-5:00 p.m. weekdays April-October, open until 6:00 p.m. on weekends; 10:00 a.m.-5:00 p.m. daily in spring, 10:00 a.m.-4:00 p.m. daily in fall and winter.

Admission & Fees: Adults $10.50, seniors 65+ $7, children 3-12 $8. Admission is half-price on Wednesdays. Yellow Rose Train: one way $2, all day pass $3, Country Carousel $2, Parrot Paradise $1, Tasmanian Tower $5. Parking $5.

Directions: From I-30, take Exit 12A (Forest Park Zoo/Texas Christian/University Drive) South. Follow University Drive for 0.9 miles to Forest Park, turn left onto Colonial Parkway, and follow for 0.4 miles into zoo parking lot.

Don't Miss: Texas Wild!, World of Primates, Asian Falls, African Savanna, Herpetarium, Raptor Canyon.

For Kids: Parrot Paradise, Play Barn, Yellow Rose train, Country Carousel, Tasmanian Tower.

Authors' Tips: The front portion of the zoo can be a bit confusing to navigate. The easiest way to tour the zoo, without doubling back, is to begin with the World of Primates building. The path leads past all the back outdoor yards, the African animals, and eventually, the outdoor gorilla habitat. Continue on to the meerkats and giraffes, then turn back towards the elephants and Asia. This trail passes all the other major exhibits, finishing in the back of the zoo at Texas Wild!

Edutainment: Texas Wild! has more than just animals. The Hall of Wonders is a natural history museum, where attractions include a theater that presents a unique film showcasing the ever-changing weather in Texas. Another theater, at the tail end of your journey, summarizes the major themes of the exhibit. Colorful narration for both films is provided by animated animal characters.

OPENED IN 1909, THE FORT WORTH ZOO HAS A LONG HISTORY IN north central Texas. While the city of Fort Worth is often overshadowed by neighboring Dallas, its zoo consistently receives more praise. This was not always the case, however. In 1991, the American Zoological Association assumed management of the facility's daily operations, and the zoo temporarily closed down to construct new exhibits. Since then, with its funding restored, the zoo has opened eleven significant new exhibits. Recently, the Fort Worth Zoo solidified its reputation for excellence when it was named the number one attraction in the metropolitan area by a recent *Zagat Survey* travel guide.

FEATURED EXHIBITS

They say everything is bigger in Texas, and **Texas Wild!** is no exception. Spread across more than six acres, the exhibit is part amusement park, part zoo, and part museum. The zoo portion re-creates six of the Lone Star State's major ecosystems. The *Hill Country* of Central Texas begins with a small stream that's home to turtles and Guadeloupe bass. A nearby eerie cemetery where fake vultures perch atop gravestones welcomes visitors to an authentic nineteenth-century *Texas Town*. The long row of Old West buildings includes a post office, jail, ice cream parlor, and general store. A restaurant at the end of the street has a second floor hotel balcony where a relaxing cowboy props his feet up. Texas longhorn cattle and quarter horses live in pens just behind the hotel. *High Plains and Prairies*, found in the state's Panhandle region, is home to white-tailed deer, sandhill cranes, and wild turkeys, in a grassy yard beyond a stream. Black-tailed prairie dogs, burrowing owls, swift foxes, and black-footed ferrets are displayed in a shack that appears to have been struck by a tornado. From there, the path leads to the *Pineywoods and Swamps*, where alligators and otters swim in side-by-side crystal clear streams. Red wolves can be seen from within a visitor shelter, but spotting them in their deep, dense forest may be a challenge. Another long window looks out at black bears, whose grassy habitat is divided by another stream. Bubble windows extend into the otter and bear exhibits to bring kids closer to these fascinating creatures. At the *Gulf Coast*, an old bait shack exhibits redfish, gulf killfish, a sea turtle, and a touch pool with a rotating cast of characters. Outside, at the marina, roseate spoonbills often perch on a tugboat. You can watch white and brown pelicans from the surrounding dock. Dangerous predators, all originally indigenous to Texas though some have not been seen in the wild here for decades, are found in *Brush Country*. Jaguars, coyotes, coatis, bald eagles, bobcats, ocelots, and cougars are found in net-enclosed habitats that resemble the rugged Spanish mission areas of southern Texas. A walk-through aviary that includes a falconry wing with rare aplomado falcons is just up the path. Finally, a cool breeze greets visitors as they enter the *Mountains and Deserts* mine shaft. Texas horned lizards (often mistakenly called "horned frogs" or "horned toads"), the mascot of nearby Texas Christian University, and other small creatures are found along the dark cave walls. Every corner reveals a surprise; one turn reveals an angry rattlesnake! Texas leaf-cutter and fiery red ant colonies are fun to watch, as are dozens of fluttering fruit bats. Insect wall inhabitants include dung beetles and millipedes. Small aquatic exhibits display Pecos pupfish, turtles, black-spotted newts, and an indigo snake. In one last corner of this damp cave, there are several spider species, including jumping, black widow, and brown recluse spiders.

The **World of Primates** is, at press time, the only place in the U.S. where you can see all four great ape species: gorillas, chimpanzees, bonobos, and orangutans. The highlight of this 2½-acre facility is an indoor tropical rain forest, the gorillas' main habitat. Under a triangular glass roof, this lush jungle includes tall palm trees and man-made buttress trees. The gorillas' tri-level home is separated from visitors by a wide moat fed by four loud, crashing waterfalls. Colorful African birds, including weaver birds and brilliant blue rollers, fly freely throughout the exhibit. Windows allow the chimps, bonobos (also known as pygmy chimps), and orangutans to be seen at close range in their rocky indoor habitats, while a colobus monkey troop is displayed behind harp wire. Outside, an elevated boardwalk encircles the building, passing by grassy island habitats for each of the great apes, gibbons (lesser apes), and brightly colored mandrills. These lush islands are separated by cascading streams and waterfalls.

Asian Falls offers a panoramic stroll past many of Asia's largest animals. Adult bull elephants and a herd of females reside in separate quarters in this 3½-acre complex. *Asian Rhino Ridge*, which features greater one-horned rhinos, is up the boardwalk. A visitor bridge passes above the rhinos, who can often be found in their deep pool. Visitors can get closer by following a set of stairs down to a ground level viewing area, which also allows for peeks into the back of the elephant yard. Higher on the hill, there are yards for sarus cranes, muntjac deer, wild lowland anoa cattle, and a small aviary for birds of paradise. A deep canyon with a forty-foot waterfall divides two lush yards for tigers. One side has a pair of white Bengal tigers, best seen through a window. The other side features Malaysian tigers across a wide overlook. Sun bears, the smallest bear species, live in a similar densely planted ravine, at the end of your tour.

Raptor Canyon brings visitors close to powerful birds of prey. Next to a pair of Andean condors, king vultures share their rocky cliff habitat with magpie jays. Milky eagle owls enjoy a tall, forested home. The last two exhibits are specially designed to give their occupants full flight opportunities. Impressive South American harpy eagles and bateleur eagles from Africa can fly from one side of their habitat to the other, right over the guest walkway.

With over 600 reptiles and amphibians of more than 160 different varieties, Fort Worth's **Herpetarium** is one of the nation's largest reptile houses. The collection is world famous, not only for its size and variety, but also for its breeding success with rare and endangered species. A special panel invites visitors to push a button to guess whether exhibited snakes are venomous or harmless. Impressed tortoises, crocodile newts, and Puerto Rican crested toads are just a few of the exceedingly rare animals found here. The collection is arranged geographically, covering Eurasia, Africa, Australasia, Tropical America, and North America. A separate nursery gallery exhibits the newest reptile babies. Outside, gharial crocodiles float in a large pool next to Komodo dragons and Philippine crocodiles.

Like most of the zoo's large animal exhibits, the **African Savanna** yards are fronted by beautiful winding streams. Ever-active meerkats dig in a dirt-filled enclosure behind a waist-high glass wall. Both white and black rhinos live in large, shaded yards. A wooden deck is positioned over the stream to allow visitors a closer look at giraffes and African land birds. At the trail's end, hippos can be found in a deep pool, across from the giraffes. Cheetahs, warthogs, and bongo antelope are also part of this exhibit, but can only be seen from the World of Primates outdoor boardwalk mentioned earlier.

OTHER EXHIBITS

More animals from the African plains inhabit the **African Diorama**, a pair of unique split-level exhibits. Zebras and warthogs share a large yard in front of watchful lions, who lurk above them. A similar set-up displays lesser kudu antelope and long-necked gerenuk gazelles in a lower paddock, with another rocky grotto of lions up behind them. Another trail that bisects these predator/prey exhibits provides a closer view of the lions, Nubian ibexes in a steep cliff habitat, and Galapagos tortoises.

Kangaroos and wallabies hop through an open yard in the **Australian Outback**. An adjacent building features marine life from the **Great Barrier Reef**. Three types of sharks, forty-five fish species, thirty kinds of corals and eight invertebrates are found in the building's three saltwater tanks.

Flamingo Bay exhibits two species of these pink birds in separate lagoons divided by a visitor walkway. Few zoos offer such a close look at beautiful flamingos. Near Raptor Canyon, macaw parrots, tamarin monkeys, toucans, waterfowl in two ponds, cranes, and other birds inhabit a set of aviaries.

FOR THE KIDS

Texas Wild! offers several kid-friendly activities. The *Play Barn* is a bi-level playground for kids to explore. While playing here, kids will encounter baby chicks and mice, and learn about farming in Texas. The small *Petting Yard* has pens for pigs, cows and goats, and armadillos, all available for petting. The **Yellow Rose Train** travels to and from the front of the zoo, while the **Country Carousel** is a cowboy-themed merry-go-round.

The boardwalk in **Parrot Paradise** surrounds a rock outcropping, with trees and a shallow pool. Hundreds of small parakeets and cockatiels fly around visitors in the large net dome. The birds can be fed for an additional fee.

Just outside the Great Barrier Reef is a twenty-five-foot-high rock climbing wall called **Tasmanian Tower**. There is an aquatic-themed sand playground nearby.

IN PROGRESS

Coinciding with the zoo's centennial anniversary in 2009, Fort Worth is scheduled to open the **Museum of Living Art** (MOLA for short), a new herpetarium, as we go to press. This major project will house around 900 scaly creatures and enhance the zoo's already stellar reputation for reptilians. The building will be surrounded by outdoor spaces for Aldabra tortoises, Komodo dragons, gharial crocodiles, and saltwater crocodiles. State-of-the-art temperature controls and larger exhibits will allow the zoo to expand its breeding programs, and resulting babies will be showcased in a nursery. New animals will be added, including king cobras, Chinese giant salamanders, gliding frogs, and crocodile lizards. Outside the building, an outdoor courtyard will feature South American jungle animals, an insect gallery, and a new food court. Long windows in the dining area will look into the gharial and saltwater crocodile habitats.

Houston Zoo

1513 North MacGregor Drive
Houston, Texas 77030
(713) 533-6500
www.houstonzoo.org

Hours: 9:00 a.m-7:00 p.m. daily during Daylight Savings Time, last ticket sold at 6:00 p.m.; 9:00 a.m.-6:00 p.m. daily, rest of year, last ticket sold at 5:00 p.m. Children's Zoo and carousel close 30 minutes before the rest of the zoo. Closed Christmas Day.

Archerfish is one of 100-plus species in Kipp Aquarium.

Admission & Fees: Adults $10, seniors 65+ $5.75, children 2-11 $5. Family package $35 (admission for two adults and two children, four carousel tokens, souvenir guide book). Carousel $2/two tokens.

Directions: From South Freeway (TX-288), take the Texas Medical Center/MacGregor Way exit. Follow for 0.2 miles on North MacGregor Way, then stay right on Hermann Loop Drive for 0.6 miles. Turn right onto North MacGregor Drive and follow for 0.4 miles to the zoo, on the left. From I-45, take Exit 46B (TX-288 S/Lake Jackson), get on TX-288 South and follow above directions. From I-10 eastbound, take Exit 768B on the left, merge onto I-45 South and follow above directions. From I-10 westbound, take Exit 770A on the left, get on US-59 South and follow for 3.1 miles. Take the exit for TX-288 S/Lake Jackson/Freeport, get on TX-288 south and follow above directions. The zoo can also be reached via the METRORail train system and Metro bus system. The Hermann Park/Rice University and Memorial Hermann Hospital/Houston Zoo Stations serve the zoo. Save your METRORail ticket for $1 off zoo admission.

Don't Miss: Natural Encounters, Koala Crossing, World of Primates, Asian Elephant Habitat, Carnivore Country, Reptile and Amphibian Building, Tropical Bird House, Aquarium.

For Kids: Children's Zoo, wildlife carousel.

Authors' Tips: Admission to the zoo is free on five holidays: Martin Luther King Day, Memorial Day, Independence Day, Labor Day, and the Friday after Thanksgiving. Technologically savvy visitors can download a series of podcasts off the zoo's website or iTunes. The informative podcasts give details about some of the zoo's exhibits and most popular animals.

Edutainment: This zoo has an extensive animal encounter program. There are events around the zoo every half hour from 10:00 a.m. to 4:00 p.m. One of the country's only public piranha feedings is popular with visitors, as are the big cat training sessions. Other feedings and chats feature babirusa pigs, sea lions, margay cats, pelicans, and koalas. Times and shows change daily, so check your zoo map or a kiosk just inside the zoo entrance for the current roster.

FOUNDED IN 1922, THE HOUSTON ZOO IS LOCATED JUST SOUTH OF downtown in Hermann Park, adjacent to Rice University. It's surprising to many that Houston is the nation's fourth largest city. Less surprisingly, given this, the zoo's annual attendance figures are among the top ten in the nation. With over 4,500 animals of more than 800 species, the Houston Zoo has one of the most diverse collections in the country. There are several defining architectural features on the beautiful grounds, the best of which is a picturesque reflecting pool surrounded by benches and gardens. This tranquil area, wonderful for a relaxing break from walking the fifty-five-acre zoo, runs directly down the middle of the zoo, just behind the entrance plaza.

FEATURED EXHIBITS

Relaxing music sets the mood in **Carruth Natural Encounters,** which was named "Exhibit of the Year" in 2007 by the AZA. Fourteen distinct habitats, many of them with combinations of species not seen elsewhere, are found in and around the building. Just inside, a chalkboard lists the day's events, near a crashing waterfall where fish and turtles swim in a pool beneath. From a dry rocky streambed, Asian small-clawed otters can run and dive into a deep glass-fronted pool. Agoutis, small guinea pig-like rodents, scurry across the ground in an indoor rain forest while sloths, tamarin monkeys, doves, pheasant-like turacos, and green toucan-like aracari birds inhabit the trees above. Straw-colored fruit bats and tarantulas live nearby in a darkened cave. Undoubtedly, the most interesting and popular spot here is the glass-fronted piranha pool. Courageous kids (or anyone small enough to fit) can crawl through a clear acrylic tunnel that passes directly beneath these carnivorous fish. Freshwater stingrays, pacu fish, and electric eels swim in neighboring pools, but the upcoming desert draws even more attention. Antelope ground squirrels seem to be constantly on the move, in contrast to the vulturine guinea fowl, springhaas (rabbit-like rodents), and rock hyraxes, small rodent-like desert creatures from Africa. Three sets of underground tunnel displays exhibit honey ants, naked mole-rats, and large Damara mole-rats. A small stage, built to resemble a house's front porch, is used for animal demonstrations. Just beyond the porch are clownfish and other reef fish swimming in a brightly lit semicircular tank. One of the nation's best meerkat exhibits is directly outside, with plenty of views of these dynamic mongoose relatives in an ultra-long, glass-fronted, dirt-filled habitat. Also outside is a tropical rain forest home to more tamarin monkeys, birds, and sail-fin lizards. The animals are rotated in and out of this jungle exhibit several times a day, so every visit may reveal a new animal.

Koala Crossing, near Natural Encounters' exit, is a long habitat for Queensland koalas, where the glass wall slants inward for a closer view. In 2000, a joey (baby koala) was born here, making the Houston Zoo, at press time, one of only ten zoos worldwide to successfully breed koalas.

Set in the heart of the zoo, **Wortham World of Primates** shows off primates from around the world. Madagascar's ecosystem is re-created with a lush island inhabited by ring-tailed lemurs. Nimble sifaka lemurs were added in 2007, in a habitat equipped for their high-energy ways – they love to leap from tree to tree. The boardwalk path rises slowly as it passes net enclosures of South American tamarin monkeys, marmoset monkeys, and howler monkeys. In the African section, another island enclosure exhibits termite-eating patas monkeys. Baboon-like mandrills and DeBrazza's guenon monkeys dwell together among dense palm trees across from red-capped mangabey monkeys. As the boardwalk reaches treetop level, the tall mesh enclosures curve around two gazebos that visitors can enter for views into these exhibits. A final African enclosure displays red-tailed guenon monkeys and Allen's swamp monkeys. The Asian trek begins with long-armed siamangs. Though not primates, the babirusa pigs are a popular addition to the path. The largest (and final) exhibit is an orangutan island. These intelligent red apes are visible from an overlook, or from much closer through glass.

The star of the **McNair Asian Elephant Habitat** is Mac, the largest elephant calf ever born in captivity. Born in October 2006 at 384 pounds, Mac lives with his mom Shanti, and a couple of other elephants in an exhibit that's currently in the midst of expansion (see below), to give more space to the creatures (they will remain on exhibit during construction). A breeding herd of Masai giraffes, the tallest and darkest of the nine giraffe species, is exhibited nearby.

Carnivore Country occupies a large central portion of the zoo. The featured habitats include two large grottoes for Malayan tigers and African lions. Both can be viewed across a wide stream or through glass along a path between the two cat habitats. Small mesh enclosures in front of the habitats have been installed to accommodate public training sessions with the big cats. A stairway leads down to underground windows that look out across the lions' rocky outcropping. Behind the tigers, a row of tall, densely planted cages displays more felines; most interesting are the ocelots and margays, both small to mid-size spotted cats. Clouded leopards and a cat-like fossa, actually a mongoose relative, are also displayed. Just around the corner are canyon habitats for cougars and a jaguar, both visible behind glass. Opposite the felines are two bear species. Grizzly bears have a deep pool to wade in under a light canopy. Spectacled bears dwell on a grassy bluff, with trees to climb near a cascading waterfall. African wild dogs live behind the lions.

A leucistic alligator (white, but not albino – leucistic animals have colored rather than red eyes) is the featured animal at the **Reptile and Amphibian House**. The 'gator basks under cypress moss in the building's centerpiece exhibit, visible from both sides of the surrounding rectangular path. Rhinoceros vipers, black mamba snakes, African rock pythons, anacondas, rattlesnakes, and several newt species are just a few of the more than 150 animals inhabiting over eighty displays. Outside, two rain forest-esque exhibits hold crocodile monitor lizards and Komodo dragons.

The small, round **Kipp Aquarium** displays over a hundred species of fish in beautiful salt- and freshwater aquatic habitats. Among the best exhibits are a large circular reef tank for nurse sharks and an Amazon flooded forest with more piranhas. Other distinctive displays include moon jellyfish, sea turtles, rockfish and lionfish sharing a poisonous fish tank, seahorses, an octopus, several chambered nautiluses, and fishes from the Indian Ocean. A trio of tanks showcases different levels of an Australian coral reef.

The best of the zoo's many beautiful bird exhibits is the **Tropical Bird House**. Over a hundred colorful exotic birds live in naturalistic habitats in two galleries enhanced with background murals. You'll see various kingfishers, finches, and other vividly tinted birds, but the main attraction is the iridescent golden-headed quetzal, the national symbol of Guatemala. Houston is one of only a few zoos to display these stunning birds and at press time, the only one to successfully breed them. Between the galleries, visitors cross a wooden suspension bridge that leads into a lush jungle room, where, along with other avians, luminous orange cock-of-the-rocks fly among reproductions of ancient Mayan ruins.

OTHER EXHIBITS

Two wide decks overlook the **sea lion** pool, directly inside the zoo entrance. Keeper chats and shows are conducted here every day, so this blue tarp-covered pool is generally a hot spot.

Most of the zoo's bird collection lives in outdoor aviaries surrounding the Tropical Bird House. In a grove of banana trees, the **Fisher Bird Garden** includes seventeen aviaries and is home to king vultures, great hornbills, and crowned pigeons. The fascinating collection in the **Birds of the World** aviaries includes pheasants and pheasant-like birds such as curassows as well as the largest collection of colorful turacos in the nation. Don't miss the Attwater's prairie chickens, a colorful native Texas bird that is, at press time, displayed in only two zoos in the nation, both in Texas. Other bird exhibits include a lush flamingo pool, four tall cages of macaws, and **Duck Lake**, with rare Hawaiian Nene geese.

On opposite sides of the zoo are rows of large, fenced paddocks that exhibit a variety of hoofed animals. Okapis, rare forest-dwelling relatives of giraffes, are the feature species at the south side, and are joined by bongo antelope, yellow-backed duiker antelope, warthogs, and a mixed-species South American exhibit that includes giant anteaters, maned wolves, and lowland tapirs. Across the path, at the end of the row, are Ankole cattle. The huge horns on these African natives make those of a Texas longhorn look tame. The northern enclosures have the some of the tallest and smallest antelope species in the world. Giant elands share space with tiny dik-diks, as nyalas and blue duikers graze next door.

FOR THE KIDS

The **McGovern Children's Zoo** takes kids from Houston to the far reaches of Texas ecosystems. It all begins in the *City*, with metal sculptures in a garden maze. A water play park mimics the impressive fountain in Hermann Park. White-tailed deer, turkeys, porcupines, pheasant-like chachalaca birds, owls, and raccoon-like coatis are all displayed along a rising boardwalk in the *Forest*. At the top of the path is a walk-through aviary with local birds, and overlooks of raccoons and bald eagles. The trail descends to the *Coast*, where river otters swim in pools in a swamp setting. You'll hear the pelicans and gulls before you see them; these two common avian Gulf residents relax on a marina dock. In an adjacent building there are tanks with seahorses and ocean fish, as well as a small touch pool with an assortment of sea creatures. Back outside, circular windows let you peer into a bog filled with alligators. In the *Prairie*, three capsule-shaped bubble windows let kids pop up in the prairie dog habitat. Surrounding canyon walls serve to divide exhibits for roadrunners, swift foxes, and a cave of bats in the *Desert*. Finally, geese, llamas, and donkeys explore dusty pens in the *Farm*, and goats and sheep are available for petting. Several themed playgrounds are fun for kids to explore.

There's a **wildlife carousel** just outside the Children's Zoo. Temporary exhibits are housed in the **Brown Education Center**, and six cameras show live video from the exhibits and animal demonstrations in Natural Encounters.

IN PROGRESS

At press time, the Houston Zoo estimates that the Elephant Habitat will be under construction until 2009. When completed, its exhibit space will expand six-fold and occupy the entire southeastern corner of the zoo. In the first stage, they'll add a third yard and increase the size of the existing two yards. Work has begun on the new elephant barn, which will include a glass viewing area so visitors can watch the pachyderms when they are inside.

M'Kubwa, an Eastern lowland gorilla who lived to be fifty-one years old, was a Houston icon during his nineteen-year stay at the zoo. In 2009, five years after his death, the zoo plans to bring back apes as part of a new **African Forest**. The ambitious project, which will encompass thirteen acres, will open in several phases. The first phase will feature a chimpanzee troop and a new giraffe yard. Further phases will add okapis, bongo antelope, gorillas, leopards, red river hogs, underwater views of hippos and Nile crocodiles, and a huge walk-through aviary.

San Antonio Zoo & Aquarium

3903 North St. Mary's Street
San Antonio, Texas 78212
(512) 734-7184
www.sazoo-aq.org

Hours: 9:00 a.m.-6:00 p.m. daily, Memorial Day-Labor Day, grounds open until 8:00 p.m.; 9:00 a.m.-5:00 p.m. daily, rest of year, grounds open to 6:00 p.m.

Admission & Fees: Adults $9, seniors 62+ and children 3-11 $7, handicapped: adults 15+ $6, children 3-14 $4.50; military $1 discount. Brackenridge Eagle train: adults $2.75, children $2.25; Butterflies! $1, lory nectar $1.

Directions: From I-35, take Exit 158A and merge onto US-281 North. Follow US-281 for 1.3 miles, then take the St. Mary's Street exit. Follow St. Mary's Street for 1 mile to zoo, on the right. From I-10, proceed until it merges with I-35 in

Capybara in Amazonia Rain Forest.

central San Antonio, then follow above directions. From I-37, proceed until it becomes US-281 North, then follow above directions.

Don't Miss: Africa Live!, African Rift Valley and Plains, Amazonia Rain Forest, Tropical Bird House, Gibbon Forest, Cats of the World, Cranes of the World, Komodo dragons.

For Kids: Tiny Tot Nature Spot, Lory Landing, Fun Farm Petting Zoo, Brackenridge Eagle train.

Authors' Tips: The Ice Cream Deck in Tiny Tot Nature Spot is a great place to cool off with a cone while watching the flamingos. Bring along swimsuits for kids; the Riverbank (see below) is a fun "wet" area that kids won't want to miss.

Edutainment: "Keeper and Education Connections" is a program that provides information about animals. There's a wide variety of choices throughout the day, many in Tiny Tot Nature Spot. These informal chats, listed on the zoo map, feature a variety of animals, including bears, gibbons, elephants, snakes, okapis, and capybaras.

HOME OF THE ALAMO, RIVER WALK, SPANISH MISSIONS, AND several renowned theme parks, San Antonio has long been a major family vacation destination. The San Antonio Zoo is part of the city's history. It opened in 1914 at an enviable location near the headwaters of the San Antonio River. Built in an abandoned rock quarry that once supplied the limestone for the Alamo, many exhibits are backed by spectacular rocky cliffs. The grounds also include refreshing waterways, shaded by towering oak, pecan, and cypress trees.

FEATURED EXHIBITS

Africa Live! brings two of the continent's largest semi-aquatic animals up close for observation. Under a crashing waterfall, the path leads into a cave, where underwater viewing of hippos and Nile crocodiles awaits. In a replica of the Semliki River of central Africa, both animals are displayed in deep streams. As you wind through the cave, you'll encounter many smaller animals as well. The deadly snakes – including green mambas, African rock pythons, and rhinoceros and gaboon vipers, – are all marked with eye-catching, mesmerizing patterns and colors. Elephant shrews, dwarf crocodiles, bullfrogs, African cichlid fish, lungfish, dung beetles, and scorpions are also featured. Outside, *Nanyuki Market* resembles its African namesake.

The zoo's collection of African animals is quite extensive. In addition to the hippos, two nearby exhibits showcase animals from Africa. The **Rift Valley Tract** is a multi-level habitat, best seen from *Treetop Lookout,* an observation deck at the exhibit's highest point. To get there, visitors climb through a large mesh aviary inhabited by more than a dozen species of birds. Near the overlook, aardvarks and crested porcupines rest in small grottoes. After the panoramic view from this lookout, the path leads to black-footed cats and a sloping hillside home for cheetahs. The cheetahs are visible again from a bridge, from which you can also see white rhinos. Black rhinos, which tend to be more aggressive, are displayed next, in several yards. A smaller **African Plains** exhibit is further down the trail. Giraffes, Grevy's zebras, topi antelope, ostriches, crowned cranes, and marabou storks inhabit an arid savanna enhanced by sporadic foliage. Nearby is a small aviary for crowned hornbill birds, an elephant exhibit, and another grotto with aardwolves, rarely exhibited hyena-like insectivores from eastern and southern Africa.

South America is also well represented here, particularly in the **Amazonia Rain Forest**. For the best experience, we recommend you enter the cave along the main path for a close encounter with a fearsome jaguar. The cave exits into a spacious flight cage, where turtles and fish swim in a stream below trees filled with scarlet ibises, green oropendolas, and other colorful birds, and a giant anteater rambles along the shoreline. From here, you can cross the bridge to a nocturnal exhibit that displays short-tailed fruit bats, sloths, and owl monkeys in dark enclosures. Just outside is a small pool for dwarf caiman crocodiles, and enclosures for saki monkeys, spotted ocelot cats, and a troop of spider monkeys. Another giant flight cage houses a pair of Andean condors, the world's largest flying birds. An impressive collection of small monkeys, including three tamarin species (golden lion, cotton-top, and pied), inhabits a set of wire enclosures around a flooded forest habitat that's home to a green anaconda snake. Finally, Maguiri storks and capybaras share a stream habitat, where the huge aquatic rodents can show off their excellent swimming abilities.

San Antonio has one of the largest and most diverse bird collections in the country. Many of these birds call the **Hixon Tropical Birdhouse** home. Inside, a ring of natural habitats, backed by colorful murals, re-create bird environments from around the world. Terns and plovers wade in a shoreline setting, barbets and weaver birds perch near an African hut, and tawny frogmouths and other Australian birds rest in a eucalyptus forest. Other rare and colorful birds here include Guam kingfishers, and quetzal birds, the national symbol of Guatemala. Over a dozen other birds have free flying rights in the building, though they generally stay in the central forest.

Gibbon Forest is a unique mixed-species exhibit, where a lush jungle has been created in front of the sand-colored rock quarry cliffs. Ropes and branches span the higher reaches of this tall net enclosure, giving the acrobatic gibbons plenty of options for swinging. At ground level, a rock wall splits the habitat into two sections. While the gibbons have access to the entire exhibit, small muntjac deer live in the brush on one side, and the other is home to Asian small-clawed otters. The otters can swim in a small pond close to the viewing area.

Cats of the World takes visitors into an artificial cave populated by exotic felines, including fishing cats, clouded leopards, and snow leopards. Cat-like fossas, actually closely related to mongooses, are also shown here. Also seen from windows in this cave are black-and-white ruffed lemurs (usually on an island) and red ruffed lemurs in another nearby exhibit.

Cranes of the World houses just a small sample of the many cranes at this zoo. Across shallow ponds, four species are visible: blue, Manchurian (or red-crowned), hooded, and whooping cranes, the largest and one of the rarest crane species.

The **Komodo dragons** have both a glass-fronted outdoor habitat and an indoor space in a covered hut next to Gibbon Forest. In an exciting development for this zoo, baby dragons hatched here in 2007. A separate room in the hut is home to another large reptile, a reticulated python.

OTHER EXHIBITS

In the zoo's entrance area, you'll see a wide variety of animals in both indoor and outdoor exhibits. A large flock of Caribbean flamingos lives right inside the entrance gate. Four species of bears, black, grizzly, Asian black, and spectacled, inhabit a curving row of enclosures called the **Bear Grottoes**. On the other side of Gibbon Forest is a spacious habitat for endangered François' langur monkeys from Vietnam. In the middle courtyard is the first of two popular buildings, the **Aquarium**, which has a nice collection of saltwater and freshwater fish. Animals displayed here include seahorses, electric eels, archerfish, rare Rift Valley cichlid fish, and piranhas and other Amazon fish. In the **Reptile House**, visitors can see a wide variety of snakes, frogs, and turtles, and a fine collection of vipers from all over the world. In **Butterflies!**, hundreds of winged wonders fly through a structure that was rebuilt after a tree collapsed on it in 2005. In a row of older cages, several intriguing primates are displayed, including gibbons and Wolf's guenon, colobus, and golden-bellied mangabey monkeys.

The rest of the extensive bird collection is distributed throughout the zoo. A row of grassy yards surrounded by moats hold larger birds, including several stork species, crowned cranes, bald eagles, flamingos, and a few non-birds: American alligators, Orinoco crocodiles, and false gharial crocodiles. Other outdoor aviaries display owls, hornbill birds, macaws, and some beautiful birds you've probably never seen before. A set of side aviaries is designated for stunning birds of paradise. The **Wetlands** section, which includes more alligators, is closed in September during egret breeding season, when hundreds of egrets invade the zoo and create quite a mess! From above and below water, visitors can watch river otters swim near the bird aviaries.

This zoo has always had a fine collection of **hoofed animals**. More African animals, including warthogs, spiral-horned addax antelope, addra gazelles, yellow-backed duiker antelope, goat-like Nubian ibexes, and an exotic okapi, a forest-dwelling giraffe relative, are all exhibited near the African exhibits described above. Nearby, bush dogs (small South American canines), Arabian sand gazelles, and muntjac deer represent other continents. Sumatran tigers, lions, and spotted hyenas live in large adjacent exhibits along the same loop. Two Australian icons, kangaroos and emus, live in a very realistic habitat with red dirt and shrubs: it's strikingly similar to the landscape of Australia's Red Center. Two types of wallabies, colorful flightless cassowary birds, and another bird aviary represent more Australasian wildlife.

FOR THE KIDS

Kronkosky's Tiny Tot Nature Spot is the first children's zoo specifically designed for kids under five. Within its seven major areas, however, kids of any age (and adults) are likely to have fun. Children have their own entrance, where they hop on stone lily pads across a stream that runs beneath a low trellis. From there, they can explore *Tropical Waters,* a pair of caves with tanks of giant Amazon fish, or go to *My Backyard,* a small barnyard with goats, sheep, and other domestic animals available for petting. Inevitably, kids spend the most time in the *Discovery House,* partly due to its air conditioning! Inside are three distinct sections, starting with a *Pond,* where kids can enter a giant "aquarium" or go fishing in a stream for magnetic toy fish. In the next room, children learn all about being on the *Zoo Staff.* They can dress up like zookeepers, prepare animal food, or even pretend to be veterinarians. Naked mole-rats and prairie dogs live in the *Underground Room,* where worms and roots dangle from the walls. Outside, near the *Campground* tents, two tropical habitats exhibit raccoon-like coatimundis and squirrel monkeys. The most exciting area for kids, though, is the *Riverbank,* a huge curving shallow stream that invites any and all to jump in and get wet. Parents can watch comfortably from a shaded sandy beach. Finally you'll come to a lagoon for flamingos, which are fed daily in mid-afternoon.

Lory Landing, open 10:00 a.m.-4:00 p.m. daily, is a wonderful opportunity for kids to interact with colorful parrots. From a wooden ramp, kids can watch several species of lorikeets and lories. Cups of nectar to feed the birds can be purchased at the

Hungry Hippo concession stand just outside the zoo, near the parking lot, you'll find the terminal of the **Brackenridge Eagle**, three miniature trains that journey through Brackenridge Park (home to the zoo), skirting the banks of the San Antonio River.

IN PROGRESS

The hippo and crocodile habitats are one part of Africa Live! Construction has already begun on a rain forest section, which will feature okapis and small duiker antelope, as well as multiple net enclosures for birds, colobus monkeys, aardwolves, and leopards. Eventually, a café and amphitheater will look out onto a savanna where gazelles will intermingle with both white and black rhinos, near side exhibits of African wild dogs and meerkats. The elephant exhibit may also be expanded in the future.

Caldwell Zoo

2203 Martin Luther King Boulevard
Tyler, Texas 75702
(903) 534-2169
www.caldwellzoo.com

Hours: 9:00 a.m.-5:00 p.m. daily March -Labor Day, exhibits open to 6:00 p.m.; 9:00 a.m.-4:00 p.m. daily, rest of year, exhibits close at 4:30 p.m. Closed Thanksgiving, Christmas, and New Years Day.

Admission & Fees: Adults $8.50, seniors 55+ $7.25, children 3-12 $5. Seed stick for Wild Bird Walkabout $1.

Directions: From I-20 eastbound, take Exit 556 South (US-69/Tyler/Lindale), follow for 8 miles, and turn left onto Martin Luther King Boulevard; zoo is immediately ahead on the left. From I-20 westbound, take Exit 571A South (US-271/Tyler), and follow for 10.8 miles. Turn right onto East Martin Luther King Boulevard. Follow Martin Luther King Boulevard for 2.2 miles: zoo is on the left.

Don't Miss: East Africa, Native Texas habitats, entry plaza islands.

For Kids: Wild Bird Walkabout, Petting Pen.

East African crowned crane

Authors' Tips: In addition to enjoying the wonderful views from the African-themed Chakula Café, take time to sit outside in a rocking chair in the entry plaza. From these comfy wooden rockers, relaxing patrons can observe the entry plaza islands. See South America first, then enter East Africa near the cheetahs. After you check out the giraffes and elephants, head down to the lemurs and toward the lions. The path then loops past the rest of the African animals, into Texas, and finally back to the front entrance.

Edutainment: Penguin feedings are held daily at the African Reptile/Aquarium building.

LOCATED ABOUT AN HOUR EAST OF DALLAS, THE CALDWELL ZOO provides diversion for families traveling across northern Texas. It is inexpensive, compact, and exhibits a wide variety of exotic animals in beautiful naturalistic habitats. The animals are arranged into three continental regions. Upon entering the zoo, visitors start along any of the three paths that lead to Native Texas, East Africa, and South America.

This zoo is a testament to the generosity, vision, and dedication of D. K. Caldwell, who opened the facility in 1954 for the children of the Caldwell Playschool and all of East Texas. Owned and operated by the Caldwell Foundation, the zoo is designed especially for children and was open free of charge for more than forty years. Admission prices were finally implemented in 2003 to help offset growing expenses and to facilitate expansion plans. The admission cost is still quite low in comparison to other zoos, and the zoo is well worth the price.

FEATURED EXHIBITS

The largest and most impressive exhibit is the open savanna of **East Africa**. Wildebeest, greater kudu and impala antelope, warthogs, rare Grevy's zebras, and various ground-dwelling savanna birds graze on a central grassland. In front of the antelope yard, African elephants occupy a dusty island, while giraffes tramp in front of a tall fence made of inverted logs. An elephant-viewing walkway leads to their pool, and into the elephant barn for indoor viewing. The *Chakula Café* provides the best view of the entire African area; you can see giraffes and elephants in the foreground, the antelope savanna just behind, and lions in the distance. Past an interpretive building that displays African cultural artifacts, a pretty plaza hosts African lesser flamingos in a shallow lagoon. Down the hill, a large fenced aviary has an impressive number of birds, including ibises and crowned cranes, as well as petite dik-dik antelope. From an elevated vista, you can watch black rhinos in two spacious yards. The long, grassy cheetah yard provides its residents with plenty of running space and has viewing windows on both ends. A unique mixed-species exhibit – displaying blue monkeys and black-backed jackals – is around the corner from a lush lemur island. In the *African Reptile/Aquarium* building, black-footed penguins and African cichlid fish swim in two glass-fronted indoor brooks. Behind the brooks is a desert habitat for spurred tortoises, more dik-dik antelope, and a variety of ground-dwelling and perching birds. Windows onto the outdoor savanna make a spectacular background. Lions are visible from here, but are better seen from an outdoor viewing station, where you can see their natural prey, zebras and antelope, behind them. A boardwalk leads on through a natural marsh and under towering pine trees to a complex where four striking species are exhibited in habitats enhanced by tall trees, water holes, rocky cliffs, and waterfalls. At the first viewing stop, you'll find a mixed-species exhibit: bongo and yellow-backed duiker antelope roam the ground, while colobus monkeys hang out in the branches above. Leopards are up next. Their exhibit is backed by windows that give them a view of the antelope. A much larger viewing area provides a final overview of all these animals.

A boardwalk takes visitors to the animals of **Native Texas**. A series of naturalistic habitats built into the rocks allow for close viewing of raccoon-like coatis, gray foxes, a variety of birds, and otters. The rocky otter exhibit, with waterfalls and underwater viewing, is especially beautiful. Opposite this exhibit, the boardwalk overhangs a waterfowl pond that counts pelicans among its many residents. The expansive *Texas Plains* prairie yard exhibits wild turkeys, deer, longhorn cattle, and American bison. The boardwalk continues on to several habitats that resemble rocky crags. Here, predatory birds displayed behind thin harp wire include owls, crested caracaras, and hawks. A pair of bald eagles, also birds of prey, can be seen nearby, usually perched on a thick log. Four feline habitats are landscaped with branches, waterfalls, and streams; they provide excellent opportunities to see bobcats, ocelots, mountain lions, and jaguars. The walkway broadens as it curves around the bison yard to a natural swamp populated by alligators and turtles.

An energetic troop of squirrel monkeys inhabits one of two **entry plaza islands**. Pelicans, spoonbills, and other colorful birds live in the waterfall-fed stream that surrounds the monkeys. Across the dividing bridge is the other island, which hosts a flock of flamingos. Use the walkway to get great views of both islands.

OTHER EXHIBITS

Smaller animals from the Lone Star state are on display in the **Texas Reptile/ Aquarium**, part of the Native Texas area. Catfish, gars, and other fish from local ponds and streams swim in a wide, rocky aquarium. Numerous snakes, lizards, and turtles are displayed in habitat dioramas, which are organized by the region of the state the animals come from. An assortment of rattlesnakes and other venomous snakes are among the most attention-grabbing residents.

The third zoogeographic area, **South America**, is arranged along an uphill path shaded by overhanging tree branches. Upon entering this "Little Amazon," visitors pass macaws perched in the trees, and toucans and endangered golden lion tamarin monkeys in small enclosures. A large flight cage is filled with tropical wading birds such as roseate spoonbills, scarlet ibises, and purple gallinules. The main exhibit here is a long, multi-species habitat that follows a curving path up the hill. Giant anteaters, seriema birds, king vultures, and capybaras (large aquatic rodents) are among the animals that share this fenced enclosure.

FOR THE KIDS

In **Wild Bird Walkabout**, over 400 parakeets and cockatiels fly and perch among the tree branches. Kids can feed these colorful Australian parrots a seed stick, available for a small fee. Near the South American area is the **Petting Pen**, a small goat contact yard. Nearby, a couple of small playgrounds are surrounded by sand. Buckets encourage children to play in the sand as much as on the playground equipment.

IN PROGRESS

The zoo is changing the South American area into a **Children's Garden** with animal contact areas, water play areas, a playground, and other animal exhibits.

BEST OF THE REST

Little Rock Zoo

1 Jonesboro Drive
Little Rock, Arkansas 72205
(501) 666-2406
www.littlerockzoo.com

In the capital of the Natural State, natural habitats are scattered throughout its renowned zoo. The *Great Ape Display* features chimpanzees, orangutans, and gorillas in lushly planted deep grottoes. Visitors view the display from a high walkway atop the grotto walls. Other primate displays throughout the zoo include island exhibits of siamangs, spider monkeys, and lemurs. The *Big Cat Habitat* features lions, Amur tigers, and jaguars. Large animals include Asian elephants, both white and black rhinos, giraffes, and zebras. There are a number of unusual animals, including red pandas, giant anteaters, warthogs, pronghorn antelope, and Australian wombats, as well as a *Reptile House*.

BREC's Baton Rouge Zoo

3601 Thomas Road
Baker, Louisiana 70807
(225) 775-3877
www.brzoo.org

Located just north of Louisiana's capital city, this zoo offers a wide variety of activities for children and adults. The *KidsZoo* has a playground, and a contact yard where kids can pet farm animals. Families can also take a scenic ride on the *Cypress Bayou Railroad*, or watch the *elephant show*, presented twice daily. On its spacious 145 acres, the zoo has an impressive collection of both large and small cats, including white tigers. Birds are found in abundance here: there's the *Birds of the World* complex, *Birds of Prey* exhibits, and a walk-through *Parrot Paradise*. Separate areas display wildlife of South America, with maned wolves; Australia, with kangaroos; and Africa, with lions, giraffes, zebras, pygmy hippos, and rhinos. Local wildlife is shown in *L'aquarium de Louisiane*, with exhibits of fish, reptiles, and amphibians native to the Bayou State. Next door is the *Otter Pond*, with impressive underwater views of playful river otters.

El Paso Zoo

4001 East Paisano Drive
El Paso, Texas 79905
(915) 521-1850
www.elpasozoo.org

Located less than a mile from the Mexican border, this small zoo displays a wide variety of animals on just eighteen acres. Asian animals are its primary focus; nearly half the zoo grounds are used to display Asian elephants, Indo-Chinese tigers, Amur leopards, Sumatran orangutans, sun bears, Malayan tapirs, siamangs, and Asian hoofstock in an area enhanced with Oriental buildings. South America is also well represented with *Spider Monkey Island*, jaguars, ocelots, Galapagos tortoises, and a *South American Pavilion* with beautiful naturalistic indoor habitats for small mammals, monkeys, and a variety of tropical birds and Amazon fish. *World of the Sea Lion* features California sea lions in a twenty-foot-deep pool with underwater viewing and a large amphitheater. As we go to press, plans call for the zoo to double in size by 2009. Additions will include a new reptile house and an *African Savanna* featuring lions, zebras, and giraffes.

Cameron Park Zoo

1701 North 4th Street
Waco, Texas 76707
(254) 750-8400
www.cameronparkzoo.com

Often overlooked since there are so many larger zoos nearby, this zoo focuses exclusively on animals from Africa and North America, and each area is very well done. The best exhibit here is *Brazos River Country*, named for the river that borders the zoo. Native animals of all sorts are found in this large habitat, from saltwater fish to black bears. Caracara birds, ocelot cats, wild javelina pigs (also known as collared peccaries), and a nocturnal barn are also found along the trail. Most fun is the otter pool, where kids can slide down a glass slide right through the otter's pond! Bison graze among teepees, and several large carnivores – jaguars, cougars, and alligators – are very popular with visitors. Elephants, white rhinos, lions, giraffes, and antelope each enjoy large grassy habitats in *Africa*. An excellent collection of reptiles, especially desert dwellers, is housed in the *Herpetarium*. Gibbons and lemurs inhabit two beautiful island exhibits, and Sumatran tigers can be seen through harp wire, which provides excellent visibility.

Zoos Bring Together Animals from Around the World

Wombat (l) is native to Australia. It is a marsupial, like a kangaroo.

Aardvark (r) is an African native with an Africaans name that means "earth pig."

They can both be found at the Brookfield Zoo.

Great Lakes Area Zoos

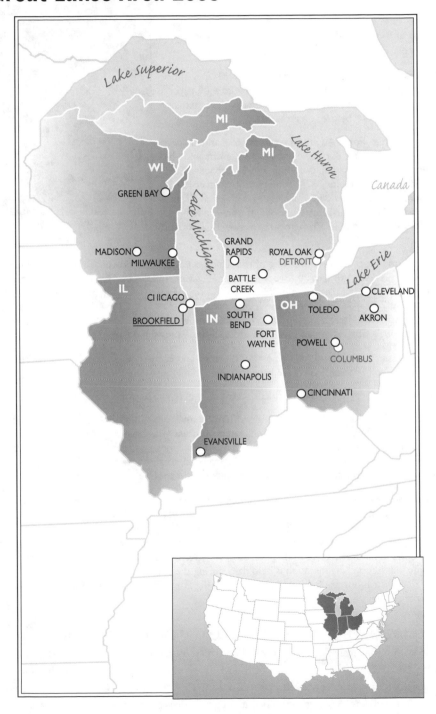

Lake Superior

MI

WI

MI

Lake Huron

Canada

GREEN BAY ○

Lake Michigan

GRAND
RAPIDS ○

ROYAL OAK ○
DETROIT

Lake Erie

MADISON ○
MILWAUKEE ○

BATTLE
CREEK ○

○ CLEVELAND

IL

CHICAGO ○
BROOKFIELD ○

IN

SOUTH
BEND ○

FORT
WAYNE ○

OH

○
TOLEDO

○ AKRON

POWELL ○
COLUMBUS

○ INDIANAPOLIS

○ CINCINNATI

○
EVANSVILLE

Brookfield Zoo

3300 Golf Road
Brookfield, Illinois 60513
(708) 688-800 or (800) 201-0784
www.brookfieldzoo.org

A gibbon in the zoo's Tropic World.

Hours: 9:30 a.m.-6:00 p.m. daily, Memorial Day-Labor Day; 10:00 a.m. -5:00 p.m. daily, rest of year; to 6:00 p.m. on weekends in April, September, and October. Indoor exhibits close half an hour before the grounds do.

Admission & Fees: Adults $11, seniors 65+ and children 3-11 $7. Parking $8. Butterflies: adults $3, seniors and children $2; Motor Safari: adults $3, children $2; carousel $2.50; Hamill Play Zoo: adults $3.50, seniors and children $2.50; Children's Zoo: adults $1.50, seniors and children $1, free admission November-February; dolphin show: adults $3, seniors and children $2.50; members receive discounts on some of the above fees.

Directions: Located 14 miles west of the Chicago Loop. From downtown, take I-290 (Eisenhower Expressway) to Exit 20 (Brookfield Zoo/1st Avenue), follow 1st Avenue for 2.6 miles, and turn right onto 31st Street. Zoo parking is on the right. From I-294 (Tri-State Tollway), take the Brookfield Zoo exit (31st Street) and follow signs along 31st Street for 4.5 miles to the zoo. By mass transit, take Metra's Burlington North train line, get off at the "Zoo Stop" (Hollywood Station), and walk northeast two blocks to the zoo. Bus Routes 304 and 331 also serve the zoo.

Don't Miss: Tropic World, Habitat Africa! (Savanna and Forest), Seven Seas Panorama, The Living Coast, Wolf Woods, The Fragile Kingdom, Australia House, The Swamp.

For the Kids: Play Zoo, Children's Zoo, carousel, water play area, playgrounds.

Authors' Tips: Keep an eye out for "Zoo Gem" animals around the zoo: signs in front of their respective exhibits explain Brookfield's longtime success with breeding okapis, aardvarks, black rhinos, and other species. This zoo is very large, so don't hesitate to hop on the Motor Safari: it makes several convenient stops. Narration is provided, so guests will not only get a quick look at the zoo, but will also learn a lot about its history and about individual animals.

Edutainment: Dolphin shows are presented in the Seven Seas Dolphinarium, up to five showtimes daily in summer. Near the dolphins' underwater gallery, the Dolphin Research Boat Theater gives a video tour of the zoo's long-running wild dolphin study in Florida. Brookfield's "Zoo Chats" are among the most extensive keeper/visitor interaction programs in the nation, with daily chats at all of the zoo's most popular destinations. In the Children's Zoo, an entertaining "Animals in Action" presentation is held daily during the summer, while milking and wool-spinning demonstrations are held year round in the Big Barn. Check zoo map for times and locations of shows.

THE BROOKFIELD ZOO OPENED IN 1934 AS ONE OF THE NATION'S first barless naturalistic zoos. Located fourteen miles west of Chicago's skyscrapers, this 216-acre suburban zoo is one of the Midwest's largest and best. From the centrally located, picturesque **Roosevelt Fountain**, long flower- and tree-lined malls stretch out in four directions. Adding to the beautiful grounds is **Salt Creek Wilderness**, a scenic forest on the zoo's west side. Following the quarter-mile *Ellen Thorne Smith Nature Trail*, which surrounds man-made *Indian Lake*, visitors see may turtles, raccoons, frogs, and trumpeter swans and other waterfowl. At trail's end, a boardwalk overlooks *Dragonfly Marsh*, a cattail-filled wetland with more than 12,000 plants.

FEATURED EXHIBITS

Tropic World, a rain forest building that's longer than a football field, has been the zoo's most popular exhibit since it opened in 1980. Visitors walk along a treetop-level path where you'll feel like you're looking down into a jungle valley. Sporadic thunderstorms can occur in each continent's exhibit as often as three times a day. Pass under a fifty-foot crashing waterfall to reach the *South American* rain forest. Free-ranging cotton-top tamarin monkeys can cross above the visitor path on a set of ropes. Spider monkeys and capuchin monkeys live in the trees, and a giant anteater and Brazilian tapir wander below. *Asia* is first glimpsed from a circular deck overlooking a flooded mangrove forest. White-cheeked gibbons swing through the branches of over half a dozen trees. Orangutans have their own island, and small-clawed otters swim in the water below. Red-capped mangabey and colobus monkeys live in *Africa's* rain forest, which boasts the building's tallest trees. Mandrills and sooty mangabey monkeys roam the forest floor, along with a pygmy hippo. The building's capstone exhibit is a rocky mountain home for a lowland gorilla family. Visible from a bamboo bridge and from a progressively climbing walkway, the large troop is always in close proximity to the visitors. Syke's guenon monkeys and a small troop of colobus monkeys inhabit a side habitat.

Habitat Africa! The Savanna is set in the fictitious Makundi National Park. ("Makundi" is Swahili for "gathering place for people and animals.") At the *Waterhole*, a giraffe family comes into view. Children can try the interactive displays – a fourteen-foot-tall *Giraffe's-Eye View Scope* and a path where you can pretend to be a zebra in search of water. The entrance to the indoor *kopje* exhibits lies between two large rocks. Inside, tiny klipspringer antelope and free-flying birds come quite close to the boardwalk. Side windows offer views of the giraffes and of African wild dogs outside. In smaller exhibits, visitors can look for dwarf mongooses, lizards, and pancake tortoises. Get a great view of the mongooses by climbing through a small crevice in the rocks to a large bubble window. Back outside, the highly endangered African wild dogs are visible again from an overlook and through a wide window in an African tourist lodge. The gravel path then winds among thorn trees to the best overlook of the giraffes. Nearby, waterbuck antelope, ostriches, and warthogs share a grassland exhibit. A small building holds one of the few breeding groups of aardvarks in North America. Inside, the aardvarks can be seen both above ground, and below in their burrow.

Habitat Africa! The Forest re-creates the Congo's Ituri Forest. Thick jungle plants signal the shift from savanna to rain forest. The exhibit chronicles three kinds of people who live in the dense jungle: two vastly different tribes, and visiting researchers. A trickling stream runs parallel to the visitor path, which leads to overlooks of yellow-backed duiker antelope and okapis, endangered forest-dwellers that are related to giraffes. Brookfield was the first zoo in the U.S. to breed okapis. In a well concealed building, dwarf crocodiles and Congo peafowl are shaded by overhanging foliage. Dense plant life hides blue duiker antelope, located near small exhibits of chameleons and tortoises. A mock research station sits in front of the okapi indoor exhibit. The okapis, as well as Congo buffalo and red river hogs, are seen on an outdoor path leading to the *Ways of Knowing Trail*, a short interactive journey revealing the secrets of surviving in the dense African jungle.

Back in 1960, Brookfield became the first inland zoo to exhibit dolphins. **Seven Seas Panorama**'s dolphin shows are still a big hit. The 2,000-seat *Dolphinarium* is landscaped with palm trees and other tropical plants to resemble a Caribbean coast. A wide underwater gallery enables people to watch the dolphins during and between shows. *Pinniped Point*, a re-creation of the shores of America's Pacific Northwest, is home to sea lions, harbor seals, and a gray seal. Another underwater gallery displays these animals as they swim in their rocky pools.

The sounds of crashing waves and cackling gulls ring through **The Living Coast**'s outdoor entry plaza. Water flows down the blue walls at the start of an underwater journey to three of South America's ocean environments. The *Open Ocean* is home to a school of lookdown fish, bonnethead sharks, and green sea turtles. At *Nearshore Waters*, a tall aquarium displays a wide variety of fish. Penguins are sometimes visible swimming up above, between the strands of kelp. Leopard sharks and moray eels often hide in the rocky underwater cliffs nooks, so look closely for them. Side exhibits for cardinal fish, seahorses, and zooplankton, tiny shrimp and other sea creatures that make up the bulk of many whales' diets, are nearby. Do not miss the *Surf Zone*, where a wave crashes in every ninety seconds from above the pathway. In our opinion, the best exhibit in the building is *Rocky Shores*. Under a geodesic dome, endangered Humboldt penguins, Inca terns, and gray gulls dwell along a towering cliff face. The penguins often dive in the deep pool, but are also visible resting on shore near their nesting sites. Beneath an overhanging cliff are smaller exhibits for chinchillas, vampire bats, boas, and degus, a small, furry species of rodent. Near the exit, *Penguin Cove* gives visitors a glimpse at the penguins' nest burrows. Outdoors, Andean condors inhabit a spacious flight cage.

Endangered Mexican gray wolves roam the **Regenstein Wolf Woods**. The wolves have two acres to explore, but at least a few are usually perched atop a massive, centrally located hill. Guests have plenty of opportunities to view the wolves: from two long overlooks, through a fence along the *Nature Trail*, and through a darkened one-way mirror. If the wolves are not in view, guests can operate cameras located within the exhibit and then watch the wolves on a video monitor in the visitor shelter. Heated rocks and several dens make this a great exhibit for the wolves, too.

The Fragile Kingdom is a three-part exhibit dedicated to carnivores of all sizes. *The Fragile Desert* is an indoor replica of arid African deserts, exhibiting rarely seen bat-eared foxes, meerkats, and African porcupines. An exhibit of naked mole-rats is built into the rocks below the foxes. These bald but social creatures inhabit what looks like a giant ant farm. A bridge crosses between a cliff home for rock hyraxes and a rocky exhibit for tawny colored caracal cats. Fennec foxes, the smallest members of the canine family, have a sandy exhibit, but are more often seen (through a small window) hiding in their den. Other residents include sand cats, dwarf mongooses, and elephant shrews. *The Fragile Rain Forest* is unforgettable, not least of all for the powerful pungent smell from the small-clawed otters and binturongs, shaggy raccoon-like arboreal creatures. Clouded leopards, fishing cats, and a python join these somewhat stinky members of the Asian rain forest. Outdoors, a set of rocky grottoes exhibit what the zoo terms *The Fragile Hunters*: Lions, snow leopards, and Amur leopards are lured close to the visitor windows by heated rocks. Amur tigers and termite-slurping sloth bears are visible across deep moats.

The **Australia House** was the first U.S. exhibit dedicated exclusively to Australian animals. Exhibits of lizards and snakes, and an aviary for pigeons and parrots, line the walls. In the nocturnal section, a winding path circles echidnas (also known as spiny anteaters), boobook owls, and wombats. Very few zoos in the nation exhibit wombats. The highlight of this space, for most people, is the walk-through bat exhibit, where over thirty fruit bats fly freely behind a thin wire barrier just in front of the visitor boardwalk. Outdoors, there are several yards for kangaroos and emus.

North American wetland animals dwell among cypress trees in **The Swamp**. Walking across a squishy floor, visitors pass through a cloud of fog to reach a typical Southern swamp. First up is a bog habitat for egrets and herons. Sirens, a rare type of salamander, and several species of snakes are displayed along a path that leads to an overlook of water birds: wood storks, double-crested cormorants, and white ibises. In *Slice of the Swamp*, side-by-side tanks exhibit a multitude of small aquatic species, including crawdads, snails, turtles, and fish. A sharp eye might spot frogs and anole lizards in the leaves above, too. Secretive golden mice and a long-tailed weasel can be even more difficult to spot. American alligators, probably the most popular of all swamp creatures, have two exhibits. An abandoned log mill serves as a swamp shack that's full of small critters and overlooks an aviary with ducks, turtles, and a number of backyard perching birds. Also represented here is a southern Illinois wetland, where river otters play under a waterfall and a snapping turtle lives beside an aquarium full of fish.

OTHER EXHIBITS

At the **Pachyderm House**, you'll see black rhinos, pygmy and Nile hippos, tapirs, and African elephants indoors or out, depending on the weather. The **Perching Birds** house displays honeyeaters, hanging parrots, red birds of paradise, and tawny frogmouths. Its walk-through aviary has macaws, hummingbirds, and various tanager species. Reptiles and more birds inhabit **Feathers and Scales,** a combination exhibit building. Its largest exhibit is a desert habitat for burrowing owls, woodpeckers, quails, and double striped thick-knees, ground birds that look something like roadrunners. Critically endangered Guam kingfishers (another species the zoo successfully breeds) are also displayed, along with two blocks of small reptile exhibits.

Among the most popular outdoor exhibits are the **Bear Grottoes**, where baby polar bears are a common sight. Alaskan brown bears live next door. An island mountain, **Baboon Island**, is found directly behind The Swamp. A large group of Guinea baboons inhabits its gigantic boulders.

The **31ˢᵗ Street Yards**, which border that thoroughfare, are home to most of the zoo's collection of hoofstock. Double-humped Bactrian camels, American bison, addax and waterbuck antelope, and both Grant's and Grevy's zebras live in a long row of paddocks. **Butterflies!** is a narrow walk-through seasonal exhibit where many colorful species flit among streams and flowers.

FOR THE KIDS

The **Hamill Family Play Zoo**, a combination zoo, museum, nature park, and school, is a revolutionary children's zoo exhibit. Throughout this complex, trained "play partners" (zoo staff) lead many different activities, which change seasonally. The play zoo is divided into three distinct areas. In the *Zoo Within A Zoo,* kids can dress up as various zoo workers. In *Zooscape Mountain*, wearing zookeeper uniforms, children can "clean" empty animal cages next to chinchilla, snake, and kookaburra exhibits. In the *Animal Hospital*, they can don lab coats to examine x-rays and even perform operations on stuffed animals. In the greenhouse, kids participate in plant care. Children can also sit in the zoo director's chair and pretend to run the zoo exactly as they wish. Domestic pets, including dogs, cats, and rabbits, live in the *Zoo At Home*, a two-room house. At *Nature Swap*, nature items found outside, such as pine cones, can be traded for fossil rocks. Other animal exhibits include parrots, and small reptiles such as bearded dragons and turtles. At *Lemur Leap*, kids can don lemur coats and leap like lemurs, in front of an indoor/outdoor exhibit for several lemur species. Surrounding the building is *Play Gardens*, where children participate in a number of hands-on activities. Building animal homes using sticks and other natural materials is a challenge, as is climbing on a bug sculpture. Kids can easily spend an entire day exploring this exhibit's many features.

The small **Children's Zoo** is a great place for children to interact with domestic animals and to get close to animals native to North America. A turkey vulture, red-tailed hawk, opossum, and owls are some of the favorites displayed in a long row of old-fashioned wire cages. The skunks, raccoons, and woodchucks, displayed in a rocky grotto, are also popular. In the *Big Barn*, cows are milked twice daily. Goats and calves can be petted at the *Walk-In Farmyard*. Draft horses, reindeer, llamas, and a baby chick hatchery are also featured here.

There's an enormous **carousel** near the zoo's North Gate. Above its exotic mounts, murals in the center of the carousel portray each of Brookfield's major exhibits. The Brookfield Zoo also boasts three **playgrounds**, including a **water play area**.

IN PROGRESS

A new master plan will rejuvenate the zoo: every one of its original buildings is scheduled to be either renovated or replaced. The bear grottoes will go first. **Great Bear**

Wilderness is scheduled to open in 2009 as we go to press, and will be located next to Wolf Woods. The polar and brown bears will move from the grottoes to this Native American-inspired exhibit. Bald eagles and bison (which appear in the zoo's logo) will also find a home here. Planned for May 2010 as we go to press, the current Children's Zoo will be re-created as an exciting new **Children's Experience** with connections to the Hamill Family Play Zoo. Also planned is a new arrival experience at the North Gate, and a new bird and reptile display near the Formal Pool. Eventually, **Elephant Trails** will replace the existing Pachyderm House, providing more than five acres of space for the zoo's elephants, rhinos, and large antelope. The elephant herd will move freely through four separate habitats. In due course, the entire northwest corner of the zoo will be devoted to elephants.

Lincoln Park Zoo

2200 North Cannon Drive
Chicago, Illinois 60614
(312) 742-2000
www.lpzoo.com

Hours: Grounds 9:00 a.m.-6:00 p.m. daily April-October, to 7:00 p.m. summer weekends; 9:00 a.m.-5:00 p.m. daily, rest of year. Buildings and farm open 10:00 a.m.- 5:00 p.m. daily, April-October, to 6:30 p.m. summer weekends; 10:00 a.m.-4:30 p.m. daily, rest of year.

Zookeeper and seal during a keeper chat.

Admission & Fees: Free. Parking: up to 30 minutes free, under 3 hours $14, 3-4 hours $16, 4-5 hours $20, over 5 hours $24. 30-minute paddleboat rental: $12 for a 4-seater or $16 for a 2-seat swan boat, African safari (simulator) ride $5 ($4 for members), Endangered Species Carousel $2.50, children's train $2.

Directions: Located just north of downtown Chicago. From Lake Shore Drive, take the Fullerton Avenue exit, then turn left into zoo parking lot. From I-94, take Exit 47A (Fullerton Avenue) and turn left onto West Fullerton Avenue. Follow for 2.5 miles (it becomes West Fullerton Parkway). Turn right onto North Cannon Drive and follow for 0.4 miles to the zoo. Chicago Transit Authority has stops near the zoo. From the "L" train, take the Brown line train to the Fullerton stop, then walk east on Fullerton for six blocks (approximately 15 minutes). The zoo is on the right. Bus routes 151 and 156 both serve the zoo.

Don't Miss: Center for African Apes, African Journey, Lion House, Primate House, Small Mammal-Reptile House, Seal Pool.

For Kids: Children's Zoo, Farm-in-the-Zoo, paddleboats, Endangered Species Carousel, African safari ride, children's train.

Authors' Tips: Café Brauer is a great place to eat and enjoy the view; the ice cream and cold drinks available here will cool anyone off on a hot day. Outside the brick building is a terrace overlooking South Pond and a great view of the Chicago skyline. There are plenty of shady spots around the zoo to have a picnic, relax, and read – it's hard to beat the atmosphere.

Edutainment: For anyone who has never been to a farm, the cow-milking demonstration in the Dairy Barn is a must. Also in Farm-in-the-Zoo is a gardening seminar, where attendees can help tend a vegetable garden. Some of the more popular keeper chats are held at the seal pool and Primate House, but others can be found by the apes, reptiles, and bears.

PERHAPS NO OTHER ZOO IN THE COUNTRY HAS A BETTER SETTING than the Lincoln Park Zoo. Located just off the shore of Lake Michigan, in the nation's third largest city, this zoo draws over three million visitors every year. Its popularity is partly due to its admission price (or lack thereof): this is one of the last free zoos in America. Several of its gates remain open throughout the day, and joggers are a common sight. Being in the shadow of Chicago's beautiful skyline has its advantages, but space is not one of them. Over the course of nearly 140 years, however, the zoo has developed an impressive animal collection, fitting a lot into its thirty-five acres, which makes a trip to this zoo enjoyable no matter how long you stay.

Despite opening in 1868, the zoo has repeatedly updated its exhibits to modern standards – in the 1970s, 1990s, and again in the past decade. The combination of historic building exteriors with spacious, lush indoor exhibits makes this a fascinating place. The Lincoln Park Zoo is one of America's best small zoos.

FEATURED EXHIBITS

Few zoos (or cities) have as remarkable a history with gorillas as Lincoln Park and Chicago. Over the years, several of the zoo's gorilla icons, especially Bushman and Otto, have captured the hearts of Windy City residents – they were frequent subjects of local newspaper and TV stories. The zoo's current silverbacks live in the breathtaking **Regenstein Center for African Apes**, an indoor/outdoor paradise for gorillas and chimpanzees. The *Gorilla Bamboo Forest* is the largest and best of the three outdoor habitats. These magnificent apes are sometimes visible only inches away, through a huge window at the bottom of their hill. At the top of the hill is a forest, from which a waterfall emerges. Gorilla babies are common here – nearly fifty have been born in the past forty years. Gorillas and chimps rotate time between the second and third habitats, covered with stiff netting. Each habitat has an adjoining indoor section, connected by a sliding glass door that often stays open all day. The indoor exhibits are fully visible through floor-to-ceiling windows. Unique triangular immersion windows extend into the outdoor habitats – pop in to take a closer look at the apes.

Regenstein African Journey is just what its name implies – an expedition through each of the continent's major ecosystems. First up is the *Savanna*, where wild dogs and warthogs live in yards no more than a few feet apart. Giraffes, gazelles, and ostriches roam an elevated plain that slopes down to two vantage points for visitors. Inside a building, the *Rainforest* environment is home to colobus monkeys and ibis birds. After crossing a bridge and ducking under a tree, the indoor path leads you to pools for dwarf crocodiles and pygmy hippos, each with hundreds of fish to accompany them and underwater viewing for visitors. Creepy orb spiders and hissing cockroaches, both from Madagascar, are two exhibits some would prefer to miss! A ramp leads to the *Dry Thorn Forest*, where klipspringer antelope, lovebirds, and rock hyraxes, which look like rodents but are actually most closely related to elephants, all live in a kopje habitat. Aardvarks and meerkats are displayed in front of the giraffes' indoor exhibit. Near the building's exit, colorful cichlid fish from Kenya's *Lake Malawi* swim in a large tank. A shady enclosure of black rhinos is just outside, near the giraffes.

The historic **Kovler Lion House**, built in 1912, is a landmark at the zoo's main entrance. Two outdoor yards, one for Siberian (also known as Amur) tigers and one for lions, grace the building's entry plaza. Each of these yards is connected to indoor exhibits in the *Great Hall*, where the historic architecture is eye-catching. Both sides of the hall are lined with attractive indoor enclosures displaying jaguars, servals, and Amur leopards, all enhanced with realistic rock work and murals that depict the landscape of each cat's homeland. On the building's north end is a row of newly expanded habitats for pumas, petite Pallas' cats, red pandas, snow leopards, and one of the nation's only exhibits of sandy-colored Afghanistan leopards.

The **Helen Brach Primate House** is another of the zoo's historic buildings. Its interior was renovated in the 1990s to include natural habitats lush with living plants, artificial tree trunks, trickling waterfalls, and background murals that make the rain forest seem to extend as far as the eye can see. The habitats, forty feet tall with floor-to-ceiling windows, feature Geoffrey's tamarin monkeys, howler monkeys, gibbons, swamp monkeys, and DeBrazza's monkeys. A definite visitor favorite is the massive male drill. The drill is a baboon-like species similar to a mandrill, except that their faces are black, not multicolored.

Near the entrance to the **Regenstein Small Mammal-Reptile House**, swans and flamingos live in outdoor lagoons. Inside, the first of three sections spotlights reptiles and amphibians. A circular set of enclosures displays poison dart frogs, skinks, and box turtles. Larger enclosures hold ground boas, rattlesnakes, and beaded lizards. In addition to its other animals, the small mammal section's highlights are the nocturnal exhibits, which include armadillos and slow lorises, furry primates with big, owl-like eyes. Dwarf mongooses and naked mole-rats are shown in large colonies, as are fruit bats, who have a dark cave habitat. Sand cats live nearby. The third section is a mixed-species rain forest. Here, aquatic animals live on the ground or in the water below, and arboreal (tree-dwelling) animals live in the trees above. These aquatic/arboreal, above/below pairs include Asian otters with multi-colored Prevost's squirrels, white-faced saki monkeys with slow-moving caimans, and howler monkeys with snake-necked turtles and red devil fish. A row of small desert habitats displays fennec foxes, wallabies, and red-footed tortoises. Don't overlook the tarantulas and leaf-cutter ants, by the large man-made tree near the exit – they're easy to miss. The worker ants are usually hard at work cutting leaves to bring back to the rest of the colony.

The most famous site in the zoo is probably the **Kovler Seal Pool**, a traditional meeting place for Chicago businessmen over the years. Today, gray and harbor seals swim in a pool with waves that overflow its sides, creating a refreshing splashing sound.

In addition to great water-level viewing, visitors can take a tunnel to an underwater gallery, or watch from elevated amphitheatre seating.

OTHER EXHIBITS

The 1904 **McCormick Bird House** is another impressively renovated building. Exotic birds from around the world are found in ten unique habitats, from the *Seashore* to the *Deep Forest*. Each habitat is enhanced with lush plantings and background murals. Feathered gems include paradise whydahs (long-tailed brown-and-black finches from Ethiopia) in the *Savanna*, wrinkled hornbills in a *Mountain Clearing*, and highly endangered Guam rails, a wading bird, in the *Riverbank* habitat. The *Tropical River* has a walk-through aviary where a waterfall cascades into the river and colorful birds such as rare Bali mynahs and Nicobar pigeons fly freely.

In addition to the Bird House, there are three other fine bird exhibits at the Lincoln Park Zoo. The **Regenstein Birds of Prey Exhibit** features three towering flight cages for bald eagles, owls, vultures, and storks. At the **Kovler Penguin & Seabird House**, aptly named chinstrap penguins swim past visitors, along with king and rockhopper penguins. In an adjacent room, a rocky cliff habitat displays tufted puffins, razorbills, and penguin-like common murres.

Polar, **spectacled**, and **sun bears** each have habitats near African Journey. **Hoofed animals** are displayed along a looped path at the far south end of the zoo. Large yards hold Grevy's zebras, white-lipped (or Thorold's) deer, goat-like Sichuan takins, sable antelope, and long-horned Arabian oryxes. Side yards display alpacas, smaller relatives of llamas, and a mob of red kangaroos. A herd of double-humped Bactrian camels lives just outside the African Journey exit, by the rhinos.

FOR THE KIDS

The **Pritzker Family Children's Zoo** was the nation's first year-round zoo for children. Renovated in 2005, its theme is now *At Home in the Woods*. At the first exhibit, endangered red wolves enjoy a densely forested home. It takes a patient and persistent observer to spot these slender canines. Past a flowing stream in the otter habitat, the path leads to a building with underwater views of both the otters and several beavers. In the building's center is a maze of platforms resembling falling leaves. Each "leaf" connects to another, forming a challenging climbing structure for adventurous kids. At the end of the exhibit, black bears dwell in a long, boomerang-shaped enclosure. Kids can climb into a log to get a closer look at the bears.

Farm-in-the-Zoo, a working replica of a Midwestern farm, is just across the *Lester E. Fisher Bridge*, named for the zoo's late director. Several buildings illustrate Illinois' rich agricultural history. There are great photo opportunities in the *Big Barn*; kids can climb onto a tractor or into a giant broken eggshell. The *Livestock Barn* has pigs, horses, and cattle, but the *Dairy Barn* is by far the most popular, with its dairy cows, especially fun to watch during milking. Outside, there's a small goat contact yard.

There are several rides near each zoo entrance: *paddleboats* by the Farm, a *train* near the seals, a *carousel* by the main entrance, and a *simulator ride* by the camels.

IN PROGRESS

In the near future, the zoo plans to restore the **South Pond**, an important natural area of the zoo. This project will restore eight acres of wetlands and prairie grasses that will serve as a home for native wildlife, including the more than a hundred bird species that inhabit the pond. When complete, this pond will be an excellent educational resource for local students.

Fort Wayne Children's Zoo

3411 Sherman Boulevard
Fort Wayne, Indiana 46808
(260) 427-6800
www.kidszoo.org

Hours: 9:00 a.m.-5:00 p.m. daily, mid-April to mid-October (call or check website for exact dates). In late October, there are special Halloween hours. Closed rest of the year.

Kangaroos in Australian Adventure's walk-through yard.

Admission & Fees: Adults $9.50, seniors 60+ $8.50, children 2-14 $6.50. Sky Safari, train, river, and carousel rides $2; pony ride $4; goat feeding: bottles $1, cones 50¢. Participates in reciprocity program.

Directions: From I-69, take Exit 111A (Lima Road/US-27). Follow US-27 for 0.8 miles, then take a slight right onto North Wells Street. Follow North Wells Street for 0.8 miles, then turn right onto Franke Park Drive. Follow Franke Park Drive to the zoo parking lot.

Don't Miss: Australian Adventure, Indonesian Rain Forest, African Journey, Sea Lion Beach.

For Kids: Indiana Family Farm, train ride, pony ride, Endangered Species Carousel, River Ride, Sky Safari ride.

Authors' Tips: There are two Dairy Queen restaurants on the grounds; in the Indonesian Rain Forest and the Australian Adventure areas. DQ's regular menu is available, including Blizzards. The Peacock Patio Snack Shop, serving pizzas and fruit bowls, is also a popular place to eat.

Edutainment: Regularly scheduled "Creature Features" include twice-daily sea lion training sessions and goat milking demonstrations on weekdays, and keeper chats featuring tigers, giraffes, orangutans, Komodo dragons, and other animals at their respective exhibits. Twice a week, at the "Dive Chat" show, guests can talk to an underwater scuba diver in the Great Barrier Reef Aquarium. A schedule is distributed along with the zoo map at the front gate.

IN CONCEPT AND NAME, THIS ZOO IS FOR YOUNGSTERS, BUT ITS many unique exhibits are enjoyed by adults as well. Its position as a "children's zoo," however, has brought it widespread publicity, with national periodicals *Family Fun* and *Child Magazine* ranking this zoo one of America's top ten zoos for kids. Extending out from the inner Central Zoo are three excellent continental exhibit areas, each with its own popular and fun themed ride.

FEATURED EXHIBITS

The **Australian Adventure** is one of the country's largest and best displays of Australian animals, as well as a most convincing virtual journey to the "Land Down Under." The trip begins in the *Australia Welcome Center*, where the continent's geography and wildlife are introduced in displays aimed specifically at kids. Next door, the *Great Barrier Reef Aquarium* displays hundreds of colorful reef fish. In a larger tank, three species of sharks swim by menacingly, while smaller tanks show fascinating sea nettles and moon jellyfish. Outdoors, the space resembles a genuine Outback courtyard, and all the buildings are covered with typical Aussie red tiles. In one of these structures, you'll find *Australia After Dark*, home to unusual echidnas (also known as spiny anteaters), striped possums, and a long bat cave with only thin, nearly invisible wire separating fruit bats from humans. The outdoor tour begins with a stroll through the screened-in *Walkabout*, where hundreds of colorful lorikeets fly in flocks around their visitors. Further on, a semi-circular path cuts through the *Walk-Thru Kangaroo* yard, where there are no physical barriers between people and gray kangaroos. A side exhibit displays dingoes, the wild dogs of Australia. On the narrated *River Ride,* visitors float in dugout canoes around the perimeter of this fascinating exhibit.

Asian wildlife is the theme of the **Indonesian Rain Forest**, where the centerpiece is the *Jungle Dome Aviary*, a domed rain forest building with free-flying tropical birds. Upon entering this lush jungle habitat, pick up a Field Guide folder to help identify the fifteen avian species, flying fox fruit bats, and even the tropical plants of this humid, realistic rain forest. Birds to keep an eye out for include fairy bluebirds, pekin robins, and jambu fruit doves. In a side room under the dome, *Dr. Diversity's Rain Forest Research Station* displays butterfly collections, live exotic insects, and educational exhibits, all surrounding a giant elephant skeleton. Also exhibited here are Komodo dragons, the world's largest lizards. Down the hall, the indoor *Orangutan Valley* features the namesake Sumatran red apes. Just outside the aviary, a colorful *Endangered Species Carousel* plays circus music, inviting children to select an unusual animal to ride. In a large wooded habitat with a dry streambed, rare Sumatran tigers are on the prowl past several viewing huts for visitors. On the *Tree Tops Trail*, an elevated boardwalk, visitors encounter shaggy, slow-moving binturongs, looking something like raccoons, as well as rare birds and siamangs and other Asian primates, all in naturalistic mesh habitats.

Until the new African Journey opens (see "In Progress," below), the **African Village** will host an interesting variety of animals from that continent. The village features thatched-roof mud huts intermingled with the exhibits of pretty African birds, Allen's swamp and DeBrazza's monkeys, and African leopards. A long elevated boardwalk takes you to a giraffe enclosure.

The most appealing exhibit in the Central Zoo area is **Sea Lion Beach**, home to several playful California sea lions, best seen through long underwater glass panels. Waterfalls, wildflowers, evergreen trees, and artificial rock work make this place feel like the rocky California coastline. There is also plenty of room here for the popular sea lion training demonstrations, held twice daily.

OTHER EXHIBITS

The **Central Zoo** hub is the site of a variety of interesting animal exhibits. Just inside the entrance gate is a prairie dog pit, a popular exhibit with children. Another favorite is *Monkey Island*, a moated habitat for playful and animated capuchin monkeys. You'll also find other primates, such as ring-tailed lemurs, saki monkeys, and tiny tamarins. More tree-dwelling animals in mesh enclosures here include bobcats and furry red pandas.

Another highlight of the central zoo is the aquatic animal area, which includes the sea lions mentioned above. There are fascinating underwater views of American alligators, river otters, and black-footed penguins. On land, giant Aldabra tortoises occupy a nearby yard, as do a small mob of Bennett's wallabies.

The walk-through aviary is filled with colorful birds, including bright scarlet ibises. Small aviaries scattered around the central zoo house toucans, red-tailed hawks, turkey vultures, and even an unusual, plump Eurasian eagle owl.

FOR THE KIDS

While the entire zoo is nominally for kids, the **Indiana Family Farm** is the most child-oriented area. The Hoosier State is known for farming, and this corner of the zoo pays tribute to that tradition, with large red barns, a farmhouse, a windmill, and a tractor. The much-loved *Contact Area* holds a herd of goats to pet and feed, but there are also horses, sheep, cattle, rabbits, and pigs to see and touch in and around the barns. A chicken coop has many adorable chicks for kids to admire.

A miniature replica of an 1863 locomotive takes passengers on a **train ride** all around Franke Park. Up a hill, **pony rides** are available. Near the entrance to the future African Journey area, the **Sky Safari** ski lift ride takes passengers to heights of almost forty feet. Eventually, this flight will provide views of the African animals, but until then, it gives you an overview of the exhibit's construction.

IN PROGRESS

After passing through a misty oasis area, the brand new **African Journey** will begin with the *Safari Trail*. There, a narrow bridge will lead to the marshland habitat of swamp monkeys, pelicans, and water-dwelling sitatunga antelope. Next, a group of gigantic boulders will mimic the famous kopjes of the Serengeti Plains, where vultures, serval cats, and rarely exhibited honey badgers (or ratels) will be displayed. Children will be able to scoot through a tunnel to spy on a colony of banded mongooses. The centerpiece of this kopje, however, will be the amazing lion habitat, where only a glass wall will keep the thousand-pound "king of beasts" from curious children. A similarly naturalistic habitat will display spotted hyenas. An elevated boardwalk will lead to a special giraffe-feeding area, sure to be a popular spot. From the path across the African grassland, zebras, wildebeest, and ostriches will be visible, roaming through their ten-acre savanna. At the *Zebra Research Station*, kids will enjoy operating remote video cameras to observe the savanna animals. This new area is scheduled to open at the beginning of the 2009 season as we go to press.

Indianapolis Zoo

1200 West Washington Street
Indianapolis, Indiana 46222
(317) 630-2001
www.indianapoliszoo.com

A 30-foot diameter glass dome lets visitors watch dolphins from below their performance pool.

Hours: 9:00 a.m.-5:00 p.m. weekdays, 9:00 a.m.-6:00 p.m. weekends/holidays, Memorial Day-Labor Day; 9:00 a.m.-4:00 p.m. weekdays, 9:00 a.m.-5:00 p.m. weekends, mid-March-May and September-November; Noon-9 p.m., December; 9:00 a.m.-4:00 p.m. daily, rest of winter (closed Mondays and Tuesdays in January and February). Closed Thanksgiving, Christmas Eve and Day, and New Year's Eve and Day.

Admission & Fees: Adults $13.50, seniors 62+ and children 2-12 $8.50. Parking: $5. Train, pony, coaster, 4-D simulator and carousel rides: $2.25 each (discount ticket packages available).

Directions: From the north or east, take I-65 to Exit 114 (West Street). Follow this south to Washington Street, then west one mile to the zoo. From the south or west, take I-70 to Exit 79A (West Street). Follow north on West Street to Washington Street, then west one mile.

Don't Miss: Oceans, Dolphin Adventure (including Dolphin Show and Underwater Dome), walruses, Plains, Deserts.

For Kids: Encounters biome, Enchanted Mill Children's Play Area, train ride, carousel, 4-D simulator ride, Kombo family coaster, pony ride.

Authors' Tips: Many good dining choices, including Café on the Commons with outdoor viewing of lemurs and flamingos, and Dog 'N Suds fast food. Be sure to pick up your free tickets for the Dolphin Show upon entry to the zoo.

Edutainment: Daily Dolphin Shows are held in the 1,500-seat Dolphin Adventure Theater – the world's largest enclosed structure of its kind. This behavioral demonstration is one of the zoo's highlights. The 600-seat Arena presents twice daily "Creature Feature" shows, while the nearby amphitheatre features summertime "Birds of Prey" and "Backyard Animals" shows. Around the zoo, informal animal chats include a daily elephant bathing demonstration.

ONE OF THE NATION'S NEWEST ZOOS, THE INDIANAPOLIS ZOO opened in 1988. It's the envy of many zoos, due to its downtown location, and because the facility was built using the latest exhibit technology. When it comes to displaying animals at close range in naturalistic habitats, Indianapolis is among the best.

This zoo was the first in the nation to arrange its animals according to "biomes," or specific ecosystems where animals live. Nearly all of the world's creatures inhabit one of the four biomes represented here: Oceans, Forests, Deserts, and Plains.

FEATURED EXHIBITS

This zoo's crown jewel is the semi-circular **Oceans** complex, redesigned in 2007.

Not just a fish aquarium, it also exhibits aquatic mammals and penguins. A rocky pool in front of the building replicates the northern California coastline and is populated with California sea lions, gray seals, and harbor seals. Visitors who enter the building are greeted by a twenty-six-foot-wide shark exhibit, filled with a school of bonnethead sharks (small members of the hammerhead family). The *Coral Reef* exhibit, with hundreds of colorful Atlantic reef fish and moray eels, features an inverted bubble window that kids can climb into for a closer look. To the left, moon jellies drift slowly in liquid space, lit by fluorescent purple lighting. Around the corner, the building's highlight is the huge *Firestone Gallery*, where children and adults alike wait patiently around the shark petting pool to carefully touch a bigger-than-expected dog shark. All around, the walls are covered with displays presenting extensive information about sharks of the world. The *Seahorses* gallery has three tall cylinder aquariums for these fascinating animals, as well as a wall of corals, anemones, and Nemo's clownfish relatives. The same sea lions and seals seen outside are even more amusing when observed from an underwater viewing window. In the *Penguin Exhibit*, the glass floor of the visitor walkway is below the water's surface, allowing the three penguin species to dive down, swim under your feet, and then pop up on the other side. Polar bears are seen above and below water from another split-level viewing panel. When they dive towards the spectators behind the window, this area becomes one of the most crowded places in the zoo. The polar bears' rocky wintry habitat can also be seen from outside.

Besides their (at least) twice daily shows, the zoo's dolphins can be observed from below the performance pool, where a thirty-foot-diameter glass dome offers complete 360-degree viewing of these fascinating animals. Just outside is the rocky cove habitat for gigantic **walruses**. This is one of a very few zoos to exhibit these popular tusked creatures. An underwater viewing gallery lets visitors watch this group, which at press time included Nereus, the abandoned walrus from Alaska who starred in the 2005 Animal Planet program *Growing Up Walrus*.

From the initial **Plains** observation point, visitors can watch zebras, antelope, ostriches, and other African birds in their shared grassland habitat. A winding path, lined by tall grass, leads to another veldt yard with gazelles and giraffes, in a herd that often includes baby giraffes. For a small fee, the giraffes can be hand-fed at scheduled times throughout the day. Lions can be seen at close range through thin harp wire. Across the path, a bouncing rope bridge takes visitors to an overlook right in the midst of the white rhinos' rocky habitat. Also nearby are African wild dogs and a popular troop of Guinea baboons, who are especially amusing when they groom or chase each other. Large man-made boulders are used to simulate kopjes in the lion, baboon, and rhino exhibits. The *African Elephant Reserve* is one of the nation's best elephant exhibits, with pools, waterfalls, and a large yard for the herd (including a rare bull elephant) to wander. This zoo is a leader in elephant breeding, with at least four successful elephant pregnancies, including the world's first African elephant conceived by artificial insemination. The smaller **Australian Plains** features kangaroos, emus, and black swans in an expansive exhibit. A highlight here is the *Lorikeet Aviary*, where a small fee buys the thrill of hand-feeding the rainbow-colored Australian parrots, who will often perch all over you!

The **Deserts** dome is covered by an eighty-foot transparent roof, which creates a warm, dry climate. Desert gravel from Arizona lines the winding path through rock formations, canyons, and many desert plant species, including palms and cacti. Small finches, quail, tortoises, and lizards roam freely. A 2006 redesign added the popular *Meerkats* exhibit. A side door off the main path leads to the *Drop Dead Gorgeous Snakes!* exhibit, with both educational displays and a dark gallery of venomous vipers from around the world. Outside, big Aldabra tortoises occupy a hillside yard.

OTHER EXHIBITS

The lush **Forests** biome represents both tropical and temperate forests of the world. One highlight is the exhibit of Amur tigers, which features natural vegetation, waterfalls, and a long stream. Thin harp wire barriers provide visitors with nearly unimpeded views of the big cats. An adjacent small yard displays muntjacs (small Asian deer) and adorable red pandas. Also in this area is a combination exhibit of gibbons, swinging in the trees, and Asian otters in the stream below them. Most popular, however, is the Kodiak bear. This playful giant can be seen across a moat or through a large viewing window. Nearby, a towering flight cage displays bald eagles and turkey vultures.

In the **Commons Plaza**, two pretty islands on either side of the zoo's Café on the Commons are inhabited by Chilean flamingos and four species of endangered lemurs, ancient primates from Madagascar, including ultra-rare blue-eyed black lemurs.

FOR THE KIDS

The **Encounters** biome is the place where visitors, especially children, can interact with domestic animals from around the world. A set of outdoor corrals feature exotic domesticated animals such as llamas, a Scottish Highland cow, a Norwegian fjord horse, and a Dutch belted cow. The outside petting yard has a large flock of African pygmy goats, as well as guinea pigs and rabbits. Inside the Encounters building, visitors can meet the zoo's education program animals, including an African serval cat and an armadillo, at *Critter Corner*.

The wide choice of rides includes a train ride taking visitors on a behind-the-scenes tour of the zoo, an endangered animals carousel, seasonal pony rides, a high-tech 4-D simulator ride, and *Kombo*, described as a "family coaster."

Perhaps even more enjoyable than the rides, during the summer kids flock to the **Enchanted Mill Children's Play Area**. This colorful playground has both "dry" and "wet" areas. The latter leaves daring youngsters thoroughly soaked on hot days.

IN PROGRESS

Because it already completed major revisions in 2002 (Elephant Reserve), 2005 (Dolphin Dome), and 2007 (Oceans), the zoo has no plans for extensive changes in the immediate future. However, as we go to press, they hope to add a major great apes exhibit in 2013, featuring gorillas, chimpanzees, and bonobos (pygmy chimps).

Binder Park Zoo

7400 Division Drive
Battle Creek, Michigan 49014
(269) 979-1351
www.binderparkzoo.org

Hours: 9:00 a.m.-5:00 p.m. weekdays, 9:00 a.m.-6:00 p.m. Saturdays and holidays, 11:00 a.m.-6:00 p.m. Sundays, late April–early October. Closed rest of the year. Call or check website for dates, and for special holiday program hours.

Twelve species share the zoo's 18-acre African Savanna.

Admission & Fees: Adults $11.95, seniors $10.95, children 2-10 $9.95. Train ride, carousel $2 each. Giraffe biscuits $1, or six for $5.

Directions: From I-94, take Exit 100 South (MI-294/Beadle Lake Road). Follow Beadle Lake Road for 3 miles, then turn right into the zoo parking lot.

Don't Miss: Wild Africa.

For Kids: Miller Children's Zoo, Z.O. & O. Railroad, Binda Conservation Carousel.

Authors' Tips: Modeled after a cozy lodge, Beulah's Restaurant has indoor seating by a field-stone fireplace. We recommend that you ride the free Wilderness Tram to Wild Africa. Not only does it save you a long, uphill walk, it makes you feel like you're arriving in exotic Africa.

Edutainment: The Binda Conservation Discovery Center has interactive graphics and exhibits. Its 15-minute "Wildlife Discovery Theater" shows feature zoo animals. Zookeepers give inside looks at their favorites in "Zookeeper Tails" at various exhibits. Informal "Critter Chats" are held around the zoo, giving visitors the chance to meet a zoo animal up close. For schedules and locations of presentations, check the "Today" boards at four locations around the zoo.

BATTLE CREEK, MICHIGAN IS MOST FAMOUS FOR ITS BREAKFAST cereals made by familiar companies such as Kellogg and Post. Until 1999, its Binder Park Zoo was best known as a natural, beautiful but small zoo built into the evergreen wilderness. With the June 1999 opening of its world-class Wild Africa exhibit, however, the zoo not only doubled in size, it joined the ranks of major zoos across the nation. Located about halfway between Chicago and Detroit, along Interstate highway I-94, this small zoological gem offers travelers a chance to experience a very realistic trip to Africa.

FEATURED EXHIBITS

In **Wild Africa**, you are invited to suspend your disbelief and imagine you are undertaking a real African safari. The adventure begins back in the main zoo, at the *Avenue of Flags*, where twenty-six overhead arches display large national flags from all fifty-three African nations – a fun geography lesson! At the *International Depot*, visitors board a long, zebra-striped tram for a four-minute ride to the *African Village*. Stepping off the tram, you enter an authentic trading village, with thatch- and tin-roofed buildings. Scattered about are abandoned bicycles and piles of dusty luggage.

Imagining this is Africa is suddenly very easy! The gift shop, restaurant, and even the restrooms are appropriately themed. To the right, visitors enter the headquarters for "Zuri National Park" to begin their free safari. Upon exiting this official hut, the "park" entrance gate is right outside. All along the boardwalk section of this 0.8-mile walking path are expansive views of the *African Savanna Exhibit*. Spread out below, throughout an eighteen-acre grassy valley, are over fifty animals of twelve species, including giraffes, zebras, six types of antelope, and four large bird species, including ostriches. Visitors are invited, for a small fee, to feed biscuits to the giraffes at *Twiga Overlook*. Just beyond the *Ranger Station* with its many kid-focused activities, such as a giraffe periscope, a pack of African wild dogs comes into view in their hillside exhibit. At the *Kima University Research Camp*, the researchers appear to have left their food trays out, as they are now playthings in the forest-dwelling red-capped mangabey monkey habitat. Past the Research Camp's tents, there's a walk-through aviary with over two hundred African songbirds of ten different species. After a long walk through the woods, the path leads to a large yard of black storks and small black duiker antelope, roaming around and beneath the now-stilted boardwalk. At *Monkey Valley*, a large wraparound enclosure lets visitors watch the colobus monkeys and black mangabeys frolic around them. The *Forest Aviary* is built over the ruins of an abandoned logging camp. Von der Decken's hornbills and gorgeous violet-backed starlings are two notable species here. After walking through a long lantern-lit gold mine – actually a tunnel under the main road – you'll arrive at your final adventure, the *Forest Farm*. Here, a herdsman's farmyard includes corrals of guinea fowl, Nubian goats, fat-tailed sheep, and impressive long-horned Watusi cattle, all available for petting.

OTHER EXHIBITS

Red kangaroos inhabit a large central grassland that gives them plenty of room to hop around. Behind them, smaller enclosures display Australian kookaburras, a prairie dog town, and cuddly red pandas from China. The **Australian Yard** features more Australians – wallabies, emus, and Cape Barren geese – in a grassy meadow, while white cockatoos perch in a nearby tree.

The **Binda Conservation Discovery Center** is the zoo's education building. It also exhibits a variety of small monkeys, fish, frogs, and reptiles, including a pair of large Burmese pythons.

Ring-tailed, ruffed, and brown **lemurs**, all endangered primates from the island of Madagascar, live side-by-side in enclosures that resemble a thicket. Aldabra giant tortoises, also island creatures, occupy a small yard in front of pretty Harper Pond.

Across the pond, your vantage point into the **cheetah** enclosure is slightly elevated, making it easy to find these slender cats in their grassy savanna. A boardwalk continues through woods to a forest clearing where Mongolian wild horses (or Przewalski's wild horses) graze. Across the path, gibbons swing and play in a spacious mesh enclosure.

The three-quarter-mile **Swamp Adventure** is a long boardwalk with scenic views of natural marsh, stream, and forest environments. Along the way, bald eagles inhabit a mesh flight cage, and trumpeter swans swim in a pond. Graphic displays aimed at children make it fun to learn about swamp life.

Near the International Depot, a boardwalk extends into a native conifer forest for great views of a **Mexican gray wolf** pack. This rare subspecies recently went extinct in the wild, but with the help of zoos, they've been reintroduced to their native habitat.

FOR THE KIDS

The highlight of the **Miller Children's Zoo** is the five-story replica of a brachiosaurus dinosaur. This two-acre area is also home to exhibits of llamas, pot-bellied pigs, and other domestic animals. Kids can pet and feed sheep and pygmy goats. Other activities include a fossil dig, tunnels that let you pop up inside the rabbit pen, and an attractive playground with a tunnel slide. The **Z.O.&O. Railroad** ride loops through the heart of the Children's Zoo, passes through a dark tunnel, and then traverses the surrounding evergreen forest.

In a covered, all-weather building, the new **Binda Conservation Carousel**, just finished in 2007, has thirty-six hand-carved endangered animals to ride, as well as two handicapped-accessible chariots.

IN PROGRESS

As we go to press, a new, naturalistic exhibit is under construction for the **snow leopards**. These rare plush-coated cats from the Himalayas will receive a new habitat that will triple their living space and more accurately replicate their natural home. Visitors will enter a shaded blind to watch the leopards climb a twenty-foot-high tree trunk or rest on a geothermally cooled boulder. Also under construction is a new 300-seat modern **Wildlife Discovery Theater**. At press time, both the new snow leopard habitat and the new theater are scheduled to open in 2008.

Detroit Zoological Park

8450 West 10 Mile Road
Royal Oak, Michigan 48067
(248) 541-5717
www.detroitzoo.org

Hours: 10:00 a.m.-5:00 p.m. daily, April-October (to 8:00 p.m. on Wednesdays, July August); 10:00 a.m.-4:00 p.m. daily, rest of year. Closed Thanksgiving, Christmas Day, and New Year's Day.

In Polar Passage, visitors watch as bears swim over them.

Admission & Fees: Adults $11, seniors 62+ $9, children 2-12 $7. Railroad $2 each way, Wild Adventure Ride $4 (must be at least 36" tall to ride). Zoo-Plus (admission plus two Railroad rides *or* one Wild Adventure ride) and Zoo-It-All (admission plus one Railroad ride *and* one Wild Adventure ride) packages will save $1 per person. Parking $5. Participates in reciprocity program.

Directions: Located north of Detroit in the suburban city of Royal Oak. From I-696, take Exit

16 (Detroit Zoo), and turn left at the light. Turn left again at the next light, onto 10 Mile Road, and follow to the zoo. Parking is available on 10 Mile Road, in a four-story garage, and in a small lot adjacent to the garage.

Don't Miss: Arctic Ring of Life, Amphibiville, Great Apes of Harambee, African Grasslands, Australian Outback Adventure.

For Kids: Farm animals, prairie dog exhibit, Ford Education Center, Wild Adventure Ride, Tadpole PlayVenture (seasonal).

Authors' Tips: This 125-acre zoo is laid out in a long, narrow rectangle, making a round-trip walk an imposing task. We strongly suggest catching a ride on the Tauber Family Railroad for the 1¼ mile trip from the Main Train Station to the African Train Station at the far end of the zoo, then walking back through the zoo (or vice versa). Ordinarily, early morning is the best time to see the polar bears swim, so make the Polar Passage tunnel your first stop.

Edutainment: Make sure to talk to as many zoo docents as possible. Sporting red shirts, these volunteers are easy to find at all major exhibits. They are extremely knowledgeable and give valuable information on both the animal species and individuals at the zoo.

OPENED IN 1928, THE DETROIT ZOO WAS THE FIRST U.S. ZOO TO emphasize barless, moated exhibits, rather than cages. Today, many visitors' first impression here is that they have entered a theme park. With a four-level parking garage and a landscaped entrance court that includes a train station, fountains, and a gift shop, it could easily be mistaken for one.

The attractive grounds include wild waterfowl lakes, spacious grassy knolls, and huge stone grottoes. The famous **Rackham Memorial Fountain** in the center of the park, with its bronze bear sculptures, is a favorite spot for photos. At the front entrance, a 150-foot-tall water tower is a local landmark. Painted with colorful animal graphics, it is visible for miles around.

FEATURED EXHIBITS

Arctic Ring of Life is, in our opinion, quite simply the best, most intricate, and largest polar bear exhibit ever created. This four-acre habitat reflects all three of the natural environments where polar bears are found. The snow-white bears, which are among the world's largest land carnivores, are easy to spot in the tall grasses of *Tundra Land Bear*, a unique exhibit that depicts these bears' summer habitat. Arctic foxes and snowy owls have small habitats along the trail, amongst several vantage points into the bears' enclosure. The path continues to a rocky coastline exhibit of harp and harbor seals, before curving down to the *Nunavut Gallery*. Inside, Inuit sculptures and artifacts sit beside twenty-foot-tall windows revealing the clear blue water of the *Open Sea*  *Bear* habitat. The highlight of this amazing exhibit is the first-of-its-kind *Polar Passage*, a seventy-foot glass tunnel passing through the bears' 300,000-gallon pool. Mesmerized visitors can watch both bears and seals swimming above and around them in the chilly forty-five-degree water. Glass barriers are cleverly hidden, creating the impression that predators and prey share the same aquatic environment. At the end of the tunnel, visitors can experience the arctic chill for themselves by pressing a hand to the ice-covered cave walls. Snowshoes hang in the *Exploration Station*, where another great underwater view of the bears awaits, and an inverted bubble window juts into the seals' pool. Outside in the *Pack Ice Bear* habitat, an iceberg-making machine generates ice to make the bears' harsh winter environment that much more realistic.

Great Apes of Harambee is the home to the largest chimpanzee exhibit in the nation. The *Fossil Trail* encircles the chimps' large habitat and provides eight distinct views into the exhibit. These boisterous apes have a varied environment with tall trees to climb, a thick forest to hide in, and an open meadow to explore. The grassy slopes are enhanced with heated rocks, artificial kapok trees, and man-made termite mounds. Detroit is one of only a few zoos to exhibit gorillas with other primates. Diana monkeys and baboon-like mandrills share a rocky elevated habitat with a troop of gorillas. Inside the *African Apes* building, skulls and handprints illustrate the differences and similarities between the apes displayed here and humans. Large glass panels allow visitors to watch the zoo's resident chimpanzees in their two-story indoor quarters, and to see both gorillas and chimps from closer vantage points in their outdoor spaces.

In most zoos, amphibians are exhibited in a reptile building. Here, these semi-aquatic creatures live in **Amphibiville**, the nation's premier display of amphibians. Exhibiting over a thousand frogs, toads, newts, and salamanders, the building is also home to the National Amphibian Conservation Center, a nationwide organization that's working to halt the alarming decrease in amphibian species around the world. Amphibiville, a building that's shaped like a lily pad, is the place to see amphibians of all sizes – from the largest (four-foot-long Japanese salamanders) to the smallest (golden mantella frogs that fit on a penny). Most of the animals here are displayed nowhere else, such as Texas blind cave salamanders and Wyoming toads. It takes a sharp eye to find the frogs in the exhibit's final stop, a steamy walk-through jungle. Just outside this building is a fine example of a Michigan wetland. On a stroll along its boardwalk, visitors can watch trumpeter swans gracefully gliding along the water surface, while native frogs croak in the cattails.

New animals and attractions have rejuvenated the **African Grasslands** exhibit. Egyptian hieroglyphics and statues along the exterior of the *Giraffe House* pay homage to the first civilization to build a zoo. From a newly constructed deck, opened in 2007, visitors can feed the giraffes at scheduled times throughout the day. Near a hippo display, aardvarks dig large burrows throughout their enclosure, which sometimes makes them hard to spot. Exhibits of warthogs and African wild dogs abut a spacious yard of thin-striped Grevy's zebras and burgundy-colored blesbok antelope. White rhinos, the world's second largest land mammal, inhabit a large yard that was formerly the elephant enclosure. Not far from here is the *African Swamp*, where cranes, storks, and flamingos wade in a lake, and six vulture species share an adjacent yard.

In the **Australian Outback Adventure**, only knee-high cables line the visitor walkway, and the resident kangaroos and wallabies wander barrier-free through their shady yard. A chart at the *Kangaroo Activity Plaza* measures how far you can jump, compared with a kangaroo. Anyone who can exceed the kangaroo's twenty-seven-foot leap should enter the Olympics!

OTHER EXHIBITS

The **Holden Museum of Living Reptiles** is one of the zoo's most popular attractions. A round central exhibit holds the largest of the building's animals; Siamese crocodiles, caimans, and iguanas. Nearly eighty other species of reptiles are displayed along the wall.

The **Wildlife Interpretive Gallery** is more art display than zoo exhibit. Two levels of animal-inspired artwork line the walls, while a small theater plays several film clips, including one about the zoo's history. Attached to this gallery are the **Butterfly Garden** and **Free Flight Aviary**. More birds can be found inside the triangular **Penguinarium**, where three Antarctic penguin species inhabit coastal habitats.

Most of the zoo's large carnivores have occupied the same grottoes since 1928. Grizzly and black bears live in a row of traditional but spacious zoo habitats. The African lion exhibit is unique, giving them a steep cliff to rest on, high above the visitor path. Siberian (also known as Amur) tigers prowl in a more modern exhibit, complete with a waterfall and plenty of shade.

Spread across the zoo are many exhibits designated by geography. The **South American** yard has tapirs, guanacos, rheas, and vultures. Other South American animals live nearby, such as, giant anteaters, tiny pudu deer, flamingos, raccoon-like coatimundis, and water-dwelling capybaras, the world's largest rodents. A mixed-species **Asian** yard displays two-humped Bactrian camels and herds of white-lipped and fallow deer. Across the zoo, nearly extinct Przewalski's wild horses, also known as Mongolian wild horses, roam an open plain. Bison and elk, in large paddocks, represent **North America**. Michigan, the Wolverine State, pays tribute to its mascot with a nearby wolverine exhibit. Japanese snow monkeys, also known as Japanese macaques, live in a mountain exhibit, complete with a waterfall and hot springs. Other primates throughout the zoo include gibbons, lion-tailed macaque monkeys, and lemurs. You'll find otters, bald eagles, red pandas, peccaries, and tree kangaroos here as well.

Wolverines

FOR THE KIDS

Horses, cattle, sheep, and other **farm animals** live in pens outside a barn near the wolverines. Pot-bellied pigs and chickens are also displayed elsewhere in the barnyard.

Kids can crawl underneath a two-tiered **prairie dog** habitat, and then emerge into any of three acrylic bubble windows inside the enclosure to get a closer look at these social rodents. Inside the **Ford Education Center** is the **Wild Adventure Ride**, a virtual reality thrill ride with a nature theme. This education building also houses a theater, an exhibit gallery, and an interpretive studio. The **Tadpole PlayVenture** is a playground for toddlers, themed to complement Amphibiville's animals.

IN PROGRESS

The zoo plans to eventually add more big cats and primates to its collection. Other future attractions could include a meerkat exhibit, hummingbirds, and a zoo-themed carousel.

Cincinnati Zoo and Botanical Garden

3400 Vine Street
Cincinnati, Ohio 45220
(513) 281-4700
www.cincyzoo.org

Harry is the third Sumatran rhino born in Cincinnati.

Hours: 9:00 a.m.-6:00 p.m. daily, Memorial Day-Labor Day; 9:00 a.m.-5:00 p.m. daily, rest of year. Closed Thanksgiving and Christmas.

Admission & Fees: Adults $13, seniors 62+ $11, children 2-12 $8. Safari shuttle $1.50, train ride $3, carousel $2, bird feeding $1, parking $6.50. Participates in reciprocity program.

Directions: From I-71, take Exit 5 (Dana Avenue), and turn right onto Dana Avenue. Follow Dana Avenue for 0.6 miles, and turn left onto Victory Parkway. Follow Victory Parkway for 0.3 miles, then turn right onto Rockdale Avenue. Follow Rockdale Avenue, which becomes Forest Avenue, for 1.2 miles, then turn left onto Dury Avenue. Zoo parking lot is on the right. From I-75, take Exit 6 (Mitchell Avenue), follow Mitchell Avenue for 0.3 miles, then turn right onto Vine Street. Follow Vine Street for 0.7 miles, then turn left onto Forest Avenue. Follow Forest Avenue for 0.2 miles, then turn right onto Dury Avenue. Zoo parking lot is on the right.

Don't Miss: Sumatran rhinos, Jungle Trails, "Cheetah Encounter" show (seasonal), Insect World, Manatee Springs, Vanishing Giants, Gorilla World, Eagle Eyrie, Cat House.

For Kids: Children's Zoo, train ride, Conservation Carousel, 4-D Special FX Theater.

Authors' Tips: As its name implies, the zoo is also a botanical garden – one of the first in the country to combine these attractions. In addition to its vast animal collection, you can also enjoy the grounds' 12 themed gardens. A pollinator garden attracts butterflies and hummingbirds, while the Garden of Peace reflects the cultural and spiritual history of the Middle East.

Edutainment: In addition to a twice-daily "Cheetah Encounter" show (see below) throughout the summer, the zoo also presents an award-winning "Great American Wings of Wonder" bird show, featuring 24 species of birds, reptiles, and mammals. "Meet-A-Zookeeper" chats are conducted at all the major exhibits. Special encounters include snake and alligator feedings at the Reptile House, cat feedings at the Cat House, an elephant bathing demonstration, and manatee divers at Manatee Springs. Check your map for times and locations.

THE SECOND OLDEST ZOO IN THE UNITED STATES (IT OPENED IN 1875), the Cincinnati Zoo has consistently been ranked as one of America's best. Moreover, the zoo is so old that three of its buildings have been designated as National Historic Landmarks. One of these is the **Passenger Pigeon Memorial**. This former birdhouse, built in 1875, is now a monument to extinct animals – particularly the passenger pigeon and the Carolina parakeet. The very last members of these species, Incas the parakeet and Martha the pigeon, died at this zoo in 1914 and 1918, respectively. Their remains were mounted and are displayed here.

The zoo has long been a leader in the field of breeding endangered species. High-tech reproduction methods are researched and applied at the **Center for Reproduction of Endangered Wildlife** (CREW), on zoo grounds. CREW has an interactive exhibit area that's open to the public – it's worth a visit.

FEATURED EXHIBITS

Cincinnati has long been one of only a few institutions to exhibit **Sumatran rhinos**. Unique for their coarse red hair, and notoriously difficult to breed, these rhinos are, as of 2007, only exhibited at this zoo. In 2001, after several miscarriages, the zoo finally successfully achieved the first captive birth of a Sumatran rhino in over a century. Andalas, the historic rhino calf, has since been sent back to his native Indonesia to begin a breeding program, but the Cincinnati rhinos continue to thrive, and have produced more babies. The family lives in two side-by-side exhibits covered by massive shade structures, creating an almost sunless environment, just like a rain forest floor. This sheltered setting, and plenty of mud wallows, protect the rhinos' sensitive skin from sunburn.

African and Asian primates are displayed in the **Jungle Trails** exhibit. A mist-covered path, enveloped by bamboo and ferns, descends toward a swaying rope bridge, where lemurs inhabit a lush island. Sumatran orangutans and white-handed gibbons swing together from tropical-vine-strangled trees and ropes. A giant elephant skull is visible in the swamp habitat that houses saddle-bill storks and duiker antelope. Side exhibits for macaque monkeys, colobus monkeys, and more gibbons are visible along the pathway. Rarely exhibited bonobos – pygmy chimpanzees – can be seen up close on a wooded hillside with a jungle stream, or through a large window in a viewing cave. The Asian and African areas both have nocturnal exhibits of smaller primates, reptiles, and birds in beautiful jungle buildings that also serve as winter quarters for the outdoor animals.

Even on safari in Africa, few people ever see a cheetah running at top speed, chasing a gazelle. "Cheetah Encounter," a summer-only presentation, provides this opportunity, though an artificial lure replaces the gazelle as the cheetah's target. Cincinnati is only the second zoo in the world to showcase the speed of this sleek cat. The dash is just one part of an entertaining show that highlights cheetah characteristics that are similar to those of domestic dogs and cats.

The most innovative exhibit here is **Insect World**, which was named "Exhibit of the Year" by the AZA when it first opened. It's the largest and best display of living insects in the United States. In a museum-like setting, educational graphics, hands-on activities, and insect exhibits are combined to address such topics as *How Insects Feed*, *Who Eats Insects*, *Camouflage and Mimicry*, and *Insect Lifestyles*. A special scale reports visitors' weights in insects. One six-year-old girl weighed in at over 8.5 million insects! Insect World is often noted for its exotic insects, including Southeast Asian walking sticks, Hercules beetles, and inch-long bullet ants, one of the world's most venomous insects. Altogether, over a hundred species are displayed. Noteworthy exhibits include naked mole-rats, the *Butterfly Rain Forest* (which also includes hummingbirds), and a leaf-cutter ant display in which a miniature video camera mounted in the exhibit magnifies the ants on a video screen.

Live palm trees overhang the walkway to **Manatee Springs**. American crocodiles and alligators float in their pool or relax on a shaded shoreline. Manatees steal the spotlight as guests enter their climate-controlled indoor habitat. Wide windows, including a bubble window, allow for great views into these sea cows' freshwater habitat. Graphics showcase the history of Florida's ecosystems, with a special emphasis on the ecological role of manatees. A standout exhibit features Florida's invasive species, headlined by large Burmese pythons, foreign invaders now common in the Everglades. Smaller exhibits for fish, iguanas, and milk snakes are nearby. A scrubland habitat filled with Eastern diamondback rattlesnakes is the last exhibit you'll pass before exiting the building.

Schott Vanishing Giants is the aptly named home of enormous endangered Asian elephants. Built in 1902, this Indian-mosque inspired building is home to a herd of female elephants. Outside, a winding visitor trail surrounds a half-acre yard, with occasional views of the elephants, who can splash in a 38,000-gallon pool or scratch their backs on a large rocky outcropping.

Gorilla World was one of the first zoo exhibits to take gorillas outdoors. With almost fifty births (and counting) since 1967, this animal, more than any other, has contributed to Cincinnati's reputation as the country's "sexiest zoo." Two groups of gorillas rotate time in this spacious exhibit, backed by an imposing rock wall. Unlike many newer exhibits, which use glass barriers, here a fifteen-foot deep moat stretching the length of the exhibit is all that separates curious visitors from the apes. Beneath a two-tiered viewing shelter, the world's largest primates seem to be especially close. Crowned guenon and colobus monkeys romp in a tall glass-fronted exhibit near the exit.

Eagle Eyrie uses the steep slope of Wildlife Canyon as the base for its two massive flight cages. Barrier-free visitor decks project into the forested homes of bald and Stellar's sea eagles. This is one of only a few zoo exhibits where eagles can fully take flight. Enormous nests bring the birds close to the viewing deck, but getting a clear look at the eagles in their dense forest can still be difficult at times.

OTHER EXHIBITS

Wings of Wonder is the zoo's renovated bird house. Inside, traditional galleries display feathered specimens from around the globe, including penguins, kingfishers, hornbill birds, the magnificent bird of paradise, and toucanets, smaller relatives of toucans. Just outside is an Australian mixed-species exhibit, where birds of all sizes and shapes, including lorikeets, seven species of parrots, imperial pigeons, and magpie geese surround visitors as they walk along an elevated boardwalk. While you're in this walk-through aviary, don't overlook the wallabies at your feet. Seed sticks to feed the birds are available for a small fee.

The **Cat House** is home to many of the world's most endangered small cats. Mesh-covered outdoor enclosures surround the building, and each indoor habitat features naturalistic rock work and beautiful mural backdrops that portray the cats' native homes. Siberian lynx, clouded leopards, pumas, and Pallas' cats are all here. This zoo has a highly successful breeding program for spotted ocelot cats, also featured here.

The gazebo-style **Reptile House** is the oldest zoo building in America. Here, Chinese alligators live on a small circular island beneath a dome that resembles the U.S. Capitol building. One wall is lined with a row of terrariums housing snakes, lizards, and frogs from across the globe.

Most of the zoo's African animals live in **Flamingo Cove**, a set of yards radiating from a central hub. Both black and Indian rhinos, which vary in size and number of horns, are found along the looping path. Grevy's zebras (distinguished from other zebras by their white bellies), bongo antelope, and okapis (forest-dwelling cousins of giraffes) are also here. An African wetland displays both greater and lesser flamingos (the lesser have black beaks), geese, and ducks.

The rest of the zoo's hoofed animals are in **Wildlife Canyon,** which includes the above-mentioned Sumatran rhinos. Rare mammals on display include goat-like takins, red river hogs, Mhorr and slender horned gazelles, highly endangered scimitar-horned oryxes, and a non-mammalian species: emus. Along this sunken path, you can also take a look up at Eagle Eyrie.

The **Nocturnal House** was the world's first light-reversal display of nocturnal animals. Among the creatures you'll see are barn owls, fennec foxes, vampire bats, and binturongs, which look like a cross between a bear and a cat. In the largest exhibit, fruit bats flutter about above pig-like aardvarks.

Tiger Canyon displays Malaysian tigers, white Bengal tigers, and African wild dogs, whre they live in a series of grassy gullies. Two rocky grottoes have been combined and renovated to create **Lords of the Arctic**, a spacious home for the zoo's polar bears. With crashing waterfalls and two large pools, these water-loving giants have no shortage of places to cool off. Three twenty-foot-high windows allow for underwater viewing into the bear's deeper pool. The **Bearline** hosts more grottoes for spectacled and black bears.

A long, raised platform weaves through **Siegfried & Roy's White Lions of Timbavati**. These lions are not truly white, but have a noticeably light tint. While a population of white lions was recently discovered in South Africa, Cincinnati's lions are from the private collection of Las Vegas entertainers, Siegfried & Roy. The lions have plenty of room to roam in this expansive exhibit, but more often than not, they can be found resting on a set of tiered wooden platforms.

Island exhibits are found throughout the zoo. Mueller's gibbons and siamangs enjoy tall bamboo climbing structures on the **Gibbon Islands.** Japanese macaque monkeys have a rocky home surrounded by water near the Reptile House. Other popular animals around the zoo include lemurs, giant anteaters, and red pandas, which enjoy two densely planted enclosures. Utilized as the zoo's main education building, the new **Schott Education Center**, which opened in 2007, also contains *Discovery Forest*, a three-story rain forest environment. South American monkeys climb among live plants in this circular enclosure, located in the building's atrium.

FOR THE KIDS

The **Spaulding Children's Zoo** is divided into several areas that are designed to connect kids with many varieties of wildlife. California sea lions can be seen both from above and below water in *Seal Falls*. Enjoy close encounters with animals in both the *Discovery Center* (where zoo staff members show off a variety of critters) and *Blakely's Barn* (where common and exotic domestic species are housed). *Wolf Woods*, the newest component of the Children's Zoo, focuses on the conservation of several native Ohio species, as well as two creatures from the American southwest. North American river otters are the highlight of the local animal display, but the walk-through turkey cage and skunk exhibit are also interesting. In the second part of Wolf Woods, a breeding pack of Mexican gray wolves can be seen in their forested hillside, from an outdoor overlook or from inside a trapper's cabin. Native to Arizona, thick-billed parrots, the only parrot species native to the U.S., have a tall enclosure covered with stiff netting.

The old-fashioned **train ride** here is one of the best. As it circles the zoo, it travels across high trestles overlooking Flamingo Cove, and glides over **Swan Lake** on surface-level tracks, offering a panoramic view of the fountains and waterfowl. The **Conservation Carousel** offers classic merry-go-round rides for kids of all ages. The new **4-D Special FX Theater**, opened in 2007, presents changing 3-D movies with the thrill of special effects that let viewers feel and smell the adventure.

IN PROGRESS

In 2007, the zoo began an exciting renovation to the Vanishing Giants building. They moved the okapis to Flamingo Cove, and its one remaining giraffe to another zoo to create space for this new exhibit. Scheduled to open in 2009 as we go to press, the new Vanishing Giants exhibit will have an expanded elephant yard for the current herd, and an additional yard for a bull elephant, allowing the zoo to resume its elephant breeding program. The Masai giraffes will benefit from an expanded habitat in **Giraffe Ridge** in 2008, and an elevated visitor deck for giraffe feedings.

Cleveland Metroparks Zoo

3900 Wildlife Way
Cleveland, Ohio 44109
(216) 661-6500
www.clemetzoo.com

Hours: 10:00 a.m.-5:00 p.m. weekdays, to 7:00 p.m. weekends and holidays, Memorial Day-Labor Day; 10:00 a.m.-5:00 p.m. daily, rest of year. Box office closes one hour prior to closing time. Closed Christmas Day and New Year's Day.

Wolf Wilderness is home to a pack of gray wolves.

Admission & Fees: Adults $10, children 2-11 $5, April-October; adults $7, children 2-11 $5, November-March. If you're a local, call for information on free or reduced admission. Riders of RTA bus 20C get half-price admission. Boomerang Line train ride $1.50, Safari ride $4, camel ride $4, lorikeet feeding $1. Participates in reciprocity program.

Directions: From I-71, take Exit 245 (25th Street), and turn right onto 25th Street. Follow for 0.8 miles, turn left onto Wildlife Way, and follow 0.6 miles to the zoo. RTA bus 20C serves the zoo.

Don't Miss: The RainForest, Wolf Wilderness, Australian Adventure, African Savanna, Primate, Cat, & Aquatics Building.

For Kids: Australian Adventure (including Boomerang Line train), Savanna Ridge playground, Safari ride.

Authors' Tips: The RainForest is kept at a constant, humid 80 degrees. During cold weather, coat racks are available, but it is easier to leave coats and heavy sweaters in your car, since the parking lot is between the RainForest and the rest of the zoo. Free ZooTrams will take you to the far points of the zoo and are especially convenient for reaching the Primate, Cat, & Aquatics Building. You can enjoy a meal in front of the lions, where stands sell food from McDonalds and KFC Express, or at the Crocodile Café in the RainForest's bazaar-like Marketplace.

Edutainment: "Dr. Z's Wild Animal Show" features an animal cast that includes a sloth, a fennec fox, a vulture, and other exotic creatures. Shows are held three times daily in summer, and on September weekends, in the 400-seat Zoo Amphitheater. During the summer, if you go to see the sea lions in their daily demonstration up on the Northern Trek, you will receive a special commemorative sticker. In the Australian Adventure area, the Ballarat Theatre hosts regularly scheduled animal shows aimed specifically at children; show times are posted at the theatre entrance.

OPENED IN 1882, THE CLEVELAND METROPARKS ZOO HAS BEEN at its present location in hilly Brookside Park since 1914. It is one of the country's oldest zoos, and with 168 rolling, wooded acres, it is also one of the largest. Cleveland is best known in the zoo world for its extensive primate collection: With thirty-four different primate species, it has one of the largest collections in North America.

FEATURED EXHIBITS

The **RainForest** building is truly world-class and is the zoo's landmark exhibit.

The domed, copper-colored glass building has 85,000 square feet of exhibit space, making it one of the largest and best indoor exhibits we've ever seen. The roar of a twenty-five-foot waterfall can overwhelm visitors entering the building's *Atrium*. Behind the falls, "ancient temple ruins" are covered with bromeliads and other tropical plants. Habitats for four species of endangered South American tamarin monkeys are built into the wall; the monkeys are only separated from visitors by thin harp wire. To the right of the Atrium is the *Medicine Trail*, a path through a dense jungle lined with plants used in modern and traditional medicines – an illustration of one of many excellent reasons to preserve the world's rain forests. A spiral staircase inside a giant kapok tree makes a playful way to get upstairs. Enter the upper level exhibits through *The Scientist's Hut*, a Malaysian research tent that sets the exploration theme. Out the windows, saki monkeys can be seen frolicking in the trees. A screen door opens to the *Amazon River Basin*, where giant anteaters and capybaras (giant aquatic rodents) inhabit a mud bank, and trees contain prehensile-tailed porcupines and sloths. Beautiful spotted ocelot cats are visible across from a large habitat for fishing cats, whose exhibit includes underwater views so visitors can watch them as they bat fish out of the water and then devour them. The *Asian Primates* section features vine-covered "temple ruins" where François' langur monkeys are clearly visible at treetop level in their two-story exhibit. Across the path, an orangutan family has the freedom to climb a tree to the top of the building's thirty-nine-foot dome. Small-clawed otters frolic in the *Bornean Streamside*, which they share with Asian turtles.

On the RainForest's lower level, an exhibition hall displays more than 300 amphibians and reptiles, including poison dart frogs, vine snakes, caiman crocodiles, and a reticulated python. Egyptian fruit bats are visible in a long nocturnal display near the entrance. Rain forest films, shown in a small video theater, make for a nice excuse to rest your feet. Indian crested porcupines, with alarmingly long quills, live in a central exhibit that gets drenched every twelve minutes by mock thunderstorms. The *Insectarium's* most notable display, the leaf-cutter ant farm, is visible up close via a joystick-operated video camera. Easy-to-use microscopes provide glimpses of the tiniest microorganisms of the rain forest. Your tour ends near the home of the largest inhabitant, a long and imposing gharial crocodile that often can be viewed nose-to-nose through underwater windows.

Enter **Wolf Wilderness** through the 3,000-square-foot *Wolf Lodge*, a near-perfect replica of a nineteenth-century trapper's cabin. Outfitted with antiques, the cabin's front room looks like the trapper just stepped out, aside from the interpretive displays and video. In a back room, wide windows give great views of the pack of gray wolves that inhabits the dense woods outside. Upon exiting the cabin, visitors walk through a bald eagle's habitat, where America's national bird perches only a few feet away from admiring visitors. Across the path is a large glass-fronted pond, the home of a beaver, who shares this habitat with the wolves. If you can't spot the beaver swimming in the pond, this industrious rodent is usually visible inside its lodge.

While the **Australian Adventure** is the zoo's main children's area, it also includes exhibits that no one should miss. One standout is *Gum Leaf Hideout*, an Aussie-style building where a breeding group of koalas perches in live eucalyptus trees. An adjacent habitat displays endangered tree kangaroos. This area's Australian theme is strong and impressive, making it easy to believe you have actually traveled "down under." The heart of this area is the large *Wallaby Walkabout*, an outback trail where both red and gray kangaroos, wallaroos, and three types of wallabies hop around their visitors from the States. The Walkabout leads to the porch of the *Reinberger Homestead*, a convincing replica of a sprawling nineteenth-century Australian ranch house. Inside, the house is a virtual time warp into rural Australian history.

The focal point of the spacious **African Savanna** exhibit is the central *Plains* yards, where zebras, bontebok antelope and gazelles, as well as ostriches and six other African bird species and a large herd of Masai giraffes, all have room to wander. The animals can be seen from secluded lookouts off the main trail, from an elevated wooden hut, and from high above, up the hill. Windows allow for close-up viewing of the lions near their den, but the best view of these majestic cats is from a wonderful seating area near the food stands. Nearby, a flock of lesser flamingos wades in an attractive marsh. A breeding group of black rhinos lives in a large yard, not far from the other African animals, while a troop of beautiful black-and-white colobus monkeys entertains visitors from its home on historic *Monkey Island*, which is over a century old. A large Persian leopard lives nearby.

Set among tall oaks, the **Primate, Cat, & Aquatics Building** is reached by climbing the fun, but tiring, *Deckwalk* to the zoo's highest elevation. Inside, wide carpeted halls are lined with rows of glass-fronted enclosures for a wide variety of animals, including gorillas, chimpanzees, gibbons, baboons, Wolf's guenon monkeys, swamp monkeys, howler monkeys, and spider monkeys. What the enclosures lack in naturalism they make up for in excellent viewing opportunities. The *Madagascar* section is most impressive, with six different lemur species, as well as the cat-like fossa, a carnivore that preys on lemurs. Another section is decorated with a Chinese motif, perhaps to make the red pandas, snow leopards, and clouded leopards feel more at home. These latter animals can also be seen in outdoor enclosures. In the *Aquatics* section, seahorses, huge pacu fish and orange piranhas from the Amazon, and the pretty *Red Sea* reef tank are among the thirty-five aquarium exhibits. Sharks can be seen through portholes and from a special seating area. Outside, a large yard houses an impressive group of cheetahs, near a naturalistic habitat with a trickling stream and pond that hosts a couple of gorillas. Aldabra tortoises live in a pen across the path.

OTHER EXHIBITS

The **Northern Trek**, of which Wolf Wilderness is a part, is located in a far corner of the zoo. Two separate pools housing sea lions, harbor seals, and polar bears feature roaring waterfalls that splash into the rocky habitats. Grizzly bears live in a nearby grotto. The visitor path circles large yards for Bactrian camels, reindeer, and white-lipped deer, all species from northern Asia. A circle of stone grottoes exhibits Siberian (or Amur) tigers and four more species of bears: sloth, black, spectacled, and Malayan sun bears.

The **Waterfowl Lake** is filled with ducks, swans, and Chilean flamingos. Out on the lake's islands, gibbons, lemurs, and tamarin monkeys can all be seen from a bridge. Endangered bald eagles and Andean condors live near the lake in two large flight cages. The **Public Greenhouse** holds everything from jungle plants to cacti, and in the summer is also home to the popular *Butterfly Magic* exhibit.

Those who are interested in veterinary medicine for zoo animals should enjoy the walk-through, self-guided tour of the **Sarah Allison Steffee Center for Zoological Medicine**.

FOR THE KIDS

In addition to the fascinating animal exhibits described above, the **Australian Adventure** also has some unique adventures especially for children. The amazing *Yagga Tree*, also called "My Tree House," is what most children will remember best. Inside and around this fifty-five-foot-tall artificial baobab tree, kids can cross a swaying suspension bridge, climb up to a towering lookout with a cannon and captain's wheel, stop to check out the bats and snakes exhibited inside, slide down a snake slide, or squeal with fright at the gigantic animatronic crocodile "Wooly Bill" as he lurches at unsuspecting kids from within his waterfall cavern. *Kookaburra Station* is a working sheep farm, where children can watch Australian Merino sheep being sheared. Outside this large barn are contact yards where kids can pet sheep, goats, and other farm animals. In the *Lorikeet Aviary*, cups of nectar can be purchased to feed the colorful, friendly Aussie birds. The *Boomerang Line* train ride encircles the entire exhibit area, passing a number of signs with a variety of Australian slogans. There are also camel rides here in season. Camels in Australia? Not as out of place as they seem! They were once common beasts of burden in the Outback and eventually went wild. Feral populations of camels now live throughout the Australian Outback.

High above the African Savanna, *Savanna Ridge* is the location of a small, colorful playground, as well as the **Safari Ride,** an exciting motion simulator ride.

IN PROGRESS

The **African Elephant Crossing** promises to be a naturalistic, state-of-the-art habitat for the zoo's expanding herd. At five acres, the exhibit will have room for up to ten elephants, including a large bull, who would be a necessary component for a breeding program. While visitors will enjoy the realistic African village and an elevated feeding station, the elephants will benefit from two sprawling yards and pools deep enough for the massive pachyderms to totally submerge themselves. Other animals in the exciting new exhibit will include meerkats, naked mole-rats, African pythons, and several colorful species of birds. This exhibit is scheduled to open in 2010 or 2011 as we go to press.

Columbus Zoo and Aquarium

9990 Riverside Drive
Powell, Ohio 43065
(614) 645-3400
www.columbuszoo.org

Hours: 9:00 a.m.-6:00 p.m. daily, Memorial Day-Labor Day; 9:00 a.m.-5:00 p.m. daily, rest of the year. Open until 8:00 p.m. on Wednesdays in summer.

Boat ride takes visitors around the Islands of Southeast Asia exhibit. Tower in distance is a climbing structure for the zoo's orangutans.

Admission & Fees: Adults $10, seniors 60+ $8 (Tuesdays $3.50), kids under 48 inches $6; carousel, train, and boat rides $1 each; pony ride $4; Lorikeet Garden $1; parking $5.

Directions: From I-270 Outerbelt, take Exit 20 (Sawmill Road). After 0.4 miles on Sawmill Road, turn left onto Hard Road and follow for 1 mile. Turn right onto Riverside Drive (OH-257) and follow for 2.6 miles to the zoo.

Don't Miss: Asia Quest, African Forest, Manatee Coast, Australia and the Islands of Southeast Asia, Pachyderm Building, North America.

For Kids: Habitat Hollow, Stings, Wings, N' Play Things Park, carousel, pony ride, North American Train, Islands of Southeast Asia Boat Ride.

Authors' Tips: With a zoo, water park, and golf course on the property, this would be a great destination for a multi-day vacation. The animal-themed water park, Zoombezi Bay, includes Jungle Jack's Landing, which has 14 rides and attractions, including a roller coaster. There are ticket packages available at the zoo that include both water park and zoo admission at a discounted rate. During the winter, the zoo opens an ice skating rink, so bring your ice skates!

Edutainment: "Wings of Flight," a show featuring birds of prey and parrots, is scheduled twice daily on weekdays. "Discovery Reef Diver" and various "Meet the Keeper" presentations are held daily around the zoo. Check the schedule on your zoo map for times and locations.

BEST KNOWN AS "THE ZOO THAT JACK HANNA BUILT," THE Columbus Zoo is now gaining fame in its own right, due to its world-class exhibits and collection. "Jungle Jack" Hanna, the zoo's director from 1978 to 1993, is now the Director Emeritus, and his presence is still felt here. Already housing almost 800 animal species, the zoo has recently acquired more land next door to its current property with an eye to expansion – to a total of 580 acres. This massive facility already includes an adjoining water park and golf course. The zoo also manages The Wilds, a 10,000-acre nature preserve in Zanesville, eighty miles east of Columbus.

Having added a new exhibit a year from 1997 to 2006, the zoo feels very new, even though it celebrated its eightieth birthday in 2007. These new exhibits deliver a conservation message but don't neglect the fun, often combining colorful educational graphics with an entertaining ride by boat or train, from which animals on display can be seen from different perspectives.

FEATURED EXHIBITS

An imposing overhanging stone sculpture leads visitors into **Asia Quest,** an exhibit that focuses on rare and endangered Asian animals and the factors that threaten their survival. An extinction bell tolls regularly in remembrance of animal species now extinct. White-naped and red-crowned cranes each share their yards with small deer (muntjacs and tufted deer, respectively). The *Quest for Enlightenment Interpretive Center* has indoor habitats for flying foxes (which are actually bats), water monitors, and silvered leaf langurs (long-tailed monkeys), which can also be seen outdoors. An Asian market scene exposes the evils of hunting endangered animals for profit. Sun bears, the smallest of the bears, wander through an abandoned warehouse and a terraced forest. A walk-through aviary presents a close encounter with colorful pheasants, while red pandas live next door. You can spot nimble spiral-horned markhor goats climbing rocks in their enclosure, just before the habitat for small and rare Pallas' cats. The adventure ends with several views of the largest of all felines, Amur tigers.

The Columbus Zoo is famous for its success in breeding gorillas. Once housed in a separate exhibit, the gorillas are now part of the **African Forest**, which begins at the *Congo Expedition Forest Trail* base camp. Here, visitors get a peek at lanky Angolan colobus monkeys, African gray parrots, and other birds, including ibises and hammerkops (African long-legged wading birds). A thick fallen tree gives the leopards a high place to be seen at rest, before the gorillas come into view. Colo, the first gorilla ever born in captivity, back in 1956, still lives here. She is as big a local celebrity as "Jungle Jack" himself! The dozen-plus gorillas share a large outdoor habitat, filled with climbing structures, hills, and tunnels. As noted above, this zoo is a leader in gorilla reproduction. Resident gorillas have produced more than fifty offspring, and the zoo's females are also frequently utilized as surrogate mothers for orphaned gorillas from other zoos, so babies are a common sight here. Nearby, red river hogs rest in a shady canyon exhibit, bordered by the nation's best exhibit of bonobos. These slender pygmy chimpanzees can climb to heights of over thirty feet in their hillside forest habitat. Small pools bring rare black-faced drills close to tall viewing windows. The forest path concludes with three outdoor yards for okapis, forest-dwelling cousins of giraffes.

When **Manatee Coast** opened in 1999, Columbus became only the third zoo in the country to exhibit manatees. In this large pool, injured manatees are rehabilitated for reintroduction to the wild. Sharing the water with these "sea cows" are stingrays and several large schools of ocean fish. The visitor path slopes from the shallows to the deep end, concluding with a video of the zoo's efforts to save the manatees.

Creatures from the world's smallest continent are found in **Australia and the Islands of Southeast Asia**. A walk-through kangaroo yard permits close-up views of these incredible jumpers, before you come to the Queensland koalas. This is one of only a few U.S. zoos to permanently exhibit koalas. Visitors then enter *Bob and Evelyn's Roadhouse*, a realistic simulation of an Australian restaurant, where you'll meet nocturnal animals from the Australasian region. Unusual animals are in every corner, and the banded palm civets (slender cat-like carnivores) are, as of 2007, seen nowhere else in the country. Kiwi birds (also seldom exhibited), fishing cats, and tree kangaroos all live along this dark path. An Indonesian bridge leads to *The Islands* and an encounter with gibbons. Arboreal orangutans have two tall wood structures to climb, but are commonly found interacting with visitors at a ground-level window. A stream flows between two grassy plateaus in the small-clawed otter exhibit, before the path circles back to the gibbons. Black swans and other waterfowl have their own pond, near the volcanic rocks that hide Komodo dragons. On the relaxing *Islands of Southeast Asia Boat Ride*, passengers float beneath the main walkway, giving another perspective on the animals visible from the path above – and a much closer look at the waterfowl. You can feed beautiful Australian birds in *Lorikeet Garden*.

The 41,000-square-foot **Pachyderm Building**, on the edge of Asia Quest, is the largest of its kind in the nation. *Elephant Pass* is the new naturalistic habitat for the zoo's herd of Asian elephants, easily distinguished from their African cousins by their significantly smaller ears. Also here, hook-lipped black rhinos occupy three adjacent yards.

North America, the zoo's longest-standing exhibit, is still one of the best collections of animals from our continent. Across from the trumpeter swan enclosure, a wide glass window looks over Mexican gray wolves. Bison and pronghorn antelope roam a horseshoe-shaped grasslands exhibit, behind a prairie dog colony. After this open landscape, the scenery changes to a thick woodland home for grizzly and black bears. Alaskan moose, a most unusual sight in zoos, can be seen from a side trail through small trees and from an unobstructed boardwalk that looks out over a bog. The forest thickens around the exhibits of cougars, bobcats, and timber (gray) wolves. Watch wolverines from within a log cabin, and take a detour to ride the *North American Train* through the shaded forest. Past a natural wetland, home to local migratory songbirds, the towering bald eagle flight cage overlooks a pool of playful river otters.

OTHER EXHIBITS

American alligators occupy a lagoon in front of the **Reptile House** near a flamingo exhibit. Inside the building is an extensive collection of lizards and snakes. Most impressive, however, is the number of Asian turtle species. Black market poaching has brought many of these turtles close to extinction. The Columbus Zoo houses and breeds more Asian terrapins than any other U.S. zoo.

The **Shores** complex, home of Manatee Coast, also includes *Discovery Reef*, a 100,000-gallon saltwater aquarium populated with sharks, eels, and more than fifty different species of colorful fish. Jellyfish are displayed inside a submarine, next to a tide pool touch tank that encourages hands-on introductions to sea stars and horseshoe crabs.

Most of the zoo's animals are in defined large exhibit areas. However, two very popular animals can be seen elsewhere in the zoo in their own exhibits. African lions, in large enclosures, can be observed from an elevated walkway near the exit to Asia

Quest. A unique circular pool on the path between the Reptile House and African Forest displays South American Humboldt penguins.

FOR THE KIDS

In North America, children can explore **Habitat Hollow**. Outside *My House*, a replica of a typical suburban house, are statues of the four words that represent what everyone needs for survival: "Food," "Water," "Space," and "Shelter." Inside the building, kids can explore marsh, prairie, and forest habitats to learn about other things animals need to survive. The last room hosts live animal demonstrations throughout the day. Out back, an insect-filled bog leads to *My Barn*, a classic Ohio farm. In a yard connected to the barn, human kids can pet goats and sheep. Pony rides are available here, as well.

In addition to the boat and train rides, which are fun for all ages, the zoo offers a classic **Mangels-Illions carousel** from 1914 and the colorful insect-themed playground **Stings, Wings, N' Play Things Park**.

IN PROGRESS

If all goes according to plan, Columbus will become what could be called a "mega zoo" by 2012. In the zoo proper, polar bears are slated to return to the zoo in 2009, along with arctic foxes and reindeer, all housed in a new **Polar Frontier** complex. Giraffes and zebras, temporarily displaced by Asia Quest, will return to a seventy-acre **African Savanna,** scheduled to be completed in 2012. Visitors should be able to see rhinos, hippos, cheetahs, lions, and more from walking trails, paddleboats, and safari train ride. Eventually, visitors will be able to ride a zip line over jaguars and tapirs in a **South American jungle** exhibit. After this last continent is added, the Columbus Zoo may have the most complete collection of any zoo in America, with an excellent range of animals from every major continent, and representatives of every major type of animal.

Toledo Zoo

2 Hippo Way
Toledo, Ohio 43614
(419) 385-4040
www.toledozoo.org

Hours: 10:00 a.m.-5:00 p.m. daily May-Labor Day; 10:00 a.m.-4:00 p.m. daily, rest of year. Grounds stay open for an hour after posted closing time, but some animals are taken off exhibit when the gates close. Closed Thanksgiving, Christmas Day, and New Year's Day.

Hippoquarium® lets you watch hippos underwater.

Admission & Fees: Adults $10, seniors 60+ and children 2-11 $7. Train $2, African carousel (indoors) $1.50, South Side carousel $1. Parking $5. Participates in reciprocity program.

Directions: From I-75, take Exit 201A (OH-25/Collingwood Avenue). Turn left onto Collingwood Boulevard, which quickly becomes Anthony Wayne Trail (OH-25). Follow Anthony Wayne Trail for 1.9 miles. Turn right onto Hippo Way and into the zoo parking lot. From I-80, take Exit 64 (I-75), get onto I-75 North and follow above directions.

Don't Miss: African Savanna (including Hippoquarium®), Africa! (including Safari Railway), Arctic Encounter®, Kingdom of the Apes, Primate Forest, Aviary, Aquarium.

For Kids: Children's Zoo, African Animal Carousel, Historic South Side Carousel, playground.

Authors' Tips: The historic Carnivore Café is a fun place to eat a cafeteria-style meal. The indoor and outdoor seating includes tables behind the large steel bars that once caged big cats and other animals. Try to schedule your visit to the hippos for the warmest part of the day, when they are most likely to be in their pool.

Edutainment: In the summer, "Paws for Learning" dog training demonstrations featuring Eddie the Education Dog are held twice daily in the gigantic 5,000-seat amphitheatre. "Reptile and Amphibian Encounter" is another daily presentation, this one held in the Reptile House. "A Zookeeper, An Animal, And YOU!" is a children's show that's held most days. There are also enrichment and feeding presentations featuring such animals as elephants, sharks, and apes throughout the week. Check the flyer inside your zoo map for program times and locations.

MANY BUMPER STICKERS IN TOLEDO SAY "I LOVE MY ZOO," AND ITS attendance figures show that Toledo area residents do indeed enjoy their excellent zoo. With a population of under 300,000, this is the smallest city in the nation to send more than a million visitors to the zoo most years.

Opened in 1900, Toledo Zoo is famous for its historic Spanish Colonial-style buildings, constructed during the Depression as part of FDR's New Deal. Its recent fame is due to the Hippoquarium®, the world's first hippo exhibit to feature filtered water and underwater viewing. In 2000, the zoo nearly doubled in size – from thirty-five to sixty acres – expanding across the Anthony Wayne Trail highway. A convenient pedestrian bridge connects the new north side exhibits with the historic South Side zoo. Located just ten minutes off the main highway between Chicago and New York, this is a worthwhile stop for weary automobile travelers.

FEATURED EXHIBITS

Despite its excellent newer exhibits, this zoo's top exhibit is still the **African Savanna**, with its world-famous *Hippoquarium*®. A pair of hippo statues form an eye-catching archway over the entrance to this exhibit. Just inside, a window showcases a slender-snouted crocodile. Soon thereafter, the pathway opens up to a deep river exhibit, with massive Nile hippos on one side and playful Cape clawless otters on the other. A long window allows visitors to watch the hippos bask on a natural riverbank, to stare at them eye-to-eye at surface level, or to marvel at the underwater grace of these otherwise clumsy creatures as they sink eight feet to the bottom of their 375,000-gallon pool. With its filtered, crystal-clear water and visitor seating area, this exhibit provides a hippo-viewing experience that can be hypnotic. Underwater hippo births, never before seen by humans, have occurred here and are replayed on a video screen. Though somewhat less unusual, when the otters are swimming and playing underwater, they too can draw crowds. Visitors continue on into the woodlands, where turkey-like kori bustards and vultures are shown in forest habitats. Inside the large elephant holding building, an aviary is populated with African birds such as Sudan golden sparrows and emerald starlings. The elephants are sometimes inside, but are best viewed outside in their streamside habitat, which includes a deep pool. DeBrazza's monkeys live in an outdoor enclosure on the side of the building. As you continue along the river, white rhinos and dromedary camels are visible across the water. The path snakes on through tall kopje boulders, leading to windows into a sandy meerkat habitat. A large sheltered viewing bay provides a great vista of the stunning white lions in their sloping, rocky habitat. The lion brothers have white manes that almost glow. This is one of only a few zoos to display white lions; these are on loan from the collection of Siegfried & Roy.

Opened in 2004, the twelve-acre **Africa!** is highly touted as the most ambitious project in the zoo's history. The attention to detail is evident upon entering this imaginative exhibit. The thatch-roofed buildings look authentically African. A pile of abandoned luggage sits in front of the brightly painted railway station, while a rusting bicycle leans against another building. African music plays in the background, setting the mood. Behind the train station, a large oval fenced yard is home to a small pack of African wild dogs. An expansive *Observation Deck* has ample seating for diners and animal-watchers alike. From this vantage point, the entire five-acre multi-species savanna yard is visible. Grant's zebras and Masai giraffes are the most noticeable animals out in the savanna, but there are also small herds of four types of antelope: greater kudu, impala, Nile lechwe, and white-bearded gnus (also called wildebeest). Seven different types of African birds, including ostriches and crowned cranes, roam among the antelope. Most of this sprawling habitat is a grassy plain, but in the forefront a trickling stream runs through a sandy beach area. Two realistic-looking fake crocodiles bask at the streamside. Further out, a vulture may be perched atop a convincing (but fake) zebra carcass, and a (real) jeep seems to be stuck at the back of the savanna. The best way to see the animals is aboard the *Safari Railway*. On this thirteen-minute guided tour, the miniature train encircles the entire savanna, providing close views of the grazing animals, especially from a unique open-sided tunnel underneath the Observation Deck. (The tunnel's open side provides great views.)

The first new exhibit to open on the north side was **Arctic Encounter**®, a spectacular look at polar bears and other arctic creatures. The fir, spruce, and Alaska cedar trees surrounding the exhibit help make this a believable northern trek. Before you enter the building, an outdoor underwater window allows a first glimpse of the harbor and gray seals' pool. In the earth-sheltered building, a massive artificial polar bear greets visitors, his ferocious teeth bared. There are more underwater views into the seals' twelve-foot-deep pool, including a lower gallery where visitors can sit below the water surface. In the polar bear gallery, artificial ice hangs from the ceiling, while crowds build in front of the underwater windows to watch these fascinating and fearsome bears show off their dog-paddling skills. The crowd will often let out a roar of glee when one of the bears dives into a deep pool that's chilled to fifty-five degrees Fahrenheit. The *Arctic Alive* gallery is an interactive, museum-quality display, delivering facts about the animals and Inuit people of the Arctic, often in an entertaining or humorous way. Visitors can walk into an icy polar bear "den" to get nose-to-nose with the bears, visible behind a one-way mirror in their real den. In 2007, a trio of polar bear cubs was born here, and ever since, this habitat has been the most popular place in the zoo. Across the path is a beautiful log cabin, complete with a porch and a stone chimney. Inside, the cabin is decorated just as it would be out in the Old West, except for three giant windows that look out into a gray wolf habitat. The wolves are lots of fun to watch as they run back and forth in their sprawling rocky grassland.

The **Kingdom of the Apes** displays most of the world's great ape species, including large troops of gorillas and orangutans, as well as chimpanzees. In this impressive exhibit, the *Interpretive Center* has attractive graphics, video displays, and hands-on activities that allow humans to compare and contrast themselves with the different apes on display. The orangutans' spacious indoor home features gigantic windows. Outside, the chimps and orangs have naturalistic, mesh-covered grassy habitats with plenty of climbing structures. At the *Splash Zone*, orangutans can push a button to activate a shower that will soak humans on the other side of the glass! (A sign warns you of this possibility.) The highlight here is the large *Gorilla Meadow,* a replica of the gorillas' African home, with live trees and wide windows. The apes' rocky indoor areas provide opportunities for even closer viewing.

The innovative **Primate Forest** complex has three natural outdoor exhibits and an indoor room in which six different primates – colobus monkeys, Allen's swamp monkeys, François' langur monkeys, Diana monkeys, DeBrazza's monkeys, and white-cheeked gibbons – are regularly rotated through the different habitats. At each of these enclosures, signs show all six species, and visitors are invited to determine which are currently on exhibit in front of them. The outdoor habitats are filled with poles and ropes for the benefit of the playful, acrobatic inhabitants.

Inside the **Aviary** are three separate walk-through habitats, displaying birds native to each environment. While this building was constructed in 1937, its renovation in 1999 won it the "Exhibit of the Year" award from the AZA. Some of the impressive collection's winged creatures are free-flying, and some are shown behind glass or thin harp wire. Realistic hand-painted murals create a beautiful backdrop. The *Sonoran Desert* room includes burrowing owls, large black-billed magpies, and more. Birds of paradise and rhinoceros hornbill birds are the most stunning specimens in the *Australian Outback* section, where assorted pretty finches and parakeets fly around their human guests. In the *African Grasslands*, unusual birds include African quail, heron-like hammerkops, and red fodies, small colorful songbirds.

The **Aquarium** here has some of the greatest species diversity in the zoo world. In its fifty-one exhibits, it displays over 2,800 fish of more than 250 species, including moray eels, seahorses, an octopus, giant Japanese spider crabs, and an impressive variety of sharks. Freshwater tanks display spotted river stingrays, piranhas, and giant Amazon fish, along the path to a lush walk-through rain forest exhibit with sloths, iguanas, tropical birds, and cichlid fish. A dark booth where flashlight fish light up is very popular with children, while adults find the iridescent lighting of the moon jelly exhibit to be very soothing.

OTHER EXHIBITS

The first of the Depression-era structures built with Works Progress Administration funds was the **Reptile House**. When it opened in 1934, it was one of only seven reptile houses in the world. Today it houses an impressive assortment of snakes, including cobras, pythons, and pit vipers, as well as Cuban crocodiles, Gila monsters, and various turtles and amphibians. One highlight is the prehistoric tuatara. This lizard-like creature from New Zealand is considered to be the closest living relative of the dinosaurs. Near the reptiles, and easy to miss, **Cheetah Valley** features the world's fastest land animals in a spacious, sloping yard. A viewing deck provides a panoramic look at these handsome cats.

In **The Museum**, twenty varieties of invertebrates, including assassin beetles, bird-eating spiders, and giant stick insects, are displayed in *The Crawlspace: A World of Bugs*. In the nearby grand hall, the new *Amazing Amphibians*, opened in 2008, showcases a wide variety of frogs, toads, and salamanders from around the world. Standouts include the critically endangered Kihansi spray toads from Tanzania, as well as an interesting collection of local frogs, illustrating why Toledo was once known as "Frogtown, U.S.A."

Tiger Terrace is a pair of lushly planted mesh enclosures – attractive habitats for Amur tigers with a glass-fronted viewing station. Next door, a similar habitat displays shaggy Asian sloth bears. In the courtyard area, the black-footed penguin exhibit gives visitors underwater views of these African penguins. Around the corner from the bears, snow leopards inhabit a mesh-covered habitat that replicates a Himalayan mountain setting. Also in the vicinity is a yard for rare white-naped cranes, and an overgrown waterfowl pool with more than a dozen species of exotic ducks and geese. Across the highway, you'll pass the pretty **bald eagles** habitat on the way to and from the connecting bridge.

The zoo used to include "Zoological Gardens" in its title, largely because of **Ziems Conservatory**, a long greenhouse filled with palms, bromeliads, and other tropical plants. Outside, a rose garden, formal gardens, and several other gardens are horticultural delights.

FOR THE KIDS

The theme of the seasonal **Children's Zoo** is "Animals A to Zoo," with multi-colored alphabetic signs which not only help kids learn about animals, but also help them learn to read. A sign reads "G is for Goat" in front of the contact yard, where kids can pet friendly goats. "A is for Alpaca" introduces another animal here. Other creatures include pot-bellied pigs, wallabies, an arctic fox, turtles, and more. Hawks and owls are displayed in the big red barn. This children's zoo will be open from Memorial Day to Labor Day 2008 and then year-round thereafter.

In addition to the Safari Railway train (see above), the world's first **African Animal Carousel**, populated exclusively by beautiful African animals, can also be found in Africa! while across the zoo, the open-air **Historic South Side Carousel** offers another enjoyable ride for kids. There's a small **playground** across from this older and smaller merry-go-round.

IN PROGRESS

The next change at the zoo will be a renovated children's zoo, to be called **Children's Zone**, scheduled to open in 2009 as we go to press. This major upgrade will include an indoor section, making it a year-round facility. In addition to a petting zoo, there will be play areas where children can pretend to be zookeepers, a trend we've seen in other top children's zoos. There are also plans to upgrade the rhino and elephant exhibits, as well as their holding barns. The schedule calls for these improvements to be completed by 2011, as we go to press. At some point in the future, the interior of the Aquarium will undergo major improvements.

Milwaukee County Zoological Gardens

10001 West Blue Mound Road
Milwaukee, Wisconsin 53226
(414) 771-5500
www.milwaukeezoo.org

Hours: 9:00 a.m.-5:00 p.m. Monday-Saturday, 9:00 a.m.-6:00 p.m. Sundays and holidays, May-September; 9:00 a.m.-4:30 p.m. daily, rest of year.

Admission & Fees: Adults $11.25, seniors 60+ $10.25, children 3-12 $8.25, April-October; adults $9.75, seniors 60+ $8.25, children 3-12 $6.75, rest of year. Milwaukee County residents with ID:

Impala and Ruppell's griffon vulture in predator/prey exhibit in Africa.

$1.75 off every day, on Wednesdays: adults $6, children $3.50. Seal/sea lion show $2; camel and pony rides $4 each; carousel $2; Sky Safari ride $3; Zoomobile: adults $1.50, children $1; Safari train: adults $2.50, children $1.50; giraffe feeding: adults $10, children $5; Sting Ray & Shark Reef admission $2, summers only. Parking $10. Participates in reciprocity program.

Directions: From I-94, take Exit 304 (County Zoo). Turn onto WI-100 North and follow for 0.4 miles. Turn right onto West Blue Mound Road. Continue for another 0.4 miles to the zoo.

Don't Miss: Predator/prey exhibits at the African Waterhole, Africa, Asia, and South America, Big Cat Country, Apes of Africa, North America, Sting Ray & Shark Reef, Mahler Family Aviary, Aquatic & Reptile Center, Primates of the World, Small Mammals Building.

For Kids: Family Farm, Safari Train, carousel, camel ride, pony ride, Sky Safari ride.

Authors' Tips: If rain is expected, try to see the zoo's southside outdoor exhibits during good weather, saving the northside indoor exhibits for the rain. The Zoomobile offers a 25-minute guided overview of this large zoo. The Flamingo Café, a sit-down restaurant, and the Woodland Retreat and Lakeview Place offer scenic views and traditional Wisconsin bratwurst sandwiches. This zoo seems to sell more stuffed animals than any other, usually at outdoor gift stands.

Edutainment: Sea lions and a hilarious harbor seal entertain large audiences at the "Oceans of Fun Seal/Sea Lion Show," held five times daily during warm weather. The Raptory Theatre, in the Family Farm, hosts the "Birds of Prey & Friends" show twice daily. Short animal demonstrations, called "Animals in Action," are presented daily, during the summer, at seven locations around the zoo. Milking and other farm-related demonstrations are presented in the Family Farm. Animal feedings take place daily at the Small Mammals Building and the harbor seals' tank.

THE MILWAUKEE COUNTY ZOO IS WISCONSIN'S TOP TOURIST attraction. With about 1.3 million annual visitors, it is also one of the nation's most popular zoos. Its popularity is well-deserved. Within its 200 acres, all of the state's best features are on display: dense forests, beautiful lakes, and a variety of native wildlife. With over 1,750 animals, this is one of America's largest and most complete zoos.

Predator/prey exhibits, where predatory big cats, hyenas, and bears are displayed in the same viewing plane as their natural prey, are common in modern zoos. Milwaukee pioneered this exhibit style and is still a leader in the field, with an amazing variety of predator/prey displays of animals from four different continents.

FEATURED EXHIBITS

The predator/prey effect is stunning at the **African Waterhole**, where zebras, ostriches, and waterbucks and other antelope wander an arid field. Only a waterhole separates them from hungry lions or hyenas. Why don't the lions eat the zebras? A twenty-foot-deep moat prevents such a tragedy. In **Africa**, impala, gazelles, ground hornbill birds, vultures, and other birds wander a sloping grassland, as cheetahs salivate just behind them.

The **South America** yard features Baird's tapirs, alpacas, king vultures, and a variety of small animals, while just above, spotted jaguars gaze at their potential prey. In the **Asia** exhibit, Amur tigers and Asian black bears overlook herds of double-humped Bactrian camels, which are often found in their deep pool.

Among the zoo's icons is beautiful Lake Evinrude, which attracts wild Canada geese and other migratory birds. Most of the impressive **North America** exhibits are across the path from this pretty lake. Another predator/prey display here has sea lions and harbor seals swimming in a deep pool, as polar bears prowl a rocky ledge behind them. Both enclosures also offer underwater windows where you can watch these creatures swim by. The large, marshy *Moose Yard* has mule deer, wild turkeys, and of course, moose, all animals exhibited in very few U.S. zoos. To see the timber (gray) wolves of *Wolf Woods*, visitors enter a log cabin interpretive building, or stroll a wooden walkway through a thick evergreen forest. Grizzly, brown, and black bears are displayed in rocky, moated grottoes, as is a badger, Wisconsin's state animal. Dall sheep live on an artificial mountain, while caribou and elk yards replicate a forest clearing. Among all of these large animal habitats, you'll also find a small prairie dog town.

In addition to exhibits that pair them with their natural prey, most of the predators have spacious indoor homes in **Big Cat Country**. Beautiful rock work, special skylights that let in outside light, and realistic background murals make these naturalistic habitats most attractive, and floor-to-ceiling sloping glass walls allow for nose-to-nose encounters with the building's cheetahs, Amur tigers, and jaguars. The lions and spotted hyenas rotate between these striking indoor habitats and their outdoor yards. Outside, near the building's entrance, are mountain habitats for thick-furred snow leopards and red pandas, as well as viewing windows for close-up peeks at the Asian black bears and Amur tigers.

Apes of Africa, half of a two-part primate complex, houses the zoo's two most popular animals, gorillas and bonobos (pygmy chimpanzees). Their habitats are lush replicas of the West African rain forest. The visitor areas seem to be extensions of these habitats, as both are enhanced with man-made trees, root buttresses, and abundant living plants. Realistic jungle wall murals make the habitats appear even larger than they are. Only glass separates humans and apes. Visitors can peek through the bushes at the gorillas, or study them from a wide unobstructed viewing area. The bonobos enjoy climbing through the full two-story vertical range of their home. This zoo's bonobo troop numbers more than twenty individuals, and is the world's largest captive group of this highly endangered species.

Connected to the great apes building, **Primates of the World** houses baboon-like mandrills, siamangs, and colobus, pygmy marmoset, and Diana monkeys, all set in lush rain forest displays similar to the Apes of Africa habitats. A third great ape species, the orangutan, also lives here in an indoor/outdoor exhibit. The building's highlight is *Temple Monkeys of Tikal*, a large indoor/outdoor replica of the jungles and Mayan temple ruins of Tikal, Guatemala. Here, lively spider monkeys swing on vines, sailing past a back wall painted with murals of ancient pyramids.

Lately, **Sting Ray & Shark Reef** has become a big visitor magnet, attracting such large crowds that guests must often wait in long lines for the opportunity to pet a leopard shark or touch a cownose stingray. For an additional fee, you can purchase treats to feed to the barbless (and thus harmless) rays.

Like most of the zoo's fine animal houses, the **Mahler Family Aviary** is set on a wide path that passes through a dense forest. More than sixty bird species are represented in this building's varying habitats. The colorful entry plaza is styled like a "mercado," a Central American marketplace. Past it, visitors come upon a wide window displaying a large flock of Antarctic penguins, visible both above and below water. Life vests hang from the ceiling, giving viewers the sensation of being on a ship along the Antarctic coast. Inca terns, spoonbills, and Waldrapp ibises populate the walk-through *Free Flight* room, which features a splashing waterfall, running stream, and tall pine and palm trees. In the lush *Rain Forest* habitats of four continents, fairy bluebirds, fruit doves, Bali mynahs, and more fly about behind thin harp wire. In the sandy *African Savanna* habitat, plovers and other birds perch on man-made termite mounds. The most photographed environment here may be the *Shoreline*, with realistic props and a splendid lake mural. The *Island of Guam* displays beautiful birds from the South Pacific, including Micronesian kingfishers and Guam rails, one of the world's rarest birds. North American whooping cranes just outside are almost as scarce.

The centerpiece of the **Aquatic & Reptile Complex (ARC)** is *Lake Wisconsin*. This 65,000-gallon aquarium is stocked with muskies, walleyes, and other native fish, most of them larger than any Wisconsin fisherman has ever had on a line. Huge pacus and other Amazon fish swim in the *Flooded Forest*, while the 28,000-gallon *Pacific Coast Aquarium* features a kelp forest stocked with a variety of sharks and fish, including odd-looking sheephead fish. The *African Lakes* exhibit displays hundreds of pretty cichlid fish in a wide tank. The reptiles, organized into seven galleries, include Chinese alligators, rattlesnakes, cobras, and a huge anaconda snake.

The **Small Mammals Building** is a visitor favorite. The main gallery displays lemurs, meerkats, small monkeys, and dwarf mongooses. At its center is a large river otter exhibit with underwater windows. The nocturnal *Animals of the Night* hall displays one of the nation's largest collections of bats, including vampire bats, and black-footed cats, fennec foxes, springhaas (a cute rabbit-faced rodent that hops like a kangaroo), and other rare animals.

OTHER EXHIBITS

Past the predator/prey habitats are the **Pachyderms**. African elephants, black rhinos, hippos, and elusive bongo antelope (which are not pachyderms) have room to roam in arid yards. Their two long rows of indoor habitats in the *Pachyderm House* are visible from outside through glass windows. Across from the Pachyderm House, *Giraffe Experience,* another part of this exhibit, is an innovative habitat for the tallest of mammals, just enlarged in 2006. Visitors come eye-to-eye with these giraffes on an elevated platform. Twice a day, for a fee, they can even feed the graceful herbivores.

Australia is the zoo's fifth continental grouping. Indoors, tree kangaroos are displayed in front of realistic murals, and small reef aquariums represent the continent's Great Barrier Reef. Kangaroos and emus live outside, in a large, oval grassy yard.

For many years, **Macaque Island** has been a top attraction, and it's often completely surrounded by curious visitors. The nation's largest colony of Japanese macaques, better known as snow monkeys, are usually comfortable with Milwaukee's famously cold winters. They seem to enjoy entertaining spectators with their antics.

You'll find the attractive **Humboldt Penguins Exhibit** at the very front of the zoo. The penguins' round habitat represents a South American rocky coastline, while underwater windows let you watch as they zip through the water.

FOR THE KIDS

Here in America's dairyland, it's no surprise that one of the **Family Farm**'s major focal points is the *Dairy Complex*. A big red eight-sided barn, originally built in 1896, houses dairy cattle, hands-on exhibits introducing the dairy industry, and a dairy-themed play area. Ice cream and other dairy products are available in the *Dairy*

Store. Kids can also enjoy the *Goat Yard* petting area, two themed outdoor playgrounds, and the *Animal Encounter Building*, where they can pet smaller animals like opossums and snakes. Other features of this excellent children's area include a pig yard, beehive, horses, a chick hatchery, and a 520-seat stadium for the birds of prey show.

The **Safari Train** passes through thick woods, over trestles, and around Lake Evinrude on its two-mile journey. It is so popular that long lines are the norm, though they're usually fast-moving. Across from the train station is a brightly lit **carousel**. In season, camel and pony rides are available around the zoo, as is the **Sky Safari** ski lift ride, which gives an exciting view from high above the predator/prey displays.

IN PROGRESS

A new Caribbean flamingo exhibit in a pond in front of the Aviary is scheduled for 2008 as we go to press. In the near future, the zoo's front entrance area will be transformed into a structure called the **Gathering Place**, with a new glass atrium, zoo displays, and educational spaces. This new building will likely connect the main restaurant and gift shops into one seamless "gathering place" for guests.

BEST OF THE REST

Mesker Park Zoo and Botanic Garden

2421 Bement Avenue
Evansville, Indiana 47720
(812) 435-6143
www.meskerparkzoo.com

This is one of the largest zoos in Indiana. Beautiful Lake Victoria lies at the heart of the facility, where paddleboats are available for rent. You can also take a bumper boat ride here around the historic *Monkey Ship*, a one-third-scale replica of Columbus' Santa Maria. For years it served as a monkey habitat. The *Asian Plains* are inhabited by double-humped Bactrian camels, tigers, gray gibbons, and an Indian rhino. Nearby are exhibits for lions and a hippo. An observation deck overlooks the *African Panorama*, home to antelope, land birds, and cheetahs. Across the lake, the *African Rift* houses giraffes and zebras. The *Discovery Center* features clouded leopards, serval cats, and rare monkeys. A spectacular 10,000-square-foot *Amazonia* rain forest building is scheduled to open in 2008. It will include exhibits of jaguars, tapirs, bats, tropical birds, reptiles and amphibians, along with Amazon river fish, including piranhas.

Potawatomi Zoo

500 South Greenlawn Avenue
South Bend, Indiana 46615
(574) 288-4639
www.potawatomizoo.org

This twenty-three-acre zoo was established in 1902 and is the oldest in Indiana. Outdoor trails lead to exhibits showcasing the wildlife of five continents. In *Asia*, Amur and white tigers are featured in glass-fronted grottoes near Bactrian camels, white-naped cranes, red pandas, and rare Sichuan takins, mountain goats from China. The antics of the inhabitants of *Chimpanzee Island* are very popular with visitors. Other animals in *Africa* include Ankole cattle, African wild dogs, lions, warthogs, zebras, and several monkey species. Toucans, llamas, and rheas (large flightless birds) live in the small *South America* section. *North America* is well represented by prairie dogs, bison, and alligators that are visible from an elevated wooden boardwalk. With a walk-through Australian kangaroo yard, excellent *Learning Center*, and an entertaining train ride, this zoo was rated one of the nation's top 20 zoos for children by *Child Magazine*.

John Ball Zoological Garden

1300 Fulton Street West
Grand Rapids, Michigan 49504
(616) 336-4301
www.johnballzoosociety.org

Exhibits at this historic zoo (it opened in 1891) spotlight four continents. On the *South American Boardwalk*, visitors learn about ancient cultures while viewing maned wolves, llama-like guanacos, spider monkeys, and capybaras (large aquatic rodents). The *North American Trek* is impressive, featuring grizzly bears, wolverines, eagles, pumas, and an otter pool with underwater viewing. Australia is represented by a *Budgie Aviary*, where visitors can hand-feed the little birds, and the walk-through *Australia Trail*, with free-roaming wallabies. *Jambo Africa* is a veldt exhibit with warthogs, bongo antelope, and African land birds. The *Mokomboso Valley Chimpanzee Exhibit* has a large habitat for one of the nation's largest troops of chimps. Among the best small zoo aquariums in the country, *Living Shores* displays the aquatic residents of a Michigan stream, the Pacific Northwest coast, and penguins from South America's Patagonia. The *Treasures of the Tropics* reptile and amphibian building exhibits a Komodo dragon.

Akron Zoological Park

500 Edgewood Avenue
Akron, Ohio 44307
(330) 375-2550
www.akronzoo.org

This small zoo is beautifully themed, and uses some unique exhibit concepts. Just inside the front gate, the *Legends of the Wild* trail displays animals in attractive naturalistic habitats, while explaining the legends and beliefs associated with these creatures. For example, Andean condors are exhibited next to a sign relating the ancient Incan belief that condors carry the sun into the sky each morning. Other legends described involve penguins, flamingos, jaguars, fruit bats, and other fascinating creatures. *Komodo Kingdom* displays three large and interesting reptiles: Galapagos tortoises, Chinese alligators, and of course, Komodo dragons. *Tiger Valley* features Sumatran tigers, lions, and sun bears, while red pandas are the stars of a smaller *Asian Trail*. The *Wild Prairie* includes otters, prairie dogs, bald eagles, and a *Farmland* petting yard.

Northeastern Wisconsin (NEW) Zoo

4378 Reforestation Road
Green Bay, Wisconsin 54313
(920) 448-7878
www.thenewzoo.com

Though this zoo once concentrated on North American animals, the NEW Zoo has expanded to include more exotic creatures, including snow leopards, red pandas, wallabies, warthogs, a *Giraffe Encounter* feeding station, and an African lion exhibit where the lions are viewed from realistic African huts. The *North American Plains* includes prairie dogs, elk, and bison. Despite the exotic new additions, the best exhibit here is still *Wisconsin/Northern Trails*, with its many native animals. Among the inhabitants are red wolves, mountain lions, red foxes, black bears, otters, badgers, white-tailed deer, a *North American Aviary*, and Alaskan moose.

Henry Vilas Zoo

702 South Randall Avenue
Madison, Wisconsin 53715
(608) 266-4733
www.vilaszoo.org

Madison, Wisconsin's capital, is famous as an educational center, so it is appropriate that its free zoo has an excellent learning center in the *Discovery Center/Herpetarium*. The Herpetarium provides underwater views of alligators, anaconda snakes, and Wisconsin lake fish. At *Discovering Primates*, there are interactive activities, videos, and exhibits of chimpanzees, orangutans, colobus monkeys, and lemurs. The zoo's signature exhibit, however, is the *Tropical Rainforest Aviary*, an indoor jungle with colorful South American birds and aquarium exhibits of freshwater stingrays, turtles, piranhas, and giant Amazon fish. The *Big Cat Complex* includes lions and tigers and … harbor seals! Four species of bears (polar, grizzly, black, and spectacled) live in nearby side-by-side rocky grottoes. The *North American Prairie* exhibits bison, prairie dogs, and of course, badgers, the state animal of Wisconsin. The zoo's many large mammals include white rhinos, Malayan tapirs, giraffes, Bactrian camels, and Rocky Mountain goats, who enjoy a mountain habitat that's forty feet high. There is also a penguin pool and a renovated *Children's Zoo*.

North Central Zoos

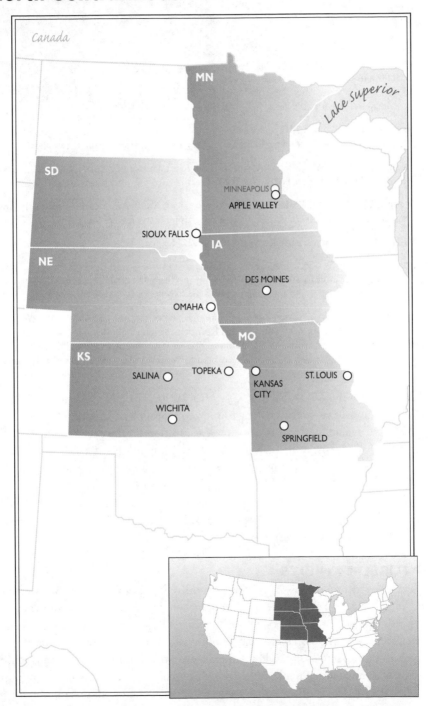

Canada

MN

Lake Superior

SD

MINNEAPOLIS ○
APPLE VALLEY

SIOUX FALLS ○

IA

NE

DES MOINES
○

OMAHA ○

MO

KS

SALINA ○   TOPEKA ○   KANSAS ○   ST. LOUIS ○
                         CITY

WICHITA
○

SPRINGFIELD
○

Sedgwick County Zoo

5555 Zoo Boulevard
Wichita, Kansas 67212
(316) 660-9453
www.scz.org

Bachelor gorillas share a spacious habitat.

Hours: 8:30 a.m.-5:00 p.m. daily, March-October; 10:00 a.m.-5:00 p.m. daily, rest of year. Closed one day in September for zoo fundraiser – check website for details.

Admission & Fees: Adults $10, seniors 62+ $7, children 4-11 $6. Giraffe feeding $1, boat tour $3. Participates in reciprocity program.

Directions: Located on Wichita's west side. From I-235, take Exit 10 (Zoo Boulevard), and turn left onto West Zoo Boulevard. Follow for 0.4 miles and turn left into the zoo's parking lot.

Don't Miss: Gorilla Forest, Pride of the Plains, Australia & South America, Jungle, North America, Orangutan-Chimpanzee Habitat, Penguin Cove, Amphibians & Reptiles.

For Kids: Children's Farms, Boat Tour, playground on Nganda Island.

Authors' Tips: This 247-acre zoo is one of the largest in the nation, but it is surprisingly easy to get around. The tram is free, offers a guided tour, and has five convenient stops. The waterfall in the Jungle is turned off in the morning to allow bird songs to be heard more clearly.

Edutainment: Informative "Catch-A-Keeper" animal demonstrations are held at various times each day. Highlights include elephant training, Komodo dragon behavior demonstrations, and giraffe behavior demonstrations. Animal feedings are held at almost every exhibit throughout the day, Check the daily schedule on your zoo map for times and places for these programs.

THE SEDGWICK COUNTY ZOO, WHICH OPENED IN 1971 AND SPORTS unique and innovative exhibits, is one of the zoo world's best-kept secrets. Because it is in Wichita, a small city that is not a typical vacation destination, its attendance is lower than that of most of the nation's top zoos. Though it is the state's number one outdoor family attraction and one of the country's best zoos, its fame doesn't reach far beyond the borders of Kansas. A real shame!

This well-organized zoo makes planning a tour an easy task. Almost all of its major exhibit areas branch out from the **Central Plaza,** a park-like area that provides most of the necessary visitor services.

FEATURED EXHIBITS

The zoo's feature exhibit is the new **Downing Gorilla Forest**, opened in 2004, an eight-acre slice of Equatorial Africa brought here to Kansas. The adventure begins at *Nganda Island*, an authentic-looking African village that makes this imaginary journey seem real. The stone-and-brick buildings of the village appear to have spent many years in the African sun. Old safari jeeps are parked nearby. Past a small colorful playground, you'll find several attractive exhibits along the riverbank. Families of DeBrazza's monkeys – sporting stylish goatees – and black-and-white colobus monkeys live together near greater flamingos and pelicans. A swaying suspension bridge leads to the main habitats. Along the path, you'll see rare okapis, giraffe relatives from the Congo, on the other side of the fence. Also nearby are large colorful bongo antelope, black-crowned cranes, and saddle-billed storks. Inside the *Gorilla Forest Preserve* building, visitors walk downhill, past walls painted with realistic jungle murals, and through a stand of artificial tree trunks. The main viewing room resembles a large tent, looking out on the gorillas. A wide, floor-to-ceiling, semicircular glass window allows the bachelor gorillas to come right up to surround the front of the tent, as they check out their crowd of admirers. The gorillas' spacious habitat – 31,000 square feet embellished with rock work, fallen trees, and a splashing waterfall – is a grassy hillside that slopes down towards the viewing area. The apes also make frequent use of their two large dayrooms, again with great windows for visitors. Interactive displays and educational graphics enhance the visitor area.

At the **Pride of the Plains** savanna exhibit, African lions are the main event. Visible from many angles, usually through clear glass, the pride of lions is kept alert by close proximity to their natural prey, warthogs and meerkats. The lions' main *Pride Rock* habitat is surrounded by a water moat. A 700-foot dirt path winds around giant artificial boulders, creating a wonderful African kopje environment. Plants and grasses similar to those from the African savanna add further realism, as does the old safari jeep parked here. A small theater hut plays interpretive wildlife videos. Behind clear glass walls, meerkats live in two separate habitats, creating rival groups that display territorial claims to their space. The warthogs, like the lions, can be seen from many different points along the trail. You'll pass more predators, African hunting dogs (aka African wild dogs), near the exhibit's exit.

When it opened back in 1977, the **Jungle** was only the second indoor tropical rain forest exhibit in the U.S. Many huge rain forest buildings have opened since then, but this half-acre, glass-roofed jungle is still one of the finest. Unlike other zoos' newly planted foliage, the thick tropical vegetation here is mature. This exhibit not only looks and sounds realistic, it even smells like a real jungle – and feels authentically humid. A dirt pathway crosses a suspension bridge and then winds downhill past enclosures of small monkeys, sloths, and tricolor squirrels. In the trees above, Indian flying foxes (actually bats) attract the most attention, but more than a hundred birds of over forty exotic species fly freely overhead. Freshwater stingrays inhabit a small jungle pool. The path then leads down under a lake to a glass tunnel that permits viewing of giant pacus and other Amazonian fish. A cave, featuring vampire bats, lures visitors off the main path. A waterfall splashes into a pool by an island habitat for dwarf caimans. A small side stream exhibits piranhas and other fish, while a Komodo dragon, the world's largest lizard, lives near the exit.

This zoo features the wildlife of five continents in distinctive exhibits. Two of the best, **Australia & South America**, are displayed back-to-back in completely screened-in yards. A quarter-mile of visitor paths wind around the exhibit's pools, streams, and trees. At 70,000 square feet, this is one of the largest walk-through exhibits in the world. At the entrance to *Australia*, a mid-sized attached yard holds stunning double-wattled cassowaries. These land birds are the largest animals in New Guinea. Other attached yards hold wallaroos, emus, tree kangaroos, and black swans. Among the most noticeable animals running and flying free here are brush turkeys, wallabies, and straw-necked ibises. Keas and other parrot-like birds are displayed in small enclosures, as are more tree kangaroos. The *South America* section displays what may be the nation's most complete and diverse collection of South American animals. Many beautiful birds fly freely here as well, including spoonbills, multi-colored macaws, and sun conures. Guanacos (llama relatives), giant anteaters, Chilean pudu deer, and Chacoan giant peccaries live in plain view in a series of yards. Squirrel monkeys live on an island habitat, and black-necked swans swim in the surrounding moat. The meat-eaters – a jaguar, spectacled bears, stilt-legged maned wolves, king vultures,

Maned wolves in South America exhibit.

and spectacled owls – are caged, for obvious reasons. The exhibit's largest animals, Baird's tapirs, inhabit a yard with a pool – you'll pass them on your way out.

The eleven-acre **North America** exhibit, an appropriate subject for a Kansas zoo, is one of the top displays of native animals in any U.S. zoo. The Kansas state song is "Home on the Range," so it is fitting to see, from an elevated boardwalk, the buffalo (bison) "roaming" and the deer and the (pronghorn) antelope "playing." Next to the bison is a large and well-populated prairie dog town. Other animals in this grasslands area include sandhill cranes, pumas, and elk in an expansive yard. A bridge crosses a boat canal to a more wooded section featuring rare Mexican gray wolves, river otters (note the attractive underwater viewing gallery), flight cages of bald and golden eagles, and an interpretive building displaying reptiles and other small prairie creatures. The exhibit's feature animals are the grizzly and black bears, housed in large, naturalistic habitats. The grizzlies can be seen from many vantage points, including a uniquely designed cave that provides close-up views through glass windows.

In the **Orangutan-Chimpanzee Habitat**, chimpanzees and Sumatran orangutans are seen in high indoor enclosures, with logs to climb and rocks to relax on, or outside in naturalistic enclosed yards. Inside, tall glass panels nearly encircle the apes, giving visitors a view so good that world-famous naturalist Jane Goodall selected this exhibit as the first training site for her ChimpanZoo project. Animated graphics and hands-on devices allow visitors to compare themselves to the apes on display.

To get to **Penguin Cove**, which opened in 2007, visitors must walk a pebble-and-seashell path, then pass through a gateway of barnacle-covered posts. The ambiance is that of the rocky Pacific coast of Peru or Chile. In the covered viewing area, the Humboldt penguins can be seen through a fifty-two-foot long underwater window as they "fly" underwater and build nests in small caves along the cliff. Guests can sit down and relax here, watching both the penguins and the equally endangered Inca terns that fly over them.

The **Amphibians & Reptiles** building showcases a modest collection, and is most memorable for its distinctive exhibits. A cactus garden and waterfall beautify the enclosure of giant Aldabra tortoises. A large, glass-fronted pond displays endangered tropical turtles. In the *Desert Room*, visitors are invited to sit down and look for the lizards that hide among the rocks and cacti. Other inhabitants of this building include poison dart frogs, beaded lizards, and many venomous snakes.

OTHER EXHIBITS

The **African Veldt** displays additional animals from this continent. The highlight of this area is the 40,000-gallon hippo pool, with a viewing bay where these heavy mammals can be seen underwater. At one time, this was the world's only underwater hippo exhibit. Other large animals roaming in spacious, open yards here include African elephants, black rhinos, giraffes, and Grevy's zebras. In cold weather, most of these animals can be seen indoors. Guinea baboons occupy a rectangular cage. Slender-horned gazelles, various antelope, and caracal lynx are also exhibited.

The small **Asian Forest** is scheduled for expansion. Current residents include leopards, Arabian oryxes, Malayan tapirs, and tall cranes. To the right, just inside the zoo's entrance, more than two dozen **Caribbean flamingos** wade in a pretty pond.

FOR THE KIDS

Once the whole of the Sedgwick County Zoo, the **Children's Farms** are reached by crossing a rustic covered bridge. Domestic animals from three continents are displayed in themed farmyards featuring breeds of cattle, swine, and chickens from across the globe. Some of these livestock are available for both petting and feeding. The *Asian Farm*, with bright red and yellow trim on its oriental-style barns, features Karakul sheep, domestic yaks, and water buffalo. The *African Farm* has a round thatch-roofed barn with sandy corrals holding a dromedary camel, Tunis sheep, and giant-horned Watusi cattle. Not to be outdone, the *American Farm* features a big red barn, with white fences and a spacious pasture that holds draft horses, beef cattle, and dairy cows. Inside this barn, visitors can watch cows being milked. The *Incubation and Hatching* facility holds ten different breeds of poultry.

A significant part of the zoo experience, the guided **Boat Tour** is not just for kids – but it is highly enjoyable for them. It begins with a view of the bison and pronghorns in their prairie yards. The monkeys and flamingos of Nganda Island come into view as the boat drifts under a pedestrian bridge. Then the canal joins up with a wild river, where watchful eyes can spot native great blue herons, turtles, and water snakes. This tour is the best way to see four types of lemurs, each on its own island habitat.

IN PROGRESS

As we go to press, a new restaurant is about to open in the Central Plaza, offering both indoor and outdoor seating. A new world-class tiger exhibit in the Asian Forest area is tentatively scheduled for spring 2009. Red pandas will be a part of this new exhibit. Further in the future, plans call for an expanded and modernized natural habitat for the elephants.

Minnesota Zoological Garden

13000 Zoo Boulevard
Apple Valley, Minnesota 55124
(612) 431-9200
www.mnzoo.com

Hours: 9:00 a.m.-6:00 p.m. daily, Memorial Day-Labor Day; 9:00 a.m.-4:00 p.m. weekdays, to 6:00 p.m. weekends, September-May. Closed Thanksgiving and Christmas Day.

Northern Trails' Tiger Lair gives the big cats plenty of play space: it's the largest tiger complex in the U.S.

Admission & Fees: Adults $14, seniors $9, children $8. Zoo/IMAX combo tickets: adults $21, seniors $15, children $14. Skytrail monorail $3.50, paddleboats $12 per half-hour. Parking $5. Participates in reciprocity program.

Directions: Located 20 miles south of the Twin Cities, in Apple Valley. From Minneapolis, take I-35W South to Exit 11B (MN-62E). Follow MN-62 for 1.3 miles, then merge onto MN-77S. Follow MN-77 for 9.5 miles, then merge onto CR-38E. Follow for 2 miles, then turn left into the zoo. From St. Paul, take I-35E South to Exit 92 (MN-77/Cedar Avenue). Take MN-77 south for 1.6 miles to the CR-38E/McAndrews Road exit. Follow CR-38E for 2 miles, then turn left into the zoo. Or take the MVTA bus line, #440, which connects the Mall of America and the zoo, Monday to Saturday.

Don't Miss: Russia's Grizzly Coast, Minnesota Trail, Northern Trail, Tropics Trail, Discovery Bay.

For Kids: Family Farm, Kids' Den, paddleboat rides.

Authors' Tips: Children (and others) should be sure to use the restroom before striking out on the Northern Trail, where a pair of binoculars for viewing the animals comes in handy. On the Skytrail Monorail, sit in the front cars for the best narration. Don't forget your camera; the Minnesota Zoo was named one of the best places to photograph animals by Popular Photography magazine in 2007. After enjoying the zoo, consider catching a movie at the IMAX Theater near the parking lot.

Edutainment: Dolphin shows that showcase these mammals' amazing acrobatic abilities and focus on the importance of conserving marine environments take place in the 800-seat Dolphin Stadium. In summer, the excellent "World of Birds" show is presented three times daily in the Weesner Family Amphitheater. Daily dives and shark feedings are presented in both the Coral Reef Sharks tank on Tropics Trail, and Shark Reef inside Discovery Bay. Check for show times in your zoo map.

THE MINNESOTA ZOO IS ONE OF THE COUNTRY'S LARGEST, WITH nearly five hundred acres of wooded Minnesota wilderness, which allows for numerous spacious outdoor animal habitats. Since it has only been open for just over thirty years, this relatively new zoo is starting to hit its financial stride, and is beginning to expand its collection beyond just those animals that acclimate best to the cold Minnesota climate.

FEATURED EXHIBITS

Russia's Grizzly Coast is unique: this wildlife habitat, based on the Kamchatka Peninsula of Russia's northern Pacific coast, has never before been extensively re-created in an American zoo. From its entrance plaza, visitors proceed down to a gallery with a split-level view of sea otters. Just past the otters, grizzly bears come into view. Along the path to a bear overlook, geysers shoot out of steam vents near the bears' sloping forest. An artificial lava tube shelters visitors as they enter a cave to look through windows onto a trout-filled stream for underwater views of the bears. An even closer encounter is possible at a nearby demonstration area, where keepers bring the giant bears for training sessions. Back on the path, visitors can explore a wooly mammoth dig site and view voracious wild boars up close. Three habitats for rare Amur leopards complete this captivating exhibit.

The state's rich variety of wildlife is reflected along the **Minnesota Trail**. Renovated in 2007 to improve the visitor experience and refresh the trail with new animals, the journey begins in the *North Woods Lodge*, a cozy log cabin with exhibits of soft-shell turtles and hibernating frogs. Raccoons explore the cabin porch, which comes complete with a set of trash cans and a stream they can wash their food in. Along the covered path for viewing the outdoor animals, visitors can get both above- and below-water looks at beavers. Since this state is known as the "Land of 10,000 Lakes," it is fitting that the zoo displays walleye, muskie, and pike in a *Minnesota Lake* exhibit. Otters, weasel-like fishers, and an aviary housing impressive pileated woodpeckers are all found along the soft rubber-padded path. Porcupines share a display with great horned owls, while across the path, a miniature lodge serves as a lookout point into habitats for wolves and coyotes. More secretive carnivores, rarely spotted in the wild, are ahead, including pumas, wolverines, and lynx, all in bi-level habitats. Bald eagles are the final animals you'll encounter before heading back into the North Woods Lodge.

The **Northern Trail** displays a variety of species able to handle the region's harsh winters. Along a one-mile trek, expansive habitats showcase animals from the world's coldest regions. First on the agenda is *Tiger Lair*, the largest tiger complex in the United States. Its defining feature is the huge window flanked by heated rocks, which lure the tigers in from their densely planted taiga habitat. A stream flows into a long pool at the other side of the enclosure. An entirely separate exhibit, *Tiger Base Camp* features a high boardwalk leading to a gazebo that overlooks another huge valley. Signs in the viewing area describe the Minnesota Zoo's efforts to conserve wild tigers. Here, visitors can use an antenna to find a radio collar hidden in the exhibit, much as a researcher would track tigers in the wild. A breeding herd of takins, rare mountain goats from China, inhabits a half-acre yard with two pagoda-style viewing shelters for visitors. An *Asian Steppe* exhibit displays double-humped Bactrian camels and Asian wild horses (aka Przewalski's wild horses), while bison, prairie dogs, and speedy pronghorn antelope inhabit the *North American Plains*. The camels and bison, each in large several-acre yards, especially enjoy relaxing in pools. The *Wolf Gazebo* is a rustic structure with windows that overlook the forest home of

Mexican gray wolves, while a video monitor inside shows activity in the wolves' den. Numerous musk oxen are best seen from a monorail that crosses the huge lake. A deck looks out across the water, but it is much too far to see clearly without the aid of binoculars. (You'll find coin-operated ones nearby.) Animals on display from the world's northern evergreen forests include woodland caribou and moose, both seen in naturalistic wetland habitats.

During the cold winter, many Northerners long for the warmth of the tropics, one reason for the popularity of the 1½-acre **Tropics Trail**. The Trail, which once displayed only species from Asian rain forests, now concentrates on biodiversity hotspots (threatened tropical ecosystems) from around the world. In the *Ghosts of Madagascar* exhibit, ring-tailed and ruffed lemurs (Latin for "ghosts," and so named for their ghostly faces and nocturnal habits) live in a lush jungle habitat. Radiated tortoises, tenrec hedgehogs, and hissing cockroaches complete the Madagascan section. Small chevrotain deer and tricolor squirrels share an exhibit as the path proceeds to the Asian habitats. A viewing area overlooks a rocky grotto for sun bears, and another grotto for Komodo dragons. In a spectacular panorama, long-armed gibbons inhabit the trees in the foreground of *Gibbon Island*, as pink flamingos wade in the background. The trail then comes remarkably close to small-clawed otters and black-and-white Malayan tapirs, which swim in the same deep pool. Past displays of tree kangaroos and a two-story aviary that's home to great hornbill birds, look down into the 82,500-gallon *Coral Reef Sharks* exhibit, where you may spot a shark's dorsal fin rippling the surface. In the underwater viewing area, more than a hundred species of colorful reef fish, including six types of sharks, can be seen. The fifty-five-foot-long, floor-to-ceiling windows bring sharks and humans face-to-face. From the depths of the South Pacific, the trail next leads to a mountain habitat for gorals, furry wild goats, with red pandas displayed in front of them. Rare Visayan warty pigs, the newest residents on the trail, live right across the path. Clouded leopards, Indian flying foxes (which are actually bats), a variety of jungle reptiles that includes huge water monitor lizards and Burmese pythons, and fishing cats are all housed behind glass in a row of uphill nocturnal habitats. Upon exiting them, the path leads through a huge walk-through aviary. Here, visitors get a second look at the hornbill birds, as well as close looks at crowned pigeons, mynahs, and over twenty other avian species. *South America*, the last continental region, is at the very top of the building. Golden lion and cotton-top tamarin monkeys, tree-dwelling tamandua anteaters, pudu deer, sloths, and agoutis (small rodents related to domestic guinea pigs) can be seen in separate mesh enclosures.

Dolphins are the stars of **Discovery Bay**. Only a couple of other zoos in the country exhibit dolphins. After you watch a show upstairs in the Dolphin Stadium, head downstairs, where several large windows give clear underwater views of the show's stars in their 380,000-gallon pool. Nearby, the *Estuary* is a touch tank with bamboo sharks. Visitors can handle starfish at the *Tide Pool*, where waves crash at regular intervals. A giant shark's mouth is the entrance into *Clubhouse Cove*, which displays sea dragons, clownfish, shrimp, octopi, and other small marine critters. Elsewhere,

Shark Reef includes some sharks larger than those in the Tropics Trail's shark exhibit, as well as moray eels and hundreds of other fish.

The **Skytrail Monorail** provides an excellent alternative to walking over a mile of trails, especially in the winter. Cruising along at a mere four miles per hour, the peaceful ride gives a fantastic elevated view of the grizzly bear habitat and the Northern Trail animals. From thirty feet up, visitors can appreciate the size of each exhibit and get a much better view of the distant musk oxen herd.

OTHER EXHIBITS

Japanese snow monkeys are the first animals most visitors encounter. In their grassy yard, the hardy macaques are perfectly at home in this cold climate. Between the two tiger exhibits is a small outdoor exhibit of meerkats. Termite mounds and an elephant skull provide high lookout spots for the meerkat sentries to watch for predators. Pop-up bubble windows, accessible by tunnel, allow visitors to check out the mob from within the habitat. Trumpeter swans glide on the zoo's *Main Lake*. Swan hatchlings raised here are introduced back into the wild after reaching adulthood. A 3,000 square foot butterfly exhibit is open seasonally near the Tropics Trail exit.

FOR THE KIDS

In our opinion, one of the best "working" farms at a zoo is this **Family Farm**. Kids and adults alike can board one of two tractor-pulled wagons at the *Grain Elevator*, which will take them to the farm; otherwise, it's a ten-minute walk. Seven red barns are open for visitors to explore. In the *Dairy Barn*, daily milking demonstrations are always fun to watch. Huge pigs have indoor and outdoor pens by their barn. There's a separate building for goats and sheep, as well as a chicken coop. For a home-cooked meal, head to the *Country Café* before you return to the main zoo. Horses inhabit a pen near the tractor drop-off point.

Located in the zoo's main building, on the way to Discovery Bay, the **Kids' Den** is an interactive play area for children and their parents. **Paddleboat rides** on swan boats are available seasonally on the zoo's main lake, near the Tiger Lair habitat.

IN PROGRESS

Along the way to Grizzly Coast, a new **Central Plaza** will give kids access to a new splash park in 2008. Plans call for a new restaurant and amphitheater to complete this ambitious project.

The **Heart of the Zoo,** expected to open in 2011 as we go to press, will address the zoo's two biggest problems: an outdated entrance plaza and the long stretch between the zoo entrance and the animals. This new entrance plaza will create an entirely new visitor experience. Sandhill cranes and other animals will roam a mature forest along the walking path into the zoo. Once inside, three entertaining species – meerkats, penguins, and snow monkeys (or Japanese macaques) – should give a great first impression. A new Africa section is also being planned, to be constructed later on.

Kansas City Zoological Gardens

6800 Zoo Drive
Kansas City, Missouri 64132
(816) 513-5700
www.kansascityzoo.org

Red river hogs live in Africa's Congolese Forest.

Hours: 9:30 a.m.-5:00 p.m. daily. Closed Thanksgiving, Christmas Day, and New Year's Day.

Admission & Fees: Adults $9.50, seniors 55+ $8.50, children 3-11 $6.50; all ages $6 on Tuesdays. Tram to or from Africa: 75¢ each way; train $2.50; boat $2; carousel $2; camel ride $3. Combo ride pass available for unlimited rides.

Directions: From US-71, take the 63rd Street exit. Continue east on East 63rd Street for 1.1 miles, then turn right onto Starlight Road and follow signs through Swope Park to the zoo. From I-435, take Exit 66 (63rd Street). Continue west on East 63rd Street for 2.3 miles, then turn left onto Starlight Road and follow signs through Swope Park to the Zoo.

Don't Miss: Africa, Australia.

For Kids: KidZone, train ride, boat ride, carousel, camel ride, pony ride.

Authors' Tips: The walk to Africa is long, making the tram a worthwhile step-saving investment. Even if you are up to the walk, we still recommend you take the zebra-striped tram, as this enhances the feeling that you're actually arriving in Africa!

Edutainment: "The Sea Lion Show" is held three times daily, weather permitting, at the Sea Lion Pool. In summer, the "Wild Wonders Animal Show" is presented twice daily at the Show Stage in KidZone. Elephant behavior demonstrations are presented daily at their exhibit throughout the summer. An elephant shows off its painting skills in a show on summer weekends. Chimp feedings and participatory lorikeet feedings are held daily. For show times, check the schedule included with your zoo map.

LOCATED NEAR THE CENTER OF THE COUNTRY, KANSAS CITY IS often called "the heart of the nation." Sometimes, however, the city evokes international comparisons – it's referred to as "Paris on the Plains" for its many wide boulevards, and it has more fountains than any other city in the world, except of course Rome.

Kansas City is also experiencing something of a renaissance. In the past decade, it's expanded its art museums and shopping complexes, opened a National World War I Museum, and renovated and expanded its downtown convention center. Part of the city's revitalization occurred in the mid 1990s, when the Kansas City Zoo was transformed from a small, outdated facility into one of the biggest and best zoos in the country. This newly modernized zoo offers visitors a variety of exotic experiences from across the globe.

FEATURED EXHIBITS

At ninety-five acres, this zoo's **Africa** section is one of the largest single exhibits in the nation. If you can't swing an actual trip to that continent, this place is the next best thing! What makes this such a fascinating journey is the way guests are taken to five different African nations. When the tram comes to a halt, the signs say you've arrived in the nation of Kenya. Thatched-roof huts, piles of abandoned suitcases, and old rusting bicycles make you feel as if you are on the other side of the world. In the *Nanyuki Market* area, the snack bars and souvenir shop all have a strong African theme. There's even a spot where visitors can pose and have their picture taken standing on the "Equator." A sign informs you that you're 8,040 miles from Kansas City.

If you arrive in Africa on foot, the first nation you'll encounter is *Botswana*, with its 4½-acre *Okavango Elephant Sanctuary*. In one of three tall cone-shaped huts, an elephant skeleton is displayed (the other two huts are restrooms). The elephant herd wanders through its long, narrow habitat, and the lengthy *Elephant Walk* visitor path parallels the exhibit. Only a cable fence separates you from the elephants, which makes for superb viewing. Near the huts is a large elephant watering hole. From the *Elephant Overlook,* you can see the herd's large yard and holding barns.

From Nanyuki Market, you'll find the animals of *Kenya* along a long path that encircles a sizeable, pretty lake. The sprawling savanna habitat is visible at several points along the way, starting with the market area. Roaming its seventeen acres are several varieties of antelope, including kudus, oryxes, and impala, and a variety of large African birds. Proceeding along the main path, cheetahs are the first animal you'll see, from an attractive glass-fronted viewing hut. Farther along, warthogs live in a sunken habitat. Next, Bomas, a real Kenyan village, is reproduced here with a group of authentic tribal huts and mud houses. Among these round huts are many exhibits of small African animals, including vultures, tiny dik-dik antelope, tortoises, and lemurs. A tall walk-through aviary showcases many African birds. The nearby kopje area features gigantic boulders – guests can get lost searching among these large stones for naturalistic habitats housing animals such as bat-eared foxes, black-footed and serval cats, and a mob of meerkats. The highlight here, though, is the lion pride – one of the largest in North America. Visitors can enjoy many great views of these majestic cats. From an elevated boardwalk, peek in on black rhinos, who enjoy a mud wallow in their long yard, while giraffes and zebras move about nearby in another large pen. Crossing a stream, you'll come to overlooks of hippos in their pool, and Nile crocodiles in the small *Crocodile Research Station*.

Off on a side trail, a swaying suspension bridge leads to the *Congolese Forest*, an area that represents the current Democratic Republic of the Congo, in place since 1997, though the sign (which needs to be updated) still says "Zaire." As you enter the thick forest, the tail of a crashed bush plane protrudes from a thicket to the right. The leopard enclosure runs along both sides of the visitor path, with an overhead tunnel cage so these large spotted cats can cross from one side to the other, over visitors' heads. Also in forest habitats here are beautiful bongo antelope, two types of mangabey monkeys, crowned cranes, and red river hogs. The main event, of course, is the large gorilla habitat. You can watch these great apes from an overlook, or through glass from a secretive blind.

Off the Kenyan trail, a side path follows a boardwalk across another stream to *Tanzania*, home of one of the largest chimpanzee habitats we've ever seen. From the *Gombe Stream National Park* visitor center, a forty-foot glass window provides great views of the large troop of chimps, who occupy a three-acre forested hillside. Renowned ape expert Jane Goodall called this "one of the finest chimpanzee exhibits in North America."

Beyond Kenya's hippos and crocodiles, the main trail leads to *Uganda*. In this forest clearing, African wild dogs and black-backed jackals alternate time in a large habitat, visible from opposite ends through thin harp wire. Nearby, playful Guinea baboons frolic in a large, impressive display area.

On a somewhat smaller scale, **Australia** is thoroughly represented on another circular trail. This tour begins at *Gundagai Station*, a replica of a rural Australian town, with a snack bar, gift shop, train station, and a forty-foot-long Aboriginal mural. Winding through the woods, the tall walk-through *Australian Aviary* houses black swans, cockatoos, ibises, and other rare Australian birds. In side yards, tall emus, New Guinea singing dogs, and endangered tree kangaroos are easily visible. Coming down the hill, you reach *Stoney Creek Sheep Station*, an authentic Australian farm with a broken down truck, windmill, and a rural house to tour. Also on the farm, in the *Wonders of the Outback* museum, there are kookaburras, several Australian reptiles, and animal artifacts to examine. In outdoor paddocks, visitors can pet and feed sheep. Up the hill, dromedary camels from the Australian desert occupy a large yard. The entire Australian trail encircles a sprawling kangaroo yard, where more than fifty red kangaroos are free to roam, with no physical barriers to separate them from their human guests.

OTHER EXHIBITS

The **Tiger Trail**, running through a steep valley, features animals from Asia, which explains the Asian statuary along the path. Cuddly red pandas are the first feature, and you'll encounter them twice, including in an attractive habitat behind glass. A pair of rare Sumatran tigers occupies a larger habitat nearby. Past a bend in the trail, the *Orangutan Primadome* allows some of these large red apes from Borneo to be seen outside in a large domed cage, while more orangutans are visible through glass in their indoor holding area. Other endangered and interesting species to be seen here include François' langur monkeys, tufted deer, demoiselle cranes, and a binturong (a shaggy black Asian mammal that's often called a "bear cat," though it's actually neither).

The **Sea Lion Pool** usually draws a crowd, especially just before or after a show. It makes for a refreshing stop on a hot day. Near the *Promenade* shortcut to Africa, the **Aviary Row** exhibits owls, pheasants, and other birds, while a flock of flamingos wades in a pool nearby. Near the zoo's exit, in the massive entry/exit building, is a beautiful aquarium of native Missouri fish.

FOR THE KIDS

The centerpiece of the **KidZone** children's area is the *Discovery Barn*, completed in 2006, an indoor air-conditioned family area with exhibits of small "kid-friendly" animals, including ring-tailed lemurs, squirrel monkeys, macaw parrots, marine toads, and meerkats. Fun hands-on activities include a climbing rope and a two-story twisting slide. Just outside, the three-story *Peek-A-Boo Tree* offers kids more climbing and sliding adventures. On the opposite side of the barn, many domestic animals can be petted and fed, including pot-bellied pigs, llamas, chickens, and dwarf goats. This area also features a lorikeet cage, with scheduled feedings.

Just as the tram is the most fun way to arrive in Africa, a ride on the **miniature train** is the best way to arrive in Australia. There's an **Endangered Species Carousel**, added in 2007, in the zoo's entrance plaza. The choice of rides includes mascot animals from local sports teams. For a spin on a live animal, check out the camel rides near the KidZone. In Africa's marketplace, at the *Boathouse Bar*, the **boat ride** is an enchanting way to see many of the African animals.

IN PROGRESS

If this zoo has a weakness, it has been its inconvenient entrance and parking areas. As we go to press, a redesigned entrance area is about to open that will make entering this zoo ultra-convenient. It will include attractive exhibits for river otters and trumpeter swans. Slated for later in 2008 is a new **Tropics** exhibit, which will feature saki monkeys in a rain forest environment. A major new polar bear habitat is scheduled to open in 2009. This exciting exhibit will include underwater windows, a gift shop, and an arctic-themed snack bar. In 2010, plans call for a new warm-water penguin exhibit.

Saint Louis Zoo

1 Government Drive
St. Louis, Missouri 63110
(314) 781-0900
www.stlzoo.org

Gentoo, king, and rockhopper penguins share Penguin Cove.

Hours: 8:00 a.m.-7:00 p.m. daily, Memorial Day-Labor Day; 9:00 a.m.-5:00 p.m. daily, rest of year. Closed Christmas Day and New Year's Day, shortened hours on Thanksgiving, Christmas Eve, and New Year's Eve.

Admission & Fees: Free. Sea lion show $3, Children's Zoo $4, Zooline Railroad $5, carousel $2, Zoomagination Station $2, simulator $3, 3-D movie $4. Safari Pass $12: includes Children's Zoo, sea lion show, railroad, carousel, simulator, and 3-D movie. Parking $10, and limited free street parking.

Directions: From I-44, take Exit 286 (Hampton Avenue), then follow 1 mile north to zoo. From I-64, take Exit 34D (Forest Park) and follow signs to zoo. (Note: I-64 will be undergoing extensive construction in 2008 and 2009.) From downtown, Bus #90 stops close to the zoo. From MetroLink light rail system, stop at the Forest Park/DeBaliviere station and ride Bus #90.

Don't Miss: River's Edge, Penguin and Puffin Coast, Insectarium, The Living World, Fragile Forest, Big Cat Country, Red Rocks, Bird House, Herpetarium, Cypress Swamp, Sea Lion Show, Animals Always sculpture.

For Kids: Children's Zoo, Zooline Railroad, Build-A-Bear Workshop® At the Zoo, Conservation Carousel, Zoomagination Station, simulator, 3-D movie.

Authors' Tips: Try to get to the zoo early, since the Children's Zoo and carousel are free for the first hour each day. The paths to Historic Hill are very steep. It's much easier to take the train to the Big Cat Country stop.

Edutainment: Sea lion shows, one of the best animal programs we've seen in any zoo, are presented three times daily during the summer season in a replica of San Francisco's Bay Wharf. Children's Zoo animal shows, also in summer, include sloths and flying squirrels, and are held four times daily, except on Wednesdays. Check your zoo map for a schedule of summer keeper chats. There is usually one chat per day during the week, two chats on weekends. Sea lions, penguins, and bears are all fed daily at their respective exhibits.

THE SAINT LOUIS ZOO OPENED IN 1913 IN HISTORIC FOREST PARK, which had hosted the 1904 World's Fair just a few years earlier. Today, it is one of the nation's only free zoos, as well as one of its best. *Parenting Magazine* has ranked it the country's number one family zoo, and *Child Magazine* listed it as one of the top twenty zoos for kids. Most persuasive of all, however, are its attendance figures: more than 3,000,000 guests come through the zoo's gates every year.

Atop the zoo's Historic Hill stands a statue of wildlife legend Marlin Perkins. Beginning his career here as a reptile keeper, Perkins made several stops at other zoos before returning here as Saint Louis Zoo Director in 1962. A year later, he began *Mutual of Omaha's Wild Kingdom*, a landmark television series that was the predecessor of Animal Planet and other wildlife documentaries and TV programs.

FEATURED EXHIBITS

A meandering waterway passes animals from four continental regions in **River's Edge**, the zoo's largest and most extensive project to date. Each exhibit can be seen from several vantage points. The trail, lined with dense vegetation, is enhanced with animal artifacts, a ranger station, and an African schoolhouse. Pick up a trail guide at the beginning of River's Edge: it gives valuable insight into both the animals and the interpretive exhibits along the path. (Don't forget to recycle the guide at the trail's end.) This ten-acre immersion exhibit begins in South America, at a mixed-species waterfront habitat for giant anteaters and capybaras, giant aquatic rodents. Bush dogs live nearby. Africa begins around the corner, with black rhinos in a long yard backed by a splashing waterfall. The trail provides several views of the rhinos and their neighbors, red river hogs and bat-eared foxes, who share an exhibit. Brightly colored carmine bee-eater birds perch in a densely branched aviary nearby. Further up the trail, a wide window lets visitors peer into the underwater world of hippos at

Hippo Harbor. These unexpectedly graceful pachyderms (hippopotamus means "river horse" in Greek) glide through the water mere inches from mesmerized visitors. There is also a small overlook of the hippos' shoreline; you can see them when they come ashore for food. Housed on opposite sides of the path, African predators of different stature can be compared. Slender, quick cheetahs roam a tiered hillside across from sturdy, powerful spotted hyenas. A curious mob of dwarf mongooses, Africa's smallest predator, ramble through termite mounds in front of the cheetah habitat. Finally, the trail leads to Asia and the elephant complex. The herd is divided into three habitats, each with a refreshing pool: two high-banked dusty yards and a third yard that winds close to the visitor path and ends at a spectacular waterfall. The journey concludes in North America, at a Missouri cave with a 33,000-gallon aquarium that displays fish of the Mississippi River. A nearby educational display sheds light on the Flood of 1993, and how we can prevent a future disaster.

Penguin and Puffin Coast is the first walk-through penguin habitat in the nation. No other penguin exhibit comes close to the one-of-a-kind, up-close experience here. Outside, at *Humboldt Haven*, an old bear pit has been renovated to resemble the Peruvian coast; it's now a home for Humboldt penguins and pelicans. Inside, the temperature is kept between 45 and 50 degrees Fahrenheit; visitors feel like they're immersed in an Antarctic climate. Lighting in the building shifts to create sunrises and sunsets, but is always adjusted to match the light levels at the furthest tip of the Southern Hemisphere: dimmer during our summers, lighter in winter. A four-foot glass wall is the only separation between visitors and the penguins along the rugged shoreline. In *Penguin Cove*, gentoo, king, and rockhopper penguins can be seen both above and below water as they swim in their chilled pools. The path moves on to the Northern Hemisphere and *Puffin Bay*. Horned and tufted puffins inhabit another rocky cliff face behind their own cool stream.

The **Insectarium**, one of the largest displays of invertebrates in the country, exhibits over a hundred insects in twenty separate areas. Ants, Peruvian fire sticks, cockroaches and huge rhinoceros beetles are just a few of the creepy crawlies that live here. The most popular spot is the *Butterfly Wing*, where hundreds of butterflies flutter under a geodesic dome. Also interesting is the *Not Home Alone* section, where kids can find some of the bugs that might be sharing house space with them! A huge bee colony is surrounded by colorful displays about the process of pollination.

The **Living World** education center is this zoo's most unusual exhibit. The building includes two theaters, classrooms, a lecture hall, a restaurant, and a gift shop, but the highlights are the two exhibit halls that integrate high technology and live animal displays. *An Introduction to Ecology* houses temporary exhibits. At press time, it features a "Year of the Frog" exhibit, which opened in that year (2008) to highlight the worldwide amphibian crisis. Six-foot-long Chinese giant salamanders, the world's largest salamanders, swim in a flowing sixty-foot stream. Fourteen major exhibits feature amphibians from Missouri (including eastern hellbenders – large salamanders) and elsewhere. The other exhibit hall, *An Introduction to the Animals*, provides a one-room tour of the animal kingdom. The tour begins with

The Invertebrates, a display of anemones, crabs, insects, and other invertebrates. *A Tour of a Bee* is a fascinating mini-movie made with a scanning electron microscope. *The Vertebrates* features fish, reptile, amphibian, bird, and mammal oddities such as mudskippers, lungfish, seahorses, poison dart frogs, anoles, frogmouth birds, and pygmy marmosets. In the hall's center, *The Processes of Life* display uses a leaf-cutter ant exhibit to illustrate the social behavior of animals. Life-size animated figures teach about animal communication and defenses.

Gorillas have long had an outdoor exhibit at the zoo, and a 2005 renovation added outdoor habitats for the chimpanzees and orangutans of the **Lipton Fragile Forest**. St. Louis was the first zoo to establish a bachelor group of gorillas, and that tradition continues today. The *Gorilla Habitat* houses teenage males in an expansive hillside. The flat *Chimpanzee Refuge* is home to a troop that can be seen behind glass in a long yard. The back wall of the chimp exhibit is drilled with more than thirty holes, some filled with special treats so the apes can hunt for them throughout the day. The *Orangutan Refuge* is well-designed for these most arboreal of great apes. Tall trees sprout from an angled hillside underneath mesh netting in the orangs' dense habitat. The domed *Jungle of the Apes* building is the winter home of all of the apes. A winding path through a humid rain forest leads to excellent close-up viewing opportunities. The apes' two-story habitats include rocky outcrops, tall trees, and live plants.

In **Big Cat Country,** visitors follow a raised walkway that overlooks lions, Amur tigers, and jaguars in spacious, grassy yards landscaped with rocks, trees, and cascading waterfalls. Pumas, snow leopards, and rare Amur leopards – all climbing cats – are displayed in unique wire mesh tension structures.

Historic Hill has the zoo's oldest buildings. Their exteriors retain their historic charm, but their interiors have been extensively renovated into naturalistic exhibits. The **Bird House**, built in 1930, is a great example. Inside, lush habitats are enclosed by fine steel wire, which seems to disappear due to special lighting. Thanks to this wire-and-lighting system, all of the building's stunning exotic birds are shown with no visible barriers, a collection that includes great hornbills, hyacinth macaws, peacock pheasants, and at press time, the nation's only display of horned guans.

The 1927 **Herpetarium**, with a Spanish-style façade, displays a diverse collection of reptiles and amphibians in modern naturalistic habitats. The impressive size of the collection is due to the influence of Mr. Perkins, who served as reptile curator for several years. Chinese alligators, Cuban crocodiles, false gharials, and Yacare caiman are some of the impressive collection of rare crocodilians. Lizard-like tuataras, Komodo dragons, Chinese giant salamanders, and Missouri hellbenders are some of the more interesting creatures found inside. Tortoises and Chinese alligators are exhibited side-by-side outside, on the hillside leading up to the building.

The **Red Rocks** area, named for the red boulders that back some of its yards, hosts most of the zoo's hoofed animals in spacious yards, many shared by multiple species. A number of rare animals are found here, including Speke's gazelles, goat-like Sichuan takins, okapis (related to giraffes), addax antelope, and one of only a few displays of

Somali wild asses in the nation. The zoo has had considerable breeding success with the gazelles and takins. Giraffes, kangaroos, Grevy's zebras, Bactrian camels, ostriches, lesser kudu antelope, anoa cattle, Arabian oryxes, gerenuk gazelles, bongo antelope, and three more gazelle species are also shown in this expansive area, and several pig species live here, including warthogs, Visayan warty pigs, Chacoan peccaries, and babirusa pigs. In cold weather, the giraffes and kangaroos can be seen indoors.

The Flight Cage, featured at the 1904 World's Fair, is the oldest structure in the zoo and is home to the **Love Cypress Swamp**. Sixteen North American bird species live in this lovely re-creation of a Southern marsh. Spoonbills, ibises, egrets, herons, merganser ducks, and cormorants are all visible from a low wooden boardwalk through this gigantic structure.

The **Animals Always sculpture** is the defining feature of the zoo's west entrance. Measuring 36 feet high and 130 feet wide, this is the world's largest public zoo sculpture, and makes an excellent site for a family photo. More than sixty animals and 1,300 natural elements make up the hundred-ton sculpture, which is visible from Highway 40 outside the zoo.

OTHER EXHIBITS

When the **Bear Pits** opened in 1921, their use of molded concrete to simulate natural rock formations was quickly imitated by other zoos. Today, four species of bears – polar, grizzly, spectacled, and black – live in these deep grottoes. Malayan sun bears, the smallest bears here, live in a smaller grotto across the zoo, next to the prairie dogs.

The **Primate House** is another of the Historic Hill buildings with a renovated interior. Hamadryas baboons, lion-tailed macaque monkeys, colobus monkeys, cotton-top tamarin monkeys, dusky leaf monkeys, spider monkeys, sifaka lemurs, and various other lemurs are some of the entertaining primates that live in rocky habitats behind tall windows.

Between the Bird House and the 1904 Flight Cage, an outdoor **Bird Garden** exhibits a diverse collection of birds, including several birds of prey. Bald eagles, king vultures, bateleur eagles, and cinerous vultures are housed on this winding hillside path. Also here are an overlook into a crane habitat and a small walk-through aviary. The **Sea Lion Basin** is an attractive natural coastal pool exhibiting California sea lions. River otters swim in the nearby **Chain of Lakes** exhibit, as do several swans and other waterfowl. The collection of waterfowl here is the largest in the country.

FOR THE KIDS

The **Children's Zoo** offers a wide variety of opportunities for hands-on animal interaction. Just inside its entrance, a goat-petting yard is sunken into a rocky crag, with black-and-white ruffed lemurs in an aviary-style enclosure next door (the lemurs, though, are not available for petting). The *Hip Hop Swamp* exhibit focuses on amphibians, particularly brightly colored frogs. A building holds some interesting, non-typical children's zoo animals. You'll see meerkats, naked mole-rats, armadillos, fennec foxes, and tree kangaroos, in addition to the expected rabbits and guinea pigs.

Small reptiles and amphibians are also displayed inside, as are echidnas (spine-covered egg-laying mammals). The outdoor otter pond is a popular spot, mostly due to a clear acrylic slide that passes right through the otter pool, putting children nose-to-nose with these playful creatures. A play area allows kids to replicate the behaviors of their favorite animals. They can dig like aardvarks, climb on a spider web, and slither like boas. A small stage provides some excellent chances for close looks at birds of prey, macaws, and other birds.

The **Zooline Railroad** circles the entire zoo property and passes through a couple of tunnels. Train stations are located in front of the tigers, at the entrances to River's Edge and Living World, and near the carousel. The **Conservation Carousel** has sixty-four hand-carved wooden animals to pick from. Many kids will want to stop at the **Build-A-Bear Workshop® At the Zoo**, to construct a unique toy animal.

Zoomagination Station is a complex interactive area for kids that lets their parents sit back and relax. Kids can fill bird feeders in the backyard, or pretend to be zookeepers and care for animals inside. Children can also design their own zoo enclosures, watch a puppet show, or build animal models to take home. The **motion simulator** (near the 1904 Flight Cage) and **3-D movie** (in the Living World) present unique virtual reality experiences to enhance your zoo visit.

IN PROGRESS

Saint Louis Zoo is currently developing plans for several new exhibits. A few projects are on the drawing board, but no timeline or list of animals has been set as we go to press.

Omaha's Henry Doorly Zoo

3701 South 10th Street
Omaha, Nebraska 68107
(402) 733-8401
www.omahazoo.com

Hours: 9:30 a.m.-5:00 p.m. daily. Grounds stay open two hours past closing, or to dusk. Closed Thanksgiving, Christmas Day, and New Year's Day.

Admission & Fees: Adults $11.00, seniors 62+ $9.50, children 3-11 $7.25. Combo ticket for zoo and IMAX film: adults $18.25, seniors $15.75, children $12.50. Train: adults $3.25 round trip/$1.75 one way, children $2.25/$1.25; tram $2 or $.50 a stop; carousel $1; budgie seed stick $1. Participates in reciprocity program.

Collared peccaries (prey) can safely ignore puma (predator) in the Sonoran Desert exhibit.

Directions: From I-80, take Exit 454 (13th Street) South. Follow 13th Street for 0.4 miles, passing Rosenblatt Stadium, then turn left onto Bert Murphy Avenue. Continue around the stadium for 0.2 miles, then turn left onto 10th Street. Zoo parking lot is on the right.

Don't Miss: Lied Jungle, Desert Dome, Kingdoms of the Night, Gorilla Valley, Aquarium, Orangutan Forest, Cat Complex, Bear Canyon.

For Kids: Exploration Station, Dairy World, wildlife carousel, zoo train.

Authors' Tips: The zoo is built on two levels connected by steep walkways. A step-saving tram circles the zoo, but to save time and money, visitors can take the elevator near Orangutan Forest to get to the lower section. The best food (and view) in the zoo is at Durham's Tree Tops Restaurant, where a nine-foot-tall, floor-to-ceiling window looks down into Lied Jungle.

Edutainment: Horseshoe crabs, sharks, and starfish rotate time in a small touch tank in the lobby of Scott Aquarium, open 10:00 a.m.-2:00 p.m. daily in summer. Animal presentations are given daily in the Exploration Station. The Lozier IMAX Theater is on site (admission is extra, though) and features nature-themed movies on a 61-foot-tall by 83-foot-wide screen.

OMAHA'S HENRY DOORLY ZOO HAS A KNACK FOR CREATING exhibits that become the biggest and best of their kind. In the newer exhibits, every effort is made to put as little separation as possible between visitors and animals. These innovative exhibits have led to the zoo's inclusion in the popular book, *1,000 Places to See in the U.S.A. and Canada Before You Die* (Workman Publishing Company, ©2003). It's no wonder Omaha's Henry Doorly Zoo is the most-visited tourist attraction between Chicago and Denver.

As if the zoo alone weren't enough, it shares its parking lot with Rosenblatt Stadium, home of the College World Series, making this corner of Nebraska a busy place in summer. For more animal viewing in the area, check out the Lee G. Simmons Conservation Park & Wildlife Safari, named after the zoo's longtime director. Located about half an hour west of the zoo, the park is a combination drive-through and walk-through facility focusing on North American wildlife.

FEATURED EXHIBITS

Lauded by both zoo and mainstream media as one of the best zoo exhibits ever built, **Lied Jungle** is a must-see for any zoo enthusiast. Opened in 1992, the eighty-foot-high conservatory covering 1½ acres, is, at press time, the world's largest indoor rain forest. More than 2,000 living plants make nearly a hundred animal species (and their human visitors) feel like they're in a real jungle. The journey begins in *Asia*, with views of gibbons and small-clawed otters from an elevated pathway. More gibbons are on an island just around the corner, as is a slippery swaying suspension bridge behind a waterfall. Next, in the Asian nightlife cave, clouded leopards, Indian porcupines, and pythons are displayed. Endangered François' langur monkeys share a lush island with black-and-white Malayan tapirs. *Africa* begins with a view of lemurs, shown behind nearly invisible harp wire. Across the path, pygmy hippos wade below, while uncommon blue monkeys bound through the trees above another pool, this one home to fish and giant soft-shelled turtles. Spot-necked otters have their own stream, before the path turns toward *South America,* where spider monkeys hang out in the trees above Baird's tapirs. Just ahead, another cave features more small animals, including tamarin monkeys and vampire bats. A small crevice leads to *Danger Point*, the highest viewing spot in the building. Bordering a fifty-foot waterfall, this cliff overlook of the spider monkeys is incredible! One last island is home to a family of black howler monkeys. Don't forget to look down at the enormous Amazonian fish swimming in the moat, including several ten-foot-long arapaimas.

What separates this rain forest replica from any other is the *Jungle Trail*. After you finish the elevated tour, a set of stairs leads to a dirt walkway that takes you past all the previous exhibits, this time at ground level. The overhanging trees make this journey a dark and humid one. Douroucouli monkeys are displayed as the path begins, and free-ranging golden lion tamarin monkeys and an assortment of birds may cross the trail at any time. As you pass streams and massive tree buttresses, you'll encounter underwater views of the tapirs, otters, pygmy hippos, African cichlid fish, and Philippine crocodiles.

Beneath the world's largest glazed geodesic dome lies **Desert Dome**, an immense re-creation of the world's arid desert environments. Towering cliffs and canyons divide the exhibit into distinct deserts from three continents. A sloping red sand dune, built with over 300 tons of sand, welcomes visitors to southern Africa's *Namib Desert*. Aviaries for African birds and a bat-eared fox exhibit are carved into a rock face. Just around the corner, serval cats spy on klipspringer antelope. A huge cliff face crawling with rock hyraxes, rodent-like creatures most closely related to elephants, is situated behind an oasis and across from a mob of meerkats. Inside a desert cave, the path winds past venomous snakes and other reptiles from Africa and Australia. Several cobras and taipans, the world's second-deadliest snake, are quite eye-catching, but the water dragons and frilled lizards are just as fascinating. Kookaburras are shown behind glass just as the cave opens up to Ayers Rock, the famous landmark of the *Red Center of Australia*. Yellow-footed rock wallabies hop across the rock face. Along a dirt path, the only thing that separates visitors from the rest of the exhibit is a forest of short trees, one of which often holds a perching cockatoo. Wonderfully colored Gouldian finches fly through a neighboring finch aviary. The southwestern United States' *Sonoran Desert* is the final section of this incredible exhibit. In perhaps the most visually stunning habitat, collared peccaries (or javelinas), a species of wild pig, roam past the watchful eyes of pumas. Bobcats rest in a cave as the path winds into Hummingbird Canyon. Several species of mesmerizing hummingbirds zip about in enclosures that are over twenty feet high. Also in this canyon is a waterfall and pond for wading ducks. The path opens up into a saguaro cactus forest, where sharp eyes can spot more free-roaming hummingbirds. Jackrabbits, prairie dogs, armadillos, and cottontail rabbits share a burrow-filled habitat. American badgers and kestrel falcons are displayed, before you head downstairs to…

Kingdoms of the Night, the world's largest nocturnal exhibit. Clever lighting keeps animals in sight and active, but it's dark enough to preserve the feeling that you're entering their nighttime world. A naked mole-rat colony and sleek, cat-like fossas, Madagascar's largest predatory mammal, are the first animals you'll encounter. Springhaas, a rabbit-like rodent, and aardvarks dwell on the ground, while lemur-like big-eyed greater bushbabies bounce through the overhanging branches in the

Gibbon in Lied Jungle, waterfall and visitors in background; restaurant windows above right.

African Diorama. Over 2,400 stalactites hang from the ceiling inside the *Wet Cave.* A seemingly bottomless pit is actually a sixteen-foot-deep pool filled with blind cave fish, to eerie effect. For many people, bats are equally spine-chilling. Here, more than 3,000 fruit bats inhabit a sprawling cave habitat. The sound of fluttering wings fills the air as they flap about behind thin mesh netting. Rare Japanese giant salamanders inhabit a rocky pool near a rushing underground waterfall. Wallabies and statuesque tawny frogmouth birds co-exist in the *Eucalyptus Forest.* Tiger quolls, spotted carnivorous marsupials, rest in a streamside thicket across the path. Three armadillo species prowl the floor of the *South American* forest, as more ground-dwellers, agoutis (wild relatives of domestic guinea pigs), scout for food below the sloths and arboreal tamandua anteaters overhead. In the *Dry Cave,* beams of light from above help visitors realize they are now seventy feet below ground. Arranged around a gorge are exhibits of six rarely seen bat species, including bulldog bats, named for their muscular snouts. Finally, the path leads to the *Swamp.* American alligators, including a beautiful white alligator, are visible from a swaying boardwalk. Beavers swim around a lodge and several islands. The sound of croaking bullfrogs gets louder and louder as the path approaches a frog-filled bog. Opossums rest in a tree near another pond for spectacled caimans, a species of South American crocodile. An interesting mixed-species exhibit ends the tour. Raccoons patrol the edge of a pond, filled with plenty of hungry young alligators. These alligators have to be replaced annually with younger 'gators to prevent any unfortunate mishaps!

At **Hubbard Gorilla Valley**, visitors are made to feel like *they* are caged while the gorillas run free. Passing through a set of double doors, visitors enter a long, bland, concrete hallway. Alongside the hall are four lush gorilla exhibits, with the most breathtaking views of gorillas we've ever seen. Two unusual types of windows allow the closest possible looks at these largest of the primates. Accessed via an underground tunnel, large bubble windows pop up into the exhibit. They are as popular with the gorillas as they are with kids. S-shaped windows snake into the gorillas' space and bring visitors close to these intelligent animals. Cattle egrets roam freely between the gorilla exhibits and a nearby muddy yard where red river hogs happily wallow. Wolf's guenon monkeys frolic in the trees above a cascading waterfall. Colobus and Diana monkeys share a huge indoor exhibit with the gorillas.

Creatures from the deep seas are featured in **Scott Aquarium**. Australian blue penguins, smallest of the penguin species, live in the outdoor courtyard near the entrance. Inside, king and rockhopper penguins (both from Antarctica) waddle about in up to twenty tons of man-made snow. Arctic puffins have a rocky cliff habitat next door. An octopus and several anemones are displayed in additional tanks showcasing wildlife from the cold waters of the Pacific. Slow-moving leafy sea dragons and distinctive-looking nautilus, related to squid, are also featured. The seventy-foot-long shark tunnel is easily the most popular spot in the Aquarium. Huge sand tiger sharks and quick-moving reef sharks swim through the seventy-seven-degree water, accompanied by thousands of fish. More interesting and definitely harder to spot are several species of well-camouflaged wobbegong sharks. A floor-to-ceiling tank of moon jellies is ahead, as is a shallow Indonesian reef exhibit. The building's final habitat is an Amazon flooded forest, home to more fish as well as to squirrel monkeys.

The orangutans of **Hubbard Orangutan Forest** are said to have the best view in Omaha. Side-by-side outdoor habitats have sixty-five-foot-high man-made banyan trees for centerpieces, giving these arboreal red apes a great overview of their surroundings. Sturdy vines and ropes connect the banyan trees to smaller branches, providing plenty of swinging opportunities for the orangs, and for the François' langur monkeys and gray gibbons which often share one of the net-covered exhibits. Spacious indoor enclosures make primate viewing possible all year round.

With 37,000 square feet of interior space, the **Cat Complex** is the largest feline building in North America. Although this structure is aging, its collection is still impressive. Omaha is particularly known in the zoo world for its large collection of tigers. Amur, Malaysian, and both orange and white Bengal tigers are found in this indoor/outdoor exhibit. African lions have rocky grottoes outside, as do the Amur tigers. Jaguars, pumas, snow leopards, Amur leopards, fishing cats, and more can be seen in two rows of exhibits outside the building, as well as in several covered indoor areas.

From the outdoor exhibits of the Cat Complex, visitors can peer into **Durham Bear Canyon**. Down in the canyon, polar, sun, black, and grizzly bears can all be seen up close. Special side windows let visitors get even closer, while the polar bears can also be seen swimming underwater.

OTHER EXHIBITS

The four-acre **Simmons Free Flight Aviary**, one of the world's largest, is so big, it's difficult to see the opposite end. A boardwalk bridge over a long stream takes visitors through this tropical habitat of over 120 bird species, including golden pheasants, scarlet ibises, flamingos, spoonbills, and storks. Three shaded seating areas are available for relaxed bird-watching.

The **African Veldt**'s main enclosure holds ostriches, reticulated giraffes, cranes, and black-footed penguins. The thick woodland environment is visible several times along the trail. The indoor *Giraffe Complex* includes an aviary with weaver birds and tiny dik-dik antelope. Honey badgers (also known as ratels), a species rarely seen in zoos, are displayed here. *Cheetah Valley*, a grassland habitat for cheetahs, is also part of the Veldt. **Hoofstock** yards line the path through the zoo's lower section. Included in the impressive collection are bongo antelope, warthogs, sable antelope, zebras, scimitar-horned oryxes, the world's largest captive herd of wild Asian gaur cattle, and okapis, forest-dwelling cousins of giraffes. A colony of free-ranging prairie dogs lives near this region's picnic area – picnickers can roam right among them!

Owen Sea Lion Plaza is memorable for its relaxing charm. A convenient snack bar and ice cream stand are nearby, and the plaza has a large seating area where visitors can rest and refuel while watching the California sea lions. Further along, an old baseball field has been converted into **Pachyderm Hill**, home to white rhinos and African elephants

Spider and squirrel monkeys inhabit the largest of the islands in the **Lagoon**. A covered bridge gives visitors views of the monkeys, which have access to a large concrete "tree," with ropes and long branches that connect to the smaller islands. Another island here is home to gibbons, and thousands of koi fish swim in the water below. The zoo's best photo ops are to be found in the **Garden of the Senses**. This tranquil re-creation of an old English garden is filled with animal statues of all shapes and sizes, from elephants to grasshoppers. Streams and beautiful flowers make this a peaceful, relaxing place. Among its trellises are perches for macaws and cockatoos.

FOR THE KIDS

Dairy World features a see-through cow that illustrates the milk-making process, along with an artificial cow with water-filled rubber udders for city kids to learn milking skills. Rabbits, barn owls, and other small animals are displayed in a big red barn. Outside, the *Petting Zoo*'s contact yard has goats and potbellied pigs, while llamas and ponies live nearby in large corrals. Over 400 colorful birds live in *Budgie Encounter,* home to parakeets, cockatiels, quails, pigeons, and doves. Visitors can purchase seed sticks to feed the birds. Among the many small mammal exhibits up a hill are a prairie dog town that's supervised by nearby vultures, an otter pool with underwater windows, and a small mammal building featuring cotton-top tamarin monkeys, black-footed cats, and what is, at press time, the nation's only exhibit of raccoon dogs, wild dogs from Japan and East Asia with faces that strongly resemble raccoons'. Three round cages nearby display more primates. African wild dogs can be seen from a gazebo that overlooks their ravine. **Sue's Carousel**, a wild animal-themed merry-go-round, is also in this area. Beside the gaur herd is the zoo's main train station. The **Omaha Zoo Railroad** runs from the station to the zebras and back, giving good views of the hoofstock yards along its 1.8-mile route.

Just inside the entrance, **Exploration Station** uses small exhibits and a theater to give visitors a preview of the zoo's main attractions. The theater, underneath a thatched hut, plays short clips filmed at Lied Jungle, Desert Dome, and elsewhere throughout the zoo. Surrounding the safari hut is a set of glass cases, each with an artifact from a different zoo exhibit. More animals can be found at the *Tree of Life*, a twenty-foot-tall mesh-enclosed tree that's home to an assortment of birds. Turtles and fish swim in a stream below, while other invertebrates and reptiles are displayed nearby.

IN PROGRESS

North of the Veldt, a new **Butterfly and Insect Pavilion** will open in May of 2008. Inside this 14,000-square-foot building, a thousand colorful butterflies will flutter around guests, who can also tour the insect zoo, which will display ants, giant walking sticks, and other creepy creatures.

The zoo's next major project is to transform a hillside and lagoon into an expansive **Madagascar** exhibit, set to open in 2009 as we go to press. Several lemur species, including ring-tailed, ruffed, and lively sifakas, will be found on an island and in a walk-through habitat where little will separate them from visitors. The zoo is acquiring more land, to build an expanded **African elephant** habitat. According to plans, the complex will encompass twelve acres. This gigantic rolling grassland habitat would also include the first-ever underwater views of elephants in the United States. Pachyderm Hill would be slightly remodeled to give the white rhinos more space.

BEST OF THE REST

Blank Park Zoo

7401 SW 9th Street
Des Moines, Iowa 50315
(515) 285-4722
www.blankparkzoo.com

Iowa's best zoo opened in 1963 as a small children's zoo. It reopened in 1986, following three years of renovation, as a standout mid-size zoo. The focal point here is clearly the impressive indoor *Discovery Center*. Inside, a winding trail takes visitors by *Alpine* exhibits with Siberian lynx, to a bat cave, through a rain forest with free-flying birds, and leads finally to aquariums with Amazon and coral reef fish and moon jellyfish. Outside, the *Great Cats* complex features lions, Siberian (or Amur) tigers, and snow leopards. The *African Boardwalk* takes visitors to see zebras, bongo antelope, serval cats, and even to hand-feed giraffes. The *Australian Trail* meanders through a large yard with wallabies and emus. Other interesting exhibits include the sea lion and seals pool, penguins, and Japanese macaques, also known as snow monkeys.

Rolling Hills Wildlife Adventure

625 North Hedville Road
Salina, Kansas 67401
(785) 827-9488
www.rollinghillswildlife.com

Billboards along Kansas' I-70 invite travelers to stop at Rolling Hills to experience an unusual combination of wildlife exhibits. Its sixty-five rolling acres are home to an abundance of large animals, including white and Indian rhinos, giraffes, zebras, pronghorn antelope, and a rare white camel. In the *Apes* building, orangutans and chimpanzees are featured, and mandrills are exhibited nearby. A group of feline exhibits includes two species each of leopards and tigers, including a white tiger, while lions live across the zoo. Other interesting animals on display include aardvarks, maned wolves, and African hunting dogs (aka African wild dogs). Across the parking lot, the *Wildlife Museum* charges a separate admission fee, but it's well worth the price. Inside, hundreds of mounted taxidermy specimens are set in realistic dioramas representing seven ecosystems around the world, from the *Far East* to the *Arctic* to the *Rainforest*. A 360-degree domed 3-D movie theater is part of this extensive adventure.

Topeka Zoo

635 SW Gage Boulevard
Topeka, Kansas 66606
(785) 272-7595
www.fotz.org

During the 1970s, this small zoo was known as "World Famous Topeka Zoo," primarily because of its trend-setting *Tropical Rain Forest* building, which opened in 1974 as the world's first domed rain forest exhibit. Though small compared to larger zoo rain forest exhibits, this jungle habitat is very enjoyable, with tropical birds, reptiles, and small mammals to see. Almost as groundbreaking, *Discovering Apes* features a glass tunnel for visitors that leads through the gorilla habitat. The zoo's most beautiful exhibit is probably *Black Bear Woods*, with a bi-level viewing deck. Other highlights include elephants, hippos, orangutans, lions, and a gorgeous *Children's Zoo*.

Dickerson Park Zoo

3043 North Fort Avenue
Springfield, Missouri 65803
(417) 864-1800
www.dickersonparkzoo.org

Located near the Ozark Mountains and Branson vacation area, this zoo displays its animals in continental groups. It's best known for the large elephant herd in *Tropical Asia*. Baby elephants are common here. Malayan tapirs and gibbons also live in the

Asian area. *Africa* features giraffes, zebras, warthogs, antelope, and cheetahs, while *South America* has maned wolves and rheas (large flightless birds), and *Australia* has kangaroos and emus. The forested *Missouri Habitats* have the most extensive collection; native species include wolves, coyotes, mountain lions, black bears, red foxes, and otters. Hippos, meerkats and alligators surround the *Diversity of Life* reptile building.

Great Plains Zoo & Delbridge Museum of Natural History

805 South Kiwanis Avenue
Sioux Falls, South Dakota 57104
(605) 367-7003
www.gpzoo.org

Set in South Dakota's largest city, this zoo's largest outdoor exhibit is the thirteen-acre *African Savanna*, with black rhinos, giraffes, zebras, warthogs, African wild dogs, and cheetahs. Other creatures here include tigers and snow leopards in the *Asian Cat Habitat*, *Bear Canyon*'s grizzlies, and black-footed penguins, which are very popular with visitors. This zoo's highlight, and something that sets it apart from most other zoos, is the *Delbridge Museum of Natural History*, with a collection of over 150 mounted animals from around the world. Specimens are displayed in naturalistic dioramas, including a sixteen-foot giraffe, a four-ton elephant, and even a giant panda.

Tree kangaroo (l), Flying fox bat (r)

Micronesian kingfisher

Elephant shrew

Coatimundi

Southwestern and Western Zoos

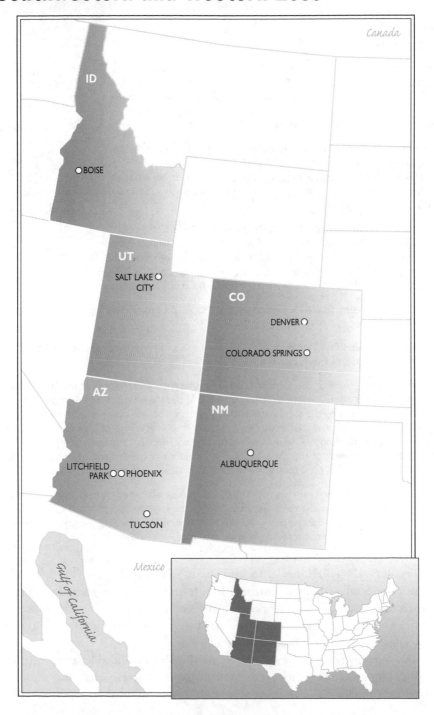

Phoenix Zoo

455 North Galvin Parkway
Phoenix, Arizona 85008
(602) 273-1341
www.phoenixzoo.org

Hours: 7:00 a.m.-2:00 p.m. weekdays, 7:00 a.m.-4:00 p.m. weekends and holidays, June-September; 9:00 a.m.-5:00 p.m. daily, October-May; zoo closes at 4:00 p.m. during the ZooLights holiday display (November-December), but reopens from 6:00 p.m.-10:00 p.m. Closed on Christmas Day, but open Christmas night for ZooLights.

Admission & Fees: Adults $14, seniors 60+ $9, children 3-12 $6. Safari train $3; Safari Cart tours $20 ($18 for members); camel ride $5 (plus $5 for an optional photo); carousel $2; bike rental $8-$30 per hour, depending on bike size; pedal boat rental $20 per hour; Stingray Bay $3 ($1 for members).

Bighorn sheep on crag in Desert Lives exhibit.

Directions: From I-10, take Exit 153B (Broadway Road/52nd Street). Turn right onto Broadway Road and follow for 0.5 miles. Turn left onto South Priest Drive and follow for 3.3 miles. Priest Drive becomes North Galvin Parkway, which leads to Papago Park. Turn left into Papago Park and follow signs to zoo. The Valley Metro Transit System bus route #3 stops right at the zoo.

Don't Miss: Arizona Trail, Africa Trail, Monkey Village, Forest of Uco, Tropical Flights, Desert Lives, Stingray Bay.

For Kids: Children's Trail, Harmony Farm, Leapin' Lagoon Sprayground, Enchanted Forest, Animal Corridors Maze, carousel, camel ride.

Authors' Tips: In summer, the zoo's early opening time gives you the opportunity to visit while the temperature is 20 to 30 degrees cooler than it is in the afternoon. Bring sun hats, sunscreen, and water bottles during the summer. Binoculars can also be very useful in this sprawling zoo. Drinking fountains are available throughout the zoo, and snack bars sell ice cream, soda, and other cooling treats. Another heat-beater is the Safari Train, a 25-minute, 2½-mile narrated tram ride through most of the zoo's 125 acres. For private, customized tours, spend a little more and take the Safari Cart tour. Note that Monkey Village closes early in summer.

Edutainment: Early each morning, the "Wild About Animals" show is held at the Enchanted Forest Amphitheater, near the zoo's entrance. Special keeper talks and animal feedings are held daily at Monkey Village and at the otter and baboon exhibits. There are additional talks and feedings on weekends. Check the schedule in your zoo map.

FAST-GROWING PHOENIX IS NOW THE NATION'S FIFTH-LARGEST city, and a top Sunbelt tourist destination. The Phoenix Zoo, located near the Scottsdale tourist area in beautiful Papago Park, has benefited from this growing visitor base. It is the largest self-supporting (that is, not funded by tax dollars) zoo in the U.S. Its many pretty lakes and palm trees make it an attractive desert oasis.

This zoo only opened in 1962, but it quickly gained worldwide fame. In 1963, a last-ditch effort was enacted to save the Arabian oryx, a desert antelope that was nearly hunted to extinction. Nine of the very last oryxes were rounded up and brought here to establish a breeding colony. More than forty years later, over 230 oryx calves have been born at this zoo. Oryxes are now displayed across the nation, and small herds have been re-introduced into the deserts of Israel and Oman. The Phoenix Zoo has been credited with saving this species from extinction.

FEATURED EXHIBITS

Arizona is justly famous for its unusual wildlife, so it's only natural that the zoo's premier exhibit is the **Arizona Trail**. Native cacti are displayed along a wide, level walkway, including towering saguaros. Bald eagles and turkey vultures perch in a large flight cage near a naturalistic habitat for coatimundis, playful raccoon relatives from the desert. Bobcats and mountain lions are visible through thin harp wire in their rocky habitats, and three large rock-strewn desert yards inhabited by coyotes, pronghorn antelope, and collared peccaries (or javelinas), a type of wild pig, can be seen from an overlook. Rare Mexican gray wolves, in a corner habitat, deserve special attention. A cluster of smaller enclosures houses prairie dogs, porcupines, Gila monsters, roadrunners, desert tortoises, and thick-billed parrots, a species native to Arizona. In one of the zoo's few exhibit buildings, the *Nocturnal Exhibit* displays bats, ringtails (also known as cacomistles), spotted skunks, and a kit fox. Quail and other desert birds move about in a walk-through aviary. A great variety of rattlesnakes are the main attraction of the indoor/outdoor reptile and amphibian area, where the animals are displayed in ten bioclimatic zones. Featured animals here include alligator lizards, Colorado River toads, and coachwhip snakes. Wild brush-tailed ground squirrels and jackrabbits roam through this exhibit, and elsewhere throughout the zoo.

One of this zoo's specialties is African animals, mostly found along the **Africa Trail**. The four-acre *Savanna* displays giraffes, gazelles, giant-horned Watusi cattle, ostriches, and vultures. Tall palm trees and giant boulders are scattered throughout the grassy slopes of this natural exhibit. The panorama can be enjoyed from convenient benches in front of the habitat. An attached, more arid yard holds Grevy's zebras and marabou storks. Across the trail, the *Baboon Kingdom* is a two-part complex displaying Hamadryas baboons and beautiful mandrills in grassy yards with high rocky backdrops. Signs offer information about the baboons, and large viewing windows allow for close-up encounters. An open, grassy pit houses an attractive duplex exhibit of lions and rare Sumatran tigers, who are often spotted cooling off in their own pool. The paved trail leads past several other African animals, including white rhinos, warthogs, meerkats, and rare Mhorr gazelles. Cheetahs and African wild dogs each enjoy lushly planted grassy habitats.

Monkey Village is a favorite for all ages, a rain forest habitat where visitors can literally enter the monkeys' world. Once inside this 10,000-square-foot enclosure, humans must stay on the roped path, while the exhibit's little squirrel monkeys are free to get as close as they please. You can't actually pet these adorable primates, but you'll still be close enough to have a truly memorable experience. Be sure to bring a camera!

Just off the Tropics Trail is the entrance to the **Forest of Uco,** a South American village with faded storefronts and a plaza fountain. Dense vegetation lines the path to the animal exhibits. First up is a scarlet macaw parrot, overlooking a low Amazon fish aquarium. The main feature of this exhibit is a spectacled bear habitat, with side viewing windows and a pretty trickling waterfall. Along the dirt path, you'll also see white-faced saki monkeys and toco toucans.

At **Tropical Flights,** an outdoor rain forest exhibit off the Tropics Trail, six tall aviaries are surrounded by lush tropical vegetation. Egyptian fruit bats, long-legged wading birds such as spoonbills and ibises, and rhinoceros hornbill birds are some of the exotic and beautiful animals on display. Highly endangered Micronesian kingfishers and Guam rails, a type of water bird, are also exhibited here. A winding path passes a cascading waterfall that runs down into the nearby lake.

A gravel detour off the Africa Trail leads to the **Desert Lives** exhibit. Two massive red rock buttes provide natural habitats for Arizona's desert bighorn sheep and the zoo's trademark animal, the Arabian oryx. Colorful signs relate the story of how the zoo revived this species from the verge of extinction. Your own binoculars or the coin-operated, high-power telescopes provided make it easier to see the animals, who are often visible in the distance, usually climbing a rocky crag. It's a breathtaking sight to see one of the bighorn sheep stand regally at the very top of a high butte.

Stingray Bay, a 12,000-gallon touch tank, installed in 2007, features over thirty cownose and southern stingrays and bamboo and nurse sharks for visitors to touch, a most unusual experience for desert-dwelling Arizonians. The rays are completely safe; their stinging barbs are kept trimmed, in a process much like trimming your fingernails. The exhibit is open seasonally, from October to May.

OTHER EXHIBITS

More interesting exhibits are found along the **Tropics Trail** around the zoo's Main Lake, including a palm grove for flamingos, spot-necked otters that splash about in a pool fed by a waterfall, and an orangutan family that lives under a net dome. In the lake, two islands are inhabited by lemurs and spider monkeys, respectively. Around the corner from the orangutans is a large Asian elephant yard, where the zoo conducts research on elephant behavior. The resident pachyderms use a large pool to cool off in the desert heat.

South American animals are highlighted on both sides of the Forest of Uco. Some of the continent's more unusual species – maned wolves, giant anteaters, and Chacoan peccaries – are on one side. The peccaries, large relatives of the local collared peccaries, or javelinas, seen on the Arizona Trail, are highly endangered and were not even documented by Western scientists until 1975. On the other side of Uco are enclosures for a black jaguar and for the jaguar's favorite dinner, capybaras, the largest members of the rodent family. Between them are exhibit yards for three species of giant tortoises.

FOR THE KIDS

Cross a red covered bridge to the highlight of the seven-acre **Nina Mason Pulliam Children's Trail**: the *Heritage Farm*, where a big red barn, school house, and tall windmill give children the feel of visiting a real working farm. The *Animal*

Nursery and *Brooder House* exhibit baby animals and poultry chicks at different stages of development. There's also a small petting zoo, with over thirty small goats, Navajo sheep, and zebu cattle. Also in nearby pens are a donkey, a large black draft horse, and a Shetland pony. Beyond the farm, you can often watch raccoons from within a viewing cave as they relax in a burrow behind their streamside habitat. Other small animals are also displayed in intimate settings, including black swans, petite tamarin monkeys, a spotted ocelot cat, a caracal lynx, an African porcupine, wallabies that hop about in the *Wallaby Walkabout*, and an island of siamangs. The playground here is enjoyed by both children and their parents. Kids can frolic on the spider web, monkey bars, and other animal-themed structures, while adults can rest and watch from a picnic area next to the refreshment center.

On the hottest Arizona days, there is no better place to be than **Leapin' Lagoon Sprayground**, a water play area where dozens of wet children laugh and squeal. Nearby, the **Piper Enchanted Forest** is a playground designed for toddlers. It has small slides and an attractive tree house to climb and play in. Also in this front plaza area is the **Phoenix Zoo Carousel**, with three dozen very unusual animals, including a hummingbird and a sea dragon, you can ride. (Hint to parents: Do the carousel before the Sprayground — wet kids are not allowed on the carousel.) Near the Forest of Uco, children enjoy the challenge of the **Animal Corridors Maze**. Appropriate for a desert zoo, camel rides (and photos of same) are available near the lake. For a fun family adventure, rent a pedal boat for a closer look at the primate islands. You can also rent a variety of individual and family size bikes for rides around the zoo.

IN PROGRESS

At press time, the Phoenix Zoo is in the midst of a major capital campaign to raise funds for improvements and upgrades. Planned projects include a new entry Oasis, with an array of aquariums and other animal exhibits, and cultural displays from around the world, as well as a state-of-the-art tiger exhibit near the Main Lake.

Arizona-Sonora Desert Museum

2021 North Kinney Road
Tucson, Arizona 85743
(520) 883-2702
www.desertmuseum.org

Hours: 7:30 a.m.-5:00 p.m. daily, March-September; 8:30 a.m.-5:00 p.m. daily, October-February, last entry 4:15 p.m. Reopens Saturday evenings 5:00 p.m.-10:00 p.m., June-August.

Saguaro cacti near the Desert Loop Trail.

Admission & Fees: Adults $9, children 6-12 $2, June-August; adults $12, children $4, September-May.

Directions: Located 14 miles west of Tucson via Gates Pass Road. From I-10, take Exit 254 (Prince Road) West, then take the frontage road (North Freeway Road) south for 3 miles. Turn right onto West Speedway Boulevard. Follow for 4.6 miles, then take a slight left onto West Gates Pass Road. Follow Gates Pass for 4.8 miles, then turn right onto North Kinney Road. Follow for 2.4 miles to the museum on the left. Large motor homes or cars towing trailers should take Exit 99 (Ajo Way) West from I-19, and then follow Kinney Road to the museum.

Don't Miss: Mountain Woodland, Riparian Corridor, Cat Canyon, Earth Sciences, Desert Loop Trail, Desert Grassland, Hummingbird Aviary, Life Underground, Walk-In Aviary.

For Kids: Cave in the Earth Sciences building, animal tracks stamp booklet.

Author's Tips: Because the desert here is the real thing, it can get very hot. If you're visiting between April and October, pack sun hats, sunscreen, and extra cash for liquid refreshments. In summer, take advantage of the unusually early opening time and plan to arrive then, when it is cooler and the animals are more active. Water fountains, concession stands, shaded ramadas, and air-conditioned indoor exhibits are spaced throughout the grounds. If there are long lines at the Orientation and Small Animal Room, bypass it and come back later in the day.

Edutainment: Held twice daily along the Desert Loop Trail, the "Raptor Free Flight" program features hawks, falcons, owls, and roadrunners, all demonstrating their natural behaviors. The fascinating indoor "Live & (sort of) On the Loose" show gives spectators a great look at venomous reptiles of the Southwest. It's an extraordinary experience to see and hear a big diamondback rattlesnake shaking its rattle in the same room with you! Other docent demonstrations and tours are given at various locations. Check the Daily Events Schedule, in the Orientation Room, for times and places.

AT FIRST BLUSH, IT MIGHT SEEM ODD TO INCLUDE A "DESERT museum" in a zoo guidebook. Though listed as one of the world's top zoos by many sources, the Arizona-Sonora Desert Museum (ASDM) is not a typical zoo. It is actually part zoo, part geology museum, and part botanical garden.

The ASDM exhibits only animals native to the Sonoran Desert of Arizona and Mexico. Far from being a barren wasteland, this desert is home to a wide variety of wildlife, and more than 300 types of animals and over 1,200 plant species are displayed here. In fact, ASDM is also frequently considered to be one of the most beautiful zoos in America. Situated in a saguaro cactus forest, it is landscaped with native desert plants and boasts a mountain backdrop. Both zoological and mainstream media say that no zoo takes better advantage of its natural surroundings than this one.

FEATURED EXHIBITS

The tour through the underground **Earth Sciences** building begins with a man-made limestone "dry" cave, complete with a running stream, large stalactites and stalagmites (no longer "growing," since this is a dry cave), and prehistoric fossils. It is so well executed that some visitors find it difficult to believe this cave isn't real. It empties into the *Ancient Arizona* room, where some impressive technology is used to interpret the geology of the desert. The dimly lit room you enter next exhibits a collection of over 14,000 minerals from the Sonoran desert, including gold nuggets and copper "leaves." In contrast to these local specimens, you'll also find a genuine moon rock on display.

The **Mountain Woodland** habitat is a replica of the animal and plant communities found on the forested mountain "islands" that pop up throughout the Sonoran Desert. It is in this rocky environment, planted with Mexican oak and pine trees, that some of ASDM's most popular animals are found, including mountain lions, black bears, white-tailed deer, and rare Mexican gray wolves. Also here are thick-billed parrots, a species native to Arizona and the only parrot species found in the United States.

The main feature of the **Desert Grassland** habitat is a large hillside prairie dog town. Visitors can watch the prairie dogs in their open exhibit as they emerge from and scurry among their many underground burrows. Burrowing owls and desert snakes are also displayed here. A large cutaway on the wall illustrates the complex underground burrow networks of the prairie dogs and burrowing owls.

On hot days, the air-conditioned **Cat Canyon** exhibit provides cooling relief for visitors. A pair of bobcats, an ocelot, and a margay cat can be seen from many angles, though it is sometimes a challenge to find them. Most unusual, and thrilling to see, is the sleek, elusive jaguarundi.

Just beyond the cats, the **Desert Loop Trail** offers visitors a chance to take a rugged half-mile hike through the desert. Along the way, graphics introduce the marvelous agave plant, as well as the region's trademark saguaro cactus. Behind a nearly invisible barrier, coyotes and javelinas (wild pigs, also known as collared peccaries) are displayed along the path in large, naturalistic exhibits that blend seamlessly into the landscape. The remarkable Invisinet® mesh fencing used to contain these animals was developed here at the Desert Museum.

The **Riparian Corridor** surprises many visitors with its aquatic exhibits. It is a reminder that streams do indeed flow in the desert, and that water is a precious commodity here. A stairway descends to indoor, underwater views of beavers on one side and river otters on the other. The otters are favorites of children, especially when they swim and dive. The beavers share their pond with native fish. Visitors can peek into their lodge, which the beavers enter from underwater. There are also small exhibits of aquatic insects. Just beyond the streamside habitats is the rocky home of curious coatis, raccoon-like scavengers of the desert. Down the path, a herd of desert bighorn sheep climb above and below visitor level, up and down an artificial mini-mountain.

The most popular exhibit here may be the large (3,300 square feet) **Hummingbird Aviary**. Seating areas let visitors relax and admire the grace and beauty of these tiny birds. Seven different hummingbird species fly freely around visitors. More than a hundred hummingbirds have hatched successfully in this aviary since it opened in 1988, so looking for the tiny hummingbird nests is a fun challenge.

The enormous **Walk-In Aviary** is impressive both inside and out. There are many places inside to sit and watch over 110 desert birds of more than forty species, including cactus wrens, Gila woodpeckers, Gambel's quail, and (Arizona) cardinals (like the team!).

Hummingbird feeds nesting chick.

The **Life Underground** exhibit is aptly named. This dark, sixty-foot tunnel is an updated version of ASDM's landmark *Tunnel* exhibit. Its goal is to answer the question, "Where do all the animals go during the heat of the day?" Behind windows into below-the-surface burrows, you'll spot several desert dwellers, including foxes, kangaroo rats, ringtails (or cacomistles), pack rats, and tarantulas.

OTHER EXHIBITS

Most visitors start their tour just inside the entrance area at the **Orientation Room**, which has interesting graphics about the desert. The nearby **Reptiles & Invertebrates** room features snakes, lizards, tarantulas, scorpions, insects, and other small creatures of the desert. There are also models of Arizona wildflowers to study.

Across the entrance plaza, another building houses an indoor/outdoor snack bar, a large gift shop, and the **Fishes & Amphibians** exhibits. Frogs, toads, turtles, and eight species of fish, all native to Sonoran Desert streams, are displayed here. An interesting exhibit features Apache trout, the state fish of Arizona.

Several interesting and informative exhibits focusing on plants of the Sonoran Desert are found throughout the park. These include the **Desert Garden**, a local favorite, the **Pollination Gardens**, which attract a multitude of bees, butterflies, and hummingbirds, and the **Cactus Garden**, with a winding walkway that passes over 100 species of cacti and other desert plants.

FOR THE KIDS

In the Earth Sciences cave, a side tunnel gives kids (and adults who are willing to squeeze a bit) a chance to experience a realistic seventy-five-foot caving experience. Children delight in clambering through its maze of narrow passageways.

Kids can pick up a booklet to gather ink stamps of various animals' tracks. At least fifteen animals have special stations at their exhibits where children can "collect" the tracks of the animals they see in a process that's much like stamping a passport.

IN PROGRESS

Built along the Desert Loop Trail, the new **Life on the Rocks** display highlights small species found in the desert's rocky environments. This revolutionary exhibit is opening in stages; some of it opened in 2007, the remainder is scheduled to open in 2008 or later as we go to press. Kids have their own canyon-like crevice to walk through as they and their parents discover the animals on exhibit. Larger animals, including a hog-nosed skunk, owls, and large rattlesnakes, are exhibited behind clear glass walls with the native desert visible behind them. Smaller species, including tarantulas, banded geckos, black widow spiders, ground squirrels, smaller snakes, and kissing bugs, are shown in innovative small displays tucked into crevices between the rocks. Visitors can lift an artificial rock, revealing, for example, a scorpion living underneath, covered by Plexiglas. In other exhibits, visitors will see Gila monsters, leaf-nosed bats, desert fish, and many more snakes and lizards, all in displays that illustrate their relationship with their rocky homes.

Cheyenne Mountain Zoological Park

4250 Cheyenne Mountain Zoo Road
Colorado Springs, Colorado 80906
(719) 633-9925
www.cmzoo.org

Visitors can feed giraffes in the zoo's African Rift Valley.

Hours: 9:00 a.m.-6:00 p.m. daily, Memorial Day-Labor Day; 9:00 a.m.-5:00 p.m. daily, rest of year. Last admission at 4:00 p.m. Zoo closes early on Thanksgiving, Christmas Eve and Christmas Day.

Admission & Fees: Adults $12, seniors 65+ $10, children 3-11 $6. Military and AAA members get a $2 discount. Zoo tram $1, carousel $2, Shongololo Choo Choo $1, pony ride $5, Safari Trail Immersion Tour $5, giraffe crackers $1 for a pack of 3.

Directions: From I-25, take Exit 138 West (South Circle Drive/Lake Avenue/CO-29 W). Follow Lake Avenue west for 2 miles to the Broadmoor Hotel. At the hotel, turn right and follow signs for just over 2 miles to the zoo.

Don't Miss: African Rift Valley, Asian Highlands, Primate World, Lion's Lair, elephant yard and building, Will Rogers Shrine of the Sun.

For Kids: My Big Backyard, Gusa Play Area, Shongololo Choo Choo, antique carousel, pony ride.

Authors' Tips: With its steep hills and high altitude, exploring this zoo on foot can be challenging. Elevation-wise, walking to the zoo's high point is equivalent to climbing a ten-story building. During the summer (and on weekends during the rest of the year), you can use the Zoo Tram, which makes eight stops around the zoo on its 15-minute circuit.

Edutainment: Various animal training demonstrations and keeper talks are held daily, featuring Komodo dragons, elephants, penguins, and more. Check the schedule posted near the front of the zoo. On the Safari Trail Immersion Tour, guests accompany a keeper down into the African Rift Valley to meet the giraffes. Make reservations early, as each tour is restricted to a maximum of ten people. Tours run daily in summer and on weekends in May and September.

LITERALLY BUILT ON A MOUNTAINSIDE, THE CHEYENNE MOUNTAIN Zoo has some very steep hills to climb. Billed as "America's Only Mountain Zoo," the altitude at its lowest point is nearly 7,000 feet, making it the nation's highest zoo. One of only a few privately owned zoos, it was founded in 1926 by Spencer Penrose, who also established the world-famous five-star Broadmoor Hotel, a place you will likely pass on your way up the mountain.

This may also be the only zoo in America that allows cars to drive through it. Admission to the zoo includes the toll for the scenic highway leading up to the **Will Rogers Shrine of the Sun**, a 1.4-mile drive. The panoramic view from the tower memorial, positioned at 8,000 feet, rivals the view from atop Pikes Peak. On a clear day, the entire Colorado Springs area is visible.

FEATURED EXHIBITS

If you like giraffes, there is no better place, outside of Africa, to see them than here in the **African Rift Valley**. Almost 200 giraffes have been born here, more than at any other zoo in the world, and there are almost always baby giraffes to see. Two fourteen-foot giraffe sculptures welcome guests to this unique place, a habitat that resembles an African thorn savanna. A boardwalk passes directly through the open habitat, and because this walkway is elevated, visitors find themselves face-to-face with more than a dozen giraffes. Special "giraffe crackers" may be purchased to hand-feed them. The giraffes will use their long, purple tongues to take crackers right out of your child's hand – what a photo op! Even if you don't feed them (or if you run out of crackers), the giraffes are amazingly friendly, sticking their faces over the fence, inviting you to pet them. Another thrill is witnessing the twice daily "Giraffe Stampede," at the beginning and end of the day, when a keeper opens the hydraulic drawbridge and the whole herd gallops into or out of the habitat. Visiting the giraffes in their holding area is also interesting – there's a life-size cutout of a pregnant giraffe to illustrate the inner workings of this fascinating animal. Along the boardwalk, you can enter and explore a massive replica of a 900-year-old baobab tree. A research station and exhibits of African bugs are inside, but kids are usually most thrilled when the "spirit of the baobab tree" talks to them! Sharing the savanna yard are zebras, lesser kudu antelope, and cattle egrets and other African birds. At the boardwalk's end, practically the whole meerkat colony stands up on its hind legs, scanning the horizon for intruders to its lovely glass-walled exhibit. Other exhibits display red river hogs, vultures, and colobus monkeys – these black-and-white primates dwell in a towering mesh enclosure. Next to their habitat is a three-story tower, accessible by elevator. From the tower's highest level, the view of the monkeys, giraffes, and even Colorado Springs below is outstanding.

The Tibetan architecture in the **Asian Highlands** creates a Himalayan atmosphere, where Amur leopards, snow leopards, and Amur tigers can be seen roaming the trees and rocks of their naturalistic hillside habitats at the top of the zoo. The Pallas' cats, which look like furry gray house cats, seem almost out of place in another large rock-strewn habitat, though it actually replicates their home in the wild quite accurately.

One of the zoo's most popular exhibits is **Primate World**. The building's carpeted interior features an audiovisual center, interactive graphics, and wide windows onto a variety of primates. While they can sometimes be seen inside, the gorillas are most enjoyable in their three-quarter-acre hillside outdoor habitat, which features both indoor and outdoor vantage points for visitors. Orangutans play on a variety of climbing structures in their forty-five-foot-high mesh enclosure, while an indoor viewing area extends directly into the habitat, allowing for close-up encounters. Lion-tailed macaque monkeys and siamangs can also be seen both inside and in their outdoor enclosures.

Using one of the original, historic bear grottoes, the **Lion's Lair** is a beautiful modern habitat for a pair of African lions. An inset with large windows allows guests to walk up close to the king of beasts. This pair has been especially prolific, producing several litters of cubs.

In a canyon-like setting, visitors look down into the **elephant yard and building**. The African elephants enjoy a large yard with a pool, and odd-looking ground hornbill birds are displayed nearby. The reason, however, that we've labeled this complex a "don't miss" is because of the breeding pair of highly endangered mountain tapirs exhibited here. There are fewer than 200 of these jet-black pig-like creatures remaining in the Andean highlands of Colombia. Cheyenne Mountain is, at press time, one of only three zoos in the world caring for these critically endangered animals.

OTHER EXHIBITS

Local mountain wildlife is featured in the **Rocky Cliffs** exhibit, near the front of the zoo. A small herd of Rocky Mountain goats lives here, on a mini-mountain made of native Colorado rock. Yellow-bellied marmots, a large species of ground squirrel, inhabit a smaller rocky habitat.

The old **Monkey Pavilion** displays an impressive collection of primates, including two varieties of gibbons, howler monkeys, black mangabey monkeys, rare guenon monkeys, and two types of lemurs. Raccoon-like coatimundis, which are not primates, are also housed here. The **Bird & Reptile House** contains large and small reptiles, beautiful exotic birds, and small mammals. Species include fishing cats, poison dart frogs, and a large open-air jungle for golden lion tamarin monkeys. Indoor and outdoor habitats at the **Aquatics** building exhibit some of the zoo's most popular animals: Komodo dragons, Nile hippos, and Asian small-clawed otters. Indoors, you'll find coral reef aquariums and the pebble beach home of a colony of African penguins.

The two-story **Lodge at Moose Lake** is the first stage of the soon-to-open Rocky Mountain Wild exhibit (see "In Progress," below). Prairie dogs and their natural predators, black-footed ferrets, live side-by-side on one side of the Lodge. While the rustic structure's ground floor serves as an event and meeting space, there's fun for all visitors upstairs in the *Wild Room*. Here you can hold a snake and meet several of the zoo's outreach animals, which include a burrowing owl and a porcupine.

Also scattered around the zoo are Asiatic black bears and spectacled bears in traditional bear grottoes, and a pretty **hummingbird garden**.

FOR THE KIDS

The innovative, colorful **My Big Backyard** complex has a variety of fun activities for children. In the nature-themed playground, options include giant ants and mushrooms to climb on and a snake to crawl through, as well as water play structures such as squirting frogs and a looping snake sprinkler. The contact area includes dwarf goats, potbelly pigs, rabbits, and guinea pigs for petting. Kids can also enjoy feeding the fish in the koi pond. *Old Gnarly* is a replica of a 1,000-year-old Ponderosa pine tree that children can enter to see small animal exhibits. Elsewhere, kids can climb to a tree house to participate in nature-related crafts.

In the small *Gusa Play Area*, representing part of the African Rift Valley, children can explore small village huts, and climb other structures decorated with African designs. Nearby, you'll find the **Shongololo Choo Choo**, a small train ride primarily for toddlers. Further up the hill, older children and toddlers will both enjoy the delightful 1937 **antique carousel** and **pony rides**.

IN PROGRESS

The next exciting addition to the zoo will be **Rocky Mountain Wild**, scheduled to open in the summer of 2008 as we go to press. An elevated walkway will nearly encircle *Moose Lake*, the wetland home of moose, the largest of the deer species. Along the way, a side path will lead to an overlook of highly endangered Mexican gray wolves in their **Wolf Woods** habitat. The winding main path will next lead to *Cougar Canyon*, a rocky habitat for mountain lions. Another wild cat, the Canada lynx, will be housed nearby. River otters will delight guests, who will benefit from clear underwater viewing panels. A fire tower, accessible by stairs and an elevator, will be the entry to a treetop-level boardwalk leading to the area's signature exhibit, a sprawling hillside habitat for grizzly bears. From a covered viewing area, these massive bears will be visible as they fish for live trout in a pool at the foot of *Grizzly Falls*. Overlooking the entire area, regal bald eagles will perch high in the trees of their mountainside habitat.

Denver Zoo

2300 Steele Street
Denver, Colorado 80205
(303) 376-4800
www.denverzoo.org

Spotted hyenas live in Predator Ridge.

Hours: 9:00 a.m.-6:00 p.m. daily, April-September; 10:00 a.m.-5:00 p.m. daily, rest of year. Last admission one hour before closing.

Admission & Fees: Adults $11, seniors 65+ $9, children 3-11 $7, April-September; adults $9, seniors $7, children $5, rest of the year. There are free admission days during the winter, approximately bi-monthly. Carousel and train ride $2 each, lorikeet nectar $1.

Directions: Located in City Park, just east of downtown Denver. From I-70, take Exit 276B (Colorado Boulevard/CO-2) South. Follow Colorado Boulevard for 2.2 miles, then turn right onto East 23rd Avenue. Follow 23rd Avenue for 0.4 miles, then turn right into zoo. From I-25, take Exit 204 (Colorado Boulevard/CO-2). Turn right onto South Colorado Boulevard and follow for 4.6 miles. Turn left onto East 23rd Avenue, follow for 0.4 miles, and turn right into zoo. Metro transit buses #5 and #44 service the zoo.

Don't Miss: Predator Ridge, Primate Panorama, Tropical Discovery, Northern Shores, Bird World, Bear Mountain, Sheep Mountain.

For Kids: African Kraal, Endangered Species Carousel, Pioneer Train, Lorikeet Adventure.

Authors' Tips: While the zoo's 80 acres aren't difficult to explore on foot, the Safari Shuttle offers a relaxing tour. The Samburu Grille near the entrance is an attractive cafeteria-style restaurant with salads, burgers, a pasta bar, and more, and indoor and outdoor seating. If you have time, the impressive Denver Museum of Natural History is within walking distance, and worth a visit.

Entertainment: The "Wildlife Show," held three times daily in summer in the Wildlife Theater, includes free-flying birds and exotic animals. Twice daily sea lion shows, in Northern Shores, are demonstrations of typical behaviors of these intelligent mammals. In the "Pachyderm Demonstrations," a black rhino and elephants take turns showing off. Keepers show how they take care of lions, wild dogs, and hyenas in "Predator Ridge Demonstrations." Public animal feedings include gorillas, red river hogs, and penguins. In Bird World's daily "Bird Bug Toss," visitors help staff toss mealworms and waxworms to the birds. There's a schedule on the back of your map.

OPENED IN 1896, THE DENVER ZOO IS THE SECOND-OLDEST ZOO in the West, and its Bear Mountain is the nation's oldest naturalistic, barless exhibit. Like its home state, the zoo has beautiful, wide open spaces. Species-wise, its specialties include birds, arctic animals, hoofstock, and especially primates. With over 1.7 million visitors annually, this is the most popular zoo between California and Chicago.

FEATURED EXHIBITS

Predator Ridge lies just inside the zoo's entrance, and it includes one of our favorite lion exhibits. A portion of Samburu National Park in Kenya is re-created here, beautifully landscaped to resemble a dry kopje. African wild dogs, spotted hyenas, and two prides of lions rotate through each others' habitats. The variety of scenery and the scents of previous occupants provide valuable mental stimulation for these intelligent carnivores. Another habitat, *Pahali Ya Mwana,* is set aside for mothers and babies: lionesses with cubs, or wild dogs or hyenas with pups. *Pahali Ya Simba* is an enjoyable discovery center with educational graphics, TV screens playing footage of wild lions in Kenya, and several small animal displays. In their large habitats, the lions and other predators can be seen from many different angles – through a long outdoor glass wall, from viewing caves, and from the discovery center. Behind nearly invisible glass windows in their small rocky habitats, African porcupines, crowned cranes, and entertaining banded mongooses appear to be uncaged.

With twenty-nine different species of monkeys, apes, and lemurs, **Primate Panorama** is one of the most extensive displays of primates we've ever seen. While species from three different continents are displayed, the bamboo and thatched-roof huts (which are actually service buildings, restrooms, and night holding rooms) create an African atmosphere. Near the entrance sign, ring-tailed lemurs live on an attractive island. The extensive *Jewels of the Emerald Forest* building uses realistic background dioramas to introduce four distinct primate environments: *Malagasy,* with a variety of lemurs, including mouse lemurs; *South American forest floor* and *forest canopy,* with marmoset and tamarin monkeys, titi monkeys, squirrel monkeys, and white-faced saki monkeys; and the *Primates of the Night,* with large-eyed owl monkeys and lemur-like slender lorises. Back outside, a series of four-story mesh tents are filled with tall trees, vines, and running streams. Larger tree-dwelling primates, gibbons and red-capped mangabey monkeys, live in these mesh habitats. Black macaque monkeys dwell in a nearby glass-fronted habitat. The *Great Apes* building houses orangutans and gorillas during inclement weather, but it's a real treat to get to see these apes in their spacious outdoor yards. The gorillas' one-acre enclosure is one of the world's largest. In front of the ape exhibits is the walk-through *Forest Aviary*, stocked with bar-headed geese, long-legged ibises, and other beautiful birds. Tucked in a corner, *Shamba* is a realistic reproduction of a West African village, and includes an exhibit of red river hogs. The *Congo Basin* has three tall mesh habitats, which provide spacious homes for DeBrazza's monkeys, colobus monkeys, African hornbill birds, and other Congo natives. The main attraction here is the troop of colorful baboon-like mandrills.

The multi-species **Tropical Discovery**, an indoor rain forest building topped by two glass pyramids, was this zoo's first major exhibit of reptiles, amphibians, fish, and insects. When it opened back in 1993, its more than a thousand animals of over 240 species nearly doubled the zoo's animal collection. Orchids, ferns, and towering palm trees are just some of the nearly 200 plant species that enrich the ten exhibits inside. The feature attraction here is *Dragons of Komodo*, at press time the world's largest indoor habitat for these dangerous giant lizards. The *Mountain Cave* exhibit features vampire and fruit bats. Under a forty-five-foot pyramid, in the *Temple Ruins*, cobras, vipers, and boas can be seen amid lush greenery. The *Mangrove Swamp* features some of nature's oddities, including archerfish, which spit water to knock down insects; fiddler crabs, which have one giant claw and one small one; and mudskippers, fish that can crawl out onto dry land. The zoo's noisiest creatures, howler monkeys, are overhead. A rainbow of colorful reef fish, moray eels, and seahorses can be seen in a *Tropical Reef* exhibit. Alligator snapping turtles, the world's largest freshwater turtles, live in the *Cypress Swamp*, while alligators themselves drift through the *Tropical Marsh*.

The three-acre **Northern Shores** replicates the coast of the Arctic Ocean. It is filled with arctic willows and tundra wildflowers. Its centerpiece, *Seal Harbor*, has a 140-foot-long sea lion pool and a second pool for harbor seals. The sea lions can be seen from above in a Pacific coastline habitat, or through windows underwater. The aquatic-themed restaurant and gift shop have a harbor town atmosphere. The stars of the Northern Shores are the polar bears, whose enormous pool includes underwater split-level viewing windows. Another fine exhibit allows river otters to be observed underwater, swimming in a stream. Set among scattered evergreens, arctic foxes enjoy a habitat with a stream running through it. At *Wolf Pack Woods*, a three-quarter-acre pine forest is home to a small pack of arctic tundra wolves. These white wolves can be seen and photographed through thin harp wire, which allows for terrific views.

Bird World, one of the country's best birdhouses, has three lush, walk-through aviaries. The wide array of tropical birds, displayed in naturalistic habitats embellished with realistic mural backgrounds, includes rhinoceros hornbill birds, magpie-like hunting cissas, and brilliantly colored golden-headed quetzal birds. Enter the *Tropical Rain Forest* through a cave to see Nicobar pigeons and other pretty birds. The *Aquatic Bird Habitat* features a cascading waterfall and displays scarlet and white ibises. The flight cages and enclosures encircling the Bird World building are also special. At the front entrance, a colony of African jackass penguins, named for their donkey-like braying, can be seen in a pool and on a rocky shoreline. On the side of the building are tall flight cages for vultures and sea eagles. Across the path from the flight cages, at the *Bird Garden,* ten mesh enclosures display multi-colored birds, such as tragopans and other pheasants. The most recognizable are the cassowaries, large and dangerous land birds with electric blue and red coloring – their powerful kick can be lethal.

Bear Mountain, which opened in 1918, was the nation's first naturalistic zoo exhibit to use artificial rock work. One of the prettiest places at the Denver Zoo, its tall grottoes, ornamented with pools and waterfalls, house grizzlies and Asian black bears. A small replication of Colorado's Mesa Verde cliff-dweller ruins is also a part of this historic exhibit, and a great photo spot. It's overrun by a popular pack of white-nosed coatis, relatives of raccoons.

The **Sheep Mountain** exhibit is home to Rocky Mountain bighorn sheep, Colorado's state animal, and their Alaskan cousins, Dall sheep. Both have thick, curly horns, used for combat during mating season. One of the two "mountains" in their exhibit is a towering alpine peak, the other is a huge pile of boulders.

OTHER EXHIBITS

The **Felines** building is actually two structures, both filled with naturalistic indoor habitats. Among its inhabitants are Amur tigers, Amur and snow leopards, serval cats, jaguars, and striped hyenas. In a central court between the buildings, you can see long-legged maned wolves. The tigers also have a large, lush grotto outside.

The Denver Zoo has one of the most diverse and interesting collections of hoofed animals in the country. Many of its fascinating **hoofstock** live along a long oval path that cuts through the center of the zoo. The majority of these spacious, tree-lined yards contain African species, many in large herds, including Grevy's zebras, bongo antelope, giraffe-necked gerenuk gazelles, and a variety of other antelope species. Cape buffalo (one of Africa's "Big Five" safari checklist animals) are displayed here, though at very few other zoos. Other animals in this area include ostriches, warthogs, kangaroos, cheetahs, and rare Mongolian wildhorses, also known as Przewalski's wild horses. Probably the rarest animals here are the multi-colored okapis, which are relatives of giraffes. Their cousins, reticulated giraffes, are found at **Giraffe Meadows**. The rest of the zoo's hoofstock are across the wide two-lane visitor path in another row of open yards. Many of the unique and unusual animals here are from North America, including musk oxen, prairie bison, and caribou.

Along a loop off the main path, plant-filled cages house majestic pumas and petite Pallas' cats. Rare and exotic Asian species in this area include Pere David's deer, yaks, Bactrian and dromedary camels, goat-like Mishmi takins, and red pandas.

Not all of the zoo's excellent bird collection is displayed in Bird World. You'll find a small lagoon filled with flamingos and other waterbirds near the carousel. Bald eagles and Andean condors are on opposite sides of a divided flight cage nearby. Across the zoo, Humboldt penguins are displayed in a small building. The zoo's dedication to breeding endangered birds is most evident in the new **Avian Propagation Center**, opened in 2007. Most of what takes place inside is off-exhibit, but there are outdoor interpretive displays and red-crowned cranes, secretary birds, and toco toucans.

Asian elephants, black rhinos, Nile hippos, and pig-like Malayan tapirs all have large yards with mud wallows around the **Pachyderm Building**. Inside, these massive mammals have rocky grotto-like stalls, some with deep pools. A central enclosure displays rock hyraxes, which resemble rabbits but are most closely related to elephants, near a mini-gallery of art painted by Mshindi, one of the only black rhinos known to paint with a brush.

Crested screamer birds and pelicans utilize the water-filled moat around **Monkey Island**, home to playful capuchin monkeys.

FOR THE KIDS

In Primate Panorama, the *African Kraal* replicates an African farmyard; guinea fowl and chickens cackle near a contact area with pettable small goats.

The popular **Pioneer Train**, the country's first natural gas-powered zoo train, offers rides that pass through a tunnel and over the surface of a pretty lake. The **Endangered Species Carousel** here is one of the largest in the nation, with four dozen exotic creatures to ride. At **Lorikeet Adventure**, six colorful species of Australian lorikeets can be fed for a small fee.

IN PROGRESS

The zoo is raising funds for a ten-acre **Asian Tropics** exhibit, which should be its most spectacular yet! At the southern edge of the zoo, five wide spacious yards will be rotating habitats for the zoo's Asian elephants and Malayan tapirs, as well as some new Indian rhinos. Guests will travel a boardwalk to see troops of noisy gibbons on a series of island habitats. Flying fox bats, fishing cats, and other small species will be on exhibit inside the *Asian Pavilion*, while a set of adjacent outdoor enclosures will feature rare and beautiful Sarus cranes and black leopards.

Rio Grande Zoo

903 10th Street SW
Albuquerque, New Mexico 87102
(505) 768-2000
www.cabq.gov/biopark/zoo/

Hours: 9:00 a.m.-5:00 p.m. weekdays, 9:00 a.m.-6:00 p.m. weekends, Memorial Day-Labor Day; 9:00 a.m.-5:00 p.m. daily, rest of year. Closed Thanksgiving, Christmas Day, and New Year's Day.

Admission & Fees: Adults $7, seniors 65+ and children 3-12 $3. Combo admission to Albuquerque Biological Park, which includes the zoo, Albuquerque Aquarium, Rio Grande Botanic Garden, and connecting train ride (no train on Mondays): adults $12, seniors and children $5. Camel ride $3 (seasonal); Thunderbird Express train ride: adults $2, children $1; lorikeet feeding $1.

Wolf's guenon monkeys live near the train station in Adventure Africa.

Directions: From I-25, take Exit 224 West (Lead Avenue). Turn west onto Lead Avenue and follow for 1.2 miles to 10th Street. Turn left onto 10th Street and follow for 0.3 miles to the zoo. From I-40, take Exit 157A (Rio Grande Boulevard) South. Go south on Rio Grande Boulevard for 0.6 miles, and take a left turn onto Central Avenue. Follow for 0.9 miles to a right turn onto 10th Street, and proceed south for 0.6 miles to zoo. City bus line services the zoo.

Don't Miss: Adventure Africa, Koala Creek, Inukshuk Bay, Seals & Sea Lions, Ape Country, Raptor Roost, Amphibians & Reptiles of the World, Tropical America.

For Kids: Climbing Gym, Jumping Waters play area, Band Shell Moat (fish feeding), lorikeet feeding, Thunderbird Express train ride, camel ride.

Authors' Tips: Don't miss the new Cottonwood Café and its New Mexican food. It is decorated with colorful stained glass windows and beautiful woodern corbels (support beams) hand-carved in the form of New Mexico's native animals.

Edutainment: In the "Animal Encounters" show, which runs spring through fall, you'll meet some of the zoo's trained animals face-to-face in the large outdoor Nature Theater. Stars include talking parrots, intelligent ravens, friendly llamas, an African porcupine, and more. Public animal feedings include seals, sea lions and polar bears.

THE RIO GRANDE RIVER, WINDING THROUGH THE HEART OF NEW Mexico, is lined by a pretty cottonwood forest called the *bosque*. The Albuquerque Biological Park, which includes the beautiful Rio Grande Zoo, is situated not far from downtown Albuquerque. Enhancing these natural surroundings, the zoo is embellished with magnificent rock work, dazzling waterfalls, Pueblo-style buildings, and sculptures of wild animals. At its center are a spectacular lake and towering band shell, both surrounded by attractive exhibits.

The Biological Park is actually a four-part complex, including the zoo, the Albuquerque Aquarium, the Rio Grande Botanic Garden, and Tingley Beach. Between them is the Tingley Beach train station, with access to three fishing lakes. Fans of aquatic creatures and beautiful flora should consider scheduling time to see one or more of these other attractions. The Rio Line train provides convenient transportation between the zoo and the rest of the Biological Park.

FEATURED EXHIBITS

Spread across six acres, the new **Adventure Africa** complex, which opened in 2005, features seventeen separate exhibits and more than twenty species of mammals and birds, all native to Africa. The walls and buildings are set along a winding path, and decorated with beautiful African artwork. Like the rest of the zoo, this area is well shaded by mature cottonwood trees. At the beginning of the impressive trail you'll find *Twiga Lookout*, a re-created African village outpost for viewing the reticulated giraffes. ("Twiga" is Swahili for "giraffe.") Visitors can observe the giraffes across a dry gulch, or enter realistic African huts to see tribal utensils, read giraffe trivia, and get a closer look at the giraffes through the hut windows. Nearby, a large herd of zebras shares an arid pasture with a few ostriches. By a white rhino habitat, a small amphitheater hosts occasional African dance presentations. The centerpiece of this exhibit is a glass-fronted chimpanzee habitat. Nearly a dozen chimps enjoy a variety of enrichment activities, playing on and around ropes, climbing trees, swinging, and exploring lush vegetation throughout their habitat. Two savanna carnivores – cheetahs and spotted hyenas – live across from each other in grassy yards. A fenced-in tunnel leads directly through an aviary housing two species of vultures and marabou storks. Another aviary features hammerkop birds, pied crows, and other birds. From inside a mud hut alcove, you can peek through windows at Cape hunting dogs (or African wild dogs) and warthogs in side-by-side enclosures. Visible from a rope-and-log bridge, the large hippo exhibit is impressive. The hippo family here has the benefit of an immense pool to cool down in. An African marketplace includes a tribal king's throne. In a tall enclosure, DeBrazza's guenon monkeys overlook red river hogs and their klipspringer antelope neighbors. Near the train station and café, both decked out with African décor, you'll find Ankole cattle and Wolf's guenon monkeys.

As visitors approach the **Koala Creek** building, they are greeted by the chatter of rainbow lorikeets from across the path. This building is home to a pair of plush Victorian koalas, who have longer fur than the more commonly seen Queensland koalas. In this sunlit glass-roofed structure, visitors along the path have a great view of the koalas and many other Australian animals, including shingleback lizards, carpet pythons, side-necked turtles, wompoo fruit doves, kookaburras, and an aquarium display of rainbowfish.

The **Inukshuk Bay** polar bear habitat features two pools and a water slide for the bears. For entertaining underwater views, visitors go down into what looks a lot like a frozen ice cave. From above water, these massive white bears can be seen trying to balance themselves on oversized floating platforms, and diving into the water to retrieve fish tossed in by a keeper.

You enter the **Seals & Sea Lions Exhibit**, a similar display, through a tall rocky cave. Inside, along an uphill path, windows provide underwater and split-level views of California sea lions and harbor seals as they swim through underwater passageways. Across the path, windows overlook a beautiful lake. As you exit the cave, you enter a replica of a California coastal town where seals and sea lions splash in the harbor waters of a rocky cove.

Ape Country is tucked around the corner from the zoo's entrance. Two groups of gorillas and one of orangutans dwell in semicircular enclosures, where they play on wooden jungle gyms and relax on grassy lawns. Baby gorillas are common here. Viewers can watch the apes at close range across a dry moat or, for a very close encounter, peer through a window in a viewing cave. Noisy siamangs, a lesser, as opposed to great, ape, live nearby in a tall mesh habitat. Their spacious enclosure is built around a two-story tree house overlook that visitors enter by crossing a bouncing wood-and-rope suspension bridge.

The shaded **Cat Walk** provides close-up views of a diverse group of large and small cats. You see African lions first, living in an open yard bordered by an elevated walkway. Next you descend to a long, curving row of large enclosures that display bobcats, servals, snow leopards, ocelots, jaguars, and mountain lions, along with non-feline residents – such as kangaroos, emus, arctic foxes, meerkats, and red pandas. The path ends at the home of the Bengal tigers, exhibited in a large, open grotto with a waterfall, trickling stream, and wading pool.

A shady alcove welcomes visitors to the **Amphibians and Reptiles of the World** exhibit. The building is well known amongst zoo professionals for displaying some of the world's most endangered reptiles in large naturalistic habitats. Sudan plated lizards and Dumeril's ground boas are among its exotic residents. The world's largest lizards, scaly Komodo dragons, are visible through a row of windows in a fifty-foot-long exhibit. The collection also includes unusual salamanders, frogs, and venomous snakes. Desert and Aldabra tortoises are exhibited just outside.

Six tall flight cages make up the **Raptor Roost** exhibit, where a variety of birds of prey, including Andean condors, Mexican spotted owls, and caracara hawks are separated from visitors only by thin wire. The bald eagles here are famous in the zoo world for their successful breeding history.

OTHER EXHIBITS

The first exhibit visitors encounter at the Rio Grande Zoo is the **Caribbean Flamingo** yard, with a shallow moat and central island. Walk under a waterfall to enter the **Seebe Tropical America exhibit**, a lush indoor rain forest. Inside, bromeliads, palms, orchids, and other tropical plants provide a humid green home for parrots, toucans, anacondas, piranhas, prehensile-tailed porcupines, spider monkeys, and three types of tamarin monkeys: golden lion, emperor, and cotton-top. The outdoor **Jenks Parrot Exhibit** is a walk-through aviary, populated by colorful parrots. Capuchin monkeys and more pretty birds, including golden pheasants, live right around the corner. Roadrunners, New Mexico's state bird, are exhibited in a small enclosure. Enter a cave-like entrance to check out the **Night Animals** displays of small and nocturnal animals (mostly primates) such as pygmy and slow lorises (which resemble slow-moving lemurs), and tree kangaroos.

Mexican gray wolves live in a large, naturalistic habitat. The zoo has received much acclaim from zoo professionals for breeding these *lobos*, some of which have been successfully reintroduced into the wild. The prairie dog exhibit across the zoo features native prickly pear cacti, also from the Southwest.

The **Asian elephant exhibit** has recently been expanded. The elephants now have a large pool, a small hill to climb, extensive rock work, and lots of room to roam. Because of its immense size, this yard is best seen from an elevated viewing station.

FOR THE KIDS

Children have a variety of fun choices at the Rio Grande Zoo, starting with the multi-colored **Climbing Gym** and adjacent **Jumping Waters** play area, where water jets squirt up seemingly randomly, leaving many happy children thoroughly soaked. At the **band shell moat**, a coin-operated dispenser sells food for waterfowl and big-mouthed koi fish. At the **lorikeet feeding** exhibit (in season), children and adults can purchase a small cup of nectar to feed the lovely Australian lorikeets.

The **Thunderbird Express** three-quarter scale train takes passengers on a tour of the Africa area, including some behind-the-scenes views. Across from the Cottonwood Café, a camel ride is also available.

IN PROGRESS

As we go to press, the zoo plans to make the expanded Asian elephant yard the cornerstone of a new **Asian exhibit** area, where visitors will encounter takins (a goat-like species of Himalayan antelope), Bactrian camels, and other Asian species. The *Zoo-Asia train depot* is already serving visitors – it connects the zoo with the other attractions of the Biological Park.

A pair of habitats will be attached to Koala Creek, homes for some Australian animals not seen in many zoos outside of their native land. As we go to press, massive **saltwater crocodiles** are still awaiting their new pool in a wing of the Koala Creek building. Nearby, an exhibit has already been built for **Tasmanian devils**. These nasty-tempered carnivorous marsupials are not exhibited in any other U.S. zoo, as we go to press, but Rio Grande hopes to receive permission from Australian authorities to acquire and exhibit them in this naturalistic rocky habitat.

Utah's Hogle Zoo

2600 East Sunnyside Avenue
Salt Lake City, Utah 84108
(801) 582-1631
www.hoglezoo.org

Tiger in Asian Highlands crosses mesh-enclosed bridge directly above the visitor path.

Hours: 9:00 a.m.-5:00 p.m. daily March-October; 9:00 a.m.-4:00 p.m. daily, rest of year. Grounds stay open 90 minutes after the gate closes. Closed Christmas Day and New Year's Day.

Admission & Fees: Adults $8, seniors 65+ and children 3-12 $6. Train ride $1 (members 75¢). Participates in reciprocity program.

Directions: From I-80, take Exit 129 (UT-186 N). Follow UT-186 north for 2.9 miles. Turn right onto East Sunnyside Avenue. Follow for 0.8 miles to the zoo.

Don't Miss: Asian Highlands, Elephant Encounter, Great Apes, Primate Forest.

For Kids: Discovery Land, Zoofari Express train.

Authors' Tips: While the grounds are compact, this zoo is hilly, so be prepared: wear good walking shoes. In the Asian Highlands, guests can experience the "local" culture by eating an Asian rice bowl at the Cat Wok Café, which has great views of the zoo's fascinating cats.

Edutainment: Entertaining and humorous 30-minute "World of Flight" bird shows are held daily (more often on weekends) during the summer in the 450-seat Wildlife Theatre. These shows are very popular; they feature not only the typical parrots and birds of prey, but also pelicans, doves, and other species. The elephants show off their intelligence in a twice-daily "Pachy-derm Program." In the twice-daily "Asian Highlands" program, keepers show how they train and provide behavioral enrichment to the Asian cats. There are also several "Meet-A-Keeper" programs that feature a wide variety of animals. Check the daily schedule for program times.

BUILT IN BEAUTIFUL EMIGRATION CANYON ON SALT LAKE CITY'S east side, Utah's Hogle Zoo is compact, but includes an extensive collection of animals, and some new and innovative exhibits. Since the background consists of scenic mountains and the canyon, photographs taken here are practically guaranteed be great. The zoo is situated right across the road from one of Utah's most historic sites, the valley overlook where Brigham Young once said, "This is the place," the primary reason that Salt Lake City is the still the center of the Mormon world.

FEATURED EXHIBITS

With the 2006 opening of **Asian Highlands**, Hogle now has one of the best collections of felines in the nation. The exhibit is carefully modeled after a Himalayan village in the mountainous region of Amur, near the border of Nepal and Tibet. All of the buildings in this village are built with stone bricks and tiled roofs, and long lines of colorful prayer flags are strung between them. From various places in the village, visitors can view see the Amur tiger, snow leopard, Amur leopard, Pallas' cats, and Siberian lynxes – all cats from the Himalayan region. Since Salt Lake City has the same seasonal climate as the cats' homeland, this is a year-round outdoor exhibit. All three of the larger cats (the tiger and both species of leopards) have spacious rocky hillside habitats, enclosed by nearly invisible mesh and enhanced with beautiful cascading waterfalls, small evergreen trees, and naturalistic log dens. You may get some spectacular photo opportunities at the tiger enclosure, as he swims in his own pool, with underwater viewing for guests, or crosses a mesh-enclosed bridge directly above the visitor path. Guests can use three LCD touch screens to learn more about the cats and about Himalayan culture and legends. In *Grandma's House*, visitors can see how the older generation lives in this Himalayan culture. The house also has a great low window, at just the right height for kids, that looks out into the Siberian lynx habitat. The lynxes often hang out close to the window.

Siberian lynx

All across the nation, zoos have been modernizing and expanding their elephant exhibits. Hogle's **Elephant Encounter** was one of the first to take up this trend, in 2005. In this two-acre re-creation of an African plain, three African elephants and a pair of white rhinos have room to roam. One of the four outdoor habitats has a ten-foot-deep swimming channel where the elephants can completely submerge themselves, if they so desire. The elephants can also climb a large mound for a view of the surrounding landscape. Resembling a rocky outcropping, the *Kopje* is a sheltered viewing station where the elephants and rhinos can be seen up close through thick glass. The pachyderms' watering hole and feeding stations are nearby, to help draw them close to the glass. In the thatch-roofed *African Lodge*, guests can look over an elephant skull, rhino horn, and other pachyderm artifacts.

The **Great Apes** building is one of the zoo's most popular places, especially since the Mother's Day 2005 birth of Acara, a baby orangutan. Because she had to deliver by C-section, mother Eve did not recognize her new daughter as her own, which meant the zoo staff had to hand-raise Acara. Due to these circumstances, Acara became a local celebrity. The orangutans and gorillas are seen through glass in their hay-floored indoor enclosure, or outside in grassy sloping yards. The outdoor yards, enhanced with climbing structures, are visible from overlooking walls, high above the apes.

In the indoor/outdoor **Primate Forest**, five species of monkeys are featured in large mesh-enclosed, tree-filled outdoor enclosures and glass-fronted naturalistic indoor habitats with rain forest backdrops. The colobus, capuchin, and spider monkeys are the most entertaining; there are also smaller golden lion tamarin monkeys and Schmidt's guenon monkeys to see.

OTHER EXHIBITS

The **Small Animal Building** is at the heart of the zoo's impressive animal collection. Under its domed roof, this large building displays nearly half of the species exhibited by the zoo, including more than thirty-five types of reptiles. In the building's *Desert Zone*, four types of rattlesnakes, Gila monsters, and other lizards and snakes are displayed behind glass. A meerkat pair digs burrows in their attractive habitat, while another meerkat shares her exhibit with African porcupines. Other desert creatures exhibited nearby include a sand cat and a bat-eared fox. The *Temperate Zone* has a number of other snakes on display, including additional rattlesnakes. Other reptiles, amphibians, and small mammals are exhibited here, including a black-footed cat and Wied's marmosets, a small species of monkey. The *Tropics Zone* also features small monkeys, an Arabian wildcat, and many more reptiles, including Siamese crocodiles. You can find some beautiful birds in the walk-through *Rainforest* room, including jungle fowl, spoonbills, and scarlet ibises.

A variety of animal exhibits surround the Small Animal Building. Kangaroos, wallabies, and Aldabra tortoises live in a pair of nearby yards, while gray wolves are exhibited behind the building.

Besides the apes and monkeys described above, the smaller **Primate Building** houses monkeys and lemurs. You can see them inside, through glass, or outside in traditional cages. The howler monkeys, gibbons, and ghostly Entellus langur monkeys are all impressive species, but the baboon-like mandrills are the feature attraction.

The mid-sized arid **Savanna** yard is home to a variety of antelope, including addax and springboks, as well as Egyptian geese, guinea fowl, and Grevy's zebras. Nearby, giraffes can be seen out in their open yard and inside the **Giraffe Building**, which has a balcony so visitors can stand eye-to-eye with these tall creatures. Across the path, a cheetah lives in a grassy hillside habitat in a corner of the zoo.

At **Penguin Cove**, African black-footed penguins waddle along rocky ledges and swim in a large oval pool. On one side of this exhibit, a plush red panda lives in a moated yard with trees to climb, while llamas live on the other side. Across the court, an old rocky grotto is inhabited by black bears, while cougars and endangered Chacoan peccaries, a wild pig from the Andes, are exhibited along the same path. Across from the Asian Highlands, the mountain theme continues with a hillside habitat for desert bighorn sheep. Double-humped Bactrian camels are displayed across from the gorillas.

FOR THE KIDS

Until recently, **Discovery Land** was the exhibit that most impressed us at Hogle. This children's area has four distinct sections, introducing kids to different animal environments. In the pretty fountain-fed *Duck Pond*, visitors can feed over half a dozen species of ducks and geese, as well as trumpeter swans and white pelicans. The *Knoll and Burrow* area features a Utah prairie dog exhibit, where kids can climb through a tunnel to pop up in a clear acrylic dome among the burrowing prairie dogs. Bats flutter about in an exhibit nearby. In the forested *Woodland Edge*, attractive North American animals include bald eagles, hawks, bobcats, Canadian lynx, a skunk, and a ringtail cat (or cacomistle), which is not actually a feline; it's related the raccoon! The most attractive section is the *Desert Canyon*, with open air adobe-style buildings that contain exhibits that include an armadillo, a rare Channel Island fox, various North American birds, native Utah fish, and assorted invertebrates, such as a scorpion. There is also a contact yard with Navajo sheep and Angora goats to pet, as well as a large animal-themed playground. The **Zoofari Express** train station is also in Discovery Land. A ride on this one-third-scale replica of an 1869 steam locomotive is the only way to see bison in an open paddock. There are replicas of Native American teepees and covered wagons along the train track.

IN PROGRESS

As we go to press, the zoo plans to open the **Conservation Carousel,** with forty-two hand-carved animals, in 2008. This, they hope, will be the next step in revolutionizing the zoo with new habitats and attractions over the next decade. The most exciting new habitat may be the **Arctic Exhibit**, which will hopefully return polar bears and sea lions to the zoo. Although their last bear passed away in 2003, this zoo has an outstanding record for breeding polar bears. Other plans call for an expansive **African Savanna**, a **Gorilla Forest**, and an upgrade to the penguin habitat.

BEST OF THE REST

Wildlife World Zoo

16501 West Northern Avenue
Litchfield Park, Arizona 85340
(623) 935-9453
www.wildlifeworld.com

Originally set up as a private breeding facility to supply rare and endangered animals to other zoos, this zoo on Phoenix's west side today boasts Arizona's largest collection of exotic creatures. Over twenty large paddocks hold an extensive collection of endangered species, including a variety of rare antelope, a breeding group of white tigers, and an assortment of other big cats. Intriguing indoor exhibits include a reptile house and a small mammal building. The zoo also has some great rides, including a train, a sky ride, and a boat tour around the *Kangaroo Walkabout*. As we go to press, there are plans for another ride in the near future, when the massive *Wildlife World Aquarium* opens. Some of this aquarium's fish will be visible along a unique log flume ride through the exhibit.

Reid Park Zoo

1020 South Randolph Way
Tucson, Arizona 85716
(520) 881-4753
www.tucsonzoo.org

Though it covers only seventeen acres, this small zoo includes a strong collection of mostly African and South American animals. In the *African Zone*, white rhinos, zebras, and ostriches are exhibited together, across from mandrills, giraffes, and lions. The African and Asian elephants, who live together here, are scheduled for an expansion to their habitat as we go to press. In the *South American Zone*, a central tropical bird aviary is encircled by exhibits of jaguars, tapirs, spectacled bears, anteaters, and more. The small *Asian Zone* features tigers, gibbons, and sun bears. Finally, the *Adaptation Zone* displays tortoises, monkeys, and polar bears, who have adapted remarkably well to the hot Arizona climate.

Zoo Boise

355 Julia Davis Drive
Boise, Idaho 83702
(208) 384-4260
www.zooboise.org

Located near Idaho's capitol building, this small zoo features local animals from the Rocky Mountain region, as well as creatures from Asia. The *North American Carnivores* complex includes eagles, hawks, owls, foxes, badgers, and raccoon-like coatis. Ocelots, servals, and bobcats can be seen in the *Small Cats* building, while Amur and snow leopards are exhibited outside. A large section of the zoo is dedicated to the *Animals of Asia*, which include Amur tigers, sloth bears, red pandas, and sika deer. This zoo is one of only a few in the country to exhibit moose, which are found across a bridge, near bighorn sheep, zebras, and the *Penguin Pavilion*.

West Coast Zoos

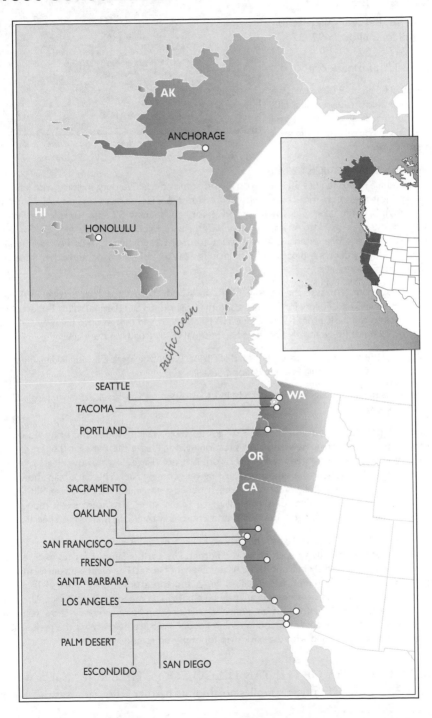

San Diego Zoo's Wild Animal Park

15500 San Pasqual Valley Road
Escondido, California 92027
(760) 747-8702
www.wildanimalpark.org

Hours: 9:00 a.m.-8:00 p.m. daily in summer and in December; 9:00 a.m.-4:00 p.m. daily, rest of the year. Grounds stay open one hour after the gate closes

Visitors can pay extra to get close to Indian rhinos and other animals on the behind-the-scenes Photo Caravan Safari.

Admission & Fees: Adults $28.50, children 3-11 $17.50. Seniors 60+ receive 10% off admission, active duty military with valid ID get in free. Journey Into Africa tour: adults $10, children $6; Conservation Carousel $2 ($4 to ride all day); Balloon Safari $15 (members $12); lorikeet feeding $2. The "Best Value Ticket" package includes Journey Into Africa and carousel: adults $34, children $24. Parking $8. For even closer encounters, more extensive animal tours are available for higher fees. For vacationers, there are multi-day tickets and packages that include SeaWorld, Disneyland, and other Southern California attractions.

Directions: From I-15, take the Via Rancho Parkway exit. Follow for 1 mile, then turn right onto San Pasqual Road. Follow for 3.4 miles, and turn right onto San Pasqual Valley Road. Follow for 1.1 miles to the park. From I-5, take Exit 51B (Vista Way) and merge onto highway CA-78E. Follow for 24 miles (it eventually becomes San Pasqual Valley Road) to the park.

Don't Miss: Journey Into Africa tour, Heart of Africa, Nairobi Village, Condor Ridge, Elephant Overlook, Lion Camp, Gorilla Habitat, Balloon Safari.

For Kids: Petting Kraal, Jameson Research Island, Conservation Carousel, Samburu Jungle Gym, Savanna Cool Zone.

Authors' Tips: This park is enormous! Wear comfortable walking shoes, and bring along binoculars for the many distant views. If you're vacationing, don't leave this park for the last day – it will wipe you out! It's a very steep walk to get from Nairobi Village down to the Heart of Africa and the Journey Into Africa tour, and an exhausting one coming back. The park map shows the most direct path, but thankfully, in late 2007 they opened a new elevator, the Great Rift Lift, to make this journey much easier. For those willing to spend some significant extra money, the behind-the-scenes tours (Cheetah Run Safari and Photo Caravan Safari) are very special.

Edutainment: The "Frequent Flyers" bird show, held three times daily, uses a rotating cast of 22 different species of birds so each show is different. The park is famous for its excellent elephant show, held twice daily in front of the Asian elephant habitat. The elephants perform tasks that demonstrate their strength and intelligence. In the three times daily "Animal Trackers" show, a zebra, a camel, and other exotic animals take part in a comedic trip to Africa. Also held three times daily, "See My Africa" is an audience-participation-heavy comedy show featuring puppets. A wide variety of animal encounters and keeper talks are held across the park. Check the schedule insert provided with the park map for show times and locations.

A SISTER FACILITY OF THE SAN DIEGO ZOO, THE ENORMOUS WILD Animal Park is located thirty-two miles north of its partner. This park was the dream of Dr. Charles Schroeder, a former veterinarian and the director of the San Diego Zoo in the 1960s. He envisioned a much larger facility, where many of the urban zoo's endangered animals could roam freely, and live and breed in large herds, as they would in the wild. Construction began in 1969, with the aim of building an off-view propagation center. But interest was so strong in this 1,800-acre facility that it was opened to the public in 1972. Today, about two million visitors come each year, many of them tourists from outside Southern California.

The facility is situated in a desert, with rolling valleys and steep rocky hills. To access much of the refuge, prepare for some hiking on its extensive network of back country trails. In the distance, hikers will see roaming herds of hoofed animals, primarily from Africa and Asia. The initial goals for this refuge have been achieved: it is now internationally famous for its breeding success with California condors, Przewalski's wild horses, tigers, and especially rhinos.

FEATURED EXHIBITS

All guests pass through **Nairobi Village**, the park's central visitor complex. Named after the capital city of Kenya, this Nairobi closely resembles its namesake in both atmosphere and traffic density! Most of the buildings have impressive thatched roofs, but the most photographed spot in the entire park is probably the *Congo River Fishing Village*, where three thatched towers anchor a bridge over a beautiful cascading waterfall, created by a natural log dam that lets the blocked water trickle through. This structure is based on a real place in Africa, where people catch fish from the bridge. The Village is built around beautiful *Mombasa Lagoon*, a central pond with animal islands that house flamingos, pelicans, lemurs, and distinctive shoebill storks. There's a real theme park atmosphere, especially at night, with many restaurants, snack bars, and gift shops. Sprinkled around the Village are various small but naturalistic habitats for interesting animals that include wild pigs such as red river hogs and babirusas, small antelope and deer, including the exotically named pudus and dik-diks, and the always popular meerkats.

Veterans of this park mourned the demise of the Wgasa Bush Line Railway. But alas, the old monorail broke down frequently, and riders complained that the fifty-minute tour was too long. In its place, the new **Journey Into Africa** tour, which opened in 2007, offers a twenty-five-minute tour aboard the *African Express*, a 104-passenger tram. These open-air tram vehicles follow a new paved path, which come one to three hundred feet closer to the animals than the old monorail did. As the tour begins in *East Africa*, the guide points out the many animals visible from the tram. This narrative is not only informative and interesting, but also quite funny. The tram passes a wide variety of antelope and gazelles, as well as wildebeest and massive white rhinos. You'll spend the most time in the *South Africa* section, where larger antelope species live in herds. Ostriches, giraffes, and ill-tempered Cape buffalo, one of the most dangerous animals in the savanna, also live here. A more forested environment represents *Central Africa*, where beautiful bongo antelope and rarely seen Vaal rhebok antelope can be sighted. Within a small pond, an island is home to pelicans and vultures, both in large numbers. The tour skirts the edge of *North Africa*, where scimitar-horned oryxes and Ankole cattle are easily recognizable by their distinctive horns. The guide will point out Africa's only native deer, the Barbary red deer. The tour ends with a view of the lions from the back of the Lion Camp exhibit. To those who miss the old monorail, don't worry. This new tour is still an extra special, extra close look at an amazing variety of African animals – an experience that's unparalleled by anything else outside of Africa.

The **Heart of Africa** is the park's most zoo-like exhibit, and one of its best. Along a winding downhill path, the tour passes four distinct African environments with twenty different bird species and eleven different mammals. In the woodland scrub, separate habitats introduce deep brown bontebok antelope, and giant elands and other gazelles. At a bend in the path, African vultures perch on a dead tree. Upon entering a forest, the trail becomes an elevated wooden walkway. The highlight of these shaded forest habitats are the elusive okapis, rare cousins of giraffes, seen up above on the hillside. Wattled cranes, yellow-backed duiker antelope, and gerenuk gazelles can also be found among the trees. As you emerge into the savanna region, a mixed-species habitat features warthogs and a large group of bat-eared foxes. The jet black ground hornbill birds here are also unusual. Nearby, you'll encounter wetlands habitats for secretary birds, kori bustards, and other long-legged birds. At a large lagoon, the trail crosses a floating bridge. If you're here with children, turn right to go to *Jameson Research Island* (see below). Otherwise, stay to the left to see colobus monkeys on *Primate Island,* and then a beautiful mass of pink – a flock of more than a hundred African flamingos. Back on land, the final animals you'll see are cheetahs, in a yard large enough for the sleek cats to show off their breathtaking speed.

Up on a high hill crest, **Condor Ridge** is the park's only exhibit of North American animals, and consists entirely of creatures from the American Southwest. Out in the park's back country, the first exhibit is an aviary with roadrunners milling about on the ground as thick-billed parrots, the country's only native parrots, perch in the pine trees above. From here, a boardwalk leads to a shaded viewing area for a set of grassland habitats. Rare black-footed ferrets are displayed quite close to their main food source, prairie dogs. Also visible from this area are porcupines, Harris' hawks, burrowing owls, and more. At the boardwalk's end, a large aviary is the trail's feature attraction – as of early 2008, the nation's only exhibit of highly endangered California condors. This facility was a major contributor in bringing these condors, America's largest flying birds, back from the brink of extinction. Next to the condor aviary is a large rocky hillside enclosure for desert bighorn sheep, another endangered animal.

Elephant Overlook is an elevated walking path between two spacious exhibit yards for Asian and African elephants, who live in side-by-side herds. The African herd was imported here from an over-populated park in Swaziland in 2003. Since then, at least five calves have been born into the expanding herd. Both species have large habitats: the Asians have two acres, the Africans have three. Both are outfitted with pools, rock formations, grassy pastures, and trees. These habitats can also be seen from the high pathway leading to the exhibits. It's rare to see so many elephants at once – the experience is breathtaking.

In **Lion Camp**, the lion pride often hangs out by a forty-foot-wide curved window, where these imposing big cats relax mere inches away from their human visitors. You can also frequently spot them sitting on top of a Land Rover parked in their habitat. The lions live in an artificial kopje, or rocky outcropping, with towering rock walls that outline part of their habitat, which also includes African acacia trees to climb, and a grassy hillside, from which they have a great view of the savanna animals below.

Cross the Congo Fishing Village bridge to reach the **Gorilla Habitat**, a wide, sloping grassy grotto shaded by mature trees. The large troop of gorillas lives just across a moat from visitors, who can watch the great apes from a long viewing area. The *Gorilla Activity Center* has many graphics that explain the plight of gorillas in the wild. On one side of the habitat is a small aviary for pretty bee-eater birds, which are skilled at catching flying insects.

There are many spectacular views in this park, but none better than the one from the **Balloon Safari**. For a fee, a giant yellow helium balloon takes as many as thirty people at a time four hundred feet up into the air, and stays there for fifteen minutes. From that height, the savanna, the lions, and the whole San Pasqual Valley are beautiful, especially at sunset. Bring your camera!

OTHER EXHIBITS

A walk through the **Hidden Jungle** takes visitors through a large glass-sided greenhouse filled with tropical plants, including beautiful bromeliads and orchids. Within this misty rain forest, colorful birds from the tropics fly freely about, among them hummingbirds, tanagers, honeycreepers, and the magnificent quetzal bird, the national symbol of Guatemala. In spring, the exhibit is also filled with thousands of beautiful butterflies. Side exhibits display leaf-cutter ants, stick insects, tarantulas, and other small creatures. Next door, **Lorikeet Landing** is another walk-in aviary, this one filled with a rainbow of lorikeet parrots. Visitors can hand feed these beautiful birds for a small fee. Near the entrance to the park is the **African Aviary**, a large walk-through jungle habitat. Most impressive here are the jet-black openbill storks, whose long bills look like pairs of pliers. A wide variety of colorful waterfowl live in the stream that passes through the exhibit. There is a smaller but similar **South American Aviary** near the Hidden Jungle, situated near a large, towering aviary-like enclosure for playful red-cheeked gibbons, a species of arboreal lesser apes.

For visitors who want some exercise, the **Kilimanjaro Safari Walk** includes miles of back country trails, leading to intriguing animals, beautiful botanical gardens, and spectacular vistas. For those interested in plant life, the *Old World Succulent Garden* and the *Baja Garden* are both filled with impressive cacti, and both have amazing views of the park. On the way, the *Epiphyllum House,* with strange jungle cacti, and the *Bonsai Pavilion* both offer interesting looks at exotic plants. Near these greenhouses, the trail traverses the beautiful *Conifer Forest*, with towering redwood trees and a cascading stream. Just beyond is *Big Cat Overlook*, one of two overlooks into a huge densely planted valley habitat for Sumatran tigers and one white Bengal tiger. After crossing a bouncy suspension bridge, the trail ends at *Kilima Point*, one of the park's best views of the hundred-acre East African savanna and its inhabitants. This fascinating and often tiring walk has many side trails, so you can set your own course; there is no pre-designated route to follow.

FOR THE KIDS

Set in Nairobi Village, the **Petting Kraal** is, in our humble opinion, the best animal contact yard in the nation. Surrounded by a tall stick fence, this petting exhibit is extra special because it gives you a chance to pet some very exotic animals. Instead of the usual goats and sheep, children get to meet blackbuck antelope and swamp deer from India, as well as various African gazelles. Unfortunately, some guests may dismiss these exotic creatures as "just deer." Nearby, windows into the **Animal Care Center** allow guests to watch zoo staff care for baby animals of all kinds.

In Nairobi Village, there's a colorful **Conservation Carousel** for children to ride. Nearby, the **Discovery Station** is a child-friendly room filled with puppets, books, and wildlife toys. Education staff here may show off a friendly small animal or help children with an animal-themed craft. Out in the Heart of Africa, **Jameson Research Island** offers similar activities for children, including animal-themed story-telling.

The **Samburu Jungle Gym** is an attractive playground adjacent to a shaded picnic area that's much appreciated by parents. There is a large climbing structure and giant animal sculptures to play on. The **Savanna Cool Zone** gives kids a chance to cool off by getting soaked. Artificial palm trees spray a cooling mist, and children can play on a slippery water-spouting turtle, crocodile, or lion.

IN PROGRESS

The old monorail tour took riders to see the animals of both Africa and Asia, while the new Journey Into Africa only covers the African sections. There are plans in development, and funds being raised, for a similar tour to see the Asian animals – perhaps a "Journey Into Asia." Living out in the *Mountain Habitat, Asian Plains*, and *Asian Waterhole* areas are many deer species, including endangered Pere David's deer, as well as ibexes and mouflon sheep up on the hillside. Riders of this new tour may get to see them, as well as Przewalski's wild horses, European bison, one-horned Indian rhinos, and two kinds of wild cattle: Javan bantengs and Indian gaurs.

Los Angeles Zoo and Botanical Gardens

5333 Zoo Drive
Los Angeles, California 90027
(323) 644-4200
www.lazoo.org

Hours: 10:00 a.m.-6:00 p.m. daily in summer; 10:00 a.m.-5:00 p.m. daily, rest of year. Closed Christmas Day.

Native to the Andes, the mountain tapir is the zoo's rarest animal: there are only 200 on the planet.

Admission & Fees: Adults $10, seniors 62+ $7, children 2-12 $5. Safari Shuttle: adults $4, seniors and physically disabled $1.50, children $1; LA Choo Choo Train $2. Participates in reciprocity program.

Directions: Located in sprawling Griffith Park, at the junction of the Ventura (CA-134) and Golden State (I-5) Freeways. From I-5, take Exit 144A (Zoo Drive) and get onto Zoo Drive. Follow for 0.5 miles, then continue on Western Heritage Way for 0.2 miles. Turn right onto Zoo Drive again and follow for 0.1 miles to the zoo parking lot. From CA-134, take Exit 5A (Victory Boulevard/I-5) and follow signs to Zoo Drive. Then follow the directions above.

Don't Miss: Campo Gorilla Reserve, Chimpanzees of Mahale Mountains, Red Ape Rain Forest, Australia, Africa, Eurasia, South America, North America, Cape Griffon vultures.

For Kids: Children's Zoo, Kids Korner, Play Park, L.A. Choo Choo Train.

Authors' Tips: If you're planning to tour all or most of this large, hilly zoo, make use of the Safari Shuttle. This tram stops at five well-spaced locations around the zoo's perimeter. Food stands are found throughout the zoo, and kids' meals are available at most of them. Mexican food is available at La Casita, and pizza at South America. This is one of only a few zoos that allows visitors to bring in food, so feel free to pack your own picnic.

Edutainment: In the World of Birds amphitheater, excellent shows are held two or three times daily, except Tuesdays. They feature various birds of prey, including an Andean condor, and talking birds such as macaw parrots. In the Children's Zoo's Adventure Theater, participatory 15-minute story-telling presentations, held twice daily, are very popular. Also aimed at children, 15-minute "Animals & You" programs provide close-up presentations of small animals at stations around the Children's Zoo. Check the show schedule in your zoo map for times and locations.

THE LOS ANGELES ZOO OPENED IN 1966 AS THE WORLD'S FIFTH-largest zoo. Back then, rare animals tended to be gathered and exhibited so quickly that even Noah would be impressed. Today, this facility's lush tropical foliage, including tall palm trees and a variety of flowering trees and bushes, make it one of the most beautiful zoos in the country. In fact, it is also accredited as a botanical garden.

The zoo is informally divided into five continental habitat regions and a sixth aquatic animals region. These groupings are very unofficial, however; there are many exceptions to the zoogeographical designations. Each of the six sections has a winding trail that loops through the exhibits. Follow your zoo map closely; it's easy to get lost here! Within each of the six sections, landscaped open paddocks are intermingled with C-shaped wire-mesh enclosures called "roundhouses." While these 1960s-era roundhouses are outdated in terms of exhibit technology, many have been attractively landscaped, and they have the advantage of allowing you to see animals all around you as you walk into the center curve of the "C."

FEATURED EXHIBITS

With the 2007 opening of **Campo Gorilla Reserve**, LA became one of a very select group of zoos to exhibit gorillas, chimpanzees, and orangutans. The new gorilla habitat features a beautiful winding visitor pathway, enhanced by various ferns, palms, and other tropical plants, and an artificially generated mist that makes the rain forest atmosphere realistically damp and cool. The zoo's gorillas are displayed in two groups: a family led by a large silverback, and a smaller bachelor group. The apes enjoy waterfalls, a stream, grassy meadows, and shady cave retreats. Visitors have five separate places to see the gorillas, including from across a lushly planted dry moat, and up close through a large slanted window in a shaded viewing station.

At nearly a full acre, the **Chimpanzees of Mahale Mountains** is one of the largest chimp exhibits in America, and one of the best. This naturalistic habitat, hailed by Dr. Jane Goodall as one of the finest in existence, attempts to bring one of Tanzania's most famous parks, Mahale Mountains National Park, to Los Angeles. More than a dozen chimpanzees have access to wide grassy meadows, rocky caves, and an artificial termite mound from which they gather food. They can also travel up the hill to their "penthouse playground," a chimp play setup on the ridge. Their habitat features a cascading waterfall and flowing stream, live tropical trees, and what appears to be an abandoned sawmill. Visitors have three viewing options when it comes to these intelligent apes: from high above; through glass at ground level from a large attractive viewing shelter; or from a fifty-seat amphitheater.

The orangutans of the **Red Ape Rain Forest** have three separate areas to explore. Lushly planted with bamboo and banana trees, the habitats resemble the apes' Indonesian homeland. To get from one area to the next, these arboreal apes climb along artificial vines and bamboo-like sway poles to a round passageway, that runs right above visitors' heads. For mental stimulation, the orangs can hunt for fruit in the tree branches, placed there by the keepers. Visitors watch these red apes from elevated bridges and decks, and from beneath a giant tent-like roof.

The **Australia** section includes eight attractive exhibits, and among the animals on display here are two of the zoo's most appealing: Komodo dragons and koalas. In one of the nation's only permanent outdoor koala exhibits, the koalas are usually visible quite close to the viewing area, perched in their trees. At ground level, tammar wallabies hop around among spiny echidnas, one of only two egg-laying mammals in the world. In a different yard, koalas share their home with gray kangaroos. Further into this small complex, *Dragons of Komodo* displays these massive lizards in a renovated roundhouse. Past a thatch-roofed entryway and authentic Balinese statues, the Komodo dragons live in a realistic replica of their Indonesian homeland. Another animal not to be missed here is the brilliantly colored double-wattled cassowary, a large flightless bird that's capable of delivering a kick fatal to humans. In a central multi-sided aviary, beautiful island hornbill birds are exhibited in the trees, above rare yellow-footed rock wallabies, a species the LA Zoo has had particular success breeding.

At the western end of the zoo, **Africa** is the largest of the geographical sections. At the area's core, Masai giraffes occupy one of the zoo's largest open yards. Lions live in a moated enclosure next door. Rare giraffe relatives, okapis, are displayed across from the food stand. A variety of hoofed animals are exhibited in open yards, including mountain bongo antelope, slightly built gerenuk gazelles, giant eland antelope, various small duiker antelope species, red river hogs, and Nubian ibex, a type of mountain goat. The island nation of Madagascar is well represented here, with ring-tailed lemurs, hyperactive sifaka lemurs, cat-like fossas, who are natural predators of lemurs, and a large group of endangered radiated tortoises. Another updated roundhouse display is an attractive home for colorful baboon-like mandrills. African monkeys in surrounding roundhouses include colobus monkeys and cherry-crowned mangabey monkeys.

Up in the zoo's northwest corner is the **Eurasia** section. The standout display here is the Sumatran tiger habitat, with an attractive waterfall. Massive Nile hippos from Africa are often submerged in their deep pool, while an Indian rhino, almost as big as the hippos, has access to paddocks on either side of the hippo exhibit. This area's four roundhouses exhibit siamangs and buff-cheeked gibbons, both arboreal lesser apes, as well as a fascinating variety of Asian eagles, including Stellar's sea eagles and Japanese mountain hawk-eagles. Asian ungulates: Japanese serows, Chinese gorals, Tadjik markhors, and Sichuan takins, some displayed in steep hillside exhibits, are fascinating to compare. Other animals include rare Visayan warty pigs and American black bears.

At the zoo's north end, the **South America** section's exhibits surround a food stand of the same name. Near the restaurant, shaggy mountain tapirs live in an open yard with a small pool. Native to the Andes mountains, these are probably the zoo's rarest animals: there are only two hundred left on the planet. Similar but less rare Central American tapirs are exhibited across the complex. A jaguar is housed in one of the roundhouses, along with two large birds: king vultures and red-legged seriemas. Extremely rare red-faced uakari monkeys, with distinctive bald faces, are also displayed here. Of the seven other types of South American monkeys found in this area, most in lush roundhouses, spider monkeys and black howler monkeys are most attention-grabbing. Other impressive species on display include long-legged maned wolves and giant Aldabra tortoises. Snow leopards from Asia live in a boulder-strewn roundhouse near the Eurasia section.

Ironically, the section displaying **North American animals** is in the zoo's southernmost corner. The most unusual North American animals here are the peninsular pronghorn antelope from the desert of Mexico's Baja California. The LA Zoo is a leader in breeding these highly endangered antelope, who live (at the zoo) in two cacti-planted large paddocks. Displayed across from the pronghorns, desert bighorn sheep are also native to the same Mexican desert. A Channel Island fox, found only on California's offshore Channel Islands, shares a nicely renovated roundhouse with its African cousins, bat-eared foxes. Two additional roundhouses feature bobcats, raccoon-like coatis, and a red-tailed hawk. The many non-American species in this area include endangered African wild dogs and a large paddock with African acacia trees for the Grevy's zebras. On either side of a yard for Speke's gazelles are rare wild pigs: Chacoan peccaries from South America and hairless babirusas from Indonesia. Another large corner paddock is shared by double-humped Bactrian camels and their South American cousins, alpacas, which look like small llamas.

The **Cape Griffon vultures** here are the nation's largest captive breeding group, housed in a large flight cage. It is well worth a stop at this off-the-main-trail exhibit, if only to see these magnificent birds spread their eight-foot wingspans for a short flight.

OTHER EXHIBITS

As visitors enter the zoo, they walk underneath a gigantic, colorful "Los Angeles Zoo" sign, reminiscent of the famous "Hollywood" sign. In the **International Marketplace**, a striking entry plaza completed in 2005, *Sea Life Cliffs* is a rocky cove habitat for harbor seals, usually visible basking on their beach or swimming underwater, where you can watch them through large windows. Across the wide path, a small pool exhibits an American alligator. Further up the path are lush, beautiful exhibits of black-necked swans and flamingos. Some say the meerkats displayed here were the inspiration for "Timon," in the Disney film *The Lion King*.

A pair of gigantic walk-through tropical flight cages comprises The **Aviary**, near the center of the zoo. A jungle path ascends to the top of a crashing waterfall, where the entire screened exhibit can be viewed, many of its gorgeous birds in flight. Among the feathered species inside are roseate spoonbills, scarlet ibises, green pheasant-like turacos, plush crested jays, and a breeding flock of flamingos.

Near the Australasian animals, the small **Aquatics** section's alligators, gray seals, river otters, and California sea lions are likely to soon say good-bye to their pool-enhanced exhibits as this area is designated as the location for the planned reptile house (see "In Progress," below). At press time, it is undetermined where these animals will be moved – elsewhere in the zoo or to other zoos.

FOR THE KIDS

The two-acre **Winnick Family Children's Zoo**, painted in bright colors, offers a wide variety of small animals, most of them perennial kid favorites. Near the front of this section, a tall, splashing waterfall is an attractive home for brown pelicans. Behind the waterfall, kids can explore a realistic cave with very convincing stalactites. Surrounding the building are habitats with barely visible barriers for thick-billed parrots, ocelot cats, and other animals. One highlight is the prairie dog town, where tunnels lead to clear acrylic domes so kids can pop up inside the exhibit, imitating the burrowing rodents. In the long *Animal Care Center*, a row of low windows provides looks at rare and unusual animals, including cotton-top and emperor tamarin monkeys, civet cats, lemur-like bushbabies, and armadillos. A small side yard displays young exotic hoofed mammals. Nearby, the dark *Desert Trail* building features arid habitats for venomous Mexican beaded lizards, African hedgehogs, and other small desert creatures. The area's most popular section is *Muriel's Ranch*, a contact yard where kids can pet goats and sheep. At *Riordan Kids Korner*, children can stop by for story-telling, puppet shows, or to meet interesting small animals.

In the Eurasia area, the animal-themed **Papiano Play Park** is surrounded by a spacious picnic area. The small **L.A. Choo Choo Train** appeals to tots.

IN PROGRESS

As we go to press, the LA Zoo is scheduled to become the nation's only zoo to display beautiful and rare **golden monkeys**. The monkeys are considered a symbol of China, much like the giant panda. These enchanting blue-faced primates, native to the same mountains as the pandas, will be displayed in a treetop forest habitat in the Eurasia section. Visitors will enter a Chinese-themed pavilion for an elevated view of the fascinating creatures. They are expected to arrive sometime in 2008.

Currently scheduled to open in 2009, the **Pachyderm Forest** will provide an expanded and modernized naturalistic habitat for a growing Asian elephant herd. With six centrally located acres, it will be one of the largest urban elephant exhibits in the nation. The elephants will enjoy a sandy beach, waterfalls, watering holes, forest paths to wander, and four separate yards. Visitors will enter this exhibit through five distinct viewing areas, each enhanced with graphics interpreting the history of elephants in five different Asian nations, including Cambodia, India, and China.

The zoo has big plans for 2010: they plan to open **Rainforest of the Americas** and **Reptile House: HISS (Herpetofauna-Invertebrate Species Survival) Center.** In the hillside Rainforest exhibit, visitors will enter through a Latin American marketplace. A small stilted exhibit building will feature freshwater stingrays, piranhas, electric eels, and other Amazonian aquatic animals. Back outside, the winding path will pass jungle habitats for jaguars, tapirs, harpy eagles, and giant otters. The new Reptile House building will have separate sections for venomous snakes, amphibians (including Japanese giant salamanders), and damp forest reptiles. Outside, a boardwalk will lead by an *Alligator Swamp*, while a smaller *Southwest Desert* building will feature rattlesnakes and lizards.

The Oakland Zoo

9777 Golf Links Road
Oakland, California 94605
(510) 632-9525
www.oaklandzoo.org

Hours: 10:00 a.m.-4:00 p.m. daily. The children's rides, train, and sky ride open at 11:00 a.m. Closed Thanksgiving and Christmas Day.

Admission & Fees: Adults $9.50, seniors 55+ and children 2-12 $6. Parking $6. Sky Ride, train ride and Tiger Coaster $2 each; other rides $1. Participates in reciprocity program.

Oakland has one of the ten best kids' zoos in the U.S.

Directions: From I-580, take Exit 29A (Golf Links Road/98th Avenue). Turn east onto Golf Links Road and follow for less than 0.1 miles. Turn right into Knowland State Park and the zoo.

Don't Miss: African Savanna, African Village, Malayan sun bears, Sky Ride.

For Kids: Children's Zoo, miniature train ride, rides area.

Authors' Tips: The Island Café offers fast food, including pizza, and peanut-butter-and-jelly and grilled-cheese sandwiches for the kids. Both this joint and the African Savanna Café have great atmosphere. Note that this zoo has short hours – some say for the benefit of the animals, who may enjoy the longer rest period between daily visitor hours.

Edutainment: On summer weekends, twice-daily shows are held in the Wildlife Theater in the Children's Zoo. Check the schedule posted at the theater.

BACK IN 1983, THE OAKLAND ZOO WAS NAMED ONE OF THE TEN worst zoos in the country by the Humane Society of the United States. Two years later, veterinarian Joel Parrott was hired as the zoo's new director. Parrott immediately began an ambitious plan to replace the outdated exhibits with new, state-of-the-art naturalistic habitats. Today, with one of the nation's best children's zoos, a trend-setting African elephant habitat, and exciting new exhibits on the horizon, this zoo is a leader in the field.

The zoo is situated in scenic, hilly Knowland State Park. Upon entering its front gate, you'll know you're in for an exotic experience. The entry plaza, **Karibu Village**, is modeled after Lamu Island, Kenya. The gift shop, the Island Café, and even the restrooms carry out the African theme. Across from the café is an attractive pond exhibit with lesser flamingos and African spoonbill birds.

FEATURED EXHIBITS

Up near the top of the zoo, the **African Savanna**'s main attraction is *Mahali Pa Tembo*, Swahili for "Place of the Elephant." This six-acre sloping habitat is one of the largest elephant exhibits in the nation. The African elephants range across a grassy slope and a barren plain spotted with trees, and enjoy a pool near the visitors' fence. *Simba Pori* ("Lion Country"), a two-acre habitat for a pride of lions, is within view of the elephants. When these big cats get tired of dozing in their open, rocky savanna, they can stroll over to the shady woodland section of their large habitat. Across the trail is a view of zebras and a pair of spacious African bird aviaries, one aviary featuring colorful songbirds (including orange bishops, violet turacos, and tambourine doves), and the other hosting larger birds such as pied crows, hadada ibises, and red-billed hornbills. Also in this exhibit area is a small herd of single-humped dromedary camels.

The **African Village**, an extension of the Savanna exhibit, re-creates a town on the savanna. Its snack bar, restrooms, and other buildings are African-style thatched-roof mud huts. In the center of the village is a large meerkat habitat, filled with boulders and tall termite mounds. Children can climb through their own tunnel to check out the meerkats through a close-up window. Across the path from the meerkats, a larger viewing station is built into the hillside and includes small glass-fronted exhibits of savanna monitor lizards and other reptiles. Adjacent to this viewing cave is a small open yard for African tortoises. Across the village, a tall enclosure is filled with playful vervet monkeys, also called "green monkeys." On the edge of town are lookout points into the large forested zebra habitat and a huge sloping eucalyptus forest exhibit for spotted hyenas.

Part of the Tropical Rain Forests complex (described below), the **Malayan sun bear** lives in an attractive and naturalistic home. Though the expansive valley enclosure is densely planted, the small black bear is easy to spot as she rambles through her lush habitat. Next door, another sprawling yard is inhabited by small Indian muntjac deer and Japanese sika deer.

The **Sky Ride** is the only way to get a good view of the zoo's bison and Tule elk, up in their hillside pasture. (They can be seen, in the distance, from certain places in the zoo, but not very well.) The ride also provides better looks at the tigers, camels, lions, and even the elephants. While you're on this fifteen-minute chairlift ride, be sure to take in the spectacular view of the Bay Area.

OTHER EXHIBITS

The **African Veldt** features a large arid yard, home to common elands (the largest of the antelope), dama gazelles, crowned cranes, Griffon vultures, Egyptian geese, and a small herd of reticulated giraffes. The tall giraffes are dwarfed by the exhibit's towering palm trees. The visitor viewing area lies across a wide water moat. Warthogs live across the path in a triangular yard.

A variety of primates is exhibited in the **Tropical Rain Forests** area. Three large, rocky habitats stand side-by-side, displaying Hamadryas baboons, squirrel monkeys, and chimpanzees. The chimps have the largest exhibit, a fully enclosed glass building, filled with structures to climb. Gibbons and their cousins, siamangs, each have their own densely planted island. Both enclosures for these loud lesser apes have tall trees and poles that allow them to climb more than forty feet up. Small cotton-top tamarin monkeys share a netted enclosure with beautiful chestnut-mandibled toucans. Other bird exhibits include colorful macaw parrots and Malayan wreathed hornbills. Among the birds are several small reptile exhibits, including a Taiwan beauty snake. The stars of this area, though, may be the Bengal tigers, visible from either end of their deep, grassy valley habitat. A much smaller cat also lives in this area: a bobcat, who is often seen napping!

FOR THE KIDS

The **Valley Children's Zoo** is one of the nation's best. As kids enter this four-acre complex, they pass giant sculptures of snakes and their eggs. Just beyond is a set of fascinating animal exhibits intermingled with children's play activities that relate to the nearby animals. Kids can climb into empty tortoise shells near the giant Aldabra tortoise yard. The pair of naturalistic river otter habitats, which include underwater viewing, also have a tunnel for children to climb into for a peek into the otters' den. Kids can hop across a pond on giant lily pads to reach a rabbit exhibit, or put their heads into a mounted oversized bunny head for a cute photo op. The *Bug House* includes a number of fascinating insect exhibits, among them a leaf-cutter ant fungus farm, a glass case filled with giant walking sticks, and a black widow spider visible only when children light up the display by pushing a large button. Outside, there are giant insect sculptures to play on and a rope spider web to climb. A fossilized skeleton of an enormous prehistoric crocodile introduces the American alligator pond, where the large 'gators can be seen underwater. More reptiles live in the small, but very well done, *Reptile & Amphibian Discovery* room, where kids enter through their own kid-sized doors. Among its excellent exhibits are desert lizards and a case with more than eighty tiny golden mantella frogs. Just beyond a pot-bellied pig pen is a large grassy contact yard, where kids can pet goats and sheep. On a steep hillside, ring-tailed lemurs occupy a large mountain habitat. A swaying suspension bridge runs parallel to the front of the lemur exhibit. On this same hill, a fifty-foot-tall flight cage lets visitors observe a colony of more than thirty flying foxes, fruit bats from Southeast Asia with a six-foot wingspan. Even when they're not flying, the large bats are lots of fun to watch, as they hang upside down just outside the visitor gazebo.

Just past the zoo's front gate, the **rides area** is a small amusement park with seven carnival-style rides, including a wildlife carousel and *Tiger Coaster*, a mild roller coaster for kids. Also in this area, at a small train depot, you can board the **miniature train** for a looping journey along one side of the zoo, past gorgeous views of distant San Francisco Bay.

IN PROGRESS

The above-mentioned miniature train will soon be part of a new adventure. It will rumble through a new **Australian Outback** exhibit, scheduled to open in 2008 as we go to press. From the train, riders will get to see wallaroos and flightless emus, and no visible barriers will separate these creatures from the train. Even more exciting, the zoo is constructing a new multi-species habitat for **giant pandas**. After years of negotiating with the Chinese government, Oakland has been approved to become the nation's fifth zoo to exhibit pandas. From a raised wooden walkway, visitors will see the panda pair in a rustic setting, with a cascading waterfall supplying a stream that will flow through their hillside habitat.

There are also impressive plans for **California!**, an extensive set of both grassland and woodland habitats for native California species both past and present. On forty additional acres high above the existing zoo, visitors will have a spectacular view of all five San Francisco Bay bridges as they wander among the exhibits of grizzly bears, mountain lions, wolves, and even black jaguars, cats that haven't been seen in California for decades. They will reach the exhibit via another sky ride that will transport them up from the zoo below.

San Diego Zoo

2920 Zoo Drive
San Diego, California 92101
(619) 231-1515
www.sandiegozoo.org

Grand Cayman blue iguanas can be seen at the zoo but are virtually extinct in the wild.

Hours: 9:00 a.m.-8:00 p.m. daily, mid-June to Labor Day; 9:00 a.m.-4:00 p.m. daily, rest of year; grounds close at 9:00 p.m. in summer, 6:00 p.m. in spring and early fall, and 5:00 p.m. in late fall and winter. Call or check website for dates.

Admission & Fees: Adults $24.50, children 3-11 $16.50, seniors 60+ receive 10% off admission prices, active duty military with valid ID get in free. Guided bus tour (includes use of express bus): adults $10, children $7 (members $8.50/$5); Skyfari Aerial Tram $3 (members free); "Best Value Ticket" package includes guided bus tour, express bus, Skyfari: adults $34, children $24; safari ride simulator $6; miniature train $2. For vacationers, there are multi-day tickets and package deals that include SeaWorld, Disneyland, Universal Studios, and the zoo's Wild Animal Park.

Directions: Located in Balboa Park. From I-5, take Exit 15C (Pershing Drive), and turn right onto 16th Street. Follow for 0.3 miles, then turn right onto Park Boulevard. Follow for 1.4 miles, then turn left onto Zoo Place and follow for 0.2 miles to zoo parking lot. From the CA-163 freeway, take Exit 1B (Park Boulevard/I-5). Follow Park Boulevard for 1 mile, then turn left onto Zoo Place. Follow for 0.2 miles to zoo parking lot. Bus Route #7 stops two blocks from zoo.

Don't Miss: Ituri Forest, Gorilla Tropics, Monkey Trails and Forest Tales, Polar Bear Plunge, Giant Panda Research Station, Tiger River, koalas, Absolutely Apes, African Rock Kopje, Reptile House and Reptile Mesa, Sun Bear Forest, guided bus tour, Skyfari.

For Kids: Children's Zoo, Skyfari Aerial Tram, Wild Earth safari simulator ride, Balboa Park Railway miniature train.

Authors' Tips: We recommend you purchase Best Value tickets, which include the guided bus tour. Located within 100-acre Balboa Park, this zoo has miles of trails winding in and out of steep canyons. Take advantage of the long moving walkways to save energy. It's a good idea to start the day by boarding one of the double-decker buses for a guided tour. The 35-minute tour, which covers more than three miles and passes the majority of the exhibits, provides a good introduction to the zoo, and drivers share interesting information and entertaining stories about the animals. After the tour, guests will be better equipped to choose which animals to visit. The zoo's restaurants and gift shops are, like everything else here, superb. The Treehouse, adjacent to Gorilla Tropics, is a four-story replica of an African plantation house on stilts. It includes two restaurants with outdoor eating areas that provide sweeping views of the zoo.

Edutainment: Outstanding free animal shows are presented several times daily. The sea lion show, "It Began With a Roar," is held in the large Wegeforth Bowl and features sea lions, harbor seals, dogs, and other animals. These animals demonstrate natural behaviors and deliver a message about the importance of environmental conservation. "The Wild Ones," with a variety of North American and exotic animals, is held in Hunte Amphitheater. "Dr. Zoolittle's Amazing Animal Adventures," a fun look at bugs that's directed at kids, is presented at the small Clark Theater in the Children's Zoo. Many other animal encounters and enrichment programs are held around the zoo. Check the insert included with the zoo map for times and locations.

THE SAN DIEGO ZOO IS ONE OF THE WORLD'S BEST. IN THE UNITED States, only New York's Bronx Zoo is in the same league. Over 4,500 animals of more than 800 species are exhibited, the greatest diversity of any zoo in the U.S. Many of the rarest and most popular animals can be viewed in some of the best reproductions of natural habitats we've ever seen. As a tourist attraction, the zoo is on a par with Disneyland and SeaWorld; many vacationers who go to those parks will also spend a day at this zoo. This means large crowds, especially in summer. But San Diego's near-perfect climate makes a visit here a pleasant experience at any time of the year.

The plant collection is so superb that the zoo is accredited as a botanical garden. Orchids, coral trees, ferns, palms, cacti, redwood trees, and many Hawaiian plants are just some of the species that contribute to the diversity of this botanical masterpiece.

FEATURED EXHIBITS

Visitors can easily spend more time in the four-acre **Ituri Forest** exhibit than anywhere else in the zoo. The centerpiece of this amazing mixed-species complex is the hippo pool, where the massive river hippos actually seem graceful when you see them underwater through the long, glass-fronted viewing gallery. The seating area is usually filled with mesmerized viewers. The hippos share their 150,000-gallon pool with tilapia fish, which help filter the water by eating hippo dung (really!). Just outside is another entertaining streamside habitat where, on both sides of the visitor path, swamp monkeys seem to enjoy playing with African spot-necked otters, while DeBrazza's guenon monkeys romp through the trees above. As if that weren't enough, on the other side of the hippo pool is a shady forest exhibit of rare okapis, endangered relatives of giraffes.

A lush African rain forest is re-created in the **Gorilla Tropics** complex. The path to the gorilla display crosses a bridge near a cascading waterfall. Two troops of lowland gorillas can be seen in their open meadow from four different angles: three from across a moat, one through a wide window in the large viewing station. The apes' habitat is planted with bamboo, banana, and fig trees. One of the world's largest walk-through flight cages, *Scripps Aviary*, has a towering mesh roof that's almost invisible from below. Inside, a treetop-level walkway provides good views of more than 130 jewel-colored African birds, including blue-breasted kingfishers, while a ground-level path provides a closer look at the ground birds, such as shoebill storks. Nearby, another great ape species, bonobos (also known as pygmy chimpanzees) share this African jungle habitat. The agile and acrobatic pygmy chimps live in a grassy hillside habitat enhanced with waterfalls, pools, and a natural playground formed by curved and twisted palm trees. This zoo is known amongst its peers for its success breeding bonobos, so expect to see some adorable babies here. The bonobos and gorillas often hang out next to the visitor windows. Colobus monkeys, crowned eagles, and rock pythons are displayed in nearby attractive habitats.

Another major exhibit, **Monkey Trails and Forest Tales**, which opened in 2005, has large mesh enclosures for nine different species of Asian and African monkeys, plus the birds, reptiles, and other mammals that share the monkeys' homelands. At the entrance to this elaborate exhibit is *Flamingo Lagoon*, with more than ninety beautiful Caribbean flamingos. Visitors enter the monkey habitats at treetop level, where these entertaining primates can be seen in their tall trees. The rare and colorful monkeys on display include Wolf's guenons, Angolan colobus monkeys, spot-nosed guenons, and golden-bellied mangabeys. A stairway leads down to the forest floor, where black mangabey monkeys and blue-faced mandrills are usually seen. Further up the trail, two rare swine species, Visayan warty pigs and Bornean bearded pigs, can be seen along both sides of the raised wooden walkway. A net enclosure displays clouded leopards. The sometimes confusing maze of exhibits ends at an African riverbed, where pygmy hippos and slender-snouted crocodiles swim with hundreds of colorful fish. Behind the hippos, a gallery of smaller jungle animals includes dwarf crocodiles, venomous green mamba snakes, scorpions, and an assortment of lizards.

The popular **Polar Bear Plunge** is a replica of a summertime Arctic tundra. To enter this four-acre exhibit, visitors first walk through an aviary, home to arctic diving ducks, including blue-billed ruddy ducks. Watch through a window as they dive in their icy stream. The exhibit's focal point is the *Plunge*, one of the world's largest polar bear habitats, with 130,000 gallons of chilled water for the white bears to dive into. Each plunge is met with shrieks of delight from the crowds gathered in the huge underwater viewing gallery. Above water on their sandy tundra bank, the bears are backed by a herd of Siberian reindeer. Other cold weather species exhibited here include Siberian red-breasted geese, Chinese red pandas, and the secretive, house cat-sized Pallas' cat, native to central Asia.

For panda lovers, the zoo's **Giant Panda Research Station** is the place to be. This is the largest collection of this species outside of China. In 1999, panda mother Bai Yun gave birth to Hua Mei, who became the first panda cub born in North America to survive to adulthood. Bai Yun has continued to produce healthy cubs for San Diego; her fourth cub was born in 2007. The pandas live in two habitats furnished with vegetation and towering trees to climb. During the unofficial "panda playtime," there are usually long, slow-moving lines on the elevated visitor pathways. The pandas can be incredibly funny, and fun to watch, as they climb trees, summersault, and roll around their habitat. Next door, the *Giant Panda Discovery Center* has interactive graphics, a climb-in panda den, and a panda-themed gift shop.

Starting from Monkey Trails (described above), **Tiger River** is a riverbed pathway through an Asian rain forest. With the sweet smell of jasmine and ginger plants hanging in the misty air, this exhibit has not only the look, sound, and feel of a real jungle, but also the fragrance. Along a winding path, visitors encounter ten exhibits featuring over a hundred animals. Freshwater crocodiles can be viewed both above and below water. Tropical birds, a large reticulated python, web-footed fishing cats, and Malayan tapirs are also displayed. The heart of this three-acre exhibit is the hillside lair of deep-orange Malayan tigers, the smallest subspecies of tiger.

Koalas

With more **koalas** than any zoo outside of Australia, San Diego has been known in the zoo world as the (non-Australian) "koala capital." A wooden walkway makes a semi-circle around a small yard shared by tree-bound koalas and ground-based wallabies. Some of these plush-coated marsupials are displayed behind glass along the opposite side of the walkway. Another yard displays tree kangaroos. Because the koalas here have been very fruitful, it is not unusual to see babies.

Absolutely Apes is home to families, including playful juveniles, of intelligent orangutans and vocal siamangs. These apes' natural habitat seems larger than it really is, because the back of the exhibit runs down the hillside, out of human sight. The spacious glass-fronted habitat is enhanced with many climbing structures, bamboo-like sway poles, and ropes for the orangs and siamangs to play on. There is almost always at least one large orangutan sitting up next to the wide visitor window, resting on a deep layer of mulch. The sway poles and mulch seem to extend right into the visitor area, as guests stand on a comfy rubberized floor that resembles the mulch groundcover in the exhibit. When the siamangs start their loud vocalizations, they can be heard all over the zoo. Near the exhibit's entrance is a tree-filled habitat of François' langur monkeys.

While kopje exhibits are becoming common in zoos today, this zoo's **East African Kopje** was one of the first. Small, agile klipspringer antelope are at home on the giant boulders, while pygmy mongooses scurry in and out of view. Native kopje birds on display include bateleur eagles and other colorful birds, spread out among two aviaries.

The world-renowned **Reptile House**, a Spanish-style structure, is unusual in that visitors do not go inside; they "window shop" around it through open-air hallways. Its extensive collection includes a variety of rattlesnakes, pythons, cobras, vipers, lizards, turtles, and frogs. In an attached exhibit room, a Komodo dragon is displayed in an exhibit that includes an artificial deer carcass, illustrating this gigantic lizard's natural diet. Behind the main building is **Reptile Mesa**, with four smaller reptile galleries and large outdoor enclosures for centenarian Galapagos tortoises, rock iguanas, desert lizards, and a swamp habitat for large Asian turtles and pointy-snouted Indian gharial crocodiles. This is, in our opinion, the best reptile exhibit in the nation.

Another Asian jungle is evoked in the **Sun Bear Forest**. The habitat is filled with giant palms, ficus trees, ginger plants, pools, waterfalls, and climbing structures. Sun bears, the world's smallest bears, and lion-tailed macaques, rare black monkeys with lion-like manes, are amusing to watch from many different viewpoints as they roam their respective enclosures. San Diego is the only zoo to have successfully bred sun bears. Also displayed here are Gabriella's crested gibbons, shaggy, raccoon-like binturongs, and Asian tropical birds in another towering aviary.

OTHER EXHIBITS

Up on **Elephant Mesa**, African and Asian elephants live together in a large central area with their own pool. Around them, corrals hold giraffes and both Central American and Malayan tapirs. Other animals in this area include giant anteaters, capybaras (giant aquatic rodents) and wild lowland anoa cattle. Short, flightless kiwi birds, the national symbol of New Zealand, live in a small nocturnal building that is one of the zoo's few indoor exhibits. Not far away, flying foxes (which are actually bats) hang upside down at the front of their cage, near the meerkats, forest hogs, and double-humped Bactrian camels.

Many of the zoo's carnivores reside in two canyons on either side of Elephant Mesa. **Bear Canyon** features spectacled bears, Transvaal lions, and small-clawed otters. Wild cats, including a black jaguar, snow leopards, pumas, Persian leopards, and lynx are found in **Cat Canyon**, along with striped hyenas, honey badgers (or ratels), raccoon-like coatimundis, Kazakhstan corsac foxes, warthogs, Japanese serow mountain goats, and Chinese goral mountain goats. Aside from its namesake bears, the animals in **Panda Canyon** include red river hogs and a dwarf cassowary, a flightless bird from New Guinea with a bright blue neck. Across from the koalas are exhibits of rare tree kangaroos, tiny Parma wallabies, and pacaranas (spotted Brazilian rodents).

In the **Wings of Australasia** complex, twenty-three lushly planted aviaries exhibit a rainbow of over ninety tropical birds from Australia, Southeast Asia, and the Pacific islands. Feathered specimens include Micronesian kingfishers, wrinkled hornbill birds, various rare lories, and the dazzlingly beautiful Raggiana birds of paradise.

Komodo dragon in zoo's world famous reptile collection.

Birds of all sizes and colors are housed in expansive aviaries and smaller enclosures scattered across the zoo. The **Owens Aviary**, featuring birds from Southeast Asia and Australia in a rain forest environment, is one of the world's largest walk-through aviaries. Nearly two hundred birds of about sixty species can be seen from two levels, and its glass-fronted stream displays pretty rainbowfish. In the popular **Hummingbird Aviary**, these tiny multicolored birds hover and dart mere inches from visitors in a compact walk-through jungle. Elsewhere, a large waterfowl pond hosts pelicans, cranes, and other wading birds. Near the pandas, a raised walkway offers high-level views of **birds of prey**, including Stellar's sea eagles, harpy eagles, and Andean condors, in spacious flight cages.

Most of the popular **Horn & Hoof Mesa** exhibits have been closed during construction of the upcoming Elephant Odyssey exhibit (see below). But around the corner, and across from the polar bears, some remnants of this row of enclosures are still worth a visit. These include Grevy's zebras, Chacoan peccaries (wild pigs from the Andes), and takins (mountain goats from China).

FOR THE KIDS

The **Children's Zoo** has a long legacy of delighting children. In fact, over forty years ago, one of this book's authors actually rode a giant tortoise here (something that's not allowed anymore). In a petting paddock, children can pet sheep and comb goats' fur. Popular small mammals displayed here include pygmy marmoset monkeys, spider monkeys, naked mole-rats, an ocelot cat, meerkats, wombats (burrowing Australian marsupials), and an otter habitat with underwater viewing. The *Mouse House* is actually a giant loaf of bread, replaced weekly, in which the mice live and which they devour, while the *Insect House* displays several intriguing bugs, including giant stick insects. Scaled to a toddler's level, two animal nurseries are highlights of the visit for most kids. Through several windows, human "moms" can sometimes be seen caring for diapered baby apes.

The rides and shows at this zoo are among the best we've ever seen. The colorful gondolas of the **Skyfari** aerial tramway carry riders on a one-third-mile cable across the zoo at a height of 170 feet. At its peak, riders get a superb panoramic view of the zoo below, downtown San Diego, and the Pacific Ocean. Nearby, the **Wild Earth safari simulator ride** attracts adventurous kids, while smaller fry like the **miniature train** ride outside the zoo's front gate.

IN PROGRESS

In late 2007, construction began on what will become one of the zoo's largest-ever exhibits, **Elephant Odyssey**. Within this seven-acre exhibit, guests will be able to enter the elephant care area, walk a winding interpretive trail, and enjoy an archeological dig site. The elephant exhibit will be part of a complex that will display at least twenty different species, including California condors, lions, and jaguars. They're considering a theme that will connect the exhibited animals with similar species that roamed Southern California during the Pleistocene era. For example, the elephants in this revolutionary exhibit will share their habitat with tapirs and capybaras: species from different continents whose ancestors lived together in prehistoric California. The exhibit is scheduled to open in the spring of 2009 as we go to press.

San Francisco Zoo

1 Zoo Road
San Francisco, California 94132
(415) 753-7080
www.sfzoo.org

Hours: 10:00 a.m.-5:00 p.m. daily. Children's Zoo closes at 4:30 p.m., Animal Resource Center open house 2:00 p.m. -3:00 p.m. on weekends.

Admission & Fees: Adults $11, seniors 65+ and youth 12-17 $8, children 3-11 $5; San Francisco residents $9, $4.50, and $2.50, respectively. Free admission to San Franciscans first Wednesday of the month. Muni bus riders get a $1 discount (save your Muni receipt!). GPS Zoo Ranger $6.95. Little Puffer steam train $3, carousel $2. Parking $6, limited street parking available. Participates in reciprocity program.

A grizzly bear fishes in Grizzly Gulch.

Directions: Located two miles south of Golden Gate Park, just off Great Highway. From the Golden Gate Bridge, take the 19th Avenue/Golden Gate Park exit and follow CA-1 South for 2.2 miles. Turn right onto Fulton Street, follow for 2.1 miles, then left onto Great Highway. After 2.5 miles, turn left onto Sloat Boulevard. Zoo is 0.2 miles up, on the right. From the Bay Bridge, follow I-80 for 2 miles to the US-101 South exit. Follow US-101 for 2.1 miles to the Daly City exit, get on I-280 South, and follow for 3.9 miles to Exit 49 (Westlake District). Get on John Daly Boulevard and proceed for 1.2 miles, turn right, and follow Skyline Boulevard (CA-35) for 1.9 miles. Turn left, follow Great Highway for 0.8 miles, then turn right onto Sloat Boulevard. Zoo is 0.2 miles up on the right. From the south, take I-280 to Exit 49 (Westlake District), get on John Daly Boulevard, and follow above directions. Zoo is serviced by Muni/BART system. Muni buses #23 and #18 stop at the zoo, and the Muni Metro L-Taraval station is a block away.

Don't Miss: African Savanna, Grizzly Gulch, Gorilla Preserve, Koala Crossing, Primate Discovery Center, Lemur Forest, Penguin Island.

For Kids: Children's Zoo, Dentzel Carousel, Little Puffer steam train, Playfield playground.

Authors' Tips: Three outdoor cafes offer an unusual variety of food that includes pastas, fish 'n chips, burritos, and sushi and other Asian dishes, as well as standard fast food. Because the zoo is located just a few hundred yards from the Pacific Ocean, be prepared for the city's famous fog to roll in at any time. Bring jackets, as it can get cold even in summer. Rent a GPS-guided handheld "Zoo Ranger" for a special tour.

Edutainment: In the Wildlife Theatre, 20- to 30-minute live animal presentations are scheduled twice daily in summer. Animal feedings are held at several exhibits, including penguins, big cats, and grizzly bears. Many entertaining and educational programs are held throughout the day in the Children's Zoo, such as "Meet the Keeper" talks and a weekend Hatchery Tour.

IN A CITY OFFERING THE GOLDEN GATE BRIDGE, CHINATOWN, cable cars, and Fisherman's Wharf among its top attractions, this zoo could easily be overlooked. Yet more than a million people each year visit the hundred-acre San Francisco Zoo. Within it, the exhibits are roughly distributed into five continental groupings, with a few obvious exceptions.

FEATURED EXHIBITS

The three-acre **African Savanna** offers a revolutionary way to view animals – from within the middle of the habitat! Visitors enter the exhibit through one of two tunnels (one on each side) and emerge on a bridge that crosses the savanna's watering hole. All around are giraffes, zebras, kudu antelope, scimitar-horned oryxes, ostriches, crowned cranes, and marabou storks – all part of the wraparound African panorama. This expansive grassland is also visible from surrounding overlooks, and the savanna's fringe is well shaded by cypress and palm trees. The walk-through *African Aviary* features exotic hammerkop birds, two ibis species, and other African birds.

The animal on California's state flag is displayed in **Grizzly Gulch**, where grizzly bears inhabit a one-acre habitat, completed in 2007. Behind a window, the bears wander their pretty flower-filled meadow, climb a rocky twenty-foot hill, fish from the mountain stream waterfall, and swim in their large pool, which is convenient to the viewing station. Well-placed heated rocks also help tempt these massive creatures close to the viewing station.

Gorilla Preserve, a circular outdoor habitat, is one of the nation's largest gorilla displays. It is lavishly landscaped with waterfalls, trees, rocky outcroppings, and even authentic African grasses. This naturalistic habitat can be viewed from above, or from behind a wall of windows.

At **Koala Crossing**, the cuddly marsupials are displayed in an outdoor eucalyptus grove. During inclement weather, they are moved inside, behind a window, on the opposite side of the viewing area. On a side wall, a video display projects information about koalas and their native environment.

This is one of the premier zoos in the country for primate-watching. In tall outdoor atrium cages and in lush meadows, the **Primate Discovery Center** displays some of the rarest and most endangered monkeys in the world, including François' langur monkeys, stunning mandrills, quick-moving patas monkeys, vocal siamangs, black howler monkeys, and lion-tailed macaque monkeys. On the lower level, emperor tamarin monkeys are exhibited behind glass.

Next to the primate center, the **Lipman Family Lemur Forest** displays five different species of lemurs: ring-tailed, black-and-white ruffed, red ruffed, white-fronted, and black. These primitive, large-eyed primates, visible at treetop-level from a raised boardwalk, have a variety of trees to climb, including a towering cypress.

Penguin Island is a 200-foot-long pool with the country's largest colony of Magellanic penguins, native to South America. More than 160 penguin chicks have hatched on the exhibit's island. Nearby, river otters swim in another aquatic exhibit.

OTHER EXHIBITS

The zoo's big cats, displayed in lushly planted outdoor grottoes surrounding the **Lion House**, include lions and tigers (both Sumatran and Siberian, also known as Amur), as well as a small enclosure of fishing cats. Lion roars from inside this 1940 building can be heard all over the zoo. Way off the main path, the **Feline Conservation Center** displays yet more cats. While the twelve mesh enclosures are quite ordinary, they are perfectly set up for breeding. The ocelots, fishing cats, and snow leopards have all had remarkable reproductive success in this remote location.

At the **Australian Walkabout,** a semi-circular path leads through a large forest clearing yard for red and gray kangaroos, wallaroos, wallabies, and flightless emus. Colorful cassowaries, flightless birds from nearby New Guinea, are displayed in an adjacent wooded enclosure.

The **South American Tropical Forest** is an impressive conversion of a stately historic towering building into a convincing lush indoor jungle. Colorful free-flying birds include ibises and spoonbills, while the impressive reptiles seen here include a fifteen-foot anaconda snake and a pair of broad-nosed caiman crocodiles. **Puente al Sur**, or "Bridge to the South," is a mixed-species exhibit of South American animals. From a bridge, visitors can see giant anteaters, black-and-white Maguari storks, black-necked swans, and capybaras (enormous aquatic rodents) in a large hillside habitat with a marshy pond. A pair of rare shaggy-coated mountain tapirs here represent approximately one percent of the world's population of this diminishing species.

Across from Grizzly Gulch, **Eagle Island** is the densely planted home of a breeding pair of bald eagles. Brown and white pelicans live in the surrounding lake. Not far away, the zoo's North American region is growing with a new bison exhibit, completed in 2007. Next to the grizzlies, the **Bear Grottoes** are five traditional stone enclosures for spectacled and polar bears. In the nearby **Elephant Seal Rehab** pool, the San Francisco Zoo participates with the Marine Mammal Center across the Bay to help care for orphaned or injured elephant seal pups from February through June. At press time, no other American zoo exhibits these massive seals.

In ordinary open exhibits around the old Pachyderm House (which is currently closed) are an Asian one-horned rhino, a Nile hippo, and a Central American (or Baird's) tapir. The latter two pachyderms each have their own pool. A small pool nearby holds a gray seal. Other animal exhibits scattered throughout the zoo include black rhinos, eland and blackbuck antelope, and warthogs, all in separate enclosures; a Caribbean flamingo pool; a row of bird aviaries with hornbills and parrots; and the **Triple Grotto** exhibit, a rocky home for chimpanzees.

FOR THE KIDS

The six-acre **Children's Zoo** is one of the most attractive areas of the zoo. With colorful barns, large animal corrals, and a heavily populated duck pond, the *Family Farm* offers many opportunities to pet and groom various rare domestic animals, including Navajo-Churro sheep and Nigerian dwarf goats. The rarest animal here is an American Cream draft horse. The *Native American Animals* exhibit features small creatures native to the Americas: squirrel monkeys, wild turkeys, and coatis (relatives of raccoons). Even more popular are the residents of the back-to-back *Meerkat and Prairie Dog Exhibit*. Both of these burrowing mammals are shown behind glass walls in large colonies, where they pop in and out of the red soil. Many interactive activities here teach children about these fascinating animals, including a sandbox to dig in, kid-size burrows, and a cutaway model of the prairie dog den. Hawks and eagles from the animal shows stand guard outside the *Koret Animal Resource Center*, where the zoo's education animals are cared for and trained. It is worth a stop here to look through the windows; you may get a peek at some ultra-rare and beautiful San Francisco garter snakes. On the educational *Nature Trail*, teenage volunteers provide close-up views of a variety of uncaged animals. The popular *Insect Zoo* consists of a large room full of glass terrariums housing a wide assortment of bugs and spiders, including giant walking sticks, various tarantulas, termites, silkworms, and a working beehive. Outside, there is a large rope spider web to climb on.

When the kids tire of animals and bugs, they can ride the antique 1921 **Dentzel Carousel** just outside the Children's Zoo. An even more historic ride is available on **Little Puffer**, a 1904 miniature steam train. There is also a large playground in the **Playfield** area.

IN PROGRESS

A new state-of-the-art **rhino and hippo exhibit** will soon improve the lives of the Asian rhino and Nile hippo. Using land from the former elephant yard, this greatly expanded exhibit will allow the zoo to bring in companions for these animals. As this book goes to press, the new exhibit is under construction and scheduled to open in late summer of 2008.

The zoo has a large walk-through aviary, **Binnowee Landing**, which has been closed for renovations. It is likely to reopen soon.

Honolulu Zoo

151 Kapahulu Avenue
Honolulu, Hawaii 96815
(808) 971-7171
www.honoluluzoo.org

Hours: 9:00 a.m.-4:30 p.m. daily. Closed Christmas Day.

Admission & Fees: Adults $8, students 13+ (with ID) $4, children 6-12 $1, family pass $25. Parking: 25¢ per hour. Free parking also available, at the Shell parking lot on Monsarrat Avenue.

Nene geese, Hawaii's state bird, have a sanctuary here.

Directions: If you're staying in a Waikiki hotel, get on Kalakaua Avenue (the main drag along the ocean) and walk towards Diamond Head crater. The zoo is at the intersection with Kapahulu Avenue, in Queen Kapi'olani Park. From I-H1, take Exit 25A (Waikiki/Honolulu Zoo). Quickly take a slight left onto South King Street, then turn right onto Kapahulu Avenue. Follow Kapahulu Avenue for 1.3 miles to the zoo parking lot on the left.

Don't Miss: African Savanna, Kipuka Nene Sanctuary, orangutan habitat.

For Kids: Keiki (children's) Zoo, small playground outside the Keiki Zoo.

Authors' Tips: There are many opportunities to shoot memorable photos of exotic animals, like zebras and giraffes, with the famous Diamond Head crater in the background.

Edutainment: Volunteers and zookeepers give animal presentations and share information about specific animals throughout the zoo. Check signs within the zoo for times and places of these activities.

LOCATION, LOCATION, LOCATION – THAT'S THE STORY OF THE Honolulu Zoo. Its placement on Waikiki Beach is ideal for attracting many of Hawaii's millions of annual tourists, including a large number of foreign visitors. Another advantage to this locale is the near-perfect tropical climate. This makes the zoo well-suited for exhibiting tropical species from around the world. In fact, it has been exceptionally successful at breeding very rare birds and reptiles from the tropics. The great climate also means the zoo is filled with lush tropical greenery, stately palms, and beautiful and fragrant flowers.

There is, however, a drawback to the zoo's location. Hawaii has a notoriously fragile ecosystem of native plants and animals. Among the major threats to the state's wildlife are animals introduced from elsewhere. Hawaiians look warily at Guam, where non-native snakes invaded the island and nearly devastated several bird species. Because of this threat, there are strict state regulations dictating which animals can be exhibited and bred, both in the zoo and elsewhere in the state. Despite these restrictions, the zoo has accumulated an impressive and attractive collection of animals, and has become the third most popular tourist attraction on the island.

FEATURED EXHIBITS

The excellent **African Savanna** is a twelve-acre re-creation of four different African environments. At the entrance, a sign welcomes you to the "Karibuni Reserve," enhancing the feeling that you're actually traveling to Africa. The *riverine environment* here includes a riverbank exhibit of waterbuck antelope, a pool of hippos with close-up views for visitors, and Nile crocodiles, visible through underwater glass. An African marsh displays wading birds, including flamingos, spoonbills, and pelicans. The *grassland environment* is dominated by a large savanna yard, populated by giraffes, zebras, kudu antelope, ostriches, and other African land birds. A white rhino lives nearby, as do muddy warthogs. Down a side path, sleek cheetahs can be seen from within a cave, or from an open overlook higher up. A tour of the *kopje environment* takes visitors through a winding, deep gully cut into artificial rock. Agile klipspringer antelope and crested porcupines can be found among the boulders. Visible through glass walls between the stones, a small pride of lions usually rests in the shade. Nearby, spotted hyenas are best seen through another large wall of glass. Intermingled among the rocks are a set of small open-air habitats featuring a variety of native kopje lizards, including savanna monitors and agama lizards. Next to a small plaza that includes a refreshment stand, a mob of meerkats is visible through a large glass wall. Finally, the *forest environment* begins with a sprawling one-acre naturalistic chimpanzee habitat. Visitors get a 180-degree view of this entertaining troop of chimps through glass panels. Nearby ground hornbills (short black land birds) inhabit an attractive exhibit just finished in 2007. The *Manyara Bird Sanctuary* is an enjoyable walk-through aviary filled with fascinating African birds, including hammerkops and rainbow-colored turacos. In a side exhibit, a serval, looking like a miniature cheetah, keeps the birds alert – servals are their natural predators. Endangered black rhinos are visible from many vantage points. At the end of this fascinating trail, a pack of wild dogs can be seen both from an overlook and through wide glass windows from within a cave.

The **Kipuka Nene Sanctuary** is home to nearly a dozen Nene geese – Hawaii's state bird. To local residents, the Nene is almost sacred, so seeing one of these endangered birds in the wild is a real treat. Seeing them in this attractive grassy exhibit with a shallow pool is nearly as exciting. Just across from the geese, you'll see Hawaiian hawks, which are even rarer, and sometimes predators of young Nene.

Rusti the orangutan is a local celebrity in Honolulu. After spending eight sad years in a substandard mainland private zoo, he was rescued and eventually brought here. But until this **orangutan habitat** was built in 2005, it appeared Rusti would be moving on. Then, on behalf of the many heartbroken Oahu children, the Mayor of Honolulu intervened, leading to the construction of this modern exhibit for Rusti and his new companion, Violet. Their spacious open-air cage gives the happy orangutan couple great opportunities for exercise.

OTHER EXHIBITS

This zoo hosts many tourists from Asia, who, it has found, tend to be especially partial to beautiful birds. To satisfy these and other bird lovers, the zoo showcases a large collection of pretty tropical birds – a majority from the surrounding Pacific Rim nations, which find the Pacific climate of Hawaii just delightful. Just inside the zoo's entrance is a tropical pool filled with Caribbean flamingos. Around the corner, the *World of Ducks* pond has more than a dozen varieties of wading ducks, including Hawaiian Koloa ducks. In this same area, long rows of bird cages include the *Toucan Trail* (housing toucans, king vultures, and other South American beauties), *Birds of the World*, and *Paradise Row*, the home of the zoo's famous birds-of-paradise. Honolulu has had great success breeding these spectacularly beautiful birds.

Cutting across the middle of the zoo is an impressive collection of reptiles. Most prominent is the **Komodo dragon exhibit** and breeding center. Honolulu's tropical climate makes this a superb place to breed the world's largest lizards. Baby dragons can be seen across the zoo in the **Herpetarium**, where a low row of terrariums display various tropical lizards and other reptiles. Between these two reptile exhibits, large alligators drift in their pool. Next to the 'gators, another spacious lagoon holds gharials, Indian crocodiles with unusually skinny snouts. The zoo is well known in the zoo world for exhibiting all four of the world's largest tortoise species, including many Galapagos and Aldabra tortoises.

The orangutans mentioned above are actually the centerpiece of a small collection of primate exhibits, which also includes gibbons, siamangs, lemurs, long-limbed spider monkeys, and endangered François' langurs, small black monkeys from China.

Near the Komodo dragons, Sumatran tigers enjoy an attractive habitat that's recently been renovated and expanded. Other Asian animals around the zoo include elephants and a sun bear.

FOR THE KIDS

Redesigned and expanded in 2006, the **Keiki Zoo** is perfect for little keikis ("children" in Hawaiian). Here, kids can get up close to a wide variety of exotic domestic animals, including pot-bellied pigs, miniature zebu cattle, and dwarf goats. Keikis are encouraged to learn while enjoying farm- and zoo-related activities, such as milking a cow or even bathing a pony. Crawl-through tunnels let kids pop up in clear bubble domes among the guinea pigs or in the koi fish tank.

IN PROGRESS

The new orangutan exhibit was the first Asian habitat to be renovated. Soon, the zoo hopes to do the same for its largest animals, elephants. A larger exhibit would be necessary for housing a bull, should a male be born here through artificial insemination. At press time, the elephant expansion project is half-done, and the new holding area completed. But it may be a few more years before visitors see the elephants in their new exhibit.

Oregon Zoo

4001 SW Canyon Road
Portland, Oregon 97221
(503) 226-1561
www.oregonzoo.org

Packy the elephant is a zoo favorite.

Hours: 8:00 a.m.-6:00 p.m. daily, Memorial Day-Labor Day; 9:00 a.m.-6:00 p.m. daily, mid-April–Memorial Day and Labor Day–mid-September; 9:00 a.m.-4:00 p.m. daily, mid-September–mid-April. The zoo grounds close one hour after the gates do. Closed Christmas Day.

Admission & Fees: Adults $9.75, seniors 65+ $8.25, children 3-11 $6.75. Note: 25¢ of admission fee goes to local conservation projects. Zoo Loop train: adults $3, seniors and children $2.50; Washington Park train: adults $4, seniors and children $3; 3-D thrill ride $4.50; lorikeet feeding $1; parking $2.

Directions: From I-5 northbound, take Exit 300A (I-405 South). From I-5 southbound, take Exit 302B (I-405 North). Follow I-405 to Exit 1D (US-26/Beaverton). On US-26, proceed for 1.6 miles to the first exit, Exit 72 (Zoo/Forestry Center). Merge left onto SW Canyon Road. The zoo will be on the right almost immediately.

Don't Miss: Great Northwest, Asian elephants, Africa Savanna, Africa Rain Forest, Amazon Flooded Forest, Island Pigs of Asia.

For Kids: Washington Park and Zoo Railway, Family Farm, Lorikeet Landing, African Goat Kraal, 3-D thrill ride.

Authors' Tips: If you can, visit on a "three-buck Tuesday," the second Tuesday of each month, when the admission is only $3. No need to worry about the weather, as most exhibits have sheltered viewing areas in case of rain. The zoo's gift shop makes and sells fudge – stop by to taste the many delicious flavors! Visit on Mother's or Father's Day to see which animal mom or dad receives the "parent of the year" award.

Edutainment: During the summer, the excellent "Wild Life Live" show, featuring birds of prey, is presented at the Concert Lawn's Bandshell. There are farm-themed demonstrations such as sheep shearing in the Family Farm three times daily.

OPENED IN 1887, THIS SIXTY-FOUR-ACRE ZOO IS THE OLDEST ZOO west of the Mississippi River. Formerly known as the Metro Washington Park Zoo, it was renamed "Oregon Zoo" in 1998 to better reflect its location and emphasis on conserving the state's native wildlife. The zoo is helping to restore several animals that are either rare or extinct in Oregon, including California condors, sea otters, western pond turtles, and Oregon silverspot butterflies. Although it's located just outside of downtown Portland, the zoo feels a thousand miles away from any major metropolitan area.

FEATURED EXHIBITS

The **Great Northwest** exhibit perfectly represents the zoo's commitment to Pacific Northwest species. Your journey begins in the Cascade Mountains and finishes on the shores of the Pacific. Just outside the zoo's entrance plaza is *Cascade Crest*, an alpine meadow home to Rocky Mountain goats. After crossing a hundred-foot suspension bridge, visitors approach an overlook of *Black Bear Ridge*, an exhibit set in a sloping wooded ravine. Along the trail, bobcats are visible in their heated den, before you descend deeper into the gorge. *Eagle Canyon,* which was named "Exhibit of the Year" a few years ago by the AZA, shows the relationship between bald eagles and salmon. A beautiful waterfall statue illustrates the difficult upstream journey salmon must make to reach their spawning grounds. A fork in the trail leads to either an elevated look at the eagles, or a face-to-face encounter with the salmon. The path continues on to the *Cascade Stream and Pond*, a marsh wetland with a variety of animals. Underwater views of otters and beavers immediately draw your attention. Inside a small interpretive building, a long dark hallway is lined with terrariums of fish, amphibians, and reptiles. Most notable here are the western pond turtles, a rare native species that the zoo breeds and releases into the nearby Columbia River Gorge. An exhibit set in an old mining cabin reveals the nocturnal ringtail cat, or cacomistle. Back outside, you pass through a net-covered marsh aviary populated with ducks and herons, and on to a closer view of the black bears. Across the path from the bears, at *Cougar Crossing*, thin piano wire separates visitors from the shy, elusive mountain lions. Rock wall ledges and trees give these cougars plenty of high places to hide, but a small windowed cave brings visitors close to their heated den. Walk through the *Family Farm* (see below) to *Elk Meadow*, home to a herd of Roosevelt elk and a pack of gray wolves. Finally, the sound of crashing waves welcomes visitors to *Steller Cove*. A tide pool stocked with anemones and urchins lies beside a tunnel that leads to underwater views of Steller sea lions. Reaching lengths of twelve feet and weighing more than two tons, these magnificent pinnipeds dwarf their more familiar California sea lion cousins. Watch from an elevated platform or step down to touch the glass as they swim by. A ramp leads down to an underwater kelp forest filled with sea cucumbers, perch, rockfish, crabs, and sea stars. A neighboring pool holds southern sea otters, once native to Oregon but now found only off the California coast.

No zoo in America has had more success with breeding **Asian elephants**. Packy, born here in 1962, was the first elephant born in the Western Hemisphere in forty-four years. Nearly thirty calves have been birthed here since Packy, including seven of his offspring. Adult bull elephants are usually found in a front yard or inside the building. The herd of females lives in the larger back yard, which boasts an 80,000-gallon pool. A long path travels the length of the enclosure, climbs a hill for a bird's eye view, and eventually reaches the *Lilah Callen Holden Elephant Museum*, which offers historical information on both wild and captive elephants, along with a giant mastodon skeleton. Most interesting here is the Oregon Zoo's elephant family tree, which traces the lineage of its resident pachyderms back more than fifty years.

Africa Savanna is a four-acre replica of the dry East African plains. The domed *Howard Vollum Aviary* exhibits nearly twenty species of birds, including beautiful, brightly colored turacos. Visitors can stroll inside the aviary, or peer into the exhibit from treetop level while eating in the *AfriCafé*. A winding path leads past black rhinos, a hippo pool, and a spacious exhibit of Damara zebras. From the *Treetops*, an elevated deck gives an excellent overview of zebras and reticulated giraffes, who share their exhibit with ground hornbill birds and gazelles. In additional enclosures high above the savanna, you'll find naked mole-rats, weaver birds, and DeBrazza's guenon monkeys.

The **Africa Rain Forest** re-creates a very different environment, the West African tropics. Here, colobus and Allen's swamp monkeys are exhibited in a forest stream habitat. A walk-through aviary, home to colorful saddle-bill storks and tiny duiker antelope, leads to the *Bamboo du Jon Swamp* building. Inside this humid jungle, visitors encounter a pool for slender-snouted crocodiles. Nearby exhibits hold lungfish, monitor lizards, and cichlid fish.

The multi-species **Amazon Flooded Forest** was the first exhibit of its kind. Combining land, aquatic, and arboreal animals, this glass-fronted habitat showcases the diversity of the South American jungle. Small crocodilian caimans, Arrau turtles, and hundreds of fish inhabit a stream, while plump little agoutis scurry across the dense forest floor. Howler and saki monkeys hang in the trees above the flood. Separate enclosures display pygmy marmosets (the world's smallest monkey), emerald tree boas, and an enormous green anaconda. Just around the corner lies the *South America Forest*, a lush jungle environment for spotted ocelot cats.

Endangered swine are highlighted in **Island Pigs of Asia**. Visayan warty pigs, found only on six Philippine islands, are sometimes referred to as "punk rock pigs," because of their spiky manes, which resemble mohawks. Named for the distinctive warts on their face, these charcoal-colored pigs were only recognized as a distinct species in 1993. A nearby bamboo forest is home to an equally unique variety of swine, the babirusa. Males of this hairless Indonesian species are easily identified by their four tusks, two of them protruding through the snout. These protective tusks can grow to up to a foot long.

OTHER EXHIBITS

Visitors enter an ice cave to view polar bears in the **Bears** complex. From above the path, a model bear paw reaches down as if grabbing for a seal, an illustration of these white bears pursuing their prey. Long glass windows provide great views into two separate habitats – one gives an underwater perspective, the other looks into the bears' land enclosure. Next door, smaller sun bears enjoy an environment enhanced with logs and artificial trees.

Cats of the Amur Region features two of the world's most endangered animals, both from far Eastern Russia. Siberian (or Amur) tigers rest under birch trees in a long, moated exhibit. Amur leopards can be seen through glass as they roam their jagged, rocky enclosure. There are only forty of these beautiful cats left in the wild.

Chimpanzees and orangutans are the star inhabitants of the **Primates** building. The chimps can also be seen outside in a hilly grassland exhibit, next to a row of enclosures housing mandrills and gibbons. Popular Humboldt penguins reside in the **Penguinarium**. An **Insect Zoo**, renovated in 2007, is one of only a few insectariums in the country. Near the African Rain Forest exit is an indoor habitat of Matschie's tree kangaroos.

FOR THE KIDS

Reflecting Oregon's agricultural traditions, the **Family Farm** represents an historic heritage farm. Outside the massive barn are pens for Shetland sheep and Pygora goats, both available for petting. Kids can climb up on a tractor or help with a vegetable garden next to a farmhouse. Kids also pet pygmy goats in the *African Goat Kraal*, located in the Africa Savanna section.

Lorikeet Landing is a walk-through aviary where visitors can feed a flock of loud parrots. Nine lorikeet species, including the stunning brown-and-yellow Duyvenbode's lory, fly freely in this L-shaped enclosure. Purchase your cup of nectar early on, since the birds are only allowed a set amount each day.

In our humble opinion, the nation's best zoo train ride is the **Washington Park and Zoo Railway**. During the spring and fall, visitors can ride the zoo loop, a one-mile route around the zoo's perimeter. In summer, catch the Washington Park run, a four-mile trip passing through the park to the International Rose Test Garden and Japanese Garden. The latter route has fantastic views of Mount Hood and Mount St. Helens. The railway operates three trains – the *Zooliner*, the *Oregon Steam Locomotive*, and the *Oregon Express*. For older kids, the zoo also has a 3-D thrill ride, where changing adventures (usually nature-themed and always wild) are presented in the high-tech **SimEx-Iwerks Simulation Theater**.

IN PROGRESS

A new native village will serve as the entrance to the entire African complex. A fork in the path will lead to either the existing Africa Savanna or the new **Predators of the Serengeti** (scheduled to open in 2009 as we go to press). After an absence of over twelve years, lions will return to the zoo in this new exhibit displaying carnivores of all sizes. Two other large predators, cheetahs and wild dogs, will also live here, along with smaller caracal lynx, mongooses, toucan-like red-billed hornbills, and rock pythons.

The zoo's oldest remaining exhibit, the Primates building, will continue to receive piece-by-piece updates to become the **Fragile Forests** complex (tentatively planned for 2010). The outdoor exhibits for the mandrills and langurs will be combined to create *Red Ape Reserve*, a large outdoor habitat for orangutans and gibbons (scheduled to open in 2008). The remaining areas, including the chimpanzees' space, will be transformed into equatorial forest habitats.

Woodland Park Zoological Gardens

5500 Phinney Avenue North
Seattle, Washington 98103
(206) 684-4800 or 684-4026
www.zoo.org

Hours: 9:30 a.m.-6:00 p.m. daily May 1-September 30; 9:30 a.m.-4:00 p.m., rest of year. Closed Christmas Day.

The Northern Trail's grizzly habitat was modeled on the entrance to Alaska's Denali National Park.

Admission & Fees: Adults $15, children $10, May-September; adults $11, children $8, rest of year. Carousel $2, bird feeding $1. Parking $4. Participates in reciprocity program.

Directions: From I-5, take Exit 169 (NE 50th Street), then go west on 50th Street for 1.3 miles to the zoo. Seattle's Metro Transit bus #5 stops near to zoo.

Don't Miss: Northern Trail, Tropical Rain Forest (includes Jaguar Cove and gorillas), Tropical Asia, African Savanna.

For Kids: Zoomazium, Willawong Station, Historic Carousel.

Touring Tips: With Seattle known for its frequent rain, the zoo has a tour designed specifically for rainy days. Check the zoo's website for the Rainy Day Tour map. After hours, summer concerts on the North Meadow stage are extremely popular. For those with an interest in flowers, 260 varieties of roses can be found in the Rose Garden just outside the South Entrance.

Edutainment: Several times each day, keepers bring out raptors of all sizes at the Raptor Center for educational presentations, weather permitting.

SEATTLE, WASHINGTON IS WELL KNOWN AS THE HOME OF THREE companies that have changed the business world – Microsoft, Boeing, and Starbucks.

Nestled north of downtown, near Green Lake, the Woodland Park Zoo has its own legacy. This ninety-two-acre institution is often credited with beginning the shift of zoo exhibits from bars and barren cages to naturalistic depictions of the animals' native habitats. Several exhibits here use cleverly hidden barriers and an elevated terrain to create the perception of multiple animals sharing the same environment. Only the Bronx Zoo in New York has garnered more exhibit awards from the Association of Zoos & Aquariums.

FEATURED EXHIBITS

The **Northern Trail** is an exhibit featuring many animals from the Pacific Northwest. Wolves inhabit a slightly elevated forest, with a herd of elk seen behind them. Three tall net enclosures hold arctic foxes, porcupines, and snowy owls. No doubt the shining star of the trail is the grizzly bear exhibit, designed after the entrance to Denali National Park in Alaska. The bears have fallen trees and a shallow rock-bed stream that flows through their expansive hillside habitat, ending in a pool at the *Taiga Viewing Shelter*. You get several views of the bears along the banks of the stream – including from within a cave – and can watch them catch trout from the pool at the Shelter. Across the trail, otters have their own pool, glass-fronted for underwater viewing. Nearby, Rocky Mountain goats inhabit a grassy hillside with stony cliffs. A boardwalk leads to a bald eagle aviary and ends at a circular platform offering an unobstructed view of the herd of elk mentioned above.

At the **Tropical Rain Forest** complex, a towering artificial kapok tree serves as the entrance to *Jaguar Cove*. Fifteen hundred plants of over one hundred species provide shade for these large cats. The glass-fronted exhibit uses a cave for close-up views, but the last vantage point is most spectacular, featuring a waterfall and the world's first underwater viewing of jaguars. Unlike most cats, jaguars love to both hunt and swim in water. They can spy on trout while resting on a fallen log that overhangs their pool. From a

Jaguar in Jaguar Cove.

tree high above the viewing path, the jaguars often watch visitors walking by.

The Tropical Rain Forest complex continues with a path that loops by two groups of lowland gorillas, who live in separate enclosures. It was this exhibit, more than any other, which established this zoo as a leader in exhibit design. Famous primatologists Jane Goodall and the late Dian Fossey were consultants for this display – the first to give gorillas a naturalistic outdoor space. The gorillas are often seen near the viewing glass, where they can find shelter from inclement weather. They can be identified from a sign showing the age, birthplace, and a picture of each gorilla. Kids can mimic the gorillas by climbing on nearby ropes. Leaf-eating black-and-white colobus monkeys inhabit a tall net structure. Lemurs and small red-flanked duiker antelope live on islands near the entrance to the *Rain Forest* building. Inside it, skylights above each exhibit provide natural light to ocelots (small spotted cats), anacondas, toucans, and most of the zoo's perching bird species. An elevated walk-through aviary concludes this jungle tour.

One of the largest collections of bamboo in the Northwest lines the trails of **Tropical Asia,** with its *Elephant Forest* often hidden from view behind a wall of bamboo. The mixed (both African and Asian) elephant herd has a long but narrow yard. Because of its width, visitors are never far from these massive mammals. The yard's sloping elevation presents a challenge to both elephants and visitors, who follow a winding path to a seating area overlooking a large pool. When they're not outside, the elephants can be seen in their Thai-themed barn, where they receive daily baths from their keepers. They can also use their flexible trunks to grasp a pull-down cord, giving themselves showers at their leisure.

Tropical Asia continues with the *Trail of Vines.* Beyond the elephants, the path leads to Malayan tapirs. These three-toed black-and-white pachyderms have a wading pool and plenty of roaming space. Around the corner, a deep forest is home to lion-tailed macaque monkeys, so named because of the lion-like tassels at the tips of their tails. On an island exhibit, visitors next encounter vocal siamangs. These largest of the lesser apes can be heard all over the zoo due to their inflatable throat sacs. The trail concludes at the first-ever open-forest canopy for orangutans. The elevated boardwalk gives guests an eye-to-eye meeting with these large apes, as they hang out in several large trees. They also can be observed through glass at the trail's end.

Siamang

The first exhibit in the zoo that most visitors experience is the 4½-acre **African Savanna.** A re-created African village lets visitors explore the native culture with replicas of a traditional African home and school. From a window in the school, you'll get a panoramic view of giraffes, zebras, antelope, and even patas monkeys in the distance. There are several hidden alcoves along the path from the village that let you see these animals again, including a spot where you can climb rocks for a better view. A small aviary contains weaver birds, whose elaborate nests often hang overhead. The large hippopotamus pool is near the "giraffe crossing," where you can watch giraffes eagerly entering their savanna each morning. After a closer look at the quick-running patas monkeys, check out two adjacent grassland exhibits with lions on one side and African wild dogs on the other. You can see both up close through glass panels.

OTHER EXHIBITS

The zoo's oddest creatures are in the **Day and Night Exhibits** building. *Day Exhibit* showcases mostly reptiles and amphibians, including king cobras, reticulated pythons, dwarf crocodiles, and cockroaches. Vampire bats, a loris (a primitive, slow-moving Asian primate), armadillos, and sloths can be seen in the darkened *Night Exhibit* gallery.

In the **Adaptations** building, Komodo dragons are featured prominently, while clouded leopards and a kea (a rare New Zealand parrot) are also seen. Outside, Sumatran tigers, sloth bears, and sun bears each have grottoes.

Red pandas are among the rare animals that inhabit the **Temperate Forest**. Japanese serow (a species of mountain goat) and several types of Asian cranes also reside here. Wetlands birds have their own covered area, while hornbills and several pheasants occupy the *Conservation Aviary*.

A flock of Humboldt penguins lives on an island near Jaguar Cove. The **Australasia** area features an Australian yard (with wallaroos, emus, and wallabies) as well as snow leopards in a grassy bluff setting. Pairs of kookaburras and Australian parrots occupy two nearby enclosures.

FOR THE KIDS

Kids have their own entrance to **Zoomazium**, through pint-sized doors leading into this fun indoor play space. This nature-themed playground, opened in 2006, includes a climbable mountain and strangler fig tree, arts and crafts, storytelling, and live animals. *Nature Exchange* is a trading post where children can trade in items they've found in nature for a number of prizes.

In the Aboriginal language, "willawong" means "a junction of two streams." At Woodland Park, the **Willawong Station** is "a place to hand feed birds." With over a hundred Australian parakeets and cockatiels in a high-ceilinged open-flight room, there is never a dull moment, whether or not you choose to buy a seed stick to feed them.

The enclosed **Historic Carousel** offers forty-eight steeds and is open year-round.

IN PROGRESS

The Humboldt penguins will soon move to a split-view coastline exhibit. As visitors enter the renovated West Entrance, they will see the penguins on a rocky shore with nesting holes. A large fishing net will nearly engulf everyone on the path to the penguins' underwater viewing. Flamingos (arriving in 2008) and a new Desert building will also be added nearby. As we go to press, Asian one-horned rhinos are scheduled to join Tropical Asia in 2010. Though not scheduled for the immediate future, the zoo's largest upcoming project is an **Asian Highlands** zone. This area would complete and compliment the Northern Trail loop, possibly including takins (rare Himalayan goats), brown snub-nosed monkeys, snow leopards, and red pandas.

Point Defiance Zoo & Aquarium

5400 North Pearl Street
Tacoma, Washington 98407
(253) 591-5337
www.pdza.org

Sea otters float in the Rocky Shores exhibit.

Hours: 9:30 a.m.-6:00 p.m., Memorial Day weekend-Labor Day; 9:30 a.m.-5:00 p.m., April-late May and most of September; 9:30 a.m-4:00 p.m., January-March and October-December. Closed the third Friday in July (for annual fundraiser), Thanksgiving, and Christmas Day.

Admission & Fees: Adults $11, seniors 65+ $10, youth 5-12 $9, tots 3-4 $5; Pierce County residents, AAA members, and military receive $1 discount. Carousel $2.

Directions: From I-5, take Exit 132 (Highway 16 West). Exit at 6th Avenue and go straight through the light to Pearl Street. Take a right and follow Pearl Street until it dead-ends at Point Defiance Park. Signs will direct you to zoo parking lots.

Don't Miss: Asian Forest Sanctuary, Rocky Shores, Arctic Tundra, South and North Pacific Aquariums.

For Kids: Kids' Zone, Antique Carousel.

Authors' Tips: The zoo is only part of Point Defiance Park. To get the whole experience, take a trip down Five Mile Drive, an evergreen-lined road traversing the rest of the peninsula. Stop at Owen Beach or Fort Nisqually, or take a ferry to Vashon Island. Hold onto your zoo ticket for free admission to Northwest Trek (see back of ticket for information).

Edutainment: Wild Wonders Outdoor Theatre has a great Pacific Northwest outdoor activities-themed show that features a variety of species, including small, slender serval cats and an African ground hornbill bird. There is plenty of amphitheater seating, and a grassy hillside for those who prefer a more relaxed vantage point. "Close Encounters" is the zoo's keeper chat program. Times and locations for these animal appearances are shown on the zoo's map. Highlights of this program include feedings in the Aquariums, talks in the Asian Forest Sanctuary, and a squid dissection at the Marine Discovery Center.

BUILT ON THE SHORES OF PUGET SOUND, POINT DEFIANCE ZOO and Aquarium has a coastal view second to none. Focusing on animals from the Pacific Rim, this twenty-nine-acre combined zoo and aquarium is one of the best small zoos in America. Just thirty-five miles south, in Eatonville, the zoo has a four hundred-acre sister facility, Northwest Trek. It features North American animals – and offers a tram tour that passes bison, moose, and other large animals. Or if you prefer, you can walk through the woods to see smaller animals, and carnivores such as cougars, bears, and wolves.

FEATURED EXHIBITS

At the **Asian Forest Sanctuary**, eight species are rotated through six different themed exhibits, meaning different animals are found in different exhibits on any given day. The *Waterfall Panorama* is the showcase habitat, and its pool and vegetation make it best suited for the Sumatran tigers. A long stream separates the visitors' viewing platform from a grassy expanse inside the enclosure. Step into a hollowed-out ancient ruin for a possible close encounter with a tiger. The *Mineral Lick* could reveal otters or crested porcupines. Swinging gibbons and siamangs, both lesser apes, often accompany Malayan tapirs or anoa, the world's smallest wild cattle, in the *Bamboo Forest* or *Broadleaf Forest*. A pair of Asian elephants has its own separate yard, complete with a pool.

Fascinating marine animals are the stars of **Rocky Shores**. A boardwalk leads to a pool of Pacific walruses. Next door, a totem pole towers over a pool of beluga whales. These larger-than-expected mammals dazzle visitors in an underwater gallery. The Rocky Shores complex is unique in the zoo world: Point Defiance has long been the only zoo in the nation to exhibit beluga whales, and it is one of only a few with walruses. Inquisitive sea otters can often be seen floating on their backs or diving for clams. Orange-beaked horned puffins build their nests on a grassy cliff above a pool, close to the visitor path.

Several polar bears live in the **Arctic Tundra** habitat. This award-winning exhibit has two glass-windowed viewing areas, one above and the other below water level. When they're not swimming, the bears can rest atop a rocky outcropping or wade in a pebbly stream. From here, a sharp eye might catch a glimpse of a musk ox in the distance. Around the corner, water surrounds the grassy habitat of the resident arctic foxes. Further along the path, two windowed shelters overlook a reindeer herd and the aforementioned musk oxen. Few zoos exhibit these shaggy wild oxen, which form an impenetrable circle around young calves when they're threatened by a predator.

The **South Pacific Aquarium** begins in a shallow mangrove stream filled with stingrays and small fish. Step down into the *Reef* to meet a variety of large sharks. Six species, including rarely seen lemon sharks, swim in an open ocean exhibit. Only the front of the pool is well lit, so the sharks seem to appear out of nowhere as they approach the glass. Another gallery exhibits a lovely collection of seahorses. Pot-bellied and tiny seahorses are favorites with visitors, due to their unique appearance. Leafy sea dragons blend in perfectly with the kelp in their exhibit, so look closely – they can be tough to spot! Cuttlefish, which use their tentacles to propel them through the water, may also be hard to find, but be patient. It's well worth the trouble.

The **North Pacific Aquarium** holds a 160,000-gallon tank inhabited by many of the animals found just outside the zoo, in Puget Sound. Glass windows make it easy to watch flounders and sharks as they swim by. The rocky bottom has crevices for starfish and kelp plants to grip. Across the path, opposite the big tank, a long row of individual animal habitats display eels, jellyfish, spiny lobsters, and many other interesting marine animals. Finally, stairs lead up to an overlook of the Puget Sound tank and the educational *Marine Discovery Center*. Just outside the building, you'll find a tide pool populated with sea anemones.

OTHER EXHIBITS

South American penguins enjoy a coastline habitat with plenty of rocks for nesting. Covered shelters with long windows allow for comfortable viewing of red wolves, North America's rarest wild canine. Point Defiance is strongly invested in the conservation of these endangered carnivores. The **Birds of Prey** aviary displays a variety of species, including spectacled owls. Next to the Outdoor Theater, two animal exercise yards let the animals from the theater's wildlife show – everything from a beaver to a sloth – stretch their legs. A **Small Animals** area holds a Burmese python, barn owls, and a school of blind cave fish.

FOR THE KIDS

Kids' Zone is a bright and enriching place for children. The *Magical Movement* play area's colorful equipment is designed to show kids the amazing ways that animals move. Basilisk lizards and geckos hide in a row of terrariums next to the playground equipment. Kids can pet goats in *Contact Junction*, or slide down the *Otter Slide*. A partially enclosed structure exposes children to animal careers; they can pretend to be a veterinarian or a zookeeper. In summer, parents should remember to bring along a change of clothes and waterproof sandals so their children can have a blast getting soaked in the dancing lily pad fountain. Kids can choose from thirty-one animals to ride on the zoo's **Antique Carousel,** or cruise along in a sled. The zoo acquired this historic merry-go-round, originally built in 1917, after going without a carousel for twenty-seven years.

IN PROGRESS

Scheduled to open in 2008 as we go to press, *Animal Avenue* will showcase meerkats, lemurs, and thirteen other species in an area adjacent to the new Kids' Zone children's area. This section will be designed to teach children about animal families, and the roles animals play in global and local communities. **Cats of the Canopy** will eventually be home to clouded leopards. **Red Wolf Woods** will give the zoo's two red wolf packs a new forest to roam, and provide visitors with much closer views of these endangered canines.

BEST OF THE REST

Alaska Zoo

4731 O'Malley Road
Anchorage, Alaska 99507
(907) 346-2133
www.alaskazoo.org

One of the easiest ways to get acquainted with native Alaskan wildlife is to visit this zoo, located just south of Anchorage. With a few exceptions, most of the animals displayed here are native to the Alaskan wilderness. Moose, reindeer, Dall sheep, and musk oxen are some of the large hoofed animals on exhibit. Fierce predators include polar and brown bears, wolves, and wolverines. An extensive collection of predatory birds includes eagles, hawks, owls, and a Northern goshawk. Arctic foxes, snowy owls, harbor seals, and river otters are also displayed. Exotic non-Alaskan creatures from the northern climates of Asia include Amur tigers, snow leopards, double-humped Bactrian camels, and Tibetan yaks.

Fresno Chaffee Zoo

894 West Belmont Avenue
Fresno, California 93728
(559) 498-2671
www.fresnochaffeezoo.com

This zoo is best known for its *Tropical Rain Forest*, a lush jungle situated under a fifty-five-foot-high mesh screen. The naturalistic habitat showcases free-flying tropical birds and small monkeys from South America. More birds are displayed in the *African Aviary* and *Australian Aviary*. The zoo claims to have the world's first computerized *Reptile House*, where exact climate-control has led to some great successes in the zoo's reptile breeding program. Asian elephants enjoy a half-acre exhibit with a waterfall and a deep, cooling pool. *Sunda Forest* is a display of popular Asian species, including tigers, leopards, orangutans, and siamang gibbons. Other exhibits worth checking out include *Wolf Woods*, the seal and sea lion pool, and a giraffe feeding station. The "Winged Wonders" bird show is presented several times daily in a large amphitheater.

The Living Desert

47-900 Portola Avenue
Palm Desert, California 92260
(760) 346-5694
www.livingdesert.org

Located near Palm Springs, in California's desert resort area, this unique park exhibits only animals native to the hot deserts of North America and Africa. The surprisingly grassy *African Savanna* features, among other creatures, a family of giraffes and several ostriches. Plans to add lions are in the works. The African theme continues in *Village WaTuTu*, an African town where kids can pet Nubian goats. Hyenas, leopards, camels, and other animals are exhibited among the thatched huts. The *North American* section includes *Eagle Canyon*, where a path winds through naturalistic exhibits of mountain lions, Mexican wolves, wild javelina pigs (also known as collared peccaries), and of course, a golden eagle. The park's largest exhibit is *Bighorn Mountain*, home to desert bighorn sheep.

Sacramento Zoo

3930 West Land Park Drive
Sacramento, California 95822
(916) 808-5888
www.saczoo.com

Located on the south side of California's capital city, this small zoo features a central *Rare Feline Center* with jaguars, margay cats, and Geoffroy's cats, all housed in rain forest settings. Lions, Sumatran tigers, snow leopards, and hyenas are also displayed, around the corner from these rare cats. Chimpanzees, orangutans, gibbons, and other primates live in naturalistic habitats with plenty of trees and ropes to climb. Sifakas are the most unusual lemurs of the *Lemurs of the Lost World* exhibit. The *Reptile House* is impressive, as are the penguins and the bamboo-filled *Red Panda Forest*. Near the zoo entrance, a *Lake Victoria* exhibit with African flamingos and whistling ducks re-creates the beautiful flamingo-filled lakes of East Africa.

Santa Barbara Zoo

500 Ninos Drive
Santa Barbara, California 93103
(805) 962-5339
www.santabarbarazoo.org

With the San Ynez Mountains to one side, and a sweeping view of the Pacific Ocean to the other, this zoo has one of the most beautiful and dramatic settings in the country. The grounds consist of sloping lawns framed by towering palm trees and gorgeous flower beds. Many parrot-like birds can be seen in the walk-through *Tropical Aviary*, while bugs, spiders, lizards, and snakes are displayed in an adjoining exhibit, entitled *"Eeeww!"* Several animals enjoy their own pools, including small-clawed otters, Chilean flamingos, Chinese alligators, and capybaras (giant aquatic rodents). At the back of the zoo, gorillas and Baringo giraffes are featured, as are *Cats of Africa*, where you'll find lions and black-footed cats. The *California Nature Trail* boardwalk displays rare Channel Island foxes and, coming soon as we go to press, highly endangered California condors. Other residents include red pandas, Amur and snow leopards, penguins, and Asian elephants. A miniature train circles the zoo, giving grand views of the area.

APPENDIX 1.

The Top 10 U.S. Zoo Exhibits in 20 Categories

WE LIVE IN A COMPETITIVE SOCIETY. THERE ARE "TOP TEN" LISTS for everything from city populations to college sports teams. But "top" zoos are a subjective matter. Some visitors love birds. Others are more interested in reptiles, or bears. Some folks are most interested in kid-friendly attractions, while others value realism and an immersive experience. What's "best" depends on the visitor's interests.

For that reason, we do not rank zoos from best to worst, or assign them an overall numeric score. Instead, we've rated the ninety-seven zoos reviewed in this book in twenty different categories, ranging from the best representations of the earth's major geographic regions and habitats to the best exhibits of various types of animals, along with the best children's zoos and the best entertainment the zoos offer.

Of course, these ratings are still subjective, but we hope they will give you a bit more to go on than a single "top ten" list would have done.

Note: We list our choice for the overall best in each category with a short explanation for our pick. We then list our second favorite, followed by eight runners-up in alphabetical order.

African Animals and Exhibits
#1: **Kansas City Zoo**
> *In its ninety-five-acre Africa exhibit, Kansas City represents five nations with one of the most extensive collections of African animals we've ever seen.*

#2: **San Diego Wild Animal Park**
> ***Runners-up:***
> Brookfield Zoo
> Busch Gardens Africa
> Dallas Zoo
> Disney's Animal Kingdom
> Honolulu Zoo
> Jacksonville Zoo
> North Carolina Zoo
> Toledo Zoo

Asian Animals and Exhibits
#1: **Bronx Zoo**
> *With JungleWorld, Wild Asia monorail tour, Himalayan Highlands, and Tiger Mountain, the Bronx Zoo has four can't-miss Asian displays and a very extensive collection.*

#2: **Columbus Zoo**
> ***Runners-up:***
> Audubon Zoo
> Disney's Animal Kingdom
> Memphis Zoo
> Miami Metrozoo
> National Zoo
> San Diego Zoo
> Tampa's Lowry Park Zoo
> Woodland Park Zoo

North American Animals and Exhibits

#1: North Carolina Zoo

With excellent, spacious habitats, North Carolina displays the continent's key animals, from arctic polar bears to desert rattlesnakes, from swamp alligators to prairie bison, and from woodland grizzly bears to stream-dwelling otters and fish.

#2: Oklahoma City Zoo

Runners-up:

Arizona-Sonora Desert Museum
Columbus Zoo
Fort Worth Zoo
Minnesota Zoo
Oregon Zoo
Sedgwick County Zoo
Tampa's Lowry Park Zoo
Tulsa Zoo

South American Animals and Exhibits

#1: Jacksonville Zoo

Jacksonville's Range of the Jaguar takes you to a South American villa surrounded by gorgeous habitats for the continent's key animals, including rare giant otters.

#2: San Antonio Zoo

Runners-up:

Audubon Zoo
Brookfield Zoo
Los Angeles Zoo
Montgomery Zoo
National Zoo
Phoenix Zoo
Sedgwick County Zoo
Tulsa Zoo

Australian Animals and Exhibits

#1: Fort Wayne Children's Zoo

Australian Adventure introduces children and their parents to the continent in a Welcome Center, nocturnal bat flight exhibit, Great Barrier Reef aquarium, and walk-through exhibits of birds and kangaroos.

#2: Cleveland Metroparks Zoo

Runners-up:

Brookfield Zoo
Columbus Zoo
Gladys Porter Zoo
Kansas City Zoo
Los Angeles Zoo
Rio Grande Zoo
Riverbanks Zoo
San Diego Zoo

Bird Collections and Exhibits

#1: San Diego Zoo

San Diego has the nation's largest and most diverse bird collection, exhibited in two gigantic walk-through flight cages, as well as numerous smaller aviaries with gorgeous tropical birds, large birds of prey exhibits, and rare kiwis.

#2: Houston Zoo

Runners-up:

Bronx Zoo
Denver Zoo
Honolulu Zoo
National Zoo
San Antonio Zoo
San Diego Wild Animal Park
St. Louis Zoo
Toledo Zoo

Reptile & Amphibian Collections and Exhibits

#1: San Diego Zoo

The San Diego Zoo's open-air Reptile House, with its Komodo dragons, snakes, and other reptiles, is world famous, but its backyard Reptile Mesa is what we found most impressive. The Mesa includes desert lizards, large tortoises, and a swamp for Indian gharial crocodiles.

#2: Detroit Zoo

Runners-up:

Audubon Zoo
Fort Worth Zoo
Gladys Porter Zoo
Knoxville Zoo
Nashville Zoo
Omaha's Henry Doorly Zoo
Riverbanks Zoo
St. Louis Zoo

Small Mammal Collections and Exhibits

#1: National Zoo

The National Zoo's Small Mammal House is the best of its kind in the U.S. You'll also find attractive exhibits of beavers, red pandas, prairie dogs, and two types of otters around the zoo.

#2: Bronx Zoo

Runners-up:

Brookfield Zoo
Cincinnati Zoo
Knoxville Zoo
Lincoln Park Zoo
Memphis Zoo
Milwaukee County Zoo
Omaha's Henry Doorly Zoo
Philadelphia Zoo

Primates: Apes, Monkeys, and Lemurs

#1: San Diego Zoo

San Diego's Gorilla Tropics and Absolutely Apes feature three different great apes and are lauded in the zoo world and mainstream media. Its Sun Bear Forest, with lion-tailed macaque monkeys, and the newer Monkey Trails are also excellent primate exhibits.

#2: Denver Zoo

Runners-up:

Bronx Zoo
Cincinnati Zoo
Fort Worth Zoo
Lincoln Park Zoo
Los Angeles Zoo
Omaha's Henry Doorly Zoo
St. Louis Zoo
Zoo Atlanta

Cat Collections and Exhibits

#1: Cincinnati Zoo

With fifteen species of small felines, Cincinnati's Cat House is justifiably famous. Other exhibits include Tiger Canyon (with white tigers), rare white lions, and a fascinating Cheetah Encounter show.

#2: Memphis Zoo

Runners-up:

Bronx Zoo
Denver Zoo
Oklahoma City Zoo
Omaha's Henry Doorly Zoo
Philadelphia Zoo
Rio Grande Zoo
San Diego Zoo
Utah's Hogle Zoo

Bear Collections and Exhibits

#1: San Diego Zoo
> *With Polar Bear Plunge, Sun Bear Forest, spectacled bears, and of course giant pandas (which are bears, it turns out), San Diego offers the most excellent bear exhibits of any zoo.*

#2: Cleveland Zoo
> *Runners-up:*

Denver Zoo
Detroit Zoo
Memphis Zoo
Milwaukee County Zoo
National Zoo
North Carolina Zoo
Omaha's Henry Doorly Zoo
St. Louis Zoo

Pachyderms: Elephants, Rhinos, Hippos, Tapirs

#1: Miami Metrozoo
> *Miami has the greatest variety of pachyderms of any U.S. zoo. Pygmy hippos, Malayan and Baird's tapirs, Indian and black rhinos, and African and Asian elephants are displayed in spacious tropical yards.*

#2: San Diego Wild Animal Park
> *Runners-up:*

Brookfield Zoo
Denver Zoo
Disney's Animal Kingdom
Fort Worth Zoo
Kansas City Zoo
Milwaukee County Zoo
Oregon Zoo
St. Louis Zoo

Hoofed Animal Collections and Exhibits

#1: San Diego Wild Animal Park
> *The park has herds of giraffes, zebras, and a variety of African antelope roaming its 1,800 naturalistic acres, plus rarely exhibited (and dangerous) Cape buffalo.*

#2: Denver Zoo
> *Runners-up:*

Bronx Zoo
Disney's Animal Kingdom
Los Angeles Zoo
Miami Metrozoo
Montgomery Zoo
Oklahoma City Zoo
Sedgwick County Zoo
St. Louis Zoo

Marine Mammals: Dolphins, Seals, Sea Otters, Manatees

#1: Indianapolis Zoo
> *Indianapolis' dolphins inhabit the magnificent Underwater Dolphin Dome. Nearby are excellent exhibits of walruses, polar bears, and three species of seals and sea lions.*

#2: Point Defiance Zoo
> *Runners-up:*

Brookfield Zoo
Detroit Zoo
Memphis Zoo
Milwaukee County Zoo
Minnesota Zoo
Oregon Zoo
Pittsburgh Zoo
Rio Grande Zoo

Fish & Zoo Aquariums
#1: Omaha's Henry Doorly Zoo

The wide variety of species in Omaha's Kingdoms of the Seas Aquarium includes bonnethead sharks, moon jellyfish, sea dragons, and Amazon River fish. The highlight is a seventy-foot acrylic tunnel where visitors are surrounded by large sharks and rays.

#2: Pittsburgh Zoo

Runners-up:

Houston Zoo
Louisville Zoo
Milwaukee County Zoo
Minnesota Zoo
Oklahoma City Zoo
Point Defiance Zoo
Riverbanks Zoo
Toledo Zoo

Insects: Species and Exhibits
#1: Cincinnati Zoo

Cincinnati's World of the Insect was the first zoo exhibit in the nation dedicated to insects, and in our opinion, it is still the best. Features include a leaf-cutter ant display, rhinoceros beetles, and a butterfly aviary.

#2: St. Louis Zoo

Runners-up:

Arizona-Sonora Desert Museum
Dallas Zoo
Fort Worth Zoo
Oakland Zoo
Oregon Zoo
San Diego Zoo
San Francisco Zoo
Toledo Zoo

Indoor Tropical Rain Forest
(Based on animals and overall realism)

#1: Omaha's Henry Doorly Zoo

Omaha's Lied Jungle is the biggest and best indoor rain forest we've ever seen! Visitors can encounter approximately ninety animal species from three different continents, as they follow an elevated pathway through the treetops and walk down below along the Jungle Trail.

#2: Bronx Zoo

Runners-up:

Brookfield Zoo
Cleveland Metroparks Zoo
Denver Zoo
Franklin Park Zoo
Minnesota Zoo
National Zoo
Sedgwick County Zoo
Tulsa Zoo

Children's Zoos
(Based on size, quality, and uniqueness)

#1: Pittsburgh Zoo

Pittsburgh's seven-acre Kids Kingdom has just about everything: contact yards with deer, kangaroos, and goats; animal-themed playgrounds; kiddie carnival rides; and close-up animal exhibits featuring sea lions, bats, meerkats, beavers, and more.

#2: Brookfield Zoo

Runners-up:

Bronx Zoo
Erie Zoo
Houston Zoo
Knoxville Zoo
Lincoln Park Zoo
Maryland Zoo
Oakland Zoo
Phoenix Zoo

Rides

(Based on thrills, uniqueness, and variety)

#1: **Busch Gardens Africa**

Animal-themed rides at Busch Gardens include the Rhino Rally safari jeep ride and two exciting ways to see the animals of the sixty-five-acre Serengeti — via skyride and steam train. As if that weren't enough, there are also some amazing theme park rides, including five major roller coasters.

#2: **San Diego Zoo**

Runners-up:

Bronx Zoo
Dallas Zoo
Disney's Animal Kingdom
Fort Wayne Children's Zoo
Milwaukee County Zoo
Philadelphia Zoo
San Diego Wild Animal Park
Tampa's Lowry Park Zoo

Shows

(Based on entertainment value and variety)

#1: **Disney's Animal Kingdom**

Disney's Animal Kingdom includes two excellent live animal shows: the Flights of Wonder bird show and Pocahontas and Her Forest Friends. Although they don't include live animals, three Disney-film-inspired shows are Broadway quality and animal-oriented.

#2: **San Diego Wild Animal Park**

Runners-up:

Brookfield Zoo
Cincinnati Zoo
Denver Zoo
Indianapolis Zoo
Memphis Zoo
Milwaukee County Zoo
Minnesota Zoo
San Diego Zoo

APPENDIX 2.

Each Author's Picks for the Top 25 U.S. Zoo Exhibits

WHAT CONSTITUTES THE BEST IN ZOO EXHIBITS? HERE ARE THE authors' favorites—selected from exhibits open by early 2008—based on the exhibits' scope, theme, realism, and size, as well as the variety, popularity, and number of animals each includes. (See box, opposite, for more on their selection criteria.)

Allen's Best of the Best

1. **Kilimanjaro Safari** – Disney's Animal Kingdom, Lake Buena Vista, FL
2. **Lied Jungle** – Omaha's Henry Doorly Zoo, Omaha, NE
3. **Africa** – Kansas City Zoo, Kansas City, MO
4. **Texas Wild!** – Fort Worth Zoo, Fort Worth, TX
5. **Kingdoms of the Night** – Omaha's Henry Doorly Zoo, Omaha, NE
6. **Wilds of Africa** – Dallas Zoo, Dallas, TX
7. **Congo Gorilla Forest** – Bronx Zoo, Bronx, NY
8. **Range of the Jaguar** – Jacksonville Zoo, Jacksonville, FL
9. **CHINA** – Memphis Zoo, Memphis, TN
10. **Journey Into Africa** – San Diego Wild Animal Park, Escondido, CA
11. **Oklahoma Trails** – Oklahoma City Zoo, Oklahoma City, OK
12. **Arctic Ring of Life** – Detroit Zoo, Royal Oak, MI
13. **Great Northwest** – Oregon Zoo, Portland, OR
14. **Desert Dome** – Omaha's Henry Doorly Zoo, Omaha, NE
15. **African Savanna** – Honolulu Zoo, Honolulu, HI
16. **North American Living Museum** – Tulsa Zoo, Tulsa, OK
17. **Serengeti Plain** – Busch Gardens Africa, Tampa, FL
18. **River's Edge** – St. Louis Zoo, St. Louis, MO
19. **Wild Africa** – Binder Park Zoo, Battle Creek, MI
20. **African Rift Valley** – Cheyenne Mountain Zoo, Colorado Springs, CO
21. **East Africa** – Caldwell Zoo, Tyler, TX
22. **Louisiana Swamp** – Audubon Zoo, New Orleans, LA
23. **Ituri Forest** – San Diego Zoo, San Diego, CA
24. **Oceans** – Indianapolis Zoo, Indianapolis, IN
25. **Asia Trail** – National Zoo, Washington, DC

Narrowing down our lists of favorite exhibits to a mere twenty-five was a very difficult process because it forced us to exclude many exhibits we consider excellent. It also made us realize that we have very different priorities for determining an exhibit's overall excellence. This likely comes from our different backgrounds. Jon has worked in three zoos and thus tends to focus on the exhibit design and the uniqueness of the animal habitats. Allen, on the other hand, is a father of four who has visited over two hundred zoos worldwide and most values the overall visitor experience and "adventure," as well as strong cultural themes. If you disagree with one of our lists, you may quite likely find the other's more in line with your tastes.

Jon's Best of the Best

1. **Congo Gorilla Forest** – Bronx Zoo, Bronx, NY
2. **Arctic Ring of Life** – Detroit Zoo, Royal Oak, MI
3. **Kingdoms of the Night** – Omaha's Henry Doorly Zoo, Omaha, NE
4. **Lied Jungle** – Omaha's Henry Doorly Zoo, Omaha, NE
5. **Asia Trail** – National Zoo, Washington, DC
6. **Kilimanjaro Safari** – Disney's Animal Kingdom, Lake Buena Vista, FL
7. **Penguin and Puffin Coast** – St. Louis Zoo, St. Louis, MO
8. **Journey Into Africa** – San Diego Wild Animal Park, Escondido, CA
9. **Northern Trail** – Woodland Park Zoo, Seattle, WA
10. **Desert Dome** – Omaha's Henry Doorly Zoo, Omaha, NE
11. **African Rift Valley** – Cheyenne Mountain Zoo, Colorado Springs, CO
12. **Wilds of Africa** – Dallas Zoo, Dallas, TX
13. **Black Bear Falls** – Knoxville Zoo, Knoxville, TN
14. **Predator Ridge** – Denver Zoo, Denver, CO
15. **Oklahoma Trails** – Oklahoma City Zoo, Oklahoma City, OK
16. **Asian Highlands** – Utah's Hogle Zoo, Salt Lake City, UT
17. **Great Northwest** – Oregon Zoo, Portland, OR
18. **Big Cat Falls** – Philadelphia Zoo, Philadelphia, PA
19. **Range of the Jaguar** – Jacksonville Zoo, Jacksonville, FL
20. **Monkey Trails & Forest Tales** – San Diego Zoo, San Diego, CA
21. **Center for African Apes** – Lincoln Park Zoo, Chicago, IL
22. **Tropic World** – Brookfield Zoo, Brookfield, IL
23. **JungleWorld** – Bronx Zoo, Bronx, NY
24. **Louisiana Swamp** – Audubon Zoo, New Orleans, LA
25. **River's Edge** – St. Louis Zoo, St. Louis, MO

Zoo Book Glossary Terms

Ape. As a rule, apes are most easily distinguished from monkeys by their lack of a tail, with one exception. The Barbary macaque (sometimes called a "Barbary ape") does not have a tail, but is still considered a monkey because it shares no other significant common traits with apes.

Atrium Enclosure/Cage. A tall, spacious enclosure, usually an enclosed cage. Such enclosures are often used to provide adequate space for monkeys or birds.

AZA. The Association of Zoos and Aquariums. The AZA is the nonprofit organization to which almost all credible North American zoos and aquariums belong. Being accredited by the AZA is a sign that a zoo is meeting the highest standards of animal care and conservation.

Binturong. Related to civets, binturongs are native to Southeast Asia and common in American zoos. They have thick black fur and are about the size of a small dog. Tree-dwelling binturongs primarily live on fruit, but will occasionally eat small animals. They are often called "bear cats," though they are not closely related to either bears or cats.

Bioclimatic Zone. Areas of the world with similar climate and similar plants and animals. Bioclimatic zones include coastal, lowland, sub-montane, montane, sub-alpine, and alpine. Zoos will often organize their animal collections by these zones.

Biome. Generally another word for "bioclimatic zone." See above.

Bubble Window. Glass or acrylic window that has a curved "bubble" shape allowing visitors (most often children) to "enter" the animals' space. Commonly used in prairie dog exhibits, but also seen in meerkat and even gorilla exhibits.

Camel, Bactrian and Dromedary. Bactrian camels have two humps, Dromedaries have one. The easiest way to keep them straight is to remember there are two humps in the letter "B," and one hump in the letter "D."

Canine. Member of the dog family, which includes wolves, foxes, jackals, and domestic dogs.

Carnivore. From the Latin for "meat eater," carnivores are animals whose diet consists mainly of meat. This can include predators, such as cats, who kill and eat other living animals; and scavengers, such as vultures, hyenas, and Komodo dragons, who primarily eat carrion.

Contact Area. A space where people can come into contact with animals. Usually refers to an enclosed petting yard where children can touch, pet, or even groom farm animals such as cows, donkeys, and (most often) goats and sheep. Usually contact areas (also called contact yards) are a major component of the children's zoo.

Ecosystem. An ecosystem is a community of living things (animals, plants, fungi) that function together with non-living things (rocks, water). Ecosystems are contained within larger *biomes* or *bioclimatic zones* (see above). Examples of ecosystems include Florida's Everglades, Australia's Great Barrier Reef, and Africa's Rift Valley savanna.

Edutainment. Combination of "*edu*cation" and "enter*tainment*." Zoos use quality animal entertainment to educate and inspire visitors, especially children, about conservation topics. Examples include sea lion shows, bird shows, keeper chats, public animal feedings, and even educational movies.

Enrichment. The addition of landscaping, plants, objects, activities, or other stimuli to an animal exhibit with the intention of creating a positive physical or physiological response in the animals, thus enriching their day-to-day lives.

Feline. Member of the cat family, which includes thirty-seven species of wild cats, as well as domestic house cats.

Geodesic Dome. A hemispherical structure, often translucent, usually used as a roof over a rain forest or desert habitat. Domes are used to allow natural light to filter in onto animals and live plants. At zoos, these domes are typically made of either acrylic plastic or glazed glass.

Great Ape. The four great ape species are gorillas, orangutans, chimpanzees, and bonobos (also called pygmy chimpanzees).

Grotto. Traditional style of animal exhibit, often used for bears and large cats. Typically, an open, bowl-like concrete structure surrounded by rock or stone walls. Old-fashioned grottoes were often dismissively referred to as "bear pits," but today's grottoes are often enhanced with live plants, waterfalls, and pools.

Herbivore. Animal that eats primarily plant matter, rather than meat. In the zoo world, hoofed animals and pachyderms are well known herbivores.

Hoofstock. Any animal with hoofed feet. Hoofed animals (or ungulates) are separated into two groups, based on the number of their toes. Odd-toed hoofstock belong to the group Perissodactyla, which includes rhinos, tapirs, and horses. Artiodactyla, or even-toed ungulates, include everything else: deer, elephants, giraffes, antelope, goats, hippos, and camels. Note that in this book, we usually describe the elephants, rhinos, hippos, and tapirs separately as "pachyderms" (see below).

Immersion Exhibit. A zoo exhibit design style, often called "landscape immersion," with the goal of making the visitor feel as if he or she has entered the world of the zoo animal, rather than vice versa. Designs use the sights, sounds, and smells of the animal's native environment to make the experience as realistic as possible.

Cultural Immersion. Designing a zoo exhibit or exhibit area to reflect not only the animals of a particular place in the world, but also the culture and people of that place. Creative use of authentic-looking architecture, cultural artifacts, and graphics attempt to give visitors a believably exotic experience.

Harp Wire. A creative barrier used in many zoo exhibits, using closely spaced high-tension vertical wire or fine cable, sometimes also called "piano wire." A harp wire barrier is much less obtrusive than wire mesh or old-fashioned steel bars.

Invertebrate. An animal lacking a backbone. Includes creatures such as insects, spiders, scorpions, crabs, lobsters, shellfish, and jellyfish.

Keeper Chat. Presentation given at a zoo, either formal or informal, where zookeepers share information about the animals they care for, both the species and (often) the individuals at the zoo. These chats may include opportunities for visitors to meet and touch or otherwise interact with exotic animals.

Kopje. A rocky "island" outcropping in the middle of a vast "sea" of grassland, most commonly found in the savannas of East Africa. In zoos, kopjes are generally re-created with gigantic artificial boulders and winding pathways that thread between them. Kopje exhibits are settings for the animals that typically inhabit them in Africa, such as meerkats and klipspringer antelope.

Lesser Ape. Lesser apes include thirteen species of gibbons, distinctive for their smaller size (compared to great apes), long arms, and booming voices.

Light-reversal. A technique used in nocturnal exhibits (see below). The process involves leaving bright lights on during the night, and then using dim lighting (at or about the brightness of moonlight) during the day. The nocturnal animals are thus tricked into thinking it is nighttime, when they are most active, during daytime visitor hours, to the delight of spectators.

Marsupial. A mammal whose young are born while they are still in the foetal stage and then develop inside an external pouch rather than a placenta. Kangaroos and opossums are some of the best-known.

Nocturnal Exhibit/Habitat. An exhibit where nocturnal animals (those that are active at night and sleep during the day) are displayed. Visitors are able to see many fascinating creatures at their most active thanks to use of *light-reversal* (see above). Bats are by far the most common animals displayed in nocturnal exhibits.

Omnivore. An animal that eats both plants and meat on a regular basis. Omnivores include pigs, raccoons, many rodents, chimpanzees, various monkeys and birds, most bears, and of course, humans.

Pampas. Fertile South American lowlands, the South American version of a savanna. The term comes from the Quechua language for "plain." Pampas are primarily found in Argentina, Uruguay, and southern Brazil. Animals native to the pampas include guanacos (relatives of llamas), ostrich-like rheas, and bush dogs.

Pachyderm. Thick-skinned, large hoofed animals, including elephants, tapirs, rhinoceroses (rhinos), and hippopotamuses (hippos).

Pinniped. Member of the seal family, consisting of sleek-bodied, semi-aquatic marine mammals. Along with many types of seals, the group also includes sea lions and walruses.

Predator/Prey Exhibit. Habitats where carnivores (usually large cats) and their potential prey animals (usually antelope, zebras, or deer) are displayed in such a way that it appears as if the animals are sharing the same space. In fact, however, hidden barriers (usually sunken moats) are used to keep the animals apart (and alive).

Ratite. A family of large flightless birds, which includes ostriches, emus, rheas, and cassowaries.

Rotating Habitat/Exhibit. A zoo habitat where different species of animals are rotated through a set of exhibits throughout the day or week. This provides animals with a constantly changing environment and presents them with new scents, which provides valuable *enrichment* (see above). The first extensive use of this concept was at the Louisville Zoo, followed by the Point Defiance Zoo. Both zoos' exhibits are profiled in this book.

Taiga. Cold northern coniferous forest environments found in Canada, Alaska, Russia (especially Siberia), and northern Europe. The most common taiga animal seen in zoos is the Amur tiger. Other taiga creatures include some eagles, caribou, wolves, and grizzly bears.

Ursid. Member of the bear family. There are eight species of ursids surviving today: giant pandas, polar bears, spectacled bears, brown bears (grizzly and Kodiak), American black bears, Asiatic black bears, sloth bears, and sun bears.

Veldt. The wide open rural spaces of southern Africa. The term is used interchangeably in South Africa with "savanna." The word comes from the Africaans word for "field."

Viewing Cave. An artificial cave-like structure, usually built into the side of an animal habitat. When visitors enter, they usually have a clear glass-fronted view of the animals in their enclosure. Zoos often use heated rocks, water holes, and other well-placed enticements to bring the animals closer to the viewing area.

Viewing Blind. A visitor viewing area that is at least somewhat shielded or camouflaged from the animals in their habitat. It is meant to recreate the exhilarating experience of seeing animals in the wild.

Animal Index

All major zoos exhibit a broad assortment of animals. But the range of creatures you will encounter as you visit America's best zoos is truly astonishing. For most display rarer animals as well, animals that you'll find in few other zoos and, in some cases, in only one. This index includes all the animals in the book. Note that some are grouped by kind ("antelope," "bird," "pig, wild," for example), while others are listed on their own. In cases in which animals are known by more than one name, we've listed them under the name used more frequently, followed by an "aka" (also known as) in parentheses; for example "Ringtail (aka cacomistle)." Page numbers in bold italics indicate a photograph; "bc" means you'll find it on the back cover. At the end, you'll find an alphabetical list of the "best of the rest" zoos.

Best of the Rest Zoos